The Joy of Feeling

Bodymind Acupressure™

Jin Shin Do®

By

Iona Marsaa Teeguarden, M.A., M.F.C.C.

Japan Publications, Inc.

© 1984, 1987 by Iona Marsaa Teeguarden

Note to the reader: Jin Shin Do® Acupressure is not intended for the diagnosis, treatment or cure of disease. It is a relaxation therapy, and a useful adjunct to licensed, qualified medical or psychological care. For any persistent pain or symptom, even a seemingly minor one, the reader is strongly encouraged to consult a medical doctor. When used in conjunction with standard medical treatment, the Jin Shin Do Acupressure technique can assist the healing process by releasing tension, decreasing stress and encouraging a sense of increased well-being.

Published by JAPAN PUBLICATIONS, INC., Tokyo and New York

Distributors:

UNITED STATES: Kodansha America, Inc., through Oxford University Press, 198 Madison Avenue, New York, N.Y.10016. CANADA: Fitzhenry & Whiteside Ltd., 195 Allstate Parkway, Markham, Ontario L3R 4T8. UNITED KINGDOM AND EUROPE: Premier Book Marketing Ltd., 1 Gower Street, London WC1E 6HA . AUSTRALIA AND NEW ZEALAND: Bookwise International, 54 Crittenden Road, Findon, South Australia 5023. THE FAR EAST AND JAPAN: Japan Publications Trading Co., Ltd., 1-2-1,Sarugaku-cho, Chiyoda-ku, Tokyo 101. Japan

First edition: May 1987
Fifth printing: January 1998

LCCC 85- 080534
ISBN 0- 87040- 634- 5

Printed in U.S.A.

Dedication

This book is dedicated to my son, Jeremy,
whose love and understanding has been a support to me
on the journey which led to writing this book.
Just by being himself,
he has helped me to trust that
sunshine does follow all the psychic storms.

Foreword

It was over seventy years ago that Carl. G. Jung discovered that the reality of the psyche could not be experienced through simply reducing it to instinctual drives and social conditioning. Yet as profound as his understanding was, the mystery of the body for the most part eluded him.

Iona Marsaa Teeguarden, in this book, takes up that mystery and continues that exploration of the bodyself as a spokesman for psychic wholeness. Her exploration leads not only to the latest theories of bodymind reality, but back in time to some of the oldest visions of Oriental medicine, in which the body was seen as a body of energy—a body of light. The journey deep into the Eastern/Taoist past circles back to our present—to the physics of modern times, and the vision of all matter as immense fields of energy.

But do not be misled by forewords. This is not a book about theories of the body. It is a practical book about how to live your life in the body, your life as a body. It is an invitation to discover the body that you are—a network of flowing rivers of energy, rivers that can be obstructed to be sure, but rivers whose blocks can be removed, whose flows can be balanced and freed. And as they are, so we are—in body, mind and heart.

What might seem at first a "how to do it" book turns out to be a "how to be it" book. Iona must be congratulated for showing us how the body can come to be truly a home for the soul.

WEYLER GREENE, Ph.D.
President, C.G. Jung Institute
Los Angeles, California
February, 1986

Contents

List of Illustrations

Preface

The story of the process which produced this book goes back to 1973 and the birth of my son—which brought great joy into my life, and gave me time to reflect on what I wanted to do with my life. I was twenty three then. I had studied piano performance and philosophy at the University of Michigan, then moved to Los Angeles in 1970 to study macrobiotics and Oriental philosophy. There, while working as a macrobiotic cook and writing a natural foods cookbook, I had tried acupressure* and acupuncture for some physical pains and problems. In my first acupressure sessions, I remember being impressed by *how it made me feel*. When I was introduced to Reichian concepts of how muscular tension can correlate with psychological armoring, I realized that acupressure could be a very powerful transformative tool, as well as providing symptomatic relief. I decided to take some classes "because it might come in handy some day." Meanwhile I was employed as a secretary and as a research assistant (on a student suicide prevention project)—quitting my job the day my son was born.

A couple months later, I took my acupressure notebooks off the shelf, and suddenly several questions crystalized. While looking for their answers, I became fascinated with acupressure theory. This simply, there began a research project which was to extend over the next dozen years. I also began to charge ($10 at first) for giving acupressure sessions—first in my home, while my son was napping at noon or sleeping at night, and then in a chiropractor's office. The first phase of research, into the "Strange Flows" and their points, culminated in a three-month visit to Japan in 1976. The same year, Ron Teeguarden and I established the first Jin Shin Do® training center (The Acupressure Workshop) in West Los Angeles, and I began writing *The Acupressure Way of Health: Jin Shin Do.*® Published in 1978, this book is a simple introduction to Jin Shin Do® Acupressure, which is my integration of a Japanese acupressure technique, Chinese acupressure theory, and Taoist philosophy and techniques.** The last chapter of this book, entitled "An Ancient, New Age Approach to the Emotions," is actually the preface to this present book, which adds psychology to the synthesis.

I had been intrigued with the bodymind connection and the psychological applications of acupressure since being introduced to these concepts by French therapist Jean-Claude Thomas in 1970. Early in my practice of acupressure, I noticed a cor-

---

* Acupressure is like acupuncture, but instead of needles it uses finger pressure on the "acupoints" to reduce stress, release tension and balance the body-mind energy. (For a more complete definition, see Chapter 1.)
** See next page.

relation between physical tension and emotional stress, and observed that sometimes the release of physical tension didn't "hold" until there was an accompanying
awareness of psychological stressors—like repressed feelings or upsetting attitudes.
Also, I found that people tended to talk about their problems during sessions, and
that they seemed to benefit from giving in to their feelings, as well as from just
letting go and relaxing. In 1979, I suddenly decided to apply for the Master's program at Antioch University in Los Angeles, with a concentration in psychology,
and an expressed intention to research the correlation between Eastern/Taoist and
Western approaches to the psyche. While doing my graduate work, I was fascinated
to not only find parallels to Taoist theories in the writings of many Western psychologists, but also discover that Taoism had influenced the development of Carl
Jung's thinking, and was referred to frequently in the writings of Abraham Maslow,
and briefly in those of Carl Rogers.

At the time, I had no idea that the next six years would be devoted to researching
the bodymind connection, nor did I anticipate all the complexities that I would
wander through on the way back to simplicity. Research into the Taoist philosophy
and acupressure theory was a process of translation, even working with English texts
and English-speaking teachers. Replete with quaint poetic images, the ancient Taoist
writings often sound like magical mystery trips—and perhaps they are! However, I
gradually discovered that, in their quest to discover the essence of being, the Taoists
had essentially developed a theory of personality, which described five main aspects
of the psyche. In researching these, and the associated feelings and meridians,† at
first I made linear diagrams. For example, I showed the feelings associated with the
Heart like this:

Gradually, these straight lines turned into circles, like those in the Emotional Kaleidoscope diagram in Chapter 2, as I began to realize that *the psyche is polar in
nature.*††

** This book describes the Taoist philosophy, *not* Taoism as a religion. Taoism is the oldest
philosophy of China, and the basis of acupressure theory. It is an integral part of the *Nei Ching*
("Yellow Emperor's Classic of Internal Medicine"), which was the first description of acupressure
theory, written down from oral tradition around the fourth century B.C. During the "Golden Age
of Taoism" (from the third century B.C. to the seventh century A.D.), Taoist therapists contributed
significantly to the development of the Chinese health arts, and Taoism continued to have a strong
influence as late as the seventeenth century A.D. Taoist yogic techniques included simple breathing
and movement exercises, as well as work with acu-points and visualization methods.

† *Meridian:* a functionally-related series of acu-points. See Chapter 1 for more complete description of meridians and acu-points, and for a chart of them.

†† We all, then, are all things, and are capable of all feelings. Therefore labeling—whether with
terms of Western psychology or with Eastern terms—is a dangerous business. In this book, words
like "hysterical" or "paranoid" are used to describe emotional states, not as labels which define
a person.

I also gradually began to realize what I had been asking for, in deciding to write a book about feelings and emotions. What was that? A whole lot of *feeling*, and a lot of change! Paying attention to my feelings, and to images which came up in dreams and during Jin Shin Do sessions, I decided to move to the mountains with my son at the end of 1980 and, in 1982, to start the Jin Shin Do® Foundation—an international association of authorized Jin Shin Do® teachers. That year also saw the initiation of the Intensive Training Program—still one of the requirements for trademark licensure and teacher authorization.

All of the thousands of students and hundreds of clients with whom I have worked, over the past dozen years, have contributed in some way to the evolution of Jin Shin Do® Bodymind Acupressure, so my heartfelt gratitude goes to them all. In my practice as an acupressurist and psychotherapist, I have been often and deeply touched by witnessing the power, wisdom, love and beauty that are found at the core of each of us, when we let ourselves get down to that core. I am especially grateful to the many persons who shared their inner processes with me, while they were receiving Jin Shin Do sessions, and I particularly want to thank the clients who have allowed me to include a description of their inner journeys in this book, in an anonymous way. Without their generosity, it would not have been possible to write this book in the way that I wanted to—by letting the stories of people's experiences illustrate the bodymind connection, rather than by just talking about it.

I want to thank all the Jin Shin Do® Foundation members, throughout the United States and in Canada and Europe, for supporting me over the years (especially the past couple of years, when so much of my energy has been focused on completing the research and writing of this book). A special gratitude goes to Arnold Porter and Camille Bertolet, whose contributions are noted in Chapters 4 and 5. (In all the other stories and examples, the names are fictitious, so as to preserve confidentiality.) My heartfelt appreciation also goes to other JSDF members who gave permission to include parts of their (Intensive Training Program) papers, describing their Jin Shin Do experiences: Kim Carter, Erica Clark, Marcia Siegel Cooper, Gail Hubatch, Claire Nance, Susan MacEwen, Jasmine Miller, Marielle Robitaille, Renee Ryan, Debby Valentine Smith, Steve Schumacher, and Pat Zulkosky.

I want to particularly thank Aminah Raheem, Ph.D. and Camille Bertolet, who participated as therapists in a few of the sessions described in this book, and I want to thank these other JSDF training program staff members for their support and help: Justin Pomeroy, Claire Nance, Nancy Marchant, Mary Ann Oughton, Fran Javurek and Jürgen Mücher, M.D., (who gets a special thanks for his suggestions regarding the physiological sections). Additionally, I want to thank another ITP staff member, Weyler Greene, Ph.D., for illuminating the connection between Jung and Taoism, and for reading and giving me valuable feedback on the manuscript (for which I also thank Ruth Scolnick and Phyllis Ross). I also am grateful to Kathleen Chaney for her map of the "5 Lands" in Chapter 3, and to Bob Simpson for his circular tree drawings in Chapters 3 and 13. There are so many more people I would like to thank personally, but even if this list were to go on for another page, I doubt I could include everyone who has been important in some way. I cannot conclude, however, without thanking my psychology professors at Antioch University, who helped me to begin researching this book while getting a thorough grounding in Western psychology. I also am grateful to the various authors and translators who have allowed quotes from their work to be used in this book. (Of course, the presence of these quotes does not imply endorsement by these writers of the ideas presented in this book.) Throughout the book, I have usually spoken of Western psychologists and Taoist philosophers in the present tense, whether they are living or not—even Chuang Tzu and Lao Tzu, who lived over two thousand years ago. This is because I feel that in a sense the great philosophers are still living; they are still speaking to us.

IONA MARSAA TEEGUARDEN, M.A., M.F.C.C.
Idyllwild, California
February, 1986

1. The Bodymind Whole and the Core Self

The Joy of Feeling is an antidote to *the fear of feeling*—an attitude so pervasive that it could be seen as an emotional plague. It is easy to fear pain and painful feelings. It is common to want to run from or repress upsetting and distressing feelings, like hurt and anger. It is even common to suppress pleasurable feelings, like love and joy—because intense feelings can be threatening, or because of the fear that pleasure will wane and pain will follow. It probably will, sometime. The problem with feeling is that we don't get to choose only pleasurable feelings. We can choose to feel or to close down our feelings. If we let ourselves feel, we will feel both sides of life.

Feelings of physical and emotional pain are especially scary if we have no tools for releasing tension and relieving pain. But not to feel is also a problem. When there is little or no real feeling, we are stuck in a joyless space, feeling out of touch with ourselves and empty inside. We want to change that, but we may not quite know how. Jin Shin Do® (pronounced "doe") acupressure facilitates physical and emotional change, partly just by helping to make it *safe to feel*. Jin Shin Do bodymind acupressure is a powerful tool for relaxing tension and for reducing stress and pain. We naturally begin to have more trust of our bodymind selves through finding that we *can* release our tensions and transform pain back into pleasure. We begin to discover the joy of feeling and of being our whole selves—able to embrace all the aspects of ourselves, all of our physical and emotional feelings.

We cannot avoid pain. There is no right way to live that will exempt us from ever feeling physical and emotional discomfort. Yet we commonly spend a lot of time looking for the *right* way to live—and alternately, perhaps, rebelling against it. Why not instead search out the *natural* way—the way that is natural to ourselves? Maybe it seems safer to follow the way that some authoritative voice guarantees is the right one. The problem is that there are a great many such voices, all quite insistent about what is the *right* way to do this and that, and all proclaiming a different right way. There is at least the necessity of choosing between the various authorities. How can we so choose, if we do not trust our inner wisdom, if we have no sense of inner authority?

In ancient China, the Confucianists tried to regulate human behavior by advocating certain standards of virtue, telling people the *right* way to behave. This implies, of course, that it is possible to find *the* right way for everyone. "Enough of all this!" said the Taoists. "Enough of trying to act in ways that are natural to others but not natural to yourself!" Life is a process of constant change. How then can there be any unchanging *right* way? Life meanders about, like a river, flowing now this way and now that. Any linear perspective on life is as artificial as a cement-bottomed canal.

> "Natures differ, and needs with them.
> Hence the wise men of old
> Did not lay down
> One measure for all."[1]

Taoism is the Natural Way. The Taoist attitude is a flexible and adaptive one. The Taoist mind is yielding, rather than fixed on certain expectations. It is integrative, rather than excluding that judged "wrong" and holding to that judged "right." The Taoists describe a psyche "oscillating with the Tao"—that is, in tune with the unity of life or nature in all its changing forms. "Tao" basically means Nature or The Whole. ("Do" is the Japanese equivalent.) A Taoist view of life sees that there are *cycles* of change; there are *patterns* within life processes. We cannot always see the whole pattern while the changes are coming down, but even the seemingly negative or painful changes may be necessary for our growth. Changes generally need not be experienced as grounds for losing our inner joy. The real joy lies just in *being*—in the freedom to feel and be our *whole* selves.

> "The right way to go easy
> Is to forget the right way
> And forget that the going is easy."[1]

The most important teacher is the Self—not the ego or self-image, but the totality and core of our bodymind being. To see this is to have a change of heart, or of values. Much of society tempts us to value fame and fortune, or the enhancement of our image, more than we value our innate natural selves. Admittedly, possessions and prestige are useful and enjoyable commodities. But if we look around, it is obvious that they don't necessarily bring joy and contentment. Neither does happiness necessarily follow in the wake of rampant social change—from the wholesale substitution of one set of standards for another. So, what shall we try now? Who can teach us what to do?

> "If one is true to one's self and follows its teaching,
> Who need be without a teacher?
> Not only those who are experienced and wise may have a teacher,
> The fools have theirs too.
> When those who are not true to themselves try to choose
>   between right and wrong,
> It is as if they set off for Yueh today and arrived yesterday."[2]

How can we tune into our inner wisdom? One channel to the inner Self is our feelings and emotions. Traditional Chinese acupressure theory, based on Taoist philosophy, says that these are manifestations of *Shen*—"the core Self or inner spirit." (*Shin* is the Japanese word for this inner Self.) Emotions are also produced by glandular and visceral reactions to changes in the environment. Therefore, our feelings and emotions can help us tune in to stresses in our life situation, and they can give us guidance about inner needs. They are the *driving energy* of the body, and they generate self-expressive behavior. The Chinese classics say that without the energy generated by feelings and emotions, the body would die. At the least, without the capacity to feel, we would not be able to respond to or participate in life.

Feelings are how we experience ourselves. Feelings are the subject of this book. Jin Shin Do acupressure is a means to being more *in touch with* our bodymind feelings, and a tool for learning to transform painful feelings into pleasurable ones. A basic discovery is that releasing muscular tension not only increases physical well-being, but also promotes emotional well-being. A further discovery is that release of tension can bring up both "negative" and "positive" feelings and emotions. Sometimes we encounter distressing feelings that, unnoticed, have been limiting our wellness and our joy of life. Then as the muscular tensions release deeply, happy or peaceful feelings arise.

For an example, let's look in on a session with Louise, whose presenting problems included low back pain. In several earlier sessions, Louise had noticed how she tended to shut her feelings down, out of a fear of hurt or rejection. At this session, she complained that her back had been hurting more, she'd been feeling unhappy and "shaky," and her boyfriend had been unsupportive. As she focused on the low back point I was holding, she said, "That's where I feel the lack of support! I feel like my whole body wants to collapse around that point. That tension has something to do with my fear." As the tension released more deeply, Louise had a dramatically transformative experience. "Now I'm feeling warmth there," she said. "It's radiating out from those points. It's like a hammock supporting me! Suddenly I feel very solid, and happier than I have for days! I used to be afraid that I'd be more vulnerable if I relaxed and opened myself. But I feel supported and protected, like I'm in touch with something very strong inside of me." Later she said, "The experience reminded me that I've been resisting something so wonderful, to hang onto feelings that are so painful. But because they're familiar, they feel safe. It made such a difference to really feel it in my body, instead of just knowing it in my head."

Getting in touch with the body and its feelings is a way to get in touch with the core Self, which is both strong and wise. Before we take off on this pathway, a central question is: what are feelings? The word "feeling," and the words for specific feelings, may mean different things to different people. Therefore, it is necessary to define these words. I am using "feeling" in its most usual sense. Feelings are all the subjective reactions, pleasurable and unpleasurable, that we can have to a situation. The varieties of feelings include moods, sensitivities, sensations, impressions and emotions. "Emotions," then, are a special class of feelings—intense feelings with strong physical and psychic manifestations. The word "feeling" is also used to mean intuition, like when we say "I had a feeling that would happen." Intuitions can derive from feelings, so the distinction between these states is not a sharp one, but intuition has more to do with perceiving possibilities. Feeling is an unreflective reply, by the core Self or the conditioned self, to a situation. Feelings and emotions are not meaningless states. They are ways of responding to a situation and transforming it.

In defining feeling and emotion, we have encountered another term to be defined: psychic. The word *psychic* is commonly used to refer to supernatural abilities—those beyond the natural or known. Literally, however, *psychic* means "of the psyche." We need look no further than our own psyches to find something which is largely "beyond the known." The psyche is the emotional, mental, and spiritual aspects of ourselves. Though it can be conceived as the non-physical part of a person, the psyche operates through physical processes. The psyche is that which governs the total organism and its interactions with the environment; thus it is almost synonymous with the "Self." According to Carl Jung (who led Western psychology "in search of a soul"), the Self is an inner regulating center which directs the development of the psyche.[3] The Self is the core of the psyche, yet in another sense it is the totality of the psyche, because it is the guiding factor behind the entire process of psychic development. The ego, which wants to be directing the whole show, is but a limited reflection of the inner Self, which the Taoists called Shen.

The Psyche

The Self is the core of the psyche and yet it is also the whole of the psyche, because it directs the entire process of self-actualization (represented by the spiral).

The focus of psychology is, of course, on psychological processes. Until recently, the body has been largely left out of Western psychotherapy. In fact, in the early days of psychology, the therapist not only did not touch the client, but even frequently sat out of sight. A few voices cried out in this mental wilderness, saying that the body is where it's happening. The body is not just the housing for the psyche. The body and psyche are one whole. Working with the body is a powerful way of encountering the psyche, for psychic events manifest in the body—in tensions, diseases, even in the general body structure.

While many psychotherapists hesitated to take the bodymind connection seriously, the prophets of bodymind wholeness—like Wilhelm Reich and, later, Alexander Lowen—demonstrated the validity of a more wholistic approach by working with it. Increasingly, bodywork became a common psychotherapeutic technique, as many therapists discovered that releasing the body helps free the psyche, just as freeing the psyche helps release the body. The word *bodymind* was coined to describe the unity of body and psyche, and made popular in the late seventies by Ken Dychtwald's landmark book *Bodymind*. The perspective that the body and psyche are one whole, and that optimal treatment of either involves considering both, was also a basic premise behind the traditional Oriental health arts. The underlying Taoist philosophy said that Shen, the inner spirit, is the ruler of the body as well as the psyche; the two are one. To treat the bodymind, the ancient Oriental healers used acupuncture, acupressure, diet, herbs, and breathing and exercise therapies.

This book will concentrate on the use of Jin Shin Do acupressure and Taoistic breathing techniques, and will introduce a simple acu-exercise method. In discussing acupressure, however, we are also discussing acupuncture, in that the traditional theory behind both techniques is the same, and the same "acu-points" are used in both methods. During several thousand years of experimentation, the Chinese located 361 key acu-points, and described their physical and psychological functions. Each system of acupressure and acupuncture regularly uses perhaps a third or half of these points. Acu–points are characterized by a particular kind of sensitivity which is felt upon finger pressure. Many of them are found within muscles; others are located at joints. Some, but not all, are nerve-related.

What do we know about these points, scientifically? Outcome studies have confirmed that stimulating the acu-points is more effective for relieving various physical and psychological symptoms than is stimulating non-points. Research has shown that the skin temperature at the acu-points is significantly different from that of the neighboring area—usually one-half to one degree Celsius higher. When stimulated, the acu-points show a "peculiar rise in skin temperature," which can last for about ten minutes. Research has also shown that there is a markedly decreased electrical resistance at these points—about 1/100 that of the surrounding area.[4] This begins to confirm the traditional Oriental view that these are points of high energy concentration, or points which conduct energy, along pathways which are called *meridians*.

Recent research has shown that stimulation of the traditional acu-points also has the interesting effect of increasing the pituitary gland's production of *endorphins*, which have been called the body's own opiate. One reason why acupressure can reduce pain is that it relaxes muscular tension. Endorphin release may be another reason. But reducing pain may not even be the principal function of endorphins. In general, endorphins seem to relax the organism so that it doesn't respond too forcefully to negative cognitive or environmental stimuli. Therefore, an increased endorphin level has been found helpful in treating various psychological problems, including depression.

The basic difference between acupuncture and acupressure is that the former uses needles to stimulate the acu-points, whereas the latter uses finger pressure. Both aim at balancing the body energy. As a generalization, acupuncture may be more effective for internal organ problems, and acupressure for release of muscular tension and emotional distress. There is also an experiential difference between acupuncture and acupressure. That is, the feelings evoked by the two methods are different. Although there may be tingling or electrical sensations with either method of point stimulation, feelings of deep energic relaxation more often accompany acupressure.

Acupressure also tends to be a more meditative experience, and one which facilitates feeling the bodymind connection. Holding points in the center of a tense muscle brings awareness to the tension and allows it to begin relaxing. As the tension releases, there often arises awareness of physical and emotional stressors that have been generating the tension. Jin Shin Do especially encourages a deep awareness of body and psyche, because it is the most slow-paced form of acupressure. Pressure is gradually applied to the points, and held long enough to give the tension a chance to release deeply. This is a process of *being with* the body, by successively feeling into and releasing the tense or problematic areas.

In this process, we discover that unblocking the body helps to unlock the psyche. We can explain this by saying that the body and psyche are one inter-connected whole, or we can go a step further and say that the body *is* the unconscious. As we grow up and become "socialized," we tend to gradually envelop our healthy core Selves in layers of muscular tension, which limit our ability to feel. When an emotion meets with disapproval or punishment, the body contracts to control the feeling and ward off its expression. The same phenomenon occurs when the intensity of a particular feeling is more than we can currently handle. Feelings which meet with such external or internal prohibitions are contracted over, or buried in tension. The muscular contraction is, however, an expression of the feeling that is being suppressed. That is how the body becomes a record of, or in a sense *is*, the unconscious mind.

For example, can you recall the feeling of anger? Can you remember how the back hunches up, the shoulder muscles feel swollen and achy, the neck is tight and rigid, the jaw juts forward, the upper arm muscles turn into taut bands, or maybe the hand wants to make a fist? Instinctively, the body goes into an attack position. Anger stimulates a surge of energy into the muscles used for hitting, grabbing, striking, biting, yelling or talking. Anger *is* energy. *If the energy is not released or used in some appropriate activity, it stays bound in the related musculature.* It also makes us seethe inside. We can deny the anger and banish it from our conscious awareness, but *the muscular tension which it has generated acts like a record of the inner frustration.*

With intense anger, the rush of energy can be so strong that the head feels like a pressure cooker. We may even "see red." Because it can be so powerful, anger is an emotion that often meets with internal and external prohibitions. Guilt is part of how we keep the anger down. Shoulder, back, arm and neck pain, as well as headaches, can be signs of a resultant frustration within the bodymind system. Sherry, for example, had migraine headaches at least once a week. Her neck and shoulders were very tense and sore. Her husband said she had to stop taking responsibility for everyone's problems. "It's like a burden on my shoulders," she agreed, but said she had been raised with a lot of guilt, and with the message that she should live for others. In her forties, Sherry was supporting her father, yet he constantly complained that she wasn't doing enough for him. There was a lot of anger about that situation, but Sherry could never really tell her father how she felt, partly because instead of listening he would just start "ranting and raving."

With the help of tense shoulder and neck muscles and at the price of migraines, Sherry had kept her anger down. After all, anger was hardly part of the "duty" her father was always talking about; it was hardly part of what Sherry had been taught she was supposed to feel. A pervasive sense of guilt kept her from giving priority to her own needs and feelings. As Sherry allowed and expressed her anger during release of her muscular tensions, the feeling of inner frustration diminished and her migraines subsided. "The headaches used to intimidate me, like many other parts of my life did," she said later. "I learned that I could feel them coming on, work with the tension right away, and have the pain recede within an hour or two instead of in a couple days. Part of it is letting go of guilt about my anger, and even of guilt about not feeling guilty!"

The unconscious includes not only repressed feelings and thoughts, but also aspects of ourselves that have never been conscious. It is rather like a surprise package which contains some delightful things we hadn't known we wanted. A lot of the reason for repressing certain feelings, and for suppressing awareness of certain aspects of ourselves, is our tendency to suppress natural emotional responses according to what we think others think. We have introjected societal opinions about what is good and bad, desirable and undesirable, usually beginning with our parents' attitudes, and continuing with those of our peers and of various authorities. As these attitudes become firmly entrenched, they function to repress not only "unacceptable" thoughts and feelings, but also unrealized potentialities.

Throughout life, so many people want to tell us what we *should* think and feel, that eventually we can lose touch with what we really *do* think and feel, as we begin to be ruled by the limiting attitudes that we have introjected. These become the tapes operating our bodymind system. Unfortunately, many of them are negative stimuli, with distressing messages. A couple of Sherry's "old tapes," for example, were "getting mad means you're bad" and "you should live for others, not for yourself."

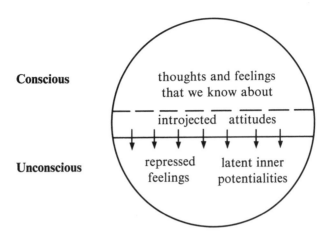

Conscious — thoughts and feelings that we know about

introjected attitudes

Unconscious — repressed feelings / latent inner potentialities

Such negative "old tapes" replay continuously to an inner audience—all the parts of ourselves. They interfere with listening to the voice of the core Self, and they hamper our relationships with others. Western psychology says that understanding and being aware of these "introjects," or old tapes, helps us to grow into our whole Selves.

Freedom

The Taoists talked about introjects too. Chuang Tzu tells the story of a disciple who traveled seven days and nights to see Lao Tzu, in the hope of finding a solution to his distress and a way out of his conflicts. When he arrived, Lao Tzu said, "Who are all those people you have brought with you?" Surprised, the man whirled around to look. Nobody was there. The "crowd of people" that he brought along was his old baggage of introjected judgments, and conventional ideas about right and wrong, good and bad.

Lao Tzu said, "You have got lost and are trying to find your way back to your own true self. You find nothing but illegible signposts pointing in all directions. I pity you." The disciple did not understand; he proceeded to meditate for ten days on cultivating qualities he thought desirable and getting rid of undesirable qualities. This only led to more conflict, confusion and despair. "Miserable!" said Lao Tzu. "All blocked up! Tied up in knots! Try to get untied!" He advised the disciple to ignore external obstructions, and to not let internal obstructions (or introjects) take effect.

The disciple groaned and said, "in my search for the Tao, I am like a sick man who takes medicine that makes him ten times worse." He asked Lao Tzu to just tell him how to begin. Lao Tzu replied: "Can you embrace the One and not lose it? Can you rest where there is rest? Do you know when to stop? Can you mind your own business without cares, without desiring reports of how others are progressing? Can you stand on your own feet? Can you duck? Can you be like an infant that cries all day without getting a sore throat, or clenches his fist all day without getting a sore hand, or gazes all day without eyestrain?" Begin by just flowing along with the current of life, like an infant, instead of trying to figure things out. "This enables you to unlearn, so that you can be led by Tao, be a child of Tao."[5]

As we grow up, our feelings are conditioned by others' judgments of what is desirable and undesirable, right and wrong, good and bad. We take these judgments into ourselves, or introject them. Then it is largely in their light that we see ourselves or our feelings as bad, and so tie ourselves up in knots of psychic and physical tension. An infant just responds to life directly, not yet being able to label feelings as "right" or "wrong." To be like an infant is to live in the here and now. That is where joy is—the joy of feeling and the joy of being.

How do we find this place of joyful simplicity and freedom? How do we become a child of the Tao, or contact the child-like core Self? Lao Tzu says we must "unlearn" and get "untied." To *unlearn* is to get free from negative attitudes which keep us out of the here and now. To get untied is to relax, and stop trying to live up to introjected expectations. Then we can feel the natural state of the core Self—a child-like joy of being that encompasses all of life's cycles of pain and pleasure.

In short, what we need to do is to free ourselves from the world, says Chuang Tzu. Freeing ourselves from the world means quieting down the hubub of the "ten thousand things," so that we can feel the joyous inner Self. It means letting go of the burden of conventional values, and throwing away distress-making ideas of right and wrong. Much of our suffering comes just from our habits of perceiving one thing as wrong or bad, and another as right or good.

When we see something as bad or wrong, we get upset. We can try to change the perceived ill by reforming the situation, the person, the society. Chuang Tzu recommends an opposite solution: drop all distinctions and embrace the "wrong" with the "right." Much energy is wasted by suffering over things that we have labeled "wrong," or by grappling for perceived rights. Much distress can be eliminated just by getting free from limiting attitudes based on outdated values, and learning to see and accept *what is.* How can we do that? Sometimes, if Chuang Tzu's allegories are an example, we can communicate, and so help each other get free from rigid mindsets. Sometimes we can do nothing except "hold fast to the Source" and "flow with the Tao."

To flow with the Tao is to flow with the changes of life. A very simple observation, but one with far-reaching implications, is that EVERYTHING CHANGES, except the fact that everything changes. Everything changes except the Tao or the Way of Nature.

> "The Way is without beginning or end, but things have their life and death —you cannot rely upon their fulfillment. One moment empty, the next moment full—you cannot depend upon their form. The years cannot be held off; time cannot be stopped. Decay, growth, fullness, and emptiness end and then begin again.... The life of things is a gallop, a headlong dash—with every moment they alter, with every moment they shift. What should you do and what should you not do? Everything will change of itself, that is certain!"[6]

Everything changes inside oneself and in the outside world, but there is a unity behind all the changing aspects of the Self and of Nature. Though life changes at a gallop, there is a WHOLENESS to it all. Chuang Tzu says, "all the ten thousand things are what they are, and thus they enfold each other."[6] All the ten thousand things are part of the Tao; all beings are energically or spiritually connected. The principle of WHOLENESS implies that wo/man is one with the environment, and similarly that the body and the psyche are one. There are no real boundaries between things—not between people, nor between the forces of nature, nor between the various aspects of oneself. All divisions—between one nation and another, between one religion and another, between one aspect of the self and another—are arbitrary. Our minds impose divisions on *what is*, because we do not realize the unity of all life.

It is by discovering and staying in touch with our inner natures that we can feel our oneness with Nature or the Tao. The ORIGINAL NATURE is child-like simplicity, freedom and joy. "It is the mirror of heaven and earth, the glass of everything," says Chuang Tzu.[7] To find the original inner nature or true Self, we must first accept all its aspects and affects.* Otherwise we are at war with ourselves—accepting some parts of ourselves and denying others. To accept all of ourselves is to be aware of our original inner nature.

One way to become aware of your inner Self is through meditation. A simple Taoist meditation involved focusing on the breath, breathing slowly, and letting your breath take you down inside yourself—down to a place of comfort inside yourself, down to the core of yourself. There, you will find an inner beauty and tranquility. You will feel a pleasant lightness, yet sense an inner power. You may discover something like a core of energy, or energy centers. Jin Shin Do acupressure is a simple technique for inducing this deep—and deeply pleasant—meditative or trance-like state. It is a means to bodymind relaxation, and it can be a shortcut to experiencing the original nature or core Self—which always knows what is so and what is needed.

The Bodymind Connection

What are you feeling? The answer might range from the physical realm to the emotional. Right now, what are you feeling? Take a couple minutes to scan your body, tuning into the feeling in your head, neck, shoulders, arms, back, chest, abdomen, pelvis, and legs. Physically, are you feeling tension or relaxation, pain or pleasure? Where in your body are you feeling these things? Now, what else are you feeling? Take a couple of minutes to just get a sense of where you are, emotionally and physically. Just feel into yourself, and let the words come up from the feelings. You might discover a sense of peace or confusion, happiness or sadness, frustration, openness—or a hundred other feelings and emotions. Where in your body are you feeling this? Suspend any skepticism you might have about the validity of this question, and tune into your body again. You may discover that there is a lightness in your body when you feel happy, a heaviness when you feel sad, a tightness somewhere when you are confused, a tenseness somewhere else when you are frustrated. Not only are the body and the psyche one interconnected whole, but also certain feelings and emotions tend to register in particular, related parts of the body.

Emotions and feelings serve a homeostatic function. In ordinary circumstances, they remain within reasonable bounds and generally enliven us. In extreme situations, when it is imperative to adjust in some way to something, emotions like anger, fear,

---

* "Affect" basically means feeling or emotion, especially a strong emotional response (as to an idea, object, person or situation).

concern, grief or excitement arise. The ancient Chinese called these "evil" emotions —but their word "evil" meant "extreme," *not* "bad." The extreme emotions stimulate the necessary activity for dealing with an emergency, or they facilitate the cathartic release of stress. They generate particular hormonal changes, stimulate related organs, and energize certain parts of the body. For example, anger stimulates the energy for confronting difficulties, while fear mobilizes the body to move away from danger.

As the difficulty is dealt with or the emergency met, the extreme emotions are transformed into harmonious, pleasant feeling states, like self-assertion, resolution, empathy, openness and joy. I call these "synergic" emotional states, because *synergic* means "working together." The synergic states are characterized by the feeling that all the aspects of oneself—and of life, too—are working together.

If the situational or psychic problem is *not* resolved, distressed feelings instead arise, calling our attention to that fact. There are dozens of these "distressed" feelings, and they can make us miserable. Unresolved anger, for example, can turn into upsetting feelings like resentment, hostility, bitterness, guilt or depression. We will begin to explore the polarities of extreme, synergic and distressed feelings, and their correlation with the "organ meridians," in the next chapter. Here I want to introduce the basic Taoist view of the bodymind connection and some parallel Western views.

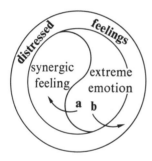

a) When released and resolved, the extreme emotions transform back to synergic feeling states.
b) When denied or clung to, they breed distressed feelings which start knocking at the door of consciousness.

"Under normal conditions, the emotions change under the pressures of external circumstances," says Kok Yuen Leung, "and because nothing is static, the emotions shift and blend continually throughout the day."[8] In a natural state, our feelings are constantly changing, in response to life events. Nothing is static; our emotional nature is no exception to the phenomenon of constant change. As a client put it, "I've been reading in one of those 'Tao books' that the kaleidoscopic shifting of emotions is natural, and that *resistance* is the problem. To flow with the Tao is to flow with your feelings too!"

This client, Charles, was recovering from a depressive disorder, which is a rather extreme example of a "distressed" feeling state. To put it simply, depression comes from not flowing with your feelings and natural emotional responses. It is an "affective" disorder characterized by a general *lack of feeling*, with symptoms like loss of appetite or sexual desire, sleep disturbances, attitudes of worthlessness or hopelessness, passivity or apathy, and decreased energy even for usual activities. Depression is the ultimate result of trying to close down our feelings and emotions. Basically, a depressive state is the opposite of aliveness, which is feeling-ness.

For many years, Charles had retreated from his feelings, and from anything new, diligently maintaining a "calm, cool and collected" front. To break the depressive spell, he had to learn to accept feelings like anger and hurt, and even joy. Early in our work together, Charles had a dream which symbolized the depressive process. He was on a submarine, with the cast of "Voyage to the Bottom of the Sea." He was an observer (as in real life), in the control room of the submarine. An "energy being" progressively took over the ship, causing the controls to fail one after another. Depression is similarly much like a force which takes over the controls of the psyche, shutting down one aspect after another, until we are powerless and can't do much of anything. But it is some part of ourselves which is shutting down the Self—perhaps the part that is afraid of feeling and prefers a safe neutrality. *Resistance* is indeed the problem. To resist your feelings is to resist your Self.

Extreme or distressed feelings just indicate that something is changing or some change is needed—whether in our attitude or in our situation, is left to discover. Resistance to change, and to changing, prolongs the emotional distress and any related physical distress. We resist changes we see as bad, and sometimes we resist changes just because the unknown seems unsafe. Similarly we resist the emotions that may be signalling these changes. We see certain emotions as *bad* and suppress them, or we start *blaming* someone else or ourselves for the "bad" feelings. Either way, we avoid our real feelings and so shut down some parts of ourselves.

But if we don't shut down some of our feelings, maybe they'll run rampant! That's why social rules and mores arose—to prevent us from getting "carried away" by our emotions and desires. Do these external restrictions work? Do they prevent violence, or help people to be happy? The Taoists thought not.

> "Happiness is as light as a feather, but nobody knows how to bear it.
> Calamity is as heavy as the earth, but nobody knows how to avoid it.
> Enough! Enough of this confronting people with virtue!
> Beware! Beware of trudging down this marked path!"[9]

The Taoists thought that imposed and introjected rules and mores cause more trouble than they prevent. For example, an introjected voice may say we are not "good" unless we act in circumscribed ways. Then we may feel guilty because we aren't always "nice," or we may feel resentful of being expected to be what we are not. The Taoists said that the self-expressive behavior generated by our feelings and emotions can more effectively be controlled by our own inner Self, or *Shen*. In this inner Self, there is a wisdom that knows the real present or past basis of our feelings, and an inner sense that knows whether an emotional response is more intense than warranted by present circumstances.

When we blindly follow social mores, or let our old tapes operate our system, this inner voice becomes faint amidst all the chatter. It is then difficult to allow Shen, the inner regulating factor, to control our behavior. For example, when we are feeling angry so often that it seems like a habit, our introjects or old tapes may be saying, "You are angry because you screwed up (and you always do)," or "you are angry because s/he is not giving you what you need (and nobody ever does)." At the same time, but more quietly, the inner Self may be saying, "This anger has its roots in the past," or "This anger comes from thinking you (they) should be something you (they) are not." Sometimes, as Charles discovered, the anger comes just from keeping a lid on yourself and your feelings until it feels like there is a volcano inside.

Often, then, resolving our emotional distress and discovering the wisdom of our inner Self requires countering old tapes—becoming aware of and "talking back" to our emotional conditioning. One big old tape that must be countered is the one which says it is good to suppress our emotions, and be continuously "cool, calm and collected." Though conditioned by social training, our feelings and emotions still are a means of receiving guidance about bodymind needs. If we can get past the introjected confusion and follow our feelings, they can lead us back in touch with real inner needs. If we don't hold onto upsetting emotions, and if we stay open to life, distressed feelings tend naturally to transform back into synergic or harmonious emotional states. For example, fear can be transformed into resolution, and the energy of anger can be used for self-assertion. Learning to let our feelings flow is part of freedom. The journey to emotional freedom and spontaneity requires courage and takes time, but it yields joy. Learning to listen to our feelings and emotions, rather than suppressing them—this is a big change. Even the Taoists, two thousand years ago, regarded the re-establishment of natural emotional responsiveness as difficult. They said this spontaneity is hard for civilized wo/man to recover because of social conditioning. As Kok Yuen Leung expresses it, "This is because Man has so consistently warped the emotional behavior of himself and his children, that he can no longer find his own way out of this distressing circumstance."[8] Or, it may be difficult to find the way out.

In this Taoist view, Man has been "tempted away from an instinctive, emotional knowledge of his place in the environment, into an arrogant belief that he stands outside the laws of Nature. His means of receiving guidance (the emotions produced by glandular reactions to external stimuli) became stunted and distorted through willful disobedience to nature, in the name of social convenience."[8] General emotional suppression might be justified as the way to self-control. But controlling destructive actions that may accompany certain emotions does not require denying instinctive emotional responses.

Emotions must be encountered to be overcome. Trying to suppress a habitual emotional response, like fear, does not work as well as listening to the emotion and paying attention to the whole series of thoughts, images and feelings that ensue. We might then discover, for example, that our frequent fears are arising out of a chronically weak, low-energy condition. Or we might discover that the habitual fearfulness stems from a traumatic experience of abandonment or rejection, and resultant introjected messages like "you can't trust anyone," or "anything good will be taken away from you." That a feeling is habitual does not, however, mean that it is never appropriate. Sometimes, paying attention to the fear, we may discover that it is a warning of some real physical or psychic danger, a signal to retreat or to be cautious. Felt fears can be resolved. Denied fears proliferate.

Denying our emotional responses also results in physical tension and distress. Traditional acupressure theory says that disease arises from rebellion against the natural way—against the way of Nature or Tao, and against Shen, our inner nature. Emotional suppression amounts to disobeying Nature's laws in the struggle for social acceptance. The alternative is paying attention to our feeling self and letting it guide us so that we can live fully, or actualize our whole potential. This requires a certain strength or determination, because it entails departing from the herd. We cannot live out our whole selves while limiting our awareness to the parts of ourselves that society likes.

What happens when the demands of society conflict with real inner needs? Acupressure theory says that the pressure of conforming to external behavior codes can result in an inner or emotional confusion which is damaging to the body. If social conditioning restrains our emotions too much, the energy becomes blocked in the functionally-related musculature and organs. Nancy was surprised by this phenomenon when she awoke one morning with a startling pain in her middle back (at the diaphragm/liver associated point). Since this area can correlate with anger and assertion problems, I asked Nancy if she had been frustrated or angry lately. At first she said no. Then she acknowledged that her financee had had several big temper tantrums and had blamed her for all their problems. But Nancy thought she had "gotten over it." She thought that if she could just be more patient things would be all right. She also felt guilty about not having accomplished more in getting their apartment organized, though her work schedule had been hectic. Towards the end of the session, she mentioned that she'd been having frequent headaches.

A week later, her back tension had increased and she had abdominal discomfort as well. The medical diagnosis was a *hiatal* (diaphragmatic) hernia, probably stress-related. Realizing that something had to change, Nancy was now willing to look more deeply into her feelings. She got in touch with the underlying and unexpressed anger which was generating the diaphragm tension, guilt and headaches. She saw that it was okay to express her needs and feelings. Thinking she should take care of everything for everyone was an old tape. Becoming more willing to assert herself, and more aware of the beginning signs of "suppression tension," Nancy was able to reverse her tension pattern. Her body became much more responsive to Jin Shin Do release, but her body tensions had had the value of stimulating needed insights and changes.

The first step towards self-awareness is simply being *able to feel.* We must begin by acknowledging our emotional responses, rather than thinking that we should not have them. "In the achieving of consciousness of one's self, most people must start back at the beginning and rediscover their feelings," says existential psychologist Rollo May. "Their connection with their feelings is as remote as if over a long-distance telephone. They do not feel directly, but only give ideas about their feelings; they are not affected by their affects; their emotions give them no motion."[10]

Being conscious or self-aware involves being able to recognize the various "affects" or emotional tones. Maturity involves being able to appropriately express or release feelings and emotions. This is not the same as acting out, or catharting all over everyone. Nor is it the same as explaining and defending feelings. The key words are "I FEEL. . . ." Right now I feel hurt, tired, angry, happy, sad, disheartened, excited. . . . Most importantly, right now I FEEL.

Perhaps you remember looking up at the stars or at a tree lighted by the moon, smelling the flowers or the fields, and feeling your Self, an alive being in a big world, with a sense of awe. Perhaps you have felt this child-like wonderment while looking out at the ocean or up at a mountain peak. This feeling of freshness and joy can be almost ground out of us as we "grow up," discover the extended world, and learn to get on in it. The *wonder* and with it the child-like *joy* can be recovered, if we are willing to risk journeying back into an increased feeling awareness of ourselves and the world. This is the antidote to rampant feelings of emptiness, dullness and boredom. "Except ye become as a little child, ye cannot enter the Kingdom of Heaven."

By Kathleen Chaney

Recovering the freedom to feel involves encountering the body, because being numb physically correlates with being numb emotionally. To feel alive and vital, we must reestablish contact with our bodily self. Although there has been a recent resurgence of interest in body awareness, an observation made by Rollo May in 1953 is still largely valid:

> "As a result of centuries of suppressing the body into an inanimate machine, subordinated to the purposes of modern industrialization, people are proud of paying no attention to the body. They treat it as an object for manipulation, as though it were a truck to be driven till it runs out of gas. The only concern they give it is a thought each week as perfunctory as a phone call to a relative to ask how he is, but with really no intention of taking the answer seriously. Nature then comes along, if we may speak metaphorically, and knocks the person down with colds or the flu or more severe illnesses, as though she were saying, 'When will you learn to listen to your body?' "[10]

Listening to the Body

We can learn to pay attention to the body not only when we are sick, but also when we feel more subtle signals like tension and fatigue. Tension is a response to physical or emotional stress or distress. Chronic tension is a subliminal state of pain. A primal response to pain is contraction of the muscles around the painful area, to decrease sensitivity there. This can be a useful response in a survival crisis, such as when an injured human being needs to escape from a ferocious animal, or an overturned automobile. But as a habitual response, this defensive contraction is fatiguing and can result in a gradual build-up of tension. When tension is chronic, *fascial adhesions* develop—that is, the fibrous connective tissues, which surround muscles and organs, actually begin to adhere together. This limits flexibility and makes the area more liable to strain, sprain or injury. Also, compensating tensions develop in other areas. As this tension or "armoring" accumulates, we begin to be as stiff as the medieval knights in their protective metal suits. For a long time, we may not be aware of how extensive our suits of muscular armoring are.

Charles, for example, was not very aware of his body tensions when he sought psychotherapy for depression. He didn't like to touch or be touched, so at first we worked just verbally. Gradually Charles became more comfortable with his feelings and, coincidentally, a nagging low back pain disappeared. Then he had a dream which pointed to the need for bodywork, by illustrating how his armoring was isolating him from life. (Before this dream, by the way, Charles was not familiar with the term "armoring," as used in bodywork and psychotherapy.) "I was with a gang, stealing some carefully-wrapped money," Charles said. He associated stealing with the feeling that he couldn't get what he needed. "To escape, I mingled with a crowd outside. But then I saw that I was wearing a suit of armor. To avoid being captured, *I had to drop the suit of armoring.*"

To change his mode of withdrawal from life, Charles had to drop the defensive, armored attitude that was reflected in his body armoring. "Then a lion was stalking me. I followed a railroad track to get away." A lion is associated with passion and courage; Charles was afraid of taking any risks and so was attracted to the "straight and narrow" paths. "At the end of the track there was a waterwheel. A gang member appeared and suggested we jump to a boat on the river below." But the boat was going to Russia—definitely an unknown place—so Charles was afraid to jump. "Then suddenly I was in the air, looking down on my other self on the track below, as the waterwheel caught that self and destroyed it." What was the dream telling him? "I might as well jump into the flow of life, because life will get me anyway!"

By the time we are adults, most of us have a fair amount of both psychological and muscular armoring, because we are generally taught how we *ought* to respond, rather than encouraged to be aware of our *natural* physical and emotional responses. The armoring process can be reversed if we can learn ways to relax and release bodymind tension, after a physical and/or emotional stress is over. Instead, if a tension persists and turns into discomfort or pain, we are often advised to ignore it, learn to live with it, or hope that it will go away soon. Tension and distress often don't just go away, until we change our attitudes to compassion for ourselves as well as others, and until we learn to listen to our bodymind feelings.

As we listen to the body, we discover that it can be an inroad to the psyche. The body and the psyche are an integrated package. The psyche communicates its wellness or dis-ease through the body—in postural, movement and breathing patterns. By paying attention to our muscular tensions and postural habits, we can get in touch with subtle, unconscious attitudes and emotions.

The word "emotion" comes from the Latin word *emovere*—from *movere*, meaning "to move," and *e-*, meaning "out." Emotions move out from the psyche; emotions also move the psyche and the spirit. But emotions are not just psychic events. Emotions also move the body, and are experienced through body feelings, movements and postures. Emotions *move* us through accompanying nerve impulses, muscular, visceral and glandular responses. In other words (those of a psychologist named

34

Dunbar), emotion is "a flow of energy which permeates (though not in equal measure), all parts of the organism."[11]

As an emotion arises, the muscles and systems which may be required for its expression are particularly energized and mobilized. For example, fear mobilizes the muscles used for flight—the lower back and legs. Concern mobilizes the brain; the muscles of the forehead may contract as though to concentrate the energy there. Grief and hurt mobilize the muscles of the chest and throat, which are used for weeping and wailing. Suppressing an emotional response, on the other hand, is accomplished partly by holding the tension in the same related muscles—those which would be used to express or release the emotion.

For example, can you recall the feeling of grief or sorrow? Can you remember how it feels to have a vast aching in the chest, or even a stabbing pain? The pectoral muscles feel sore, and there may be a searing achiness in the throat. The body wants to cry. But the people around us, or our own introjected messages, may be telling us that we shouldn't be weak, or should just stop feeling sorry for ourselves. By tensing the chest and throat muscles, we can hold back the urge to cry. We can also suppress our breathing, so that there is less oxygen intake and thus less energy available for feeling our grief. As the chest armoring builds up, however, there is an increasing feeling of inner heaviness. We become bowed down with sorrow, perhaps developing chest pains or respiratory problems. Alternatively, we can tolerate the aching or pain and breathe through it, holding the tense or sore points to help them release. We can allow tears to come and wash away our pain. Then the chest feels lighter and the spirit lightens too; the back straightens and the voice deepens; there is a pleasant feeling of openness and softness.

Each emotion mobilizes the muscles and organ systems needed for its expression. A chronic tension pattern or postural habit can be a way of repressing a certain feeling or maintaining a certain attitude. When we feel physical tension or find ourselves maintaining an uncomfortable posture, we might ask, "What am I saying through this tension or tense position?" One tension pattern says, "I am afraid of being hurt, so I will not risk really experiencing my love." Another posture says, "I am angry; this is an unfair situation (or world)." Another says, "I'm afraid that I'm not enough."

If a tense posture is a response to an on-going conflict, it cannot be dissolved without resolving the conflict. If the tension is a response to a suppressed feeling, it cannot be magically dissolved unless we can tolerate the anxiety that may come with letting that feeling out. An emotion may be anxiety-producing because it is prohibited or disapproved by others. Or just the intensity of the emotion, or a lack of support and understanding, may make the emotion seem threatening. For whatever reason, if an emotion is too anxiety-producing, then each arising of this "unacceptable" feeling is met by another tensing in functionally-related muscles, in resistance to that feeling. Tension reduces sensitivity to psychological, as well as physical, pain.

Gradually, in this psychological avoidance process, many layers of tension build up around the core Self, in order to prevent feeling more than can be tolerated. Finally, a hard surface layer of tension develops. It is like a superficial veneer, developed to prevent all the undesirable stuff from surfacing. Though the muscles are very tense and rigid to the touch, there is little or no sensation, even with firm pressure. Here the armoring process has proceeded to its logical conclusion—a numbing out. I call it the "armadillo effect." This well-developed armor is a general resistance against feeling, and a block to awareness of the core Self. As feeling returns, at first there may be increased sensitivity or soreness in the areas that were armored, because tension is a subliminal state of pain. As the tension releases more deeply, the natural movement is towards feelings of well-being.

Freeing the body helps to free the psyche, and psychological growth is accompanied by the release of physical tensions. Characteristics of personality change include an increasing acceptance of changing feelings, a growing ability to directly experience and freely express feelings, and an accompanying "physiological loosening," says Carl Rogers (a leading humanistic psychologist).[12] The aim of growthful personality change is *wholeness*. Rogers says that a crucial moment is one of integration, in which communication between the different aspects of ourselves is no longer necessary, because they become *one*—or we realize that they *are* one. When we begin to ask "just who am I?" we find there is a lot more to ourselves than we had known. It is as though we had put boxes around the different aspects of ourselves—large boxes like "body" and "emotions," and smaller boxes like "head" and "groin," "nice" and "not nice." Before we can realize that all these boxes are arbitrary divisions of one whole, we must first allow communication between the different boxes. Communication between the body and the psyche is a good place to start.

> "We are proposing welcoming the body back into the union with the self.
> This means . . . recovering an active awareness of one's body—the pleasure
> of eating or resting or the exhilaration of using toned-up muscles or the
> gratification of sexual impulses and passion—as aspects of the acting self.
> It is not the attitude of 'My *body* feels' but '*I* feel.' "[13]

Looking at illness from a wholistic perspective, Rollo May says that physical, psychological and spiritual diseases "are all aspects of the same difficulty of the self in finding itself in the world." The attitude is not "My back (neck, knee, stomach) is bothering *me*," but rather "*I sicken*" or "I am getting sick." Sometimes physical illness can relieve psychological distress by providing a focus for "floating" anxiety. On the other hand, illness seems to be an inevitable part of life; fatigue, for example, is a simple form of illness. "The battle for health must be won on the deeper level of the *integration of the self*," says May.[13] Wholeness is the harmony of body and psyche, thoughts and feelings, self and environment. This is real health.

The Taoists used acupressure, breathing and exercise techniques to listen to the body and explore the inner Self or spirit. *Jin Shin Do* in fact means "The Way of the Compassionate (Inner) Spirit." As tensions release and the body becomes more flexible, it is easier to feel the beauty and wisdom of the core spirit. Physical tensions and disharmonies are like background noise, making it hard to hear the music of the inner Self. Muscular tensions often reflect conflicts between various aspects of the Self—for example, between what you *think* you should do, and what you *feel* like doing. When communication between the body and psyche is reestablished, the real inner needs can be heard by listening to the voices of both the body and the psyche. At this point, people commonly say "I feel like myself again" or "I feel more whole."

Jin Shin Do® Bodymind Release Process (1) ————————————

In *The Acupressure Way of Health: Jin Shin Do*, I described the Jin Shin Do acupressure technique in great detail. The reader is referred to that basic manual for a step-by-step discussion of how to locate the main acu-points used in Jin Shin Do and of how to apply pressure to these points, as well as for some general balancing patterns (combinations of acu-points) which can be used to release bodymind tension.[14] Here I will give but a summary of the basics of Jin Shin Do acupressure.

The *acu-points* can be described as points of energy concentration, or points which conduct energy along pathways called "meridians" and "channels." This vital energy was called *ch'i* by the Chinese, *ki* by the Japanese, *prana* by the Indians, and *rlun* by the Tibetans. It is the same life force or energy that Wilhelm Reich called *orgone energy* and later scientists have called *bioplasma*. It can be described as an electromagnetic energy which influences balance both in the body and in the psyche.

Meridians or channels are functionally-related series of points, or pathways along which the vital energy flows. At the present time, there is no scientific evidence to satisfactorily explain what the meridians are in an anatomical sense. No mysterious extra tubes or ducts have been found in the body. Research in Japan has suggested that the meridians are located in *interfascial spaces*—spaces between the fibrous membranes which support and separate the muscles.[15] This is an interesting theory, but it does not account for all the meridian routes. What we know is that we can work through the physical body to influence the energy body, which the meridians are part of.

How does the energy, or ch'i, move along these meridians? Japanese researchers have hypothesized that the meridians are stimulated by muscular movement, or by the serial contraction of related muscles.[15] Not only physical movement, but also the flow of emotions, causes such contraction of functionally-related muscles. This brings us back to the traditional theory that emotions are the driving energy of the body and the body needs the energy generated by the emotions. In short, both physical and psychological movement stimulates the flow of the ch'i, and at the same time, the balance or imbalance of this energy in the meridians influences both the body and the psyche.

The channels, called *Strange Flows*, are like connecting links between the twelve organ meridians; they help to balance the entire bodymind energy. The Strange Flows were described in my first book on acupressure: *The Acupressure Way of Health: Jin Shin Do*.[14] This present book focuses on meridian theory. The twelve "organ meridians" distribute energy to all parts of the body. They are related to particular organs, sense organs, and muscles, and to certain feelings or attitudes, as will be described in the next chapter. In Chapters 4 through 13, these meridians will be discussed in detail, emphasizing psychological associations and describing related physical functions. Each chapter will include a diagram of the meridian showing its most important points, directions for locating these points, and stories of clients' experiences during the release of tension at these points.

1. Point Location: The large dots on the accompanying chart show the thirty main points described in *The Acupressure Way of Health: Jin Shin Do*, plus fifteen additional bilateral points (numbered 31 to 45).* All 55 of these main Jin Shin Do points are related to the Strange Flows, as well as to the organ meridians. Here I am illustrating only their organ meridian relationships, since that is the subject of this book. The small dots are functionally-related points in the area of the main points. In Chapters 4 through 13, these will be referred to by the area number and then the meridian name. For example, #19: SI means a point in the #19 area, but on the Small Intestine Meridian. (The equivalent modern acupuncture numbers will also be given.)

To locate these points, you can just feel for the most tense, sore or sensitive spot within the anatomically designated area. As your fingers become more sensitive, you may be able to feel a little hollow or groove at these points, between or within the muscles or bones. Precise point location and optimum angle of point stimulation require practical study under an experienced teacher. Yet, even when point location and technique are imperfect, Jin Shin Do acupressure will help you to get in touch with and relax the body, and to more deeply experience the psyche.**

2. Pressure and Point-Holding: Gradually apply pressure until you can feel the tension in the underlying muscles. The pressure should be firm but gentle. When you are working with someone else, ask the recipient to tell you if it is too little or too much pressure. Define "too much," for otherwise some people will not admit that anything is too much. It's too much pressure if the recipient can't relax with it, or feels like s/he's resisting your touch. Generally in Jin Shin Do the recipient lies on his or her back. To hold back points, the practitioner reaches under the back then curls the fingers up, so as to hold the points with the fingertips. (If your fingers are too weak, or the person's back is too armored, you may use your knuckles under the back points, or else have the recipient lie on his or her abdomen while you hold the back points.) Pay attention to your body position and use your body weight to hold the points, leaning into a point rather than relying just on your finger and arm strength.

When you are doing self-treatment, experiment to find a comfortable position, in which you can hold the points without tensing your body. You might apply a little pressure to the points, but focusing your attention on the points and breathing into the tense areas is more important than pressing hard. To hold back points, you can make your hand into a fist and place your knuckles under the point, leaning back into a chair or lying down. Alternatively, you can place small rubber balls under the points, or you can use an Acu-releaser device (preferably an adjustable one) to hold the back points for you.***

Generally, hold the points an average of one or two minutes, or until you feel a significant softening of the tension at the point. As the tension releases, you will feel a sensation usually described as "pulsation," which correlates with the release and movement of the blocked energy. Also, there will be a decrease of sensitivity at the point. You may need to hold a very tense point for five minutes or so, while with the

---

* Note that #s 35, 40, 41, 42 and 43 should be avoided on pregnant women.

** To assist your practice of Jin Shin Do® Bodymind Acupressure, color-coded wall charts are available from the Jin Shin Do Foundation, P.O. Box 1800, Idyllwild, California 92349, USA. Request descriptive brochure. Directory of authorized teachers also available.

*** Available from the Jin Shin Do Foundation.

Main Points of Organ Meridian

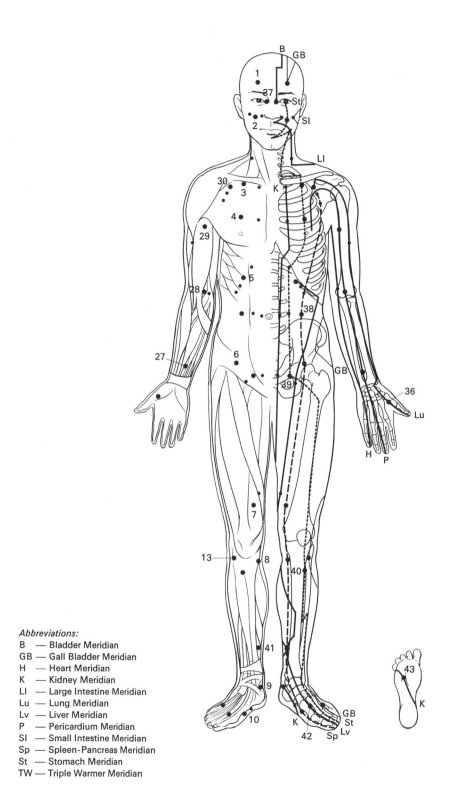

Abbreviations:

B — Bladder Meridian
GB — Gall Bladder Meridian
H — Heart Meridian
K — Kidney Meridian
LI — Large Intestine Meridian
Lu — Lung Meridian
Lv — Liver Meridian
P — Pericardium Meridian
SI — Small Intestine Meridian
Sp — Spleen-Pancreas Meridian
St — Stomach Meridian
TW — Triple Warmer Meridian

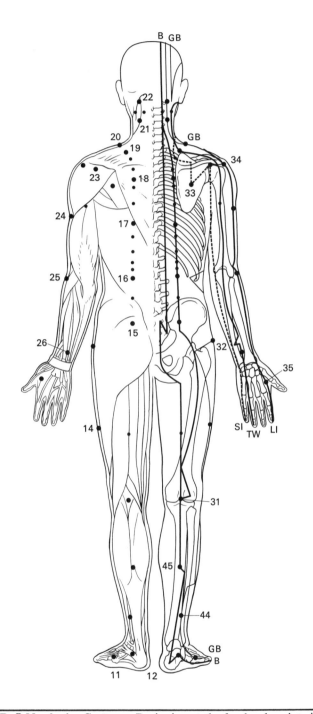

Key to the Jin Shin Do® Numbering System: Beginning at the forehead, points #s 1–30 go down the front of the body, up the back, then along the outside and inside of the arms. Beginning behind the knee, points #s 31–45 again go up the back and down the front of the body (with #35 and #36 being on the hands).

other hand you hold several *distal points*—points which are distant from that problem area but functionally related to it. These "distal points" help to release the *local point*, or problem area, much more quickly than if you just pressed on that area alone. Therefore, in Jin Shin Do you will usually be holding a local point with two or more distal points. On the meridian charts in Chapters 4 through 13, those points most commonly used as local points are shown as larger dots, and those most commonly used as distal points are shown as smaller dots. (By the way, if you cannot reach a distal point on the leg while holding a local point in the upper part of the body, simply bend the knee to bring the leg forward.)

3. Choice of Focus: A simple way to assess the level of physical tension is to check some of the main Jin Shin Do points. You can "palpate" or feel some of these points bilaterally to discover which are the most tense or sensitive. For example, you might check #s 16, 17, 18, 19, 20, 21, 22, 30, 5 and 6, noticing which are most tense or sore, and whether the right or left side feels tighter.*

An even simpler approach is to just ask the recipient what s/he would like to focus on. To find out where the most important knots of tension are, you can ask the recipient to scan the body with the "mind's eye." That means letting the attention rove from the head and neck, into the shoulders and arms, down the back, through the chest and abdomen, and into the legs, feeling for the most tense or sore places. You might also want to notice areas that are difficult to feel into, for numbness or blockage of feeling can also indicate an armored pocket of tension. As various points relax during a Jin Shin Do session, it is common to become aware of others that are tense or blocked. Pay attention to what the body is saying, and notice points that "speak up." They might be saying, among other things, "hold me"!

After choosing a few points of tension or discomfort as your initial focus, refer to the accompanying chart to see which meridian those points are located on. Then find the diagram of that meridian, at the beginning of the chapter describing its associations. For example, if you wish to focus on release of #22, you will see that this is a point on the Gall Bladder Meridian, so you will turn to its diagram in Chapter 4. This diagram will show you which distal points you might hold to help release #22. The more familiar you become with the twelve meridians described throughout this book, the more quickly you will be able to "read" the body, or know the meridian relationships of particular tensions and pains.

4. The Whole Session: When you plan to work with release of several point areas within an hour-long session, generally hold local points in the upper parts of the body first, then those in consecutively lower segments. For example, if you wanted to focus on #s 16, 18 and 21, you would first work with #21 in the neck, then move down to #18 in the upper back, and then to #16 in the lower back, as a general outline. In short, "take it from the top"! Follow this rule also in designing the course of a series of sessions. In the first couple sessions, focus on release of the neck and shoulders; in later sessions you can focus more on release of the front and back of the chest, abdomen and pelvis. You will usually be working with the arms and legs in each ses-

---

* Pulse reading is an important way of assessing the energy condition, to find out which meridians are excessive or deficient, but this requires years of experience and cannot be taught in a book.

sion, since many of the strongest distal points are located on the extremities.

It is a good idea to do basically the same thing *on both sides of the body*. For example, after working with the ♯21 on the left side, you would also work with the ♯21 on the right side of the body. *The simplest approach is to hold the distal points on the same side of the body as the local point.*

At the end of a session, you should do a final *"neck release,"* because the relaxation of this area is extremely important for bodymind well-being. You can just hold ♯20, 21 and 22 bilaterally. You can include a little shoulder release by first holding ♯23 and 19. *It is especially important that the #22s are held until they feel released;* otherwise there may be dizziness or an aching feeling in the head after the session. A nice final touch is to hold points "I" and "J" together, and then points "B" and "D." Afterwards, the recipient should relax for a few minutes, then stretch and get up slowly.

5. Approaching the Psyche via the Body: I will be giving many examples of working with the psyche, especially with feelings and images, in Chapters 4 to 13. Here is a short outline of the process of Jin Shin Do bodymind acupressure.

1. What would you like to focus on? The recipient may want to focus on the release of a physical tension, pain or problem. Or the problem may be an emotional one. In that case, good questions are: Where do you feel that in your body? How do you feel physically?

2. As tense or sore points are being held, let yourself feel the tension at each point. Feel into the point. Just *be with it.* Notice how the initial soreness and tightness can quickly change into pleasurable relaxation. Sometimes, in a deep state of relaxation, you may fall into a deeply refreshing sleep. This is especially likely if you are exhausted or "stressed out." As your bodymind heals, you will be able to choose to stay awake, for most of the session, and be *present* to the release process.

3. Be open to any feelings or images that may come up. There is always a feeling, even if it's just tension or relaxation. Likewise you are always seeing something: light, darkness, colors, or images. Avoid analyzing what you are feeling or seeing. Just allow descriptive words to come up from the experience.

4. Follow the feelings; watch the images. See what else is there. Let your feelings and images tell you about bodymind needs and inner realities.

5. Let your breathing take you down to the center of your Self—that is, into the internal energy centers. Breathe slowly and deeply, feeling your chest and abdomen expand from the inside out. Contacting your energic or psychic core is the key to resolving conflicts, releasing stress and dissolving tension. It is the key to harmonizing polarities and finding an inner freedom and joy.

2. *The Polar Nature of the Psyche —A Taoist View*

The Taoist approach to the psyche is essentially a simple one. Taoist psychology begins with life . . . being, loving, doing, creating, growing—and with death . . . loss, hurt, loneliness, meaninglessness, emptiness. From each death comes a rebirth—a renewed sense of living and loving. With each birth there is again a death—a sense of loss, or of letting go in some way. The cycles go on and on, forming a continuous spiral of change.

Meanwhile, we try to hold on. We repeatedly, if not continuously, try to hold on. We want to keep things the way they are. Or we want to keep parts of our lives the way they are—parts that we like, and even parts which we profess not to like, but which feel safe because they are familiar. What looks like misery to someone else, and even sounds like misery when we talk about it, may still feel safe because it is that to which we are accustomed. And yet we also feel stuck, trapped, distressed.

Somewhere deep inside is the awareness that we are attempting the impossible. We are trying to stop the flow of life. We are trying to make things be the way we think -they should be, or stay put—although they never do. They never have. Changes go on, and on. Just when we had given up, we fall in love, find a house, get a job, see a new pathway. Alternately, and often to no apparent purpose, we find ourselves in the process of separation from a person, place, job or whatever, In one way or another, the pathway that seemed so straightforward veers sharply, perhaps unexpectedly. Obstructions seem to proliferate. We feel bummed-out, traumatized or anxious.

Time and again, it seems that we find harmony and joy only by embracing it all— all of life, all of ourselves. There is peace in accepting the pains with the pleasures, the obstructions with the accomplishments. Hurting can be an okay experience; it can even "hurt good" when there is the inner knowing that there *is* another side—that pleasure can follow pain. So we say, "well, it can't get much worse!" or "this must be the darkness before the dawn," or "there's only one way things can go from here— up!" We can allow ourselves to feel the darkness when that is all, subjectively, that there is. Because cyclic changes are inherent in the process we call life, light follows darkness. In the psyche, light includes feelings of love and joy; darkness includes feelings of pain and distress. We cannot obstruct the planetary cyclic change of dark/ light, night/day. However, by clinging to some distressing thought or feeling, by limiting our perceptions and mindsets, we *can* obstruct the cyclic change of darkness/light in the psyche.

Taoistic *yin/yang* philosophy describes the continuous cyclic change which occurs on every level of life. Night follows day; fall and winter follow spring and summer. Tides ebb and flow. Animals are cyclically active and passive, in tune with the rhythmic changes of the earth and heavens. We do things and we rest; our muscles tense in activity and then relax. Our feelings alternate too; they are cyclically more active and more passive, extraverted and introverted, pleasurable and painful. Cyclic change characterizes all of life, including human physical and psychological processes. Opposites change into each other, and that is how life flows. All of these changes are part of life; all are necessary components of one dynamic whole.

In the Taoist view, opposites are not *opposing*. Opposites are just polar aspects of the same thing; they are *complementary*. Opposites suggest or give rise to each other. Lao Tzu explains:

> "When all in the world understand beauty to be beautiful, then ugliness exists. When all understand goodness to be good, then evil exists. Thus existence suggests non-existence; easy gives rise to difficult; short is derived from long by comparison; low is distinguished from high by position; resonance harmonizes sound; after follows before."[1]

Similarly, modern psychologist Fritz Perls says:

> "Now if we are willing to stay in the center of our world, and not have the center either in a computer or somewhere else, but really in the center, then we are ambidextrous—then we see the two poles of every event. We see that light cannot exist without non-light. If there is sameness, you can't be aware any more. If there is always light, you don't experience light any more. You have to have the rhythm of light and darkness."[2]

Observation of polarities, and of their persistent interplay in our life dramas, was the foundation of Taoist philosophy. The seemingly opposite poles of physical and psychic phenomena were called "yin" and "yang." Yin and yang symbolize the opposite but complementary forces, or energic tendencies, which generate the constant cyclic changes of life in general, and of the bodymind in particular. *Yang* forces are the more active, assertive, generating, moving, arousing energies or feelings; *yin* forces are the more passive, receptive, gestating, containing, yielding energies or feelings.

Yang forces are more active and outgoing. Yang feelings and emotions are more extraverted; energy is directed outwards and the focus is external or towards others. At an extreme, yang feelings can tie us in knots. For example, in resentment our anger is directed out towards others; the ultimate result is hostility and bitterness.

Yin forces are more passive and ingoing. Yin feelings and emotions are more introverted; energy is directed inwards and the focus is internal or towards oneself. At an extreme, yin feelings can close us down and weaken us. For example, in guilt our anger is directed internally, towards ourselves; the ultimate result is psychic impotency or depression.

If "yang" basically means active, and "yin" is passive, we could say that the *conscious* mind is more yang and the *unconscious* more yin. Western psychology, as an entity separate from philosophy, was born with Freud's discovery of this basic polarity: conscious/unconscious. The "defense mechanisms" demonstrate the dynamics of this psychic polarity. Repression and denial are ways of evicting undesirable thoughts and feelings from conscious awareness, instead depositing them in the unconscious. Other defense mechanisms give a virtuous appearance to conscious thoughts and feelings. As discussed in the preceding chapter, tension is the general mechanism for keeping unacceptable thoughts and feelings down in the unconscious (the reflection of which is the body).

The Yin-Yang of Defense Mechanisms

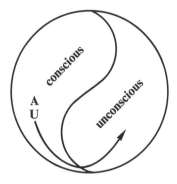

By repression, denial and avoidance, unacceptable feelings (U) are relegated to the unconscious trash can. Conscious awareness is reserved for the opposite acceptable feelings (A).

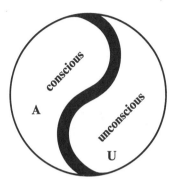

To maintain this state, we bolster the dividing line between the conscious and the unconscious, by rationalizing and by sublimating our disapproved desires and feelings.

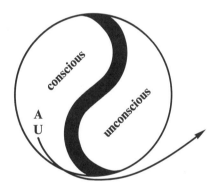

If the unsavory thoughts and feelings won't stay in the trash can, attributing them to others facilitates conscious clinging to the opposite, acceptable thoughts and feelings.

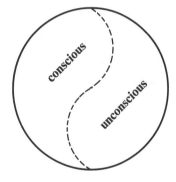

Awareness of the polar aspects of the Self erases the dividing line between conscious and unconscious, or at least reduces it to a permeable membrane.

Another kind of psychic polarity is left brain/right brain. The logical left brain is more yang; it is actively analytical and separative. The intuitive right brain is more yin; it is more passive, receptive and integrative. The left brain is good at separating thoughts and feelings into acceptable and unacceptable categories, and relegating the unacceptable ones to the unconscious trash can. One problem is: it's mostly not trash. What we call unacceptable is that which we do not know how to use. It is that which we cannot find value in—not necessarily that which is valueless. What makes something unacceptable? Chuang Tzu says:

> "A road is made by people walking on it; things are so because they are called so. What makes them so? Making them so makes them so. What makes them not so? Making them not so makes them not so. Things all must have that which is so; things all must have that which is acceptable. There is nothing that is not so, nothing that is not acceptable."[3]

Feelings considered unacceptable and so denied can be almost anything in the human emotional repertoire. Which feelings are reviled and which are esteemed varies from culture to culture, and from age to age. For example, the Puritan ethic discouraged anger and resentment; guilt was considered a fairly healthy reaction to the fact of having sinned. On the other hand, some modern ethics say that guilt is unhealthy; they encourage us to get rid of our guilt and get *in touch with* our anger. Confusing? Because its forte is integration, the intuitive right brain cooperates in the process of accepting all our seemingly opposite feelings.

A recommendation for this Taoist acceptant attitude is the fact that denying feelings does not dissolve them. Unresolved anger, for example, may manifest in general irritability, passive aggressive acts or big blow-ups. Our denied feelings seem to *seek* an outlet or create a channel of expression. An inherent urge to life seems to pervade all parts of the Self. The disowned parts tend to speak up. One way that unrealized potentialities and unresolved conflicts speak up is through distressed feelings; another way is through related physical tensions and discomforts.

Yin-Yang Symbol

Yang
(Active)

Yin
(Passive)

This symbol illustrates life's constant cyclic changes. It shows "yin," at its extreme, turning into "yang," and likewise "yang" turning into "yin." The little dots within each paisley mean that nothing is entirely "yin" or entirely "yang." The outer circle shows that these polarities are complementary; they make a whole.

When we suppress our feelings, eventually they leak out or explode. We find ourselves moaning or feeling dejected over something about which we had said, "That doesn't bother me," or "I'm handling it just fine." We are surprised by feeling sudden resentment of standards by which we had previously blamed ourselves. The existence of one extreme suggests the existence of its polar opposite. Under guilt lurks resentment. Superiority feelings compensate for inferiority feelings. Defensive pride may be a cover-up for self-pity. Anxiety or hyperexcitement alternates with depression. When the manifest feeling is at one extreme, frequently we discover that the exact opposite feeling is alive in the subconsious. When the one decreases, the opposite feeling tends to rise, until the conflict is resolved or accepted.

> "Life would be much less frantic if we were all able to recognize the diversity within ourselves, and could abandon our futile efforts to present monolithic self-portraits to the world.... An individual who 'converts' from

one viewpoint to its exact opposite appears to himself and to others to have made a gross change, but actually it involves only a very small shift in the balance of a persistent conflict."—Philip Slater[4]

The psyche is polar in nature. Why? To explain the psychological phenomena they were observing, Western psychologists Freud and Jung looked to the known laws of physics. They reasoned that the psyche, like the organism, is operated by energy, and that energy in any form must follow the same basic laws. They called the energy which operates the psyche *psychic energy*. Energy can be transformed, but not destroyed. Decreases in the energy of one element will produce complementary increases in the energy of another element. Energy seeks an equilibrium, or balance in its distribution. But perfect balance can never be attained without entropy, or inert uniformity. In human life, there is a continuous flow of energy between different poles of emotional and mental activity. Conscious and unconscious, left and right brain, distressed and harmonious feelings, shadow and light—all the aspects of the psyche seek to speak, to dance and play, to experience the dream called life.

The Taoists saw not only the psyche, but the whole relative world, as a unity of opposites, in which "everything changes except the fact that everything changes." In their perspective, yin and yang forces continuously alternate, balancing each other. "Rest is merely a state of polarity that always posits movement as its complement."[5] The Taoists saw the continuous alternation of opposites as consisting of a flow of energy between two poles. Presaging modern physics by more than two thousand years, they said that energy is the underlying dynamic of life—including the life of the psyche and the functioning of the body. This vital force or life energy, which the Chinese called *ch'i*, can be described as an electro-magnetic energy which generates physical and psychological movement. Perhaps this "ch'i" is the same thing Western psychologists called "psychic energy," for the Taoists spoke of *circulating this energy* as a way to *transforming consciousness*.

According to Carl Jung, not only are polarities inherent in life, but also growth *requires* this seeming conflict of opposite forces. In other words, all that is human, indeed everything in the universe, exists and thrives due to conflict and opposition. The seeming opposition of polar forces generates energy, and it generates growth. Since "a polarity underlies the dynamics of the psyche," we cannot avoid the "problem of opposites," says Jung:

> "All conceivable statements are made by the psyche. Among other things, the psyche appears as a dynamic process which rests on a foundation of antithesis, on a flow of energy between two poles."[6]

It is not surprising that an emphasis on polarities characterizes both Taoism and Jungian psychology, for Taoism had a strong influence on Jung's work. He began experimenting with the *I Ching* (the oldest book of Chinese philosophy) in 1920. This was a few years after he broke away from Freud, during a stormy period which is well described by a phrase from the *I Ching:* "Those at the point of an abyss feel as if their hands are in the grip of a tiger." By this time, Jung had understood that "the goal of psychic development is the self" and that "there is no linear evolution; there is only a circumambulation of the self."[7]

Two Views of Psychic Development

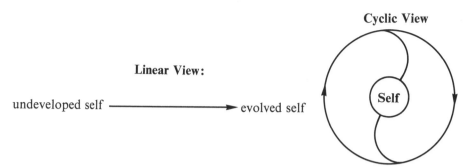

In 1923, Jung met Richard Wilhelm, who had been working on a new translation of the *I Ching*, and they discussed the ways that Chinese philosophy could shed light on the workings of the unconscious. A few years later, Jung was much impacted by Wilhelm's translation of *The Secret of the Golden Flower*, and wrote a commentary on it in an "attempt to build a bridge of psychological understanding between East and West."[8] This Taoist treatise on spiritual development describes an inward journey, towards the core Self. It gave Jung "undreamed-of confirmation" of the idea about "the circumambulation of the center."[7] Jung called the process of psychic development "individuation," and described it as a cyclic meeting and coming-to-terms with the core Self.

What stimulated Jung's interest in Taoism? Jung was searching for the common exponent behind all the psychic polarities, and he found that this was precisely the emphasis of Taoist philosophy. Referring to *Psychological Types*, his detailed work on personality theory published in 1921, Jung said: "The book on types yielded the insight that every judgement made by an individual is necessarily conditioned by his personality type and that every point of view is necessarily relative. This raised the question of the unity which must compensate this diversity, and it led me directly to the Chinese concept of *Tao*."[7] The Tao is that unity behind diversity—the unity behind all the diverse thoughts, judgements, feelings, personality types and phenomena.

An emphasis on *reconciling opposites* characterizes both Jungian psychology and Taoism. Both encourage us to look for, acknowledge and appropriately manifest all parts of our selves. Both discourage us from clinging to our habitual, comfortable, preferred self-images, which obscure part of reality. Both ask us to accept and value all the polar aspects of ourselves, so that we can see our whole Self and its participation in the Tao, or universal life process. Dualistic thought keeps us from seeing that the same force or energy imbues all the objects of nature alike, and likewise that the same internal force generates all our polar thoughts and feelings. On a universal level, we can call this unifying force *Tao* or Nature; on the bodymind level, we can call it *Shen* or the Self. Psychological development is the process of coming to know this core inner Self, which Chuang Tzu calls the "True Master":

> "Joy, anger, grief, delight, worry, regret, fickleness, inflexibility, modesty, willfulness, candor, insolence—music from empty holes, mushrooms springing up in dampness, day and night replacing each other before us, and no one knows where they sprout from. Let it be! Let it be! Morning and evening we have them, and they are the means by which we live. Without them

we would not exist; without us they would have nothing to take hold of. This comes close to the matter. But I do not know what makes them the way they are. It would seem as though they have some True Master ... (which) has identity but no form."[9]

How can we come to know our Self unless we accept its affects? How can we reconcile the conflict between the feelings we like, or the light side, and the shadow, or the dark side, unless we first accept them both? Unless we accept our polar feelings, we have but the semblance of happiness. Unless we accept the polarities inherent in the psyche and in life, we have but a fragile illusion of joy. Growth means increasing awareness and acceptance of our whole Self—all the emotional, mental and spiritual polarities. Let it all be! Accept it all! Our conflictual thoughts and feelings seem to divide us from our real Self, but accepting both sides of our psychic polarities allows us to regain contact with our core or authentic Self. Allowing the flow of our changing feelings leads us to the center, the source of all affects. At the center, we find the core inner spirit, and the joy of just *feeling* and *being*.

A client described this as the process of "finding myself under all the cover I had lived with all of my life, and the evolution of that into my 'street' person as well—the one that others see and deal with. As I experience events about me I do so now often from the center of myself, without fear, more and more able to express feelings as they exist and react naturally to events as they take place. There have been countless examples of this, more than I can remember—and they continue daily, hourly, from moment to moment even. When I do not express outwardly the true reaction within myself, when I still exhibit the 'knee-jerk' response instead of the truth, even then I know the difference. I am *consciously* aware of the dichotomy between how I am feeling and how I am *acting*. And with that, growth can continue. So, I am happier than I have ever been before in my life. I have been making decisions from that inner center, and I find greater and greater peace and joy in life all the time."

Self-Actualization and Taoist Let-Be

If all things continually change, then it seems that there might be some inherent "urge to change." On the level of the psyche, this is the urge for growth, which alternates with the desire for safety, or maintaining the status quo. Given the opportunity, each aspect of the self tends to seek growth, then a new balance or stability, then more growth, and so on. The urge to growth is the urge to wholeness. Psychic growth involves realizing the wholeness of body and psyche, and the oneness of all life. It means opening up communication between the various aspects of ourselves and actualizing our physical, mental and spiritual potentialities—by letting each aspect of ourselves BE.

Underlying this acceptant Taoist attitude is a trust that human nature, at its core, is fundamentally constructive and has an inherent tendency to grow towards realization of its full potential. This life-affirming perspective also characterizes Western humanistic psychologists. For example, Carl Rogers says that two of his most important observations are: "my confidence in the human organism, when it is functioning freely; and the existential quality of satisfying living, a theme presented by some of our modern philosophers, which was however beautifully expressed more than twenty-five centuries ago by Lao-Tzu, when he said, 'The way to do is to *be*.' "[10]

A Taoist mode of consciousness is "non-interfering" and it is "the most efficient way to perceive the intrinsic nature of the world," says Abraham Maslow, a pioneer of humanistic psychology. A *non-interfering awareness* means being able to see things *as they are*—with our perceptions determined as little as possible by subjective judgments and conditioned mindsets.

> "This kind of detached, Taoist, passive, non-interfering awareness of all the simultaneously existing aspects of the concrete, has much in common with some descriptions of the aesthetic experience and of the mystic experience. The stress is the same. Do we see the real, concrete world or do we see our own system of rubrics, motives, expectations and abstractions which we have projected onto the real world. Or, to put it very bluntly, do we see or are we blind?"[11]

According to Maslow, a characteristic of self-actualizing people is the capacity for acknowledging polar aspects of the self. These "deficit-satisfied and growth-motivated" people can simultaneously perceive the polarities, the seemingly incompatible opposites. Maslow explains:

> "It is as if less developed people lived in an Aristotelian world in which classes and concepts have sharp boundaries and are mutually exclusive and incompatible, e.g., male-female, selfish-unselfish, adult-child, kind-cruel, good-bad. A is A and everything else is not-A in the Aristotelion logic and never the twain shall meet. But seen by self-actualizing people is the fact that A and not-A interpenetrate and are one, that any person is simultaneously good and bad, male *and* female, adult *and* child."[11]

Chuang Tzu says basically the same thing:

> "Everything has its 'that,' everything has its 'this.' From the point of view of 'that' you cannot see it, but through understanding you can know it. So I say, 'that' comes out of 'this' and 'this' comes out of 'that'—which is to say that 'this' and 'that' give birth to each other. But where there is birth there must be death; where there is death there must be birth. Where there is acceptability there must be unacceptability; where there is unacceptability there must be acceptability. Where there is recognition of right there must be recognition of wrong; where there is recognition of wrong there must be recognition of right."[12]

Somewhere along the self-actualization journey, a change in perception occurs. As we fill the inner "holes" and contact the core inner Self, we begin to operate less out of deficiency needs and more out of growth needs. We begin to harmonize polarities. That is, we begin to accept opposites, in ourselves and in the world, and to see that they are complementary. Our awareness becomes less conditioned and less judgmental, so that more of reality can be embraced. Simultaneously, more aspects of the self can be embraced and more inner potential can unfold. Perls calls this the "experience of *satori*, of waking up. Suddenly the world is *there*. You wake from a trance like you wake from a dream. You're all there again."[13]

This sounds like the "peak experience" of self-actualizing people, which Maslow described after extensive research. Peak experiences are characterized by an ability to rise above parts and perceive the whole, so that conflicts are reconciled. Polar extremes begin to look like complementary parts of the whole. "What I had thought to be straight-line continua, whose extremes were polar to each other and as far apart as possible, turned out to be rather like circles or spirals, in which the polar extremes came together into a fused unity."[14]

"The more we understand the whole of Being, the more we can tolerate the simultaneous existence and perception of inconsistencies, of oppositions and of flat contradictions," Maslow continues. "These seem to be products of partial cognition, and fade away with cognition of the whole." The whole includes a whole lot of apparent contradictions. To perceive the whole is to see that all its parts are necessary.[14] Even sickness can be necessary, for it can be a pressure towards real health, which is not just the absence of disease. Similarly, emotional problems can be pressures towards psychic growth.

Accepting psychic polarities, regaining contact with the authentic core Self, becoming whole—this is growth. Maslow calls it *self-actualization* and says that a characteristic is greater creativity in everyday life. For example, he describes a psychiatrist "who delighted in his everyday job of helping people to create themselves. This man approached each patient as if he were the only one in the world, without jargon, expectations or presuppositions, with innocence and naivete and yet with great wisdom, in a Taoistic fashion."[14] Chuang Tzu similarly describes an enlightened butcher:

> "Cook Ting was cutting up an ox for Lord Wen-hui. At every touch of his hand, every heave of his shoulder, every move of his feet, every thrust of his knee—zip! zoop! he slithered the knife along with a zing, and all was in perfect rhythm, as though he were performing the dance of the Mulberry Grove or keeping time to the Ching-shou music.
>
> " 'Ah, this is marvelous!' said Lord Wen-hui. 'Imagine skill reaching such heights!'
>
> "Cook Ting laid down his knife and replied, 'What I care about is the Way, which goes beyond skill. When I first began cutting up oxen, all I could see was the ox itself. After three years I no longer saw the whole ox. And now—now I go at it by spirit and don't look with my eyes. Perception and understanding have come to a stop and spirit moves where it wants. I go along with the natural makeup, strike in the big hollows, guide the knife through the big openings, and follow things as they are.' "[15]

To Maslow, creativity means any activity or process characterized by a natural spontaneity, perception of the essential nature of things or persons, and simple enjoyment of being. This is Taoist consciousness, or the mind of *Wu-Wei*, which Chuang

Tzu says "flows like water, reflects like a mirror, and responds like an echo." The *Wei-wu-Wei* attitude means moving in harmony with life's circumstances. For the butcher, it is moving the knife in harmony with the joints and muscles; for the carpenter it is working in harmony with the grain of the wood; for the psychiatrist it is working in harmony with each patient's nature. *Wei-wu-Wei* means spontaneous movement in harmony with our inner nature and with the nature of things. In other words, it is freedom.

This reminds me of some images experienced by a client during a Jin Shin Do session. Charles said, "I feel like running away—but not really." I asked Charles to see himself running away, and then to look behind himself and see what he was running from. "Myself," he replied. What part of himself? "The happy part . . . the free part . . . I'm running in the forest. The two parts of myself are like mirror images . . . now the forest is dark." I asked Charles about the relationship of the two parts. "They merged," he said. "The guy that was running away is inside the free guy, but smaller, like his shadow. The free guy wants to go someplace, but the shadow guy doesn't want to. He's afraid to . . . he's afraid that he'll disappear, not be an individual."

Like Charles, we are often afraid of freedom, of being our whole Self. We have acquired a self-image with much effort, and have invested our sense of individuality in it. This self-image is a one-dimensional version of our real Self, and so is threatened by feeling or seeing our whole self. Clinging to the familiar self-image seems like the safest thing, but this is settling for less because this image is like a shadow of our authentic Self. There develops an increasing contrast between our real Self and that self which we have forced or allowed ourselves to become. As we accept only a portion of ourselves, we diminish ourselves and limit our freedom. This is the source of a great deal of frustration. (Interestingly, Charles' images of the free guy and the shadow guy arose during release of tensions related to frustration and anger—the diaphragm area and the Liver Meridian.)

Asked if his free self was afraid of the shadow image, Charles said, "No, it's fine with him that the other guy is part of him." I suggested that the shadow part must then have value. Charles replied, "He's the thinking part—the part that tries to make things be a certain way." He's the part that creates and maintains the self-image— in other words, he's the ego. The ego is like a shadow image of the whole Self. The value of the ego is that it helps us move through the world; the danger is that it can limit us from being all that we are. Towards the end of the session, Charles said reflectively, "That free guy running through the forest doesn't seem to know where he's going, but just *feels* the right way. Is that what they mean by Taoism?"

Yes, and what they mean by Taoism is letting oneself—all of the Self—*be*. As we watch the alternation of polar feelings and emotions, we begin to see the value of each. We begin to see that each change is necessary for the next. There is a unity to it all. Each aspect of the Self has a role to play in self-actualization; each has its importance. From these perceptions comes increased acceptance of our inner nature, and increased trust in that inner guiding factor, our core Self. There is a feeling of respect—even awe—for the dynamism of life. By accepting and respecting the innate nature of the Self, we can begin to *let ourselves—and others—be.*

No going against or tampering with the nature of things: this is the *wei-wu-wei* attitude. "Let-be" is a good translation; "non-doing" is a more popular but less accurate translation. China scholar John Blofeld gives a simple, clear definition: "The true meaning of *wei-wu-wei* is not 'doing by not doing' but acting in a manner that entails the least involvement and proceeds from the inner stillness of the heart."[16] In the *Tao of Pooh*, Benjamin Hoff points out that the Chinese character for *Wei* came from the symbols for a monkey and a clawing, grasping hand. He says, "*Wu-Wei* means no going against the nature of things; no clever tampering; no Monkeying Around." It means no "meddlesome, combative, or egotistical effort." There is no *trying*, but rather "an inner sensitivity to the natural rhythm of things."[17]

The problem with egotistical effort is that it diminishes awareness of the Tao, or the Natural Way. Wholeness depends on awareness of the natural harmony within man (between body and psyche) and within the universe (between man and Nature). The feeling of harmony goes away when our *trying* interferes with the natural balance—of our Inner Nature or of the Nature around us. Trying, without regard for the nature of things, is troublesome. The interfering mind lacks understanding of the natural way. Blofeld explains:

> "When nature is taken as a guide, a friend, living becomes almost effortless, tranquil, joyous even. Care departs; serenity takes over. *Wu Wei*, a cardinal principle of Taoists, literally means 'no action,' but not in the sense of sitting all day like a dead tree stump or a block of stone; rather it means avoiding action that is not spontaneous, acting fully and skillfully by all means but only in accordance with present need, being lively when required but never over-strenuous and certainly not strained, eschewing artfully calculated action and every activity stemming from a profit motive. A plant in need of sunlight bends towards the sun instinctively, effortlessly, its movement economical and wholly without calculation but none the less effective. So should it be with man."[18]

Lacking appreciation for *what is*, the interfering mind is prone to make comparisons and judgments, which cause distress. By just accepting how things and people are, and how they work, we can begin to move in harmony with life's circumstances, learning from all kinds of events and emotions. When we stop trying to eliminate "negative" emotions, and just listen to them, something changes. It is as though a "minus" suddenly reveals its "plus" side. Hoff says it well: "From the Taoist point of view, sourness and bitterness come from the interfering and unappreciative mind. Life itself, when understood and utilized for what it is, is sweet."[19] There is joy in it all, not just in clinging to "acceptable" feelings and situations. This is why Taoist writings are characterized by a happy serenity and a subtle sense of humor.

Maslow describes an acceptant attitude that he calls "helpful let-be":

> "It is a loving and respecting Taoism. It recognizes not only growth and the specific mechanisms which make it move in the right direction, but it also recognizes and respects the fear of growth, the slow pace of growth, the blocks, the pathology, the reasons for not growing. It recognizes the place, the necessity and the helpfulness of the outer environment without yet giving it control. It implements inner growth by knowing its mechanisms and by being willing to help *it* instead of being merely hopeful or passively optimistic about it."[20]

A common misconception of the Taoist attitude is that it was "merely hopeful or passively optimistic." But the Taoist attitude did not exclude being helpful. It was an attitude of non-attachment, but *not* an attitude of detachment. If what we judge to be helping entails *forcing* someone in some way, then the Taoists would suggest we not *try* to help, but rather wait until the person is receptive to our help. That is, don't be attached even to those changes which appear to be necessary for someone else's growth!

Wei-wu-wei means making absolutely sure that things can do what they are supposed to—and that is all. Being sure that we can do what we are supposed to means *becoming that self which we truly are*. It means doing what is necessary, for ourselves and others, and intervening in others' affairs only with caution. Practically speaking, wei-wu-wei is a matter of timing: "In motion, make use of the opportunity. Since there is no contention, there is no blame."[21] In this way, life becomes simpler and less distressed.

How can we let ourselves be all that we truly are? We each already have the most powerful of all *mandalas*, or aids to self-reflection—the body. By listening to its signals, we can get in touch with our disallowed, unconscious feelings and thoughts, and with our disowned inner potentialities. By paying attention to the messages of our physical tensions and pains, we can discover the deficiency and growth needs that we have been ignoring, and learn to trust the wisdom of the inner self. This is what Jin Shin Do is about: exploring the psyche via the body, discovering the beauty of the core Self, and learning to *let ourselves be*. Jin Shin Do acupressure is a tool for finding the joy of being all of what Kierkegaard called "that self which one truly is."

"Seeking enlightenment, a traveler sets out to climb a certain renowned, remote mountain. Although the way is long and arduous, he perseveres, for he has heard that, if he climbs long enough, he will reach his goal. Suddenly, moving downhill out of the mist, a second man appears, accompanied by three large, black dogs. So strongly do they strain against their leashes that the man almost runs to keep up. It appears that he walks them, but perhaps they lead him.

"The two travelers stop and exchange details of their routes and their aspirations. The second man is not returning from an uphill journey; he is following a downward path to fulfillment. The dogs that lead him darkly on are the emotions."[22]

The Emotional Kaleidoscope

The Taoist view of the emotions, as reflected in acupressure theory, begins with the insight that body and psyche are one interrelated whole, so that distress or well-being in the one influences the other. This perspective goes on to detail the interrelationship of particular feelings and emotions with particular parts of the body. First of all, the traditional teachings say that feelings and emotions are necessary responses, natural to the human being as s/he relates to others and to the eco-system. The emotions are glandular and visceral reactions to changes in the environment. They exist to be felt and listened to, for they are signals of changing bodymind needs. They are the driving and motivating energy of the body. When the emotions are no longer generated, the energy diminishes. Yet chronic emotional stress also depletes the energy; the resultant energy blockages and bodymind confusion can produce physical as well as psychological distress.

The bodymind is a feeling generator as well as an energy generator. The emotional, physical and energic conditions are functions of each other. Feelings and emotions arise in various parts of the bodymind. Each is accompanied by particular physical responses. Some feelings give us energy, while others decrease our energy. Some feelings open us up, while others close us down. Some feelings create tension, while others relax us. In a natural state of bodymind freedom and spontaneity, feelings and emotions change continuously—as does life, as do bodymind needs. Their manifestations are controlled by the inner spirit—Shen, the core Self. Societal rules and internalized mores, or "introjects," also control emotional manifestations—sometimes over-controlling our natural emotional responsiveness, and so causing bodymind distress.

The classics say that the emotions are produced by the "yin organs" (*tsangs*) and, further, that specific feelings and emotions are related to *particular* "yin organs" or viscera. For example, anger is related to the Liver, fear to the Kidneys, grief and anxiety to the Lungs, concern and reminiscence to the Spleen-Pancreas,* excitement and shock to the Heart and Pericardium.**[23] Each emotion most strongly affects its associated organ and the meridian, or sequence of acu-points, related to that organ. Each meridian affects certain muscles, and influences a certain sense organ, body part, and body fluid; some also influence an endocrine gland.

Each "yin organ" has a partner "yang organ" (*fou*), which is nourished by its own meridian, or energy flow. The yang meridians are related to the digestive and eliminative organs. Their psychological associations parallel their physical functions; they have to do with the processing of foods and liquids, and of psychic events. The yang organ meridians are more related to attitudes than to emotions. However, they also influence emotions, because stuck attitudes prevent the process of natural emotional transformation. For example, as we explore the physical and psychological functions of the yang meridians (in Chapters 4 through 8), we will find that tensions along the Gall Bladder Meridian can be related to anger and frustration, while tensions of the Small Intestine and Triple Warmer Meridians can be related to an inability to let joy out—or in. Over-concern and anxiety can affect the Stomach and

---

* These organs are regarded as one functional entity, because both are related to the same "meridian."

** These organs are functionally related, for both are related to "Shen" or the fire element.

Large Intestine, and fear can affect the Bladder Meridian.

The following table lists the six "yin organs," their partner "yang organs," and some of the associated feelings and emotions, along with the related sense organs and senses, body parts, and body fluids:

Yin Organ	Extreme Emotion	Synergic Feeling	Sense Organ	Body Part	Body Fluid	Partner Yang Organ
lungs	grief, anxiety	openness, letting go	nose (smell)	skin, hairs	mucus	large intestine
kidneys	fear	resolution, will power	ears (hearing)	bone, marrow	urine	bladder
liver	anger	assertion, will	eyes (sight)	tendons, ligaments	tears	gall bladder
heart & pericardium	excitement, shock	joy, happiness	tongue (speech)	vascular system	sweat	small intestine "triple warmer"
spleen-pancreas	over-concern, reminiscence	empathy, sympathy	mouth (taste)	muscles, flesh	saliva	stomach

The various feelings and emotions can be seen as forming five emotional spectra, each of which particularly relates to one of the yin organ meridians. These five spectra are depicted in the "Emotional Kaleidoscope" diagram, which summarizes my synthesis of Taoist philosophy and acupressure theory with Western psychological understanding. While future studies may result in refinement of this synthesis, its main outlines have been repeatedly confirmed in over a dozen years of my practice as an acupressure therapist, and according to the accounts of students and colleagues. I have observed that the same spectrum or range of feelings tends to be associated with tension or relaxation at certain points, in people with varying personality types. These five emotional spectra will be described, through stories and anecdotes drawn from my professional therapeutic work, as we explore the bodymind associations of the yin meridians (in Chapters 9 through 13).

Each of the five spectra on the Kaleidoscope diagram includes a range of related feelings and emotions, shown within two concentric yin-yang circles. Looking first at each *core circle*, you will see a polarity of basic emotional responses. Extreme, stress-responsive emotions are shown on the right side; the related synergic or harmonious feelings are shown on the left. *Extreme emotions* include grief, anxiety, fear, anger, over-joy or excitement, shock, concern and reminiscence. These are normal reactions to stress, but they initiate extreme activity of the sympathetic nervous system and of the related organs and parts of the body; hence they are more yang or active states. These extreme emotions need to change back into the related *synergic states*, which include openness, resolution, assertion, joy, empathy and sympathy. These "synergic states" are feelings accompanied by bodymind relaxation or a parasympathetic response; hence they are more yin or passive states.

Looking now at the *outer circles* of the spectra, you will see a number of feelings which often derive from those shown in the core circle. Here, at the periphery, are the states of psychological conflict. The extreme emotions have not been released and transformed back into the related synergic feelings. Rather, stress has turned into distress. The *distressed feelings*, shown in the outer circle, also form polarities. The

The Emotional Kaleidoscope

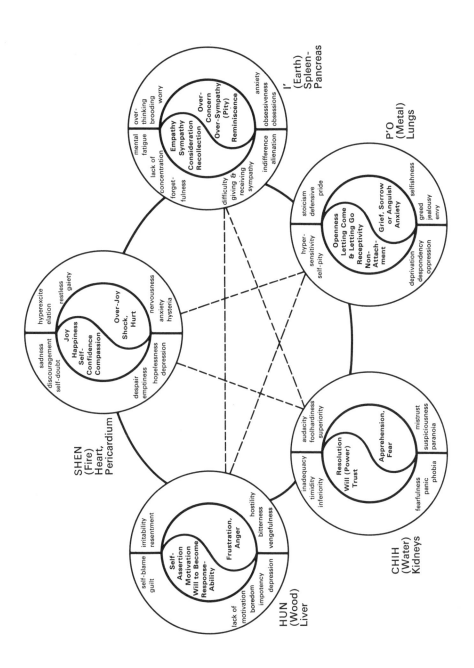

hyperactive (yang) distressed feelings are shown on the right half of the outer circle; the related hypoactive (yin) distressed feelings are shown on the left half.

The "Emotional Kaleidoscope" is an application of the traditional "five elements" theory. *It is not essential that you understand this theory before reading the rest of this book.* You will get the basic feeling of it from reading through the following chapters. Here I will give just a brief definition of this classical acupressure theory. First, what are the "elements"? The traditional "elements" were *symbols* for certain energic forces or tendencies. Therefore, the *five elements theory* might better be called the "five aspects" or "five phases" theory. Basically, it is an expansion of yin-yang theory. It describes the five phases or aspects of change, which characterize all of life. The five elements or phases are:

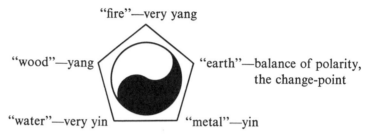

These five energic forces are aspects of Nature and of our bodymind nature. For example, the five phases of seasonal change are: spring, the time of birth or rebirth (yang); summer, the time of growth (very yang); Indian summer, the time of maturing (when the forces of nature are more equally balanced); fall, the time of gathering or harvest (yin); and winter, the time of rest (very yin). We humans also go through seasons of change, in which we are cyclically more active and more passive. We also go through cycles of (re)birth, growth, maturing, completion and resting. The five "elements" of psychic life are the five aspects of the psyche, traditionally called *Hun, Shen, I', P'o* and *Chih.* In speaking of them, we are talking about the same energic tendencies as those reflected by the "five elements" theory.

Aspect of The Psyche	"Element"	Energic Tendency	Season	Polarity	Yin Organs
Hun	wood	(re)birth	spring	yang	liver
Shen	fire	growth	summer	very yang	heart, pericardium
I'	earth	maturing	"Indian summer"	more balanced	spleen, pancreas
P'o	metal	completion	autumn	yin	lungs
Chih	water	resting	winter	very yin	kidneys

Now let's look more closely at the "Emotional Kaleidoscope" diagram, and at the feelings and emotions related to the yin organ meridians, and to the associated aspects of the psyche: Shen, I', P'o, Chih and Hun. The classics say that when the extreme emotions "change into those that are secondary to them," we can become gravely ill.[24] In my interpretation, those "secondary emotions" are the "distressed feelings" shown in the outer circles of the five emotional spectra. These distressed feelings often correlate with physical tension or disease, because they are imbalanced energic states. When we are in the throes of these feelings—like fearfulness, mistrust, guilt and resentment—our bodymind condition is more active or passive than normal.

In a balanced or "normal" state, we are able to flow with things—to tense when necessary, and then to relax. In a distressed state, in some way we are working too hard, or are too weak. Our feelings are upset and uptight (excessively yang), or they are convuluted and turned in on ourselves (excessively yin). Likewise, our muscles and organ systems are likely to be tense and overworking, or flaccid and weak. Though they may sometimes bring us misery, these distressed feelings are *not* "wrong" or "bad." They, too, have their value and reason for being, as we will discuss in later chapters.

In general, when they are chronic, the distressed feelings are the psychological factors which most negatively affect our physical condition. An estimated 80 percent of modern illnesses are stress-related, and psychological distress is commonly a part of the picture. Some of the disturbances which can be related to emotional distress include: tension and migraine headaches, painful menstruation, ulcers, asthma, rheumatoid arthritis, acne, obesity, tachycardia, hypertension (high blood pressure), insomnia, chronic pain, impotence and frigidity.[25] According to acupressure theory, the location of the physical problem suggests that there may be imbalance of related meridians and tension at related points, along with related kinds of psychic distress. The correlation of physical tensions or problems with certain psychological states is confirmed by the fact that, in acupressure practice, it often works out as well to choose points based on either emotional or physical symptoms.

It is normal to respond to life with emotion. Conditions of stress normally call forth extreme emotional and physical responses. Anger and fear, for example, arise to give us the energy to deal with threats; they are emergency responses. These and the other *extreme emotions* are *stress-responsive states*. Though sometimes our anger and fear, hurt and concern, and so on, may seem bothersome, still these emotional responses have a survival purpose. When they are not allowed to be expressed appropriately, these stress reactions turn into distress. When we hang onto or repress extreme emotions (like anger, fear and grief), distressed feelings tend to poliferate.

The *distressed feelings* are *reactive states*, for they tend to result from suppressing normal (though extreme) emotional responses. For example, look at the Chih spectrum on the Kaleidoscope diagram. In mistrust, fear is directed outward, onto others; fearfulness is directing the fear at ourselves, and so feeling that we are inadequate. Mistrust and fearfulness are reactions to unresolved fear. For another example, look at the P'o spectrum. When we can't let go to grief, the result may be self-pity and feelings of deprivation, or compensating feelings of envy and jealousy. Unresolved and unaccepted, our hurts and griefs fester, our fears and angers accumulate, our concerns multiply. Old angers give more charge to new ones; old sorrows make new problems more hurtful; old fears make new situations more fearful. Clinging to old feelings requires physical tension. Prolonged physical and emotional tension is distress.

Emotional freeflow means allowing or encouraging stress-responsive emotions to transform back into related *synergic emotions*, which are characterized by a sense of inner peace and relaxation. Ways to facilitate this emotional freeflow include opening up channels of self-expression and releasing related physical tensions. The Taoists describe a state of emotional freeflow as one of spontaneity and acceptance of inner and outer change:

> "Such a man has a free mind, a calm manner, and an unfurrowed brow. He is as cool as autumn and as mild as spring. His joy and anger flow like the changing seasons."[26]

Just as autumn changes into winter, and winter into spring, so do our feelings and emotions naturally change. The "five elements" theory describes the way that each season "gives birth to" the next—spring to summer to Indian summer to autumn to winter. Each synergic emotion also "gives birth to" the next: assertion (or the will to become) gives birth to joy, which breeds sympathy, which breeds openness . . . resolution . . . assertion. When the extreme emotions are appropriately expressed and released, they resolve back into the related synergic states. When the extreme emotions are clung to or repressed, then unresolved fear breeds anger, prolonged anger gives rise to excitement, excitement gives rise to concern, concern to anxiety, and so on.

Why do we suppress feelings and prolong distress? We could say it is to avoid hurting others, but suppressed feelings are nonetheless felt by others. In fact, the unhappy feelings generated by the unconscious stew can be *more* distressing to others than the direct, simple expression of seemingly negative feelings. Resolving feelings like hurt or anger brings us closer to each other; avoiding upset feelings drives us apart in a continuing pattern of disharmony. Persistent feelings need to somehow be expressed. A major block to freely experiencing and expressing our emotions is the tendency to judge some feelings as "right" and others as "wrong." Feelings and emotions we judge to be "wrong" are prime candidates for denial and avoidance. When such feelings are suppressed, more energy accumulates behind them so that there may be a big "charge" to their eventual expression.

The Taoists shook their heads over the destruction wrought by judgmental attitudes. Making one thing right and another wrong, affirming one feeling and denying its opposite—what is the result of all this judging? One result is that "we are tied up in knots like an old clogged drain."[27] Another result is that we have denied part of reality, and part of ourselves.

> "Our words fly off like arrows, as though we knew what was right and wrong. We cling to our own point of view, as though everything depended on it. And yet our opinions have no permanence; like autumn and winter, they gradually pass away."[27]

If we could just feel what we feel and allow the natural transformation of emotional states, then we would find ourselves continuously re-entering the synergic or peaceful, harmonious state. This state is illustrated as one side of the core polarity in the Emotional Kaleidoscope diagram, but it does not exclude its opposite. The state of feeling good, the synergic state, is not the *absence* of its opposite, but rather the *synthesis* of opposites. That is, the synergic state is *integrative*. It is related to the functions of the intuitive, integrative right brain, which does not exclude but rather coexists with the separative, logical left brain. *Acceptance* is a key to entering or experiencing the synergic states—joy and happiness, sympathy and empathy, openness, resolution and self-assertion. If we can accept our opposite judgments and opposing feelings, then we can see their pivot point.

"Tao is obscured when men understand only one of a pair of opposites, or concentrate only on a partial aspect of being. Then clear expression also becomes muddled by mere wordplay, affirming this one aspect and denying all the rest. . . .

"If I begin by looking at anything from the standpoint of the 'Not-I,' then I do not really *see* it, since it is 'not I' that sees it. If I begin from where I am and see it as I see it, then it may also become possible for me to see it as another sees it. Hence the theory of reversal—that opposites produce each other, depend on each other, and complement each other. . . .

"The wise man therefore . . . sees that in the end they are reducible to the same thing, once they are related to the pivot of Tao. When the wise man grasps this pivot, he is in the center of the circle, and there he stands while 'Yes' and 'No' pursue each other around the circumference. The pivot of Tao passes through the center where all affirmations and denials converge. He who grasps the pivot is at the still-point from which all movements and oppositions can be seen in their right relationship."[28]

The pivot or still-point of all our psychic polarities is the core Self. This Inner Nature is the center-point of all our polar thoughts and feelings. If we can just feel and accept ourselves *where we are*, then we can see how all our opposite feelings relate to core needs of the Self and so are somehow manifestations of this Self. Often, where we are is in some kind of stuck place, with distressed feelings repeating themselves as often as certain television commercials. Trying to ignore the upset feelings and just jump to peaceful or balanced states by an effort of will is usually unsuccessful. A harmonious emotional state is more easily attained by accepting and exploring all of ourselves than by trying to be a certain way.

Harmony is in the whole—someplace between or embracing right and wrong, good and bad. All our opposing feelings are part of the whole; all are manifestations of the same inner source. Simply being receptive to or accepting a bothersome feeling, then also accepting any opposite feelings we encounter, is a transformative process which leads us back to our core Self and its needs. Rather than fighting, often in vain, to control our "negative" or unacceptable feelings, we can just accept them and allow or encourage their transformation into harmonious synergic states. Restraint of our emotions is not necessary, though some restraint of our thoughts and actions may be required—especially of our tendencies to judge and then try to manipulate life, or to push the flow of life's river.

3. Five Inner Lands or Five Aspects of the Psyche

The journey towards becoming "that self which we truly are" is a journey into the psyche, which involves listening to feelings and emotions as well as thoughts. All psychic events are guides to discovering our inner selves, but making sense of feelings and emotions may not be the easiest of projects. Some feelings and emotions are direct responses of the inner self to the outer life. Others result from the repression or denial of some more basic emotional response. Still others may come up just because some part of ourself has been asleep too long. Some emotions are celebrations; others point out homework. Some seem negative; others appear to be positive. Feelings and emotions—all of them—are guiding and driving forces. They can also be like nudges, or even kicks, from some aspect of the inner self which is saying, "Wake up! Pay attention to me! Let me out, let me *be*!"

Self-actualization is a search for the center of our being, which paradoxically is meanwhile directing the search. In a way, self-actualization takes place by itself, for there is an innate urge towards living out our inherent nature. However, living out our human potential means *consciously connecting* with the core Self. Doing so depends on being willing to listen to the messages of the Self, which take the form of psychic events: feelings, emotions, intuitions, thoughts, images. To listen to these messages is to explore the psyche and seek out something not yet known—the inner Self. It is also to discover ways that the psyche and psychic events can impact on the body, and ways that the body can influence the psyche.

As we set off on this journey, perhaps we could use a map. A map could help us journey with more speed and ease. More importantly, perhaps, a map could help us to find interesting areas which we might overlook. Taoist philosophy, as reflected in acupressure theory, is one such map, showing five inner lands called Shen, I', P'o, Chih and Hun. These five aspects of the psyche are essentially five ways in which we relate to life. Our feelings and emotions are messages from one or more of these five inner lands. Each is functionally related to certain parts of the body, including an organ, sense organ, body fluid, and particular body parts or tissues. Each is also influenced by certain groups of acu-points. We can use these acu-points to help release physical or emotional tension, and to help us contact our inner nature.

Let's take a short guided tour through the five inner lands described by the Taoists—the lands of Shen, I', P'o, Chih and Hun. Like many guided tours, this one will be short. We won't stop long enough at any one place to really explore it all. We'll try to stop long enough to see and feel some of the beauty of the place, but we'll have to go back later if we want to take it all in and see the details. The tour guide is the ancient Taoist philosophy; my role is providing a modern psychological interpretation. After this introductory tour, I hope that you will be able to come back to play in these inner lands with the comfort of some feeling of familiarity.

The Firey Land of Shen

Yin Organs*	Partner Yang Organs**	Extreme Emotions	Synergic Feeling	Sound	Sense Organ	Body Fluid	Body Part	Energic Tendency
heart pericardium	small intestine "triple warmer"	excitement, shock	joy, happiness	laughing	tongue (speech)	sweat	vascular system	growth

* See Chapter 9.   ** See Chapter 5.

Shen is one of the five lands we are touring; in another way, it is all of them. Shen is the ruler of the psychic domain. It strongly influences the other four lands, which are essentially manifestations of Shen. What is the nature of Shen? Shen is characterized by a passion for life. To feel Shen is to feel the heart of the psychic domain. Shen is the emotional or spiritual name for the land of the heart. It is the lifeblood of personhood—literally and because feelings are our lifeline, are why we stay in this bodily form. The image here is fire; feelings are the FIRE of life. Feelings warm and enliven our being.

By Kathleen Chaney

Descartes said, "I think, therefore I am." No. *I feel, therefore I am*. It is by feeling that I experience my being; it is by thinking that I interpret what I observe and feel. Knowing requires the intellect, but to really *know* things also requires experiencing or *feeling* them. Sometimes, thinking is just a way of playing; it is no more (or less) important than a child's playful splashing in puddles along the wayside. Thinking is also a way of enhancing our ability to navigate the rocks and shoals of the life river. The mind can study the composition of the water, how it behaves now, and the probable past and future channels of flow. But the river itself is in constant flux, always changing. Its course is not limited to what we *think* it is or should be. The course of life's river is accessed by feeling and intuiting.

Shen, the inner spirit, is the feeling processor. Shen lets us *live*, and gives the sensation of aliveness, which is feelingness. Shen is the guiding spirit, the coordinator of impressions. Therefore, any significant stressor has an impact here, but *sudden joy* and *shock* or hurt are primary stressors of the heart. Modern stress research says that stressors include not just the hurt of changes for the worse, but also the strong joy of big changes for the better—i.e., anything which produces an intense need for readjustment. Resisting the fact of change is one way to turn stress into *dis*tress. Stress can be transformative if we listen to and learn from the psychic messages coming from our inner Selves.

Shen is like the monarch of the bodymind. Our relation to this inner ruler is a crucial one. To feel Shen is to feel ALIVE. Shen is the seat of the divine light, according to the classics. It is the essential spark of life which reflects in all our deeds and activities. The word "Shen" carries the meanings "to extend" and "to create." The core spirit wants to extend through our whole being and into the world around us. To extend our energy *is* to create. It is by extending our energy into life, by living fully, that we create ourselves and feel the joy of being.

Losing touch with Shen means losing touch with the core energy or spirit which wants to extend creatively. The result is a lack of self-confidence. A lack of trust in Shen means a lack of trust in the nature of life, for Shen is Tao within us. Losing sight of our participation in the Tao is the original dualism. Seeing ourselves as separate from the whole of Nature is an act of revolt. The classics say that all disease stems from this revolt against the Tao or Way of Nature, and against its reflection—our inner nature.

When we lose touch with Shen, we let ourselves in for various psychic addictions, becoming ruled by expectations and illusions rather than by real inner needs. We miss experiencing the here-and-now, because of the hope-hopeless cycle that is set up and perpetuated by expectations about ourselves, others and life. We live in the future, hoping; or if our illusions fold, we feel hopeless and thereby abolish the future. There is a loss of inner direction, or at least of *contact* with the inner guiding and regulating factor. There is stagnation, rather than growth and creative extension of the Self.

The classics say that emotional, mental and physical confusion shows up when Shen has no clear sense of direction, or when we have lost touch with the inner spirit. When Shen is weak, or distracted by social or physical tensions, we are more susceptible to "negative" feelings and emotions. Lack of self-confidence can also bring a sense of emptiness. Clinging to worries, anxieties, fears, angers and hurts can be a way to fill the emptiness and avoid despair. If we cannot find our way back to joy and self-confidence, then other emotions may rule instead. Trying to solve the problem by denying our seemingly negative feelings just courts depression, for it amounts to suppression of our feeling self. The only real solution is to reconnect with the core Self and allow its creative extension in the world.

> "To be useful is to realize one's true nature.
> Realization of one's true nature is happiness.
> When one reaches happiness, one is close to perfection.
> So one stops, yet does not know that one stops.
> This is Tao . . . ."[1]

The tale of King Arthur describes what happens when we lose touch with our true nature. The Land of Camelot can be seen as a metaphor for the bodymind. Arthur's kingship is like Shen's role as the bodymind ruler. Just as King Arthur has to become conscious of his ability to rule, so we must become *aware* of our own inner guiding and regulating factor. The land of Camelot is a beautiful and harmonious place, until King Arthur lets illusion take the place of reality. He attributes his shadowy or undesirable aspects to his witchy sister, and he projects his desirable qualities onto others too—beauty onto Guinevere and honor onto Lancelot. In doing so, Arthur gives up his power.

When his illusory expectations are dashed, Arthur seeks escape in restless gaiety. The carousel of excitement is not joy, but Arthur cannot find his way back to being the good ruler he had been. Because he is not in touch with his inner Self, King Arthur is increasingly being *used by* his feelings. He is being ruled by his fear, anger, jealousy and self-pity, for he has lost touch with the confidence that would allow him to accept and resolve inner conflicts. Disillusioned and confused, Arthur retreats into a hopeless, depressed place. For a while, he doesn't notice what is happening to Camelot. The people are becoming impoverished. Blight and distress are everywhere.

One day the King wakes up and looks around. He sees that the spirit of the country is a reflection of his own inner dis-ease—his lack of ease with and confidence in his inner spirit. He gathers his strength by owning the aspects of himself which he had been projecting onto Guinevere, Lancelot and the rest. He journeys forth into life again. The country wakes up as the king does. Suddenly it is like summertime in Camelot.

Growth and inner joy come with feeling and trusting Self and Tao. Real joy does not come from selecting for seeming contentment or chasing glittery glee while resisting difficulties, nor does it come from trying to avoid pain by numbing it out (and then unconsciously cycling around it). The point is not to avoid pain, and certainly not to seek it, but rather to *be fully alive*, which is a state of *feeling*—sometimes pleasure and other times pain. We can choose *to feel* or *not to feel*; we cannot choose to feel just some feelings. Our feelings arise to enliven us, and to connect us with our real inner nature. To extend this energy/spirit into the world is to grow towards the peak of our potential.

The Earthy Land of I'

Yin Organ*	Partner Yang Organ**	Extreme Emotion	Synergic Feeling	Sound	Sense Organ	Body Fluid	Body Part	Energic Tendency
spleen-pancreas	stomach	over-concern reminiscence	sympathy, consideration	singsong	mouth (taste)	saliva	muscles, flesh	maturing

* See Chapter 10. ** See Chapter 6.

It is in the land of I' (pronounced "ee") that the spirit becomes conscious of its bodily and earthly environment. The focus here is on *nourishment*, or taking the world into ourselves. Digestion is the process of taking in and using that which can be included as a part of the bodymind self. In the original feeding situation, as suckling babes, we get both physical and emotional nourishment simultaneously. Tactile contact with our mothers is a means to nourishment, and the *contact* itself is a nourishing force. We can take the world into ourselves through touching and being touched, as well as through eating.

Tactile contact is a basic need, for touching, caressing and stroking are symbols of being loved. Early evidence of the importance of touching came from John Bowlby and Renee Spitz, who studied effects of early separation and institutionalization of children in war-torn London. They found that no amount of sterile, scientifically measured food and medications would allow normal development, if the children were deprived of contact with others. Marshall Klaus, studying enforced separation of premature infants in Cleveland hospitals, found that babies who were handled did better than those who were not touched often. Random and seemingly purposeless touching had a good effect on the babies' survival rate. It also has a felicitous effect on adults.

To survive, we must be able to extend our awareness into our bodies and into the surrounding world. This is the process of fully incarnating on the earth plane—of BEING HERE. As we discover other beings dancing around in our world, we find that we need something from them, just as we need something from the earth. A project in the land of I' is finding out what this something is. I' is the aspect of ourselves which is occupied with the search for physical and emotional nourishment. To listen to this part of the psyche is to pay attention to gut-level feelings, which tell us whether we are absorbing something that the Self needs, or something it can't use and doesn't want.

I' is consciousness moving down from the transpersonal realm into the very personal realm of feeling the body and its relation to the earth and to other beings of the earth. It is the Self experiencing and realizing itself through extending itself—into the body and then horizontally into the world. This means feeling the world as an extension of the Self, and the Self as an extension of the world. It means learning to feel a *unity* with the world, and an empathetic oneness with others. The question here is: who am I in relation to the world? The quest here is feeling the ground of our being.

The image is EARTH. In the land of I', a primary concern is with *earthing* or grounding—feeling the body and its connection with the earth. What is this body? Is it a *vehicle* for the soul, or is it a *manifestation* of the spirit? A vehicle is something I use; a manifestation of myself is a part of me. The body is a manifestation of both Shen and Tao. One way of avoiding the body is living up in the head. Over-thinking can be an escape from awareness of body tension and discomfort, but—the *numbing out* also means *missing out* on the pleasures of really feeling the body—the ground of our being. An "electric head" and an automated body are unlikely routes to joy.

Traditional acupressure theory says that *over-concern* and *reminiscence* especially put stress on the stomach and pancreas. Modern research confirms that mental stress and confusion play a leading role in creating gastric distress or ulcers. The classics say that over-concern coagulates the energy and paralyzes the body. To be worried or anxious is to be stuck—overconnected with something or someone and out of touch with the whole of reality. Excessive reminiscence is also an escape from present reality; it's like watching an old movie over and over. Prolonged reminiscence concentrates consciousness and energy in the brain, which is where the past lives.

Both over-concern and reminiscence have something to do with nourishment. Reminiscence can be a way of compensating for a present lack of nourishment, by escaping in memory to a time when we felt loved and supported. We tend to become concerned when our present sources of physical and emotional nourishment are threatened—or when we *think* they are. Over-concern can also stem from a desire to please and protect those "significant others" on whom we depend for nourishment. Indifference can be the cloak under which lies a great need for emotional support and nourishment.

A journey through the land of I' requires learning that we *deserve* to be nourished, and paying attention to how various foods, persons and situations make us feel. Nourishing ourselves gives us the energy to care about others. The bodymind is deeply nourished by a feeling of *oneness* with Nature and with the beings of nature. This brings a sense of innate worthiness, which makes it easier to use our faculties of consideration and recollection for creating a life which we truly appreciate—rather than for trying to stuff ourselves into boxes to get the approval of others.

The main task in the land of I' is maturing. This means the ability to be in touch with feelings, communicate them clearly to others, and view different-ness as an opportunity for growth rather than a threat.[2]

The Metallic Land of P'o

Yin Organ*	Partner Yang Organ**	Extreme Emotion	Synergic Feeling	Sound	Sense Organ	Body Fluid	Body Part	Energic Tendency
lungs	large intestine	grief, anxiety	letting go, openness	sobbing	nose (smell)	mucous	skin, hairs	completion

* See Chapter 11. ** See Chapter 7.

In the land of P'o, the Self deals with issues of what can be called "mine." This is the realm of *desires*—the primal forces of attraction and repulsion. The focus here is on the instinctive attempt to keep what feels good for us, and to get rid of what does not feel good. P'o is the aspect of the psyche which is involved with the intake of life-giving energies or elements, and with the discharge of toxic or life-limiting ones. The respiratory system is the embodiment of this process; life depends on its rhythmic taking in of oxygen and expelling of carbon dioxide. The functions of the large intestine also illustrate the importance of this cyclic process; without its elimination of useless materials, the body would be a toxic wastepile. P'o influences our general life energy at a fundamental level.

The nature of P'o is dark and turbid, say the classics. As we enter the land of P'o, we are moving down into the unconscious, which looks like darkness and murkiness to the rational mind.* P'o has to do with all sensuous desires and impulses. It is the realm of instinct, which can—and does—operate without conscious recognition. P'o is an unsophisticated land, a land of raw energy. This energy is necessary for all the changes of consciousness, yet its primal power can feel threatening to the conscious mind. Many retreat from the power of P'o, taking on stoical attitudes of emotional restraint, which may look like non-attachment. True non-attachment begins with accepting our desires. In other words, it begins with traveling through— not skirting around—the aspect of the psyche called P'o.

In this psychic realm, the Self is refined through contact with the material plane, or with worldly desires. The image is METAL, bringing to mind the world of things. One general kind of desire is *to possess* things. Some of the focus on possessing things is survival-oriented; we need to have the means to secure food, drink, shelter and support in order to live. The basic need to possess is exaggerated, however, because the civilizing process has expanded the realm of desires beyond self-felt needs, to include a long list of wants culled from the past and present fancies of humankind. The conglomerate of individual need packages called "society" also tends to equate *worthiness* with *how much we are worth.* A more practical equation to remember is that between *possession* and *control.* Chuang Tzu says of the person ruled by the desire for possessions:

> "When he tries to extend his power over objects, those objects gain control of him. He who is controlled by objects loses control of his inner self: if he no longer values himself, how can he value others? If he no longer values others, he is abandoned. He has nothing left!"[3]

Yet, as long as we are not blinded by our desires, they generate energy and lead us on to explore life. The problem is not the desires, but being caught in their snare. Then, thinking that we have been deprived of something we need to possess, we feel oppressed or sorry for ourselves. The backside of feeling deprived is envying others who seem to have what we are denied. A Taoist antidote is to take nature as a guide and live simply. Effortless living is a correlation of being in touch with the real desires of the natural self. The basic recommendation is to travel light, rather than being burdened by a thousand cares about a hundred possessions. Inordinate desires disturb our peace and limit our openness to experience. Excess is the enemy of simplicity—and of stillness. John Blofeld summarizes this basic Taoist advice:

> "Take things as they come. Be a stranger to care, to anxiety about what you think is going to happen and, above all, to regret for anything that has already happened. Grief and disappointment come from outside yourself. Lock your door on them. Be rid of them. Having done this, you will find that stillness comes easily and of itself. No effort is needed to fix a mind that has turned away from all sources of disturbance. Do not think your

* In the *Secret of the Golden Flower*, Wilhelm and Jung described P'o as the "anima soul," which leads us down into the depths of the psyche.

life will be empty then. Quite on the contrary, you will find that the greatest joy of all is just *to be!*"[4]

Are the Taoists saying that we should suppress emotional responses like grief and disappointment? That would be violence to our inner nature, and the Taoist Way avoids *forcing* anything, including our emotional self. Besides, joy cannot be forced. Joy is found in stillness, in turning away from the longings that come from the outside—from introjected desires. Occasional disappointment is natural, and grief is a necessary response to deep loss, but excessive attachments open the door to unnecessary grief and agony. Therefore, the Taoists recommend moderation in all things—including moderation!

> "Their method is never to repress passion but quietly to transcend it. . . . Remembrance of the agonies of longings unfulfilled coupled with reflection on the tawdry nature of their objects and on the transience of such satisfactions as they sometimes bring is a most effective remedy, causing longings to melt away as soon as they arise . . . As cultivation of the Way proceeds, passions and longings diminish of themselves without the least need for repression . . . happiness comes to depend less and less upon external objects, more and more upon the joy that comes from within."[4]

When we are in a harmonious state, our emotions flow like the changing seasons, and there is a joyful ease of being. A harmonious state is one which accepts our natural emotional responsiveness, while transcending or discharging emotional grievances and longings based on introjected desires. When distressing feelings come tagging along after negative thoughts, or after bouts of inner chatter, there's a good chance that old introjected messages are stirring up our desires. Staying with an emotion until an image arises from it is one way of tuning into our real inner needs and so finding peace.

The natural rhythm is letting things come and letting things go, breathing in the oxygen of life and discharging the toxic aspects of the psychic air. The turbulent winds of change blow some things away from us, and they blow other things our way. The feeling is one of insecurity, which can be anxiety-producing. That which we lose may have seemed indispensable, and that which comes our way may seem second-best. But if we look more closely, often we find what we need unexpectedly there, amid the junk or hassles. Knowing this can decrease our anxiety. The *I Ching* says:

> "We cannot lose what really belongs to us, even if we throw it away. Therefore, we need have no anxiety. All that need concern us is that we should remain true to our own natures and not listen to others."[5]

The Watery Land of Chih

Yin Organ*	Partner Yang Organ**	Extreme Emotion	Synergic Feeling	Sound	Sense Organ	Body Fluid	Body Part	Energic Tendency
kidneys	bladder	fear	resolution, will power	groaning	ears (hearing)	urine	bone, marrow	resting

* See Chapter 12. ** See Chapter 8.

Chih is the aspect of the psyche responsible for strength of character, vitality and power of personality. It is the seat of resolution. It is that psychic force which gives us the energy to move through and around obstacles to growth, to being our real Self. The classics say this is the land of the officials who do the energetic work. The physical and psychic energy related to Chih is necessary for maintaining life, and for all bodymind movement and growth. Chih is a realm rich in energy resources.

If we imagine consciousness as a terrain, then Shen is like a mountaintop. In journeying through the lands of I' and P'o, we have been traveling down the mountain. Now, in the land of Chih, we are below sea level and in a land of many waters. The darkness increases as we move into this realm, for we are well into the unconscious here. The image is WATER: a universal symbol for the unconscious. The organs related to Chih, the kidneys and bladder, literally have a "water function," because they regulate water metabolism.

For the Taoists, water symbolizes the vital energy of life. We live in an ocean of energy which surrounds and supports us, and this energy flows within us. The patterns of energy flow in the bodymind are like rivers, streams, and canals; the points of energic concentration are like lakes, seas, ponds, wells and springs. For the Taoists, water is also an image of how to live harmoniously and growthfully. As Alan Watts put it, Taoism is the "watercourse way." If life is like a river, we need to learn to follow the flow of life's river—not to get panicked by rapids, stranded on reefs, or stuck in whirlpools, spinning madly round and round the same thing. Life is an insecure business; everything keeps changing. We are floating smoothly along, and then we run into a rock. How can we accept the difficult as well as the easy, the troubles and turbulences as well as the joys and balmy times? Lao Tzu says:

> "Nothing in the world can be compared to water for its weak and yielding nature; yet in attacking the hard and the strong, nothing proves better than it. For there is no alternative to it."[6]

Accessing our vital energy means developing awareness of an essential inner power, which we can draw on in the dark and difficult times. This power is even more primal than the power of the instincts and desires. It is the power of life itself, because accessing our vital energy means accessing the universal ocean of energy, of which we are a part and from which we can be replenished. To continuously flow around obstacles, we cannot rely only on our own individual energy reserves or else, having depleted them, we start running on "nervous energy" and damaging the bodymind. Knowing that we are part of a grand matrix of energic forces can lead to the trust that there *is* always energy available to us if we just tap into the energic Source. This is generally less stressful than trying to push the river of life.

When our reserve energy is deficient, we feel less able to navigate the rocky parts of life's river. We are liable to feel fearful, timid, inadequate and inferior. In a sense, these feelings are appropriate when our vital energy is low. The problem is the vicious cycle in which fear and inferiority feelings lower our energy level, so that we feel even weaker in relation to our environment, and so are more prone to fear and inferiority feelings. To compensate, we might project our fear outward, mistrusting or being suspicious of other persons or things. Disowning the fear can also lead to foolhardiness, which tries to override fear for ego-gratification.

The outcome of fearfulness and foolhardiness can be similar. Imagine three people in boats traveling down a river, fast approaching some forbidding rapids. The first person is fearful and feels inadequate to the challenge. S/he panics, drops the oars, and has a wet awakening as the boat enters the rapids. The second person is not in touch with any fear. Foolhardiness generates an impulse to just shoot the rapids at their fiercest point. S/he has a wet awakening too. The third person has plenty of reserve energy and resolution. S/he assesses the best way of navigating the rapids, moves through them with maximum awareness, and has a rather better chance of staying dry.

All this wetness reminds me of a personal encounter with fear, courtesy of a wet awakening. I had been feeling inadequate to the challenge of writing this book, among other things, and my reserve energy was low. I was hiking with friends, feeling weak, but not wanting to slow them down. We walked over a little dam, and then had to jump to a rock a couple feet away. Rather than listening to my fear, which was saying I presently lacked the balance and energy for this feat, I jumped— and missed. Feeling the cold water against my bruised back was shocking, and feeling unable to save myself was very scary. I was dragged out of the water, and felt a painful muscle spasm in my back (precisely in the Chih-related point). As this place was held with a few acu-points, I suddenly felt a wave of fear. As the feelings focused, I saw that they came from a part of me that wanted to give up, because it felt helpless when not understood. After a while, my inner voice suggested, "Maybe you *don't need* to be understood by everyone; maybe you can *trust your Self*." I resolved not to give up on the attempt to *be myself* in the world.

The aspect of the psyche which the Taoists called Chih is the most yin, or passive and receptive; it has to do with resting and with absorbing and storing energy. Paradoxically, it is this most passive part of ourselves which allows all our bodymind activity and movement. The project here is being in touch with our own energy, and being receptive to the energy we can absorb from our surroundings, from Nature. This produces a feeling of resolution.

The Wooded Land of Hun

Yin Organ*	Partner Yang Organ**	Extreme Emotion	Synergic Feeling	Sound	Sense Organ	Body Fluid	Body Part	Energic Tendency
liver	gall bladder	anger	assertion, will	shouting	eyes (sight)	tears	tendons, ligaments	(re)birth

* See Chapter 13. ** See Chapter 4.

As we explore the last of the five inner lands described by the Taoists, we are moving upwards into the foothills of consciousness. The rugged land of Hun is the seat of "the soul, or spiritual faculties," according to the *Nei Ching*.[7] Hun is the *actuating* force; its psychic faculties are those which allow us to carry out our functions and responsibilities.

The image is WOOD, which brings to mind a tree. A tree is a symbol for the process of self-actualization. Just as the seed of a tree already contains the adult tree, as a potential to-be-realized, so we also in a sense already are much more than we are manifesting. The psychic activity of Hun is like the force which causes a little seed to sprout, to push its way through the surrounding obstructions of the dark soil, and to finally emerge into the light, growing towards the life-giving warm rays of the sun. The energy of Hun is active and vigorous with the "new yang" energy of birth and rebirth.

By Bob Simpson

A central project in the land of Hun is developing response-ability—the *ability to respond* to life. Hun has to do with forming and enacting plans, making decisions and carrying them out. Hun energy allows us to respond appropriately to things, with a common sense which depends on being in touch with our vital energy (Chih), instinctive desires (P'o) and bodily self (I').

Hun is the developing Self directing its energy outwards, asserting and expressing itself. Hun is the motivation for appropriate verbal communication, as well as for appropriate action. Hun propels Shen. Hun is the motivation to carry out the impulses of Shen, and to live out Shen's basic message—"be/become that Self which you truly are."*

Hun has to do with initiating and completing. A deficiency of Hun energy can manifest as feelings of powerlessness; an excess can manifest as aggressive feelings. In either case, there is some difficulty with response-ability. One extreme is being unable to express oneself or take charge; the opposite extreme is a tendency towards over-control, or an egotistical desire to demonstrate power over others. The median between these extremes is self-assertion: standing one's ground or effectively taking charge, without trying to force things into an unnatural mold. Lao Tzu says that the art is to

> "Deal with a thing before it comes into existence;
> Regulate a thing before it gets into confusion . . . .
> Take care with the end as . . . with the beginning . . . ."[8]

---

* In the *Secret of the Golden Flower*, Wilhelm and Jung described Hun as the "animus soul," which moves us up into the realm of the spirit. Hun leads us to Shen, the conscious spirit.

We can aim to deal with things before they jump up and bite us, rather than just hoping problems will go away. The more we avoid dealing with situations which aren't serving the growth needs of the Self, the more we feel a reactive anger and frustration. When we direct the anger outwards by blaming others, we feel resentment and hostility. When we direct it inwards, blaming ourselves, we feel guilt and eventually depression. Getting back to an assertive center-point means acknowledging the underlying frustration and getting in touch with what needs to be expressed—in words and in our lives in general.

All of this is the worldly side of Hun activity. There is another, seemingly opposite, side. *The Secret of the Golden Flower* says that Hun has to do with "the circulation of the light" and the "return to the creative," or the development of spiritual consciousness. It also says, "When occupations come to us, we must accept them; when things come to us, we must understand them from the ground up."[9] There is no conflict between the worldly and spiritual sides of Hun activity. Living in the world is part of how we return to the creative, or get in touch with the inner spirit. We return to the creative by *creating*, not just by passively retreating from the world, in search of transcendence. Creating means expressing the Self in the world.

Our allegorical journey through five inner lands has been a homeward one. Traveling through the lands of Shen, I', P'o, Chih and Hun, we have seen many ways that the spirit experiences itself on its way back to home base. Ultimately, home base is awareness of Shen and Tao—of the inner nature and of the Nature of life. This is the return to the creative. It is a rising movement of the life energies. The motivation to find the lost Spirit, or become aware of the core Self, develops from the process of living out all the aspects of the Self.

Hun is the motivation for the journey towards being *all* of ourselves. It is the *will to become* "that self which one truly is." There is an unconscious anger that develops just from not being our Selves, or not manifesting our whole potential. The Self wants to expand and *be* what it is, and gets frustrated by unnecessary restrictions about what it *should* be. The blocked-off Hun energy starts seething inside. This corked energy can be channeled into assertiveness and creativity.

Interconnections of the Five Inner Lands

The five aspects of the psyche form an interrelated cycle, in which each gives energy to or "breeds" the next. The primal energies of *P'o* and *Chih* are the fuel for the motivating force of *Hun*, which propels us to carry out the creative impulses of *Shen*, which gives rise to the acceptant empathy of *I'*, which facilitates the openness of *P'o*, which makes more energy available for the resolution of *Chih*, which is the fuel for the assertiveness of *Hun*, which breeds joy. . . .

Innate Potentialities of Persons

It is time to depart from the metaphor of five "inner lands," and emphasize that the psyche is really more like a set of *inner forces*. The reality of the psyche can but be hinted at by a "map" or list of characteristics. There are many such maps, and many such lists. They can help us catch a glimpse of the inner forces which the *Nei Ching* describes as "mysterious powers" and "spiritual resources,"[7] and which Western psychology describes as core tendencies and innate potentialities of the person(ality).

Shen, I', P'o, Chih and Hun are five aspects of the psyche or five inner resources which allow us to develop towards realization of our full potential. The general direction of movement is towards becoming our real Selves. The same potent inner force is described by humanistic psychology as the actualizing tendency. In the Taoist view, the overall tendency is to move cyclically *through* extreme emotions, and *towards* synergic states—joy and confidence, empathy, openness, resolution, and assertion or the "will to become." A particularly meaningful parallel in Western psychology is with the directions that Carl Rogers describes people as *moving towards* in the process of therapy. Under conditions of safety, warmth and empathetic understanding, he says that people tend to move towards self-direction and trust of self, acceptance of others, openness to experience, "being complexity" and "being process." Summarizing the general pattern of movement, Rogers says:

> "It seems to mean that the individual moves toward *being*, knowingly and acceptingly, the process which he inwardly and actually *is*. He moves away from being what he is not, from being a facade. He is not trying to be more than he is, with the attendant feelings of insecurity or bombastic defensiveness. He is not trying to be less than he is, with the attendant feelings of guilt or self-deprecation. He is increasingly listening to the deepest recesses of his physiological and emotional being, and finds himself increasingly willing to be, with greater accuracy and depth, that self which he most truly is."[10]

Discovering Shen is similar to what Rogers describes as moving *"Towards Self-Direction"* and *"Towards Trust of Self."* As a person enters a more complete relationship with his inner nature, "increasingly he trusts and values the process which is himself." This leads to becoming "significant and creative" within his own sphere of life.[10] We may or may not choose to create things or theories. We *must* choose to create ourselves, if we are to be truly alive. Shen is the desire to extend ourselves creatively and live joyfully.

The aspect of the psyche which the Taoists called "I'" involves the self-actualizing characteristic Rogers describes as moving *"Towards Acceptance of Others."* In the process of growing into his whole Self, a person increasingly "values and appreciates both his own experience and that of others for what it *is*." The ultimate result is the natural development of "an acceptant attitude towards that which exists."[10] Rogers quotes Maslow's description of this state:

> "One does not complain about water because it is wet, nor about rocks because they are hard .... As the child looks out upon the world with wide, uncritical and innocent eyes, simply noting and observing what is the

case, without either arguing the matter or demanding that it be otherwise, so does the self-actualizing person look upon human nature both in himself and in others."[10]

The synergic state of P'o is openness, so the obvious parallel is with Rogers's *"Openness to Experience."* Growth requires the individual's "opening himself to internal feelings which are clearly not new to him, but which up to this time, he has never been able to experience." This is a movement towards a spontaneous way of living. "Living in an open, friendly, close relationship to his own experience" not only becomes non-threatening, but even begins to be a necessity. The person begins to *choose* familiarity with feelings. "This greater awareness of what goes on within is associated with a similar openness to experiences of external reality."[10] The harvest is an energized bodymind system, full of creative energy and able to discharge destructive feelings.

The synergic state of Chih is resolution, and the parallel is with the self-actualizing movement Rogers describes as *"Towards Being Complexity."* This is "the desire to be *all* of oneself in each moment—all the richness and complexity, with nothing hidden from oneself and nothing feared in oneself." It is the force which keeps us moving towards the "difficult, and in its absolute sense, impossible goal" of "becoming all of the complexity of one's changing self in each significant moment."[10]

"Hun" is the aspect of the psyche which gets us moving. The feeling is like what Rogers describes as *"Towards Being Process."* There is a sense of adventure, of being "more openly a process, a fluidity, a changing"—"a process of potentialities being born." The feeling is of being in flux, and of being "content to continue in this flowing current."[10] This feeling of freedom and freshness comes with appreciating oneself as a *becoming*.

4. *The Body Mandala and the Gall Bladder Meridian*

Part 1. THE BODY MANDALA

In this and the following nine chapters, we will explore the five aspects of the psyche in more detail as we travel through the related meridians. First let's get an overview of the body as a mandala or symbol for self-reflection, by looking at the "Patterns of Armoring" diagram. This tension map correlates Reichian and acupressure theories of the bodymind connection. It denotes eight main body areas, and shows some of the acu-points important for the release of each "segment."

When tension becomes chronic, usually there will be not just a tight knot in one spot, but rather something like a ring of tension around the area. If the tension at one point in one muscle does not relax, other nearby points also get affected as compensating tensions develop. *Tension tends to spread to points and muscles in the same segment.* Gradually, other points along the related meridians also become blocked.

A *segment* is a horizontal area of the body, in which the muscles and points are functionally-related. The muscles in a segment work together to make physical movements and to express feelings and emotions. Therefore, tension in one part of a segment affects the other parts. To understand this "segmental effect," you can make an experiment with the chest segment. First, try to tense the pectoral muscles [the #30s] *without creating any tension in the upper back muscles* [the #18s]. Impossible? Now try the opposite, tensing the upper back muscles without creating any tension in the pectoral muscles. At the least, this is very difficult, because the muscles in the front and back of the chest segment are functionally-related. (Relax, and breathe!)

Relaxing any one point will affect other functionally-related points. For example if tension in the #18 area relaxes, the front of the chest [including the #30s] will also be affected. If the back is to remain relaxed, the front will have to give up its tension too. Then the ring of tension in the segment can dissolve. This will affect the posture, improve the circulation of energy, and bring new levels of feeling awareness. When the armoring in any segment gives up, there comes a most pleasant feeling of freeness and well-being.

As you read the following descriptions of what the tension in each segment might be saying, you might try to find some of the related acu-points on yourself. If you find a tense or sore spot, relax and hold it for a few minutes. Feel the tension or soreness, feel into it, and be open to any feelings or images that might come up. It's like you're asking the tension, "Why do you need to be so tight?" and "Wouldn't you like to relax?"

Patterns of Armoring

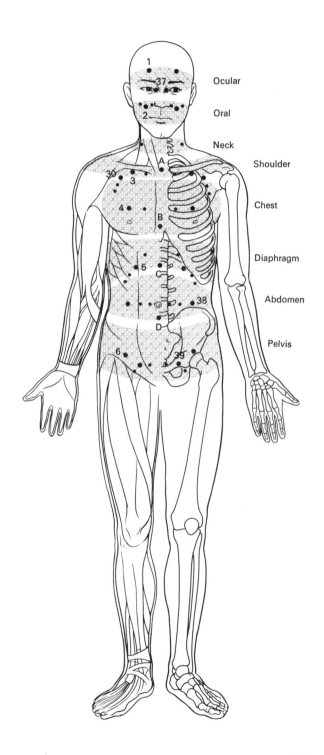

Ocular

Oral

Neck

Shoulder

Chest

Diaphragm

Abdomen

Pelvis

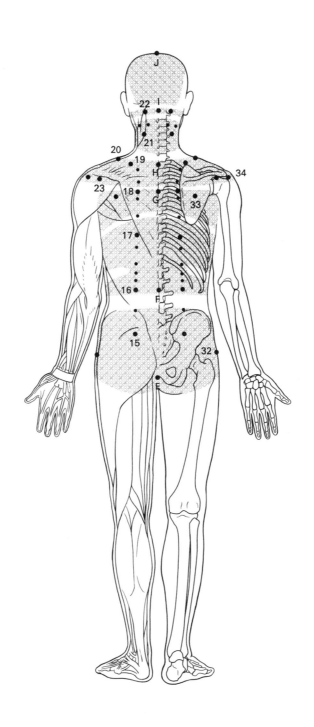

Eight Rings of Tension ─────────────────────────────

Starting at the top of the body, a ring of tension throughout the "ocular segment" can act somewhat like a blindfold. Then we don't have to see that which we don't want to look at. Sometimes we just don't want to face things which might contradict a picture that we want to have—of ourselves, our relationships, our world. We can constrict our field of vision by developing a ring of tension around the base of the skull [♯22s] and into the eyes. This also influences the *third eye*, or center of spiritual consciousness.

Tension in the jaw acts like a gag, to keep us from saying things that others might not like. Setting the jaw helps us to hold back both tears and shouts. It helps us to resist expressing ourselves in ways that might be disapproved—like by crying, grimacing, yelling, screaming, sucking, spitting or laughing. In general, the ring of tension in the "oral segment," from the neck [♯22s] through the jaws, bespeaks a need to stay in control. A couple ways of maintaining control are by keeping a set expression on our faces, and by keeping up a safe monotone of neutral verbalizations.

Releasing the ring of neck tension is also important for free Self-expression. By tightening a lasso of tension around the neck [♯21] area, we can keep threatening feelings from arising out of the heart or guts, and we can ignore the conflicts between our thoughts and feelings. Neck tension can relate to a wide variety of unconscious feelings and attitudes, because this small area is a major energy crossroads; over half of the meridians go through the neck. Eventually, tension here can act like a noose— trapping us in our own defenses, and restricting our freedom to feel and express ourselves.

Tension in the shoulder segment can be like a harness, hitching us to a cartload of responsibilities. Tension through points ♯19, 20 and 3 is like a shoulder strap. Tight shoulder straps can come from carrying excessive burdens, like heavy backpacks. These tension straps can also come from carrying psychological burdens. Perhaps we have "shouldered our responsibilities" and found them heavy. It might be that we're tired and stressed out because of taking on too much. It might be that we're creating some of the stress by resisting responsibilities, or instead, by imagining that we are individually responsible for everything that happens. The shoulder tension might be saying "I can't do it all," "I don't want to do it," or "I don't think I can do it." Knotting up the shoulder muscles can prevent us from striking out at the world—or make us want to! It also shuts down awareness of heartfelt feelings.

When we tighten the cords of tension around the chest, then we don't have to *feel* our hurt, or our love. Having the chest tied up can be less threatening than confronting heartfelt feelings. Free movement of the chest allows us to become aware of appreciation and love, and to feel more alive—but at the risk of feeling more vulnerable. In the chest segment, we encounter perhaps the most sensitive part of ourselves—the heart.

"The heart is the center or core of life, and its rule is love," says Lowen. "It is also an infant, for the heart never grows old." Chest armoring is a protection against hurt of this "infantile king."[1] It closes the doors on the emotional storehouse of the heart, and hides a pain which is a longing both for love and to love. The heart center focuses and amplifies feelings. Tension around the chest is unconsciously designed to cut off, or cut down on, anxiety-producing feelings like heartache and heartbreak.

But this tension also prevents us from fulfilling our longing for love.

Diaphragm tension is like a tight corset, which cuts off threatening feelings arising from the lower centers. The diaphragm is a main respiratory muscle. It is very susceptible to emotional stress, and to frustration and anger. The diaphragm also contracts in response to the fear of losing control, like by giving way to deep sexual feelings. According to Wilhelm Reich, diaphragm tension expresses a "no-no" attitude—"no" to full orgasmic pleasure in sex, to self-assertion in relationships, or to honest expression of anger. Chronic diaphragm armoring can reflect the rage of having held assertive emotions down for a long time, which can create a predisposition to anger.

Under the diaphragm is the solar plexus, the center of personal power. When this center is blocked, there may be powerful suppressed feelings. There may be a general inhibition about showing feelings, perhaps because of anxiety about losing control. There may even be an obsession about controlling ourselves and everyone else. The solar plexus center is a treasure house of powerful emotional and physical energy. Openness here reflects the ability to use our personal power to heighten our own experience, without crushing others.

Abdominal tension is like a belt we have tied too tightly. Constricting the waist can decrease the intensity of gut passions, and it can cut the heart off from any direct connection with genital excitation. Part of the Western ideal of a fine (especially female) figure has been to have the belly held in, so that the waist is as small as possible. Tightening the abdominal muscles has the interesting side-effect of raising the diaphragm, which helps control or suppress sexual impulses. Abdominal tension also helps hold back the impulse to cry, or at least allows us to cry quietly. Tension in the lower back [#16] can relate to fatigue, or can be a defense against fear, including the fear of attack. Chronic tension in this segment relates to a fear of feeling; openness reflects a respect of our own feelings and those of others.

Inside the lower abdomen, a couple inches below the navel, is a very important energy center called the *hara* (Japanese) or *tan t'ien* (Chinese). The hara is like a sea of generative force and vitality, which gives us the ability to adapt to change. The hara is also the body's center of gravity. It is the "center in the midst of conditions."[2] It is the center from which all movement and energy flows—"the physical embodiment of the original Life centre in man."[3] Discovering the hara means finding an inner balance-point, and implies feeling more centered psychologically as well as physically. (Directions for "hara breathing" are given in Chapter 12.)

Ropes of tension around the pelvis can act like a chastity belt, limiting our sexual feelings. As Lowen points out, deep pelvic sexual feelings are threatening to many people, who can tolerate only superficial and easily discharged feelings. Pelvic tension can correlate with sexual anxieties, problems or dysfunctions, or with stress in the relationships deriving from sexual needs. This area in general relates to primary survival needs, like the need for *discharge*—by the release of energy in sexuality, and by the elimination of waste products through intestinal and urinary functions. In the pelvis, we have arrived at the lowest energy center, the root of our being.

Back tension can be a part of the armoring in the shoulder, chest, diaphragm, abdominal and pelvic segments. All of the acu-points on the back are points of the Bladder Meridian (which we'll discuss in Chapter 8).

Rings of tension can also develop in the extremities—around the upper arm, at the elbows or wrists, around the upper thighs, at the knees, calves or ankles. Six of the organ meridians go through the legs, and six through the arms. Tension in the arms can interfere with doing physical work, and with expressing feelings by reaching out, embracing, touching, holding, giving, taking, grasping, striking or stroking. Tension in the legs can interfere with movement or with being able to "stand our ground." The legs are our primary contact with reality—our grounding. The legs are connected to and affected by the pelvis, and the arms are similarly hooked onto the shoulders.

Segments, Meridians, and Energy Centers

A feeling of wholeness depends on the free movement of energy and feeling between all the segments, and between the related energy centers and meridians. The four main energy centers emphasized in Taoist yoga are the "third eye," heart, solar plexus and "hara" centers.* The following table outlines the basic relationship of these centers with the segments and meridians.

A Taoist View of Energy Centers

Segment	Energy Center	Aspect of The Psyche	Important Meridians
ocular	Third EYE CENTER		Yang Meridians
oral, neck			Yang Meridians
shoulder			Yang Meridians
chest	HEART CENTER ("B")	SHEN	Heart & Pericardium Meridians
		P'O	Lung Meridian
diaphragm	SOLAR PLEXUS	HUN	Liver Meridian
	CENTER ("C")	I'	Spleen-Pancreas Meridian
abdomen	HARA CENTER ("D")	CHIH	Kidney Meridian
pelvis			Yin and Yang Meridians of the legs

In Jin Shin Do, the general rule is to begin from the top and work down—first releasing muscle knots and blocked points in the upper segments, and then tensions in successively lower areas. This is because release of the head, neck and shoulders is crucial to self-expression and to free circulation of energy and feelings. *Almost all the points in the upper segments—the head, neck and shoulders—are points of the yang meridians.***

Working with the yang organ meridians helps release the upper segments and allows awareness to begin moving down into the lower segments and centers. Because

---

* Three other energy centers less emphasized in Taoist literature are the crown chakra [point "J"], throat chakra [around "A"] and root chakra ["E"]. The Central Channel influences *all* the energy centers. To balance this channel, you can hold points "A," "B," and "C" with the right hand while holding "D" with the left hand; then hold point "E" with the right hand while holding "F," "G," "H," "I" and "J" with the left hand. Or you can use the release pattern for the Great Central Channel given in *The Acupressure Way of Health: Jin Shin Do*, pp. 116–117.

** The two exceptions are #3: K, a point of the Kidney Meridian, and #30, on the Lung Meridian, which is also related to the chest segment.

we want to focus on the upper segments first, in this and the next four chapters we will explore the yang meridians—the Gall Bladder, Small Intestine and Triple Warmer, Stomach, Large Intestine and Bladder. These have to do with processing physical foods and psychic events. Related tensions can correlate with digestive or eliminative problems, or with defensive attitudes.

As the above table shows, the *yin* meridians related to Shen, I', P'o, Chih and Hun are important for opening the heart, solar plexus and hara centers. We'll be meeting these energy centers in the discussions of the yang meridians, but we'll explore them in more detail when we discuss the yin meridians (in Chapters 9 through 13). The Heart, Pericardium and Lung Meridians are especially important for opening the chest segment and the heart center; the Spleen-Pancreas and Liver Meridians are most important for releasing the diaphragm segment and the solar plexus center; and Kidney Meridian points are most related to the hara center in the lower abdomen. The pelvic segment includes points of three yin meridians (the Spleen-Pancreas, Liver and Kidney) and their partner yang meridians (the Stomach, Gall Bladder and Bladder).

Before we explore first the yang meridians and then the yin meridians, let me briefly summarize the Taoist view of the inner spirit or core Self: *Shen*. In preceding chapters, I have defined "Shen" as the inner spirit and original nature, and I have described the inner Self as being like a core of energy or of energy centers. Shen is the coordinator of impressions, the guiding spirit, the director of energic activities. In acupressure theory, Shen is generally correlated with the Heart. Technically, this is but one face of Shen—*Shih Shen*, the more earthly or emotional aspect of the core spirit. *Yuan Shen* is the other and more primal aspect of Shen—the spiritual consciousness related to the "third eye" center.*

When the classics say Shen is the master of the bodymind, the reference can be to either aspect, since both have a general influence on the bodymind. Shen (in both aspects) is the core spirit. P'o, I', Hun and Chih are manifestations of this core spirit, as are all the energy centers and meridians.

Jin Shin Do® Bodymind Release Process (2)

Refer to the last part of Chapter 1, "Jin Shin Do® Bodymind Release Process," for general information on how to locate points, how much pressure to use, how long to hold points, and how to choose and combine points. The following are some concepts which are important for understanding and using the material presented in this and the following nine chapters.

Local Point: A "local point" is a sensitive or tense point in the problem area, or adjacent to the affected area. If there is no particular physical problem, the "local points" are the places where there is the most muscular tension or armoring.

Distal Point: A "distal point" is a point distant from the "local point," which helps release that tense or sore area. In Jin Shin Do, while holding a local point with one hand, we usually hold one or more distal points with the other hand. The simplest approach is to hold the local and distal points on the same side of the body,

---

* The "third eye" center is particularly influenced by the Heart, Liver and Gall Bladder meridians. "Yuan Shen" will be discussed in more detail in chapters nine and thirteen.

then repeat the pattern on the other side. For self-treatment, sometimes it may be more comfortable to hold the distal points on the opposite side from the local point, or separately.

On the meridian charts, *large dots* indicate points I most often use as *local points*, and *small dots* indicate points I most often use as *distal points*. However, any point can be a "local point" if it is tense or painful.

Source Point: Each meridian has a "source point," which may be used as a "distal point." The source point may be held together with any other point on the meridian. It may also be held by itself, to help re-establish energic balance in the related meridian. The source points have a general balancing effect, and so may be used whether the meridian is excessive or deficient.

Meridian Routes: Each meridian has a main route, with points that are close to the surface of the skin, and an internal route, as well as shorter branches or accessory routes (which connect with other meridians). On the meridian charts, the internal parts and branches are illustrated with dotted lines.

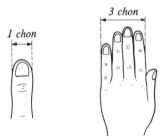

Chon: A "Chon" is a *body inch*. Together with anatomical landmarks, these "body inch" measurements are used to describe the location of acu-points. *One chon* can be measured as the width across the joint of the thumb. *Three chon* is the width across four fingers held close together. (The thumb and fingers in question are those of the recipient, so adjust your measurements accordingly.)

Each point has its own unique feeling, as you can experience for yourself.* "Hands-on" training under an experienced acupressurist is the easiest way to learn to find acu-points, but by feeling around in the areas described, you will be able to at least find the points that are most tense or sensitive on yourself. It might be enjoyable to hold some of these points, perhaps following the examples given, while reading about the meridians.

Ending a session: Hold both #22s until they feel released—or, both #20s, 21s and then 22s. Also see the last part of Chapter 1: "The Whole Session."

---

* Each point also has specific physical and psychological associations, in addition to the general associations of the related meridian, but these intriguing details are not within the scope of this book. Neither is it possible herein to explain all the many possible ways to work with the meridian points, nor to describe all the many wonderful points on each meridian. However, we will explore some easy ways to use a hundred of the most powerful points of the organ meridians.

In locating acu-points on thousands of students in the U.S., Canada and Europe, I have been impressed by the omnipresence of tension at Gall Bladder points like ♯20, 21 and 22. Tension along this meridian seems to be an indicator of the general stress level of modern civilization. This tension clamps down the back of our skulls, knots up our necks, snarls our shoulders, constricts our chests, blocks our diaphragms and makes our hip joints rigid. In fact, the Gall Bladder Meridian is a main culprit behind the entire segmental tie-up. It includes points in the head, neck, shoulders, chest, abdomen, pelvis, and legs. The only major part of the body through which this meridian does *not* travel is the arms—and they are influenced, too, by the Gall Bladder points in the shoulder and neck areas.

Tension at the base of the skull, around the ♯22s, influences the entire head and neck area, and all of the sense organs. Release of this tension brings a deep relaxation and an enhancement of the senses of sight, hearing, taste and smell. When this tension does not release, it begins to feel like a tight band around the head, from the nape of the neck through the eyes, and also through the jaws. If you isometrically tighten the muscles around your ♯22s, you can feel a compensating tension spreading into the temples and eyes and affecting the jaws. Similarly, if you grit your teeth and clench your jaws, you can feel the ♯22s tense up sympathetically. From these experiments, you can also feel how chronic tension at the ♯22s could lead to headaches, a stiff neck, and uptightness.* (Relax!)

The band of tension from the ♯22s into the eye and jaw areas acts rather like a sealing ring, for it helps seal off awareness of anxiety-producing emotions and thoughts. The alternative to excessive self-control is Self-acceptance—learning to let ourselves, and life, *be*. "This tension has to do with control issues," said one woman. "It's the feeling of holding my head up so I don't just give in and say 'yes, sir; no, sir." "The attitude of trying to fix the world the way you want it—that's what this tension is about," said a man whose headache was accompanied by tensions in the ♯22s and in the diaphragm. "Thinking I should be a savior or a knight . . . . Anger!" About a month later, when the Gall Bladder tensions were significantly released, he said, "I've realized there are two kinds of control—manipulation or *trying*, and letting things *flow*, just being aware and responsive."

Another man who suffered from frequent tension headaches realized that the knots at his ♯22s and ♯21s related to issues of control and obligation. "I feel angry when things aren't as I want them (and should have controlled them) to be, and I feel angry when there are bad feelings (for I should have managed things more happily)." That leads to feeling guilty and blaming yourself, if things turn out differently than you think they should have. It takes time to let go of this controlling attitude, and learn to instead explore and enjoy *what is*.

Common images of tension at the ♯20s include comparisons with rocks and golfballs. People sometimes ask, "Isn't that a bone?" "It's the feeling of being between a rock and a hard place," said one woman. Her trapezius muscle was so tense that a slight pressure on the ♯20s sent a pain from there to the ♯1s (which I then held as distal points). "Trying too hard, that's what it's about," another woman said. Asked

---

* All kinds of tension headaches and migraines can be associated with the Gall Bladder Meridian; migraines may also involve the Stomach Meridian; pain in the eyes and neck may involve the Liver Meridian; and pain in the back or top of the head may involve the Bladder Meridian.

Part 2. GALL BLADDER MERIDIAN———

Points of the Gall Bladder Meridian

JSD #1—This point is located in a hollow 1 *chon* above the eyebrow, up from the pupil of the eye.
["Yang White"—GB 14]*
JSD #22—Find the tense or sore point below the skull (occipital bone), between the trapezius and sternocleidomastoid muscles. Press towards #1.
["Wind Pond"—GB 20]
JSD #21—Feel for the tensest point in the middle of the neck (out from the third cervical vertebra).
[Extra point—i.e., it has no acupuncture number.]
JSD #20—Often there is a hard knot of tension here, in the trapezius muscle at the base of the neck. The point is directly up from the nipple line, and in between the front and back of the body.
["Shoulder Well"—GB 21]
JSD #5: GB—Measure down from the nipple line, and press towards the bottom of the rib cage. This point is 1 *chon* below JSD #5.
["Sun and Moon"—GB 24]
JSD #32—Find the tender point above the hip joint (or, midway between the greater trochanter of the femur and the peak of the anterior iliac crest).
["Dwelling in the Bone"—GB 29]
JSD #14—If you stand up with your hands at your sides, this point will be under your middle fingertip, behind the vastus lateralis muscle. Press toward the back edge of the thigh bone (femur).
["Wind Market"—GB 31]
JSD #13—Feel the protrusion at the top of the outer leg bone (fibula), and find the depression a little in front of and below this bone (and within the peroneus longus muscle).
["Yang Mound Spring"—GB 34]
JSD #44—Measure 3 *chon* above the outer anklebone, and press into the back edge of the fibula.
["Suspended Bell"—GB 39]

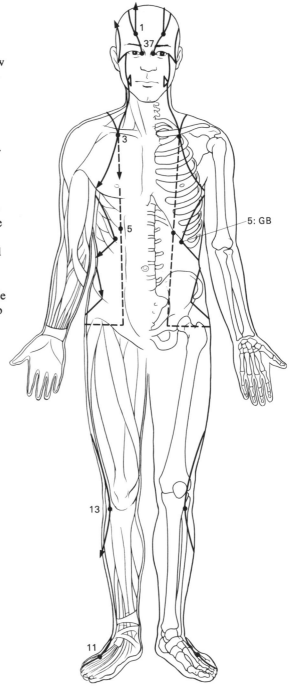

* The numbers within the brackets are the standard modern acupuncture numbers for the points. The names within quotation marks are the traditional names for the points.

Source point—In the hollow just below and in front of the outer anklebone. Press slightly upward.
["Grave Mound"—GB 40]
JSD #11—Trace up from between the fourth and fifth toes, to a sensitive point just below the junction of the fourth and fifth metatarsal bones.
["Foot Before Weeping"—GB 41]

Examples of Local-Distal Point Combinations
Try holding some of these local points with one or more of the suggested distal points:

Local point		Distal point
22	+	1, 44, 13
21	+	3, 5, 11
20	+	S., 13, 3
5 : GB	+	11, S., 17 area
32	+	14, 13, 11

S. = Source Point

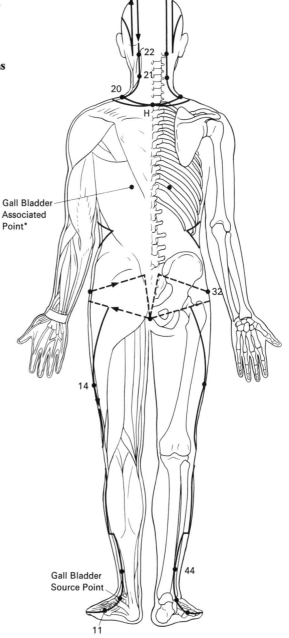

Gall Bladder Associated Point*

Gall Bladder Source Point

---

* *Gall Bladder Associated Point*—see Chapter 8 for explanation of associated points.

what the tension looked or felt like, one man saw himself "between a blue lagoon and a concrete jungle, stuck in frustration!" A woman said, "It's like a road with ruts and rocks—the hard place!" After a catharsis of old anger, she said, "I feel like I came back into myself!" She looked different too, without her frown and tight chin.

"What's that about?" Sally asked, as I was holding the #32s because of her low back pain. I replied that control issues or difficulty with taking charge were possibilities. She said that she had been very self-controlled and goal-oriented throughout her life, but oddly enough had trouble with little decisions, like what to wear. "Doesn't our society encourage us to be self-controlled?" she asked. I asked her to avoid controlling her feelings and thoughts during her session, and try to just be open to anything that might come up. The tensions in her hips and neck melted as she accepted her negative feelings, looked at the negative pictures that went with them, and then looked for positive pictures.

John, whose presenting problem was sciatica, exhibited dense and gnarly tension in the #20, #32 and #17 areas. He felt that the tightness at #20 and other neck points was related to "head-tripping," while the diaphragm blockage was about "the frustration of not expressing, and the anger of not feeling." As I worked with the tensions at #20 and #32 during one session, I asked him what his body wanted to do in these places. "I feel angry . . . I want to strike out and kick out, but I'm afraid to kick." He punched a pillow vehemently and began to kick—tentatively and carefully at first, and then with more energy as he found that the movement was surprisingly appropriate and releasing. Afterwards, tears filled his eyes at the relief of simply *feeling*.

Like the #22 tension, diaphragm tension [#5 and #17 areas] often acts like a sealing ring. "Anger" is a common response to the question: "what does this tension feel like or remind you of?" Also common are images of red; "seeing red" is a synonym for feeling angry. The diaphragmatic sealing ring is often full of canned anger or stifled sexual desires. Emotions cannot be canned as effectively as fruits and vegetables. Suppressed anger and chronic frustration tend to turn into distressing feelings like guilt and resentment.

Diaphragm tension can also be related to the Liver, Spleen or Stomach Meridians, so we will be exploring this area more in later chapters. Whether distal points of these meridians or of the Gall Bladder are used, release of the #5 and #17 areas can bring up powerful feelings. Sometimes there are images of wild animals, which are archetypal symbols of power and passion. The arising feelings are sometimes described as "the wild animalistic part," which has been submerged by the "good girl" or "good boy" part. With deep diaphragmatic breathing and release of the diaphragm armoring, there may be rhythmic body movements which look primal or sexual.

There may also be growls or shouts. Being noisy can help free the diaphragm area, and other gnarly tensions like the #22s and jaws. Another expression of sound which helps release Gall Bladder tensions is *sighing*. Think about all the decisions that you should make, all the things you should take charge of and do—and sigh, and sigh again. Can you feel how the simple act of sighing helps relieve the internal pressure? Sighing, quietly or noisily, can be done in a lot of places where shouting is unacceptable. The subject of sighing reminds me of a student in one of my first acupressure classes, who sighed regularly throughout my entire lecture. I found that disconcerting. I think I mentioned in my next lecture that *constant* sighing is a traditional sign of Gall Bladder Meridian imbalance.

This meridian stands out in my personal journey to body awareness, beginning with the memory of exquisite soreness at my ♯20s when these points were first pressed. I was twenty-one, and had decided to try acupressure for mid-back pain. I wasn't expecting to discover tensions that I hadn't known existed! The heretofore unfelt ♯20s, for example, were so painful that I felt like hitting the roof. These and other tensions seemed unyielding. They helped explain the difficulty I'd had trying to "stand up straight," stretch, and move freely. In Reichian theory, I found a word for the old tension that I had discovered in myself: "armoring." Gradually I discovered its relationship with an old habit of trying to control my feelings, which stemmed from real needs of childhood. In later Jin Shin Do sessions, as the defensive armoring of my neck and shoulders relaxed, I was surprised to feel my legs [♯14] and hips [♯32] tightening instead, as though these areas were automatic secondary lines of defense. I have also been surprised to find no apparent end to exploring the bodymind. There is always more to feel. Each time that we *become aware of* our physical and psychological defenses against feeling, it is a break-through to joy.

Control and Chaos

Control problems are a central theme of Gall Bladder Meridian blockage. Feeling a need for control and having difficulty taking charge is a polarity, the two sides of which usually co-exist in some way. Trying to exert control over things takes energy, and takes it away from some other area of life. For example, if we put a lot of energy into trying to control business or professional matters, less energy is available for taking charge in the personal arena; the opposite is also true. On the other hand, not being able to take charge in some area of life can increase the desire for control in another area. If some part of life feels chaotic and out of control, we might focus energy on some other area where it seems like we can have some control.

Heather, in her early twenties, was discontentedly dependent on her parents, and frustrated about not being able to move into the world on her own power. She was continually changing her mind about what she wanted to do, and then changing her major, while putting a lot of energy into trying to control her feelings so as not to upset her parents or her fiancé. For a while, marriage seemed like the ideal way to leave home and be independent. Heather's presenting problems included neck and shoulder tensions [♯22, 21, 20, 19: SI] and stress-related headaches. The diaphragm and abdominal areas were also tense.

For several months, it seemed that Heather basically wanted me to take charge and fix her up. She would focus her attention on tense areas and try to relax them, but she resisted considering the psychological factors that might be affecting her physical condition. Both her relationship with her parents and that with her fiancé were stressful; but feeling angry with them didn't seem nice. Heather really wanted to be nice, and to have the world be nice, so she unconsciously tried to control herself and others to make things be "nice."

When she developed allergic reactions to various foods, and to dogs (of which her parents had several), at first she wanted to see physical factors as the sole cause. She followed a nutritional program of eliminating all foods that were allergens and then gradually re-introducing them into her diet; this helped, but did not eliminate, the problem. After a doctor told her that her hypersensitive immune system symbolized a need to protect, and she read that sleeping on your abdomen could reflect the same, Heather moved full force into exploring the connection between physical and psychological factors.* "That's typical of me!" she said, when I later commented on this polar switch.

Heather began to see how her "warding-off attitude" reflected in her tendency to avoid taking charge of problems at their roots, instead trying to control the surface, or symptoms, so that things (and people) would be nice. "When the old patterns re-assert themselves, I feel frustration and a lot of tension in my shoulders [♯20] and in the deltoids," she noticed. "It helps to let myself and others have our feelings, to just let myself and others *be*, but the most important thing is doing something myself, and being grounded."

"I discovered that I have a very strong will to survive," she said. "All this suppressed energy is very powerful. I can't keep the lids on much longer." Heather was beginning to take the lids off by asserting her feelings, and not letting concern about others' opinions side-track her from her own felt course in life. Her symptoms were now much improved: her headaches were infrequent, and generally amounted to a mild achiness at the nape of the neck, and her allergic reactions were minimal. But there is always more to learn.

About a year later, a severe headache developed and I again found tension all along the Gall Bladder Meridian. Heather realized that she had been having trouble with decision-making, because of wanting to control things so they would come out "right." In her accounts of interactions with her parents and her boyfriend, I noticed a tendency to explain and defend her feelings, rather than just expressing and showing them.

I asked Heather if she might still be trying to exert control over others under the guise of self-expression: trying to control their responses by carefully explaining hers. That's like arranging your feelings, as you might arrange a dinner platter—with a heap of one feeling here, a sprig of another there, a slice of something else alongside it, so it all looks appetizing. But by the time you're done making it all pretty, and you're ready to present this well-designed platter of feelings to the other person, the feelings themselves have grown cold. If the feelings aren't there, how can they get understood? In retrospect, it's a lot of ineffective effort, compared to simply expressing and sharing feelings, in the now.

At the next session, Heather reported great improvement because of the insight about how she was *explaining* rather than just *expressing* her feelings. "My shoulders haven't felt so relaxed for a month!" she said. "The most important thing is to be true to myself. I've given up trying to control or manipulate others, so I just have myself to carry around. It's a lot lighter!" The following week, we discussed the fine line between trying to just express oneself and trying to push discussions so that they come out "right." Heather had noticed that her desire to control others often came

---

* The need to protect, fearfulness and over-concern go together. Heather's journey continues in Chapters 5, 10 (Part 2) and 12 (Part 1).

from thinking that what she wanted was obviously right or necessary. "I've always hated that in others, like in my mother. It's hard, and funny, to see it in myself!"

The next week, Heather talked about her dislike of causing negative feelings, and how she often had the impulse to try to fix upset feelings. "I need to trust my feelings to be able to just express them, without explaining and defending," she said. "If others get upset because they don't like my emotional responses, I always start thinking that my feelings are wrong." The natural next step is trying to control the bad or wrong feelings.

By the next session, Heather's tension level was markedly decreased. Her neck and diaphragm areas needed only brief acupressure attention. We focused on the shoulders (and the Small Intestine Meridian). "Remember I said I had stopped trying to control others?" Heather asked. "But I hadn't stopped trying to control myself! It's like trying to ski uphill. So I decided to just stop and see how I really feel. It's very interesting! A bigger revelation even than not trying to control others. It's even nicer not to control myself!

"Instead of just feeling what I was feeling, I would try to figure it out, and then once I figured it out, I'd try to *push* it that way! But when I put myself in a position I don't feel in my heart, people feel that. I'm actually more vulnerable, and people pounce on me more, while I'm trying to protect myself! I'm starting to sabotage those false paths now—even in simple things like the way I hold my body and the way I talk." Heather had discovered that when she was in touch with her inner self and acting from real needs, her shoulder tension would relax; when she tried to figure out and control everything, the ♯20s would feel like golfballs again.

"Control and chaos aren't different; the order is in the flow," Heather concluded. "I used to think if you controlled everything well, you could eliminate chaos. Sometimes trying to control things actually creates chaos! I think the attempt to control everything comes from feeling helpless. Just flowing with things seems like being helpless; maybe that's why people don't like it as well as having control. But it seems to me that going through life is rather like being a kayaker going through rapids, then still water, then white water—and not knowing until s/he's there which it will be. Maybe life is like that, and you can't control it to be different—like, to be all still water. Maybe that's even why we like life—why it's interesting!"

"General Gall Bladder"

The Gall Bladder Meridian is like an important and upright official who excels by his decisions and judgment, according to the *Nei Ching*; its partner, the Liver, is like a military leader who excels in his strategic planning. In the following story about "General" Gall Bladder,** a student developed this analogy further to describe the controlling attitudes which he found reflected in his own Gall Bladder tensions.

---

* Gall Bladder functions are also mentioned in Chapter 13, Part 1, which describes the closely related Liver Meridian.

** Reprinted with permission of Arnold Porter, from his paper, "Strategic Deployment of Self: Coup D'Etat in the Land of Hun."

The defensive attitudes of the "General" are attitudes we all share. The General's controlling tendencies are *our* controlling tendencies.

"Here is excessive Gall Bladder, lying awake at night, scheming, thinking about all that he must accomplish, wanting to impress people. To him, knowledge isn't just useful or interesting information, but a card that can be played towards his own advancement. Like a typical military man, Gall Bladder sees the world in terms of hierarchical structure. He wants to be at the top, by virtue of his decision-making skills.

"Having come around the long journey through Earth, Metal and Water, he is Spirit also. Now as Wood, in human form, he savors the precious gifts of individuality. His gifts are the ability to be discriminative, the ability to make and carry out decisions, to take charge of and control things, to create things. Now, having developed these valuable abilities through arduous work, he is supposed to turn them over to Shen, who like an infant monarch waits for the general to appear so that he can manifest himself on earth.

"But as generals are prone to do, Gall Bladder has become infatuated with power. He would like to control everything, push the world around, have his own way. Coup d'etat! He takes the throne himself and keeps from Shen the abilities and energies that Shen needs in order to manifest. Gall Bladder's meridian has a lot of energy; Shen's meridians (the Heart and Pericardium) have but a little. The ego is inflated; the Spirit is deprived of energy. Shen, the original spirit and true monarch of the bodymind, is confined to some aesthetic inner throne while the General gives the orders.

"But a good general does not necessarily make a good ruler. With tight neck and shoulders he sits at the helm, determined to maintain control of a stolen throne, determined to rule the Self. How tiring! How exhausting! Unfortunately he lacks the gift that his ruler waits to give him, the gift that would relax his tension and ease his life—the gift of Tao. Not having checked in with Shen, the general has not learned that there is a flow to life, and that much just ripens in its own time. There is no need to scheme and plot, at least not all the time. The overworking Gall Bladder has not learned that allowing things to come to fruition requires relaxing as well as deciding and doing.

"So how can we show the general that he doesn't have to be responsible for all of it, all the time? How can we get him to relax enough so that he can become aware of Shen and receive the gift of Tao? Some focal point is needed, to keep problems off the mind long enough to hear the voice of Shen. Focus on the finger pressure and the tense points, or on the breathing; tune into visual phenomena; listen to music or the sounds of nature. Sharing thoughts and feelings, in the here and now, also helps. It is often the withheld thoughts and feelings that, churning endlessly, preoccupy us and keep us from the here and now. To share our feelings and thoughts with another human being is to make them the business of the moment. So even that which can keep us from the present can be used as the door to the present.

"In one session, I feel Gall Bladder points ♯22 and ♯32 begin to relax after I become captivated by the light patterns moving on my eyelids. In another, as the ♯22s begin to release, I have images of mountains arising endlessly before my eyes while I am sinking into a deeper and deeper state of relaxation—a 'core state.' Inner and outer merge; the membrane between them pops. In this moment conscious and unconscious, acceptable and unacceptable, are one. The bursting of the membrane is an attunement to the time—to the Self, Now.

"So here the General has finally relaxed somewhat, and dropped some of his burden. Two things start happening: the spirit soars, and stuff begins to rise, as though from the bottom of a stagnant pond. Why is this?

"Gall Bladder likes to deploy the self strategically, trotting out the parts he judges capable, attractive, intelligent, even spiritual. He deploys these impressive parts of the Self as envoys, to further his ends and strengthen his position of control. But how about the not-so-impressive parts of the self—the injured, frightened, punished children within us, with their infantile fear, anger, hate, rage and repressed sexuality? The General has no use for these unattractive creatures, so they are kept down, out of sight, in dark concentration camps behind walls of tension. They are not useful to him.

"To him. But how about to Shen? Are these denied creatures orphans, or are they rather aspects of the Self? Doesn't Shen need them, in order to manifest himself, to be whole? As the Gall Bladder points release, I cross the border-line between the 'acceptable' and 'unacceptable' aspects of myself. I wonder if the Gall Bladder Meridian *is* that border-line, or its representative in the body. When this meridian is tense, the line is rigid and inviolable; when this meridian relaxes, the line becomes permeable. The awkward parts of ourselves can come up into the light then, to grow and to be healed by compassion. The Spirit waits to welcome these suppressed parts of itself.

"Control has been relaxed. I have stopped trying to cling to the 'acceptable.' Things that need to be dealt with have begun to float up from the unconscious depths, where I had deposited my 'unacceptable' stuff. This is scary, but made easier—in fact, made possible—by the fact that the Spirit has been released too. The energy that was withheld by the General's tense effort to control everything, and have his own way, instead becomes available to Shen. Some of the Wood energy released from the neck and shoulders has begun to energize the chest and thereby to make Fire, or ignite the Spirit. The beauty and simplicity of life become apparent. The spirit soars, thankful for trees that touch the sun, silent valleys of haze, grasses and flowers that bend in the breeze, the simple things of life—including love.

"The classics say that all the meridians 'make their decisions' in the Gall Bladder. Perhaps the foremost of these decisions is the basic one of whether to let all of oneself come out into the conscious light and grow, or whether to leave some aspects to live darkly, a life of their own, in the subterranean passages of the unconscious. As the Gall Bladder Meridian relaxes, and with it the attempt to control everything within and without, the whole bodymind can relax. In such a state of deep relaxation, I have a glimpse of the relaxed, whole Self (in which Hun and Shen are united).

> "I am on a boat going down a long, wide, flat river. There are golden trees on the shore. I want to run in them so I dive off the boat, leaving it to float. I run down the shore as the boat floats slowly on. I am dodging, weaving playfully, running naked between tree trunks in the shadow of golden leaves, dry leaves crunching underfoot. I feel like a Rosseau painting of primitive man.
>
> "I am also keeping an eye (an 'I'?) on the boat. It contains a cargo. I

envision this section of the river, and see that there are no shoals or falls. The boat can float by itself. I can run.

"The boat and its cargo are civilized and constructed, like the mind with its cargo of purpose, plotting a course for negotiating the flow of life. But what a cramp it is for a living being to be always aboard the ship, limited to its confines! I must learn to leave the boat, at least when the river is safe and the course is set."

"In this image, the General has received the gift of Tao. He is using his skills to aid Shen on his journey down the great river of Tao. But he also trusts the river, and himself! He knows when he can leave the boat behind, abandon control for a while, and run free."

Relaxation of the Gall Bladder Meridian comes with letting life flow, and with being able to alternately take charge and then relax control. The mind's cargo of purpose is important, but constantly trying to protect it is self-strangulation. Trying to control ourselves or others to do more, better, faster—often this just creates stress by meddling with the nature of things. Besides, ofttimes our efforts at control are neither necessary nor effective. Sometimes we need to set the controls on automatic and just run free—trusting the flow of life, and trusting the inner Self.

By Jeremy Teeguarden

Getting Lighter ───────────────────────────

Releasing tensions of the Gall Bladder Meridian can open the doors to a very simple but wonderful thing—feeling, and flowing with our feelings. Hyperactivity of the Gall Bladder Meridian can correlate with over-control of the feeling self. When there is also hypoactivity in most of the yin meridians, the pattern is suggestive of some kind of general emotional suppression.

Catherine's pulses were an example of this pattern. The Gall Bladder was quite excessive, while the Heart, Pericardium, Lungs and Spleen-Pancreas were deficient. Early in the session, as I held points of the Gall Bladder Meridian on the right side, Catherine said she felt very light. After a while she said, "This winter felt so sad, like it would never go away." It looked like *she* had felt sad too. I asked her to just let the sadness be there. "It's about the world, and it's about feeling like I'd lost touch with my intuitions and my Self." As I held #20 and #13 together, she said it felt like one point, and then like points very far away from each other, alternately.

As the neck tension relaxed, Catherine saw violet and blue colors, then had the image of a ladder. I asked her if she would like to visualize climbing it. "It's just blue at the top," she said a few minutes later. "There's nothing there." I asked if it was blue like the sky. What is the inner sky? Is it maybe the opening of intuition, of the spiritual, of the "third eye"? The ladder disappeared, and Catherine felt like she extended very far up, but still was in contact with the ground. "My feet feel really big," she said with amusement.

As I was completing the Gall Bladder release on the left side, she said, "I feel like my feelings can come out again! My feelings are like flowers. I'm seeing images of flower fairies. They're asking, 'Why didn't you let us out for so long?' " Through tears she continued, "I feel like a mother with her children that were lost." Then in her image all the fairies—her children, her feelings—came together into one.

"I feel so much power!" she exclaimed. She was breathing deeper now, and her chest had released quite a bit, although we hadn't worked with that area directly. To help free the chest more deeply, I held #18, #30 and "B" [with Lung, Pericardium and Heart distal points]. "I feel the power coming from inside me," Catherine continued. "It's like gold inside my chest. Part of me doesn't want to believe it!" The sense of inner power was strong enough to quiet that old doubting voice. "I feel light . . . like I'm on a mountain . . . dancing," she said, then remembered an image she'd had during meditation some years back. "There were two hands coming out from a light. I was too shy to hold them. This time I held them! I feel so strong and joyful!"

Catherine relaxed into a deep trance and was silent for the rest of the session, while I held a few points in the lower segments and legs, and then did a short neck release. I asked her to just relax for a while afterwards, and then to stretch and get up slowly. She slept for a few minutes. Afterwards, needless to say, she felt very good. She said wonderingly, "It's magic!"

5. *Triple Warmer and Small Intestine Meridians*

Part 1. TRIPLE WARMER MERIDIAN

The official of the three "warmers" has a very important function in the meridian system, although he is quite invisible upon investigation of the physical body. The *Triple Warmer* Meridian has no related organ apart from the organs of the other meridians; rather, it has the function of coordinating their activities. Here we are faced with a fact that is easier to ignore with the other "organ meridians": in the traditional Chinese theory, *the meridians are defined by their functions and by related bodymind processes, not by the physical structures of related organs.*

The three "warmers" are also called "heaters" or "burning spaces." As these names imply, the Triple Warmer helps regulate bodymind warmth, so one symptom of imbalance is increased susceptibility to coldness or fever. The "three warmers" refer to three main divisions of the body—the chest, abdomen and pelvis—and especially to the transformative processes that take place in these areas. On the physical level, these are the processes of the respiratory, circulatory, digestive and urogenital systems, which together produce and maintain the heat of the body. On another level, heat is energy.

"The burning spaces are like the officials who plan the construction of ditches and sluices, and they create waterways," says the *Nei Ching*.[1] Taken literally, this means the Triple Warmer controls the movement of fluids.* However, in the Taoist tradition, water is a symbol for energy, so "waterways" can be a metaphor for energy pathways. The Triple Warmer Meridian is in charge of the transportation of fluids *and* energy. It influences all the organs by regulating the processes of energy transformation in the three "warmers," so its imbalance implies disharmony in other organ meridians.

The Triple Warmer is called "the commander of all energies." It is in charge of the energy of the upper, middle and lower warmers, and it influences the balance of energy between the inside and outside of the body. When this meridian is hypoactive, there may be a lack of energy for activity, or an exhaustion that makes it hard to handle stress, and makes for irritability or depression. Alternately, hyperactivity of this meridian may correlate with restlessness and anxiety, or "nervous energy." In either state, there is likely to be tension at Triple Warmer points in the neck and shoulders.

---

* Therefore the Triple Warmer influences the organs involved in the movement of fluids: the Kidney, Bladder, Stomach, Small Intestine and Large Intestine, and also the Spleen (as will be explained in Chapter 10).

Triple Warmer Meridian

Points of the Triple Warmer Meridian

Source point—This point is in a depression in the middle of the outer wrist crease, between the tendons extending from the third and fourth fingers.
["Yang Pond"—TW 4]

JSD ♯26—Measure 2 *chon* above the outer wrist crease, and feel for a little muscular knot in between the bones of the forearm (radius and ulna).
["Outer Frontier Gate"—TW 5]

JSD ♯24:TW—Measure about 3 *chon* below the shoulder joint, and feel for the sore point on the back border of the deltoid muscle (above and behind JSD ♯24).
["Shoulder Meeting"—TW 13]

JSD ♯19—Feel for the sore or tense place above the inner tip of the shoulder blade (scapula), and about 1 *chon* lower than and inside of ♯20.*
["Heavenly Bone"—TW 15]

JSD –21: TW—This point is outside of JSD ♯21,* on the outer border of the sternocleidomastoid muscle, and at the level of the jaw (mandible). A "muscle knot" can often be felt at this point.
["Heavenly Window"—TW 16]

JSD ♯1: TW—At the outside tip of the eyebrow where a little hollow can be felt.
["Silk Bamboo Hollow"—TW 23]

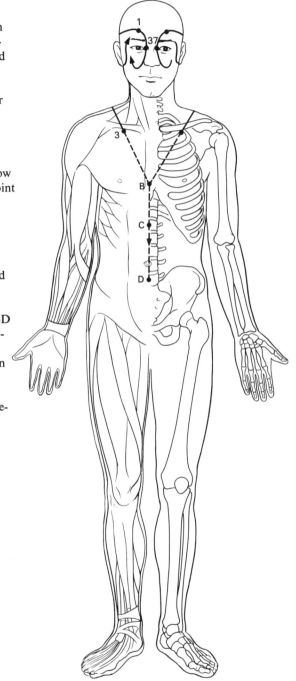

---

* See Gall Bladder Meridian, Chapter 4.

Examples of Local-Distal Point Combinations

Local point		Distal point
21: TW	+	26, 24: TW,
		1: TW, 22
19	+	26, S., 3
16 area**	+	S., 26
"D"	+	"B," "C"

S. = Source Point

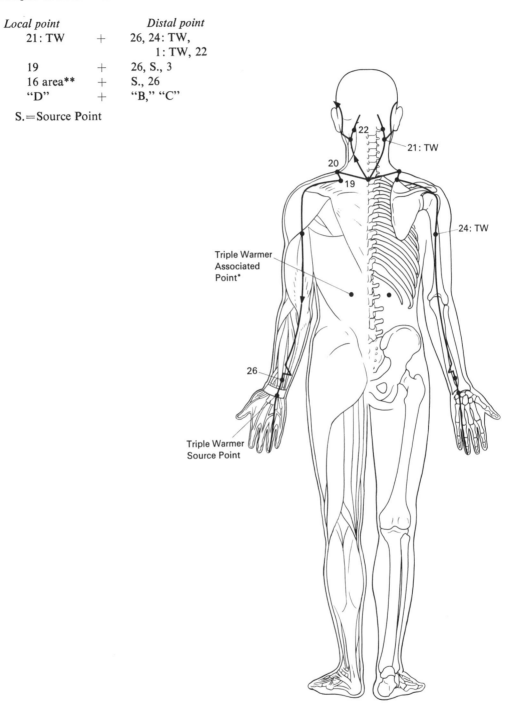

* *Triple Warmer Associated Point*—see Chapter 8 for explanation of associated points.
** Make your hand into a fist; with your knuckles on this point, lean back in a chair or lie down on your back, with your knuckles holding the point.

The Triple Warmer Meridian is part of many releases, because its points are often used in the short neck release which concludes each session.* I particularly remember one neck release I received, focusing on Triple Warmer points. The #21: TW felt so tight that it seemed impossible to let go of the tension. As these points were held [with #26 and the source point], I focused my attention on the tension. I tried to *become* the point—to really feel what it is to be tense there. At first I just felt more uncomfortably aware of the tension. Then I suddenly felt *very* tired, like I was falling into a big well of fatigue. It felt good to surrender to the fatigue—to *be* tired instead of just *knowing* that I was tired. It was a deliciously relaxing feeling. I drifted off into sleep, as the neck tension let go.

After a deep release, the bodymind needs time to stabilize in a new balance and flow of energy. In sleep, deep relaxation and meditation, we withdraw from the distractions of the world and give the bodymind a chance to rest. When the conditioned mind and ego-desires are put to sleep, the inner spirit is quieted. The vital energy can circulate more freely between the three warmers and through the meridians. In deep relaxation or meditation, we can be aware of this energy flow. Along with a joyful sense of wellness, there might be feelings of inner warmth and lightness, as the energy system is revitalized.

We might even discover that we have plenty of energy, once we stop blocking it up in knots of stress-related tension, and start letting it flow through the bodymind. This reminds me of an image that one woman had during work with the Triple Warmer Meridian. Asked what she was feeling or seeing, she said, "Just colors—blue and green." While holding #21: TW and #19 [with various distal points], I asked her to watch the colors and see if they changed. After perhaps five minutes, I asked what happened with the colors. "They changed to red and gold, and then became a red chalice," she said. "At first it was in the distance, and then it rapidly came closer." What did she want to do with the chalice? "Enter it," she said. Then she was floating in the chalice, and it got bigger and bigger until it was like an ocean.

Because her presenting problems included jaw tension as well as low energy, I also held the jaw points [with #3 and Large Intestine distal points]. The image remained. What was it saying? The chalice was a full cup—of water, and symbolically of energy. As she relaxed, she found herself in a veritable ocean of energy. "Maybe you *can* access your energy," I suggested. "Maybe the full chalice means you have access to a lot of energy." At the end of the session, she felt tingling in her left foot and then in her whole body, "like after your foot has been asleep." She enjoyed this sensation for a while, then stretched and got up slowly, feeling energized and vitalized. "Maybe some part of myself has been asleep and has just woken up," she said.

Square Pegs and Round Holes

The Triple Warmer Meridian and its partner, the Pericardium Meridian, have very general physical functions, since they regulate the interrelationship of other meridians. Likewise, these two meridians have very general psychological functions.

* See Chapter 1 of this book: "Jin Shin Do Bodymind Release Process," Part 4. Also see *The Acupressure Way of Health*, pp. 98–103 and pp. 120–123.

Lawson-Wood says they influence the relationship between parts of ourselves, and relationships between people, on all levels. He relates the Pericardium or "Circulation-Sex" Meridian particularly to intimate and sexual relationships, and the Triple Warmer to the general balance of sympathies and antipathies within social relationships. He suggests using Triple Warmer points for warming family and social ties and recovering from the depression and anxiety which can accompany a rupture of relations or estrangement.[2]

During release of this meridian, people tend to either "space out" or chatter about their problems, and these problems tend to involve relationships. Relationships bring up the general issue of conforming versus "being myself." People give us messages about how we should behave in order to fit in, and each of us has a full selection of old tapes on that theme. Relationships trigger these old messages, so that we tend to repeat old behavior patterns in an unconscious attempt to fit in. The problem is, many of the old roles and patterns no longer suit us, and so they are tension-forming.

Trying to fit a square peg into a round hole is a symbol for trying to conform to, or fit into, an unsuitable groove. This was exactly the image that came to Heather's mind when asked what the tension at ♯19 and ♯21: TW reminded her of. "In relationships I adapt, force myself into a mold, contort myself, and then wonder why I'm confused," she said. "What an energy drain!" Being a square peg in a round hole sounds uncomfortable. Not being ourselves *is* uncomfortable. Then why is it so difficult to get out of the niches that we have stuffed ourselves into? To stop playing uncomfortable roles, we have to risk facing the unfamiliar within ourselves. To develop new relationship patterns, we have to tolerate the anxiety of playing new roles. The payoff is that we stop the energy drain and we start feeling more warmth— in our relationships with others and with ourselves.

Energy Centers and the "Troll King" ————————————————

Releasing the Triple Warmer Meridian helps relax key muscle knots in the neck and shoulders, and helps awaken the internal energy centers. Relaxing the upper segments helps still the mind and—since the inner Self is less distracted by distressing thoughts—quiets the heart as well. Awareness can begin moving down into the lower segments and centers. The Triple Warmer Meridian influences communication between the vital energy centers in the three "warmers": the heart center in the chest ["B"], the solar plexus center in the upper abdomen ["C"], and the hara in the lower abdomen ["D"]. It also influences the "third eye" center, because it goes through important points in the ocular segment [♯22, ♯1, ♯1: TW and ♯37].*

The Secret of the Golden Flower says that the secret of "circulating the light" depends on being able to "fix the heart on the centre in the midst of conditions"— the hara center.[3] In other words, consciously connecting with the hara allows energy to circulate through the energy centers.

———————————————————————————————————————

* Also, there is a theory that the Triple Warmer Meridian relates to the hypothalamus, a region of the brain that is a link between the nervous system and the endocrine glands. A function of the hypothalamus is controlling the pituitary gland, which controls the other endocrine glands and the kidneys. The pituitary gland, along with the nearby pineal body (in the center of the brain), is related to the "third eye" center.

The Book of Consciousness and Life says that "heating" is also necessary for the "circulation of light":

> "Diligently heat the roots of consciousness and life.
> Kindle light in the blessed country ever close at hand,
> And there hidden, let thy true self always dwell."

Jung interprets this passage to mean that "there must be an intensification of consciousness in order that the dwelling place of the spirit may be 'illumined.' But not only consciousness, life itself must be intensified." And not only that, but there must be an intensification of energy in the "hara," for the primal energies related to this center *are* "the roots of consciousness and life."[4]

From the man who was last seen on a boat going down a long river (in the preceding chapter),* comes a dream that symbolizes the descent into the lower centers. This dream, which took place the night after a Triple Warmer release, sounds like a fairy tale. The part of the heart center is played by "Quan Yin," and that of the hara is played by the "Troll King."

The dream begins in an airplane. Two women are pilot and co-pilot of the plane, and the pilot is slumped against the door. "I point out to the co–pilot that she has power over the controls, if she wants it, because she's sitting squarely in front of them. She's not confident, so we just taxi along a winding cliff-side trail, until it becomes so narrow that we are in danger of crumpling the wing on the side of the cliff. Now we must trust to fly or we'll lose our ability. We plunge off the side of the cliff. I yell at the co-pilot to rev it up, but she fumbles with the throttle and kills it. We're falling! She gets the engine started and revs it up. Now we're flying!

"BEHOLD! There are the huge oaken doors to the Troll King's palace, just above the surf at the side of the cliff. Paradoxically, if the plane (ego?) hadn't stalled, we wouldn't have dropped low enough to see the doors below. We would have flown right over them. We bring the plane in on a small ledge. I turn to the back seat and remove a woman dressed in bridal gown and veil. She pulls back and struggles as I drag her toward the oaken doors, but there is something mock and ritualistic about my coercion and her resistance. She is Quan Yin, the goddess of compassion. I have kidnapped her to show her the lower realms. Inside, the Troll King's palace is primitive but not unpleasant. It's lighted by torches. Food is being prepared. There's music and dancing. They are preparing for a wedding. I realize: Quan Yin to the Troll King.

"The compassion energy of the heart is being wed to the powerful, volcanic, subterranean energies of the hara. Before this marriage, Quan Yin is rather wimpy— like the delicate, bound-footed ladies of the Chinese upper class. Compassion by itself lacks force. After her marriage to the Troll King, Quan Yin looks more powerful. She can have compassionate anger as well as compassionate sadness. From this comes the ability to set things straight! I wake up feeling powerful and energized after this dream."

The marriage of the heart and the hara symbolizes reclaiming the primal energies that have been hidden from conscious awareness. When we are out of touch with the hara, that energy center is like a secret underground cave. The abdomen is con-

---

* See Chapter 4, Part 2, "General Gall Bladder."

stricted and the center of gravity has shifted upward, to the chest. The physical manifestation of this shift is a "chest out—belly in" posture. In the book *HARA*, Karlfried Durckheim says this "false ordering of the inner forces" causes "the natural alternation between tension and relaxation" to be replaced by a "swing between hypertension and slackness." Speaking for Western man, he asks, "But is not the heart the natural centre of man? And is not man the being destined either to lift himself heavenwards and to master his life with his 'head' and 'will,' or failing this, to accept and endure it with his heart?" Speaking for the Eastern view, Durckheim replies:

> "Certainly he is. But right mastery and the strength to endure will be achieved only when the forces located in the upper part of his body and their centre, the ego, operate not independently and separately but are constantly held in check and guided by those that lie at a deeper level.
>
> "Man, *as a living being*, is not rooted in himself. Rather is he nourished, sustained and held in order by Nature, whose laws operate without his knowledge and assistance. Man sets himself in opposition to the order of life which fundamentally sustains him if, by an unnatural shifting of his centre of gravity, he denies that vital centre in his being which testifies to this order.
>
> ". . . Just as the growth and unfolding of the crown of a tree depends directly on its root-system, so also the vital development of man's spirit depends on his being true to his roots, that is, to an uninterrupted contact with the primal unity of Life, from which human life also springs."[5]

Part 2.   SMALL INTESTINE MERIDIAN

Tension at Small Intestine points, especially in the shoulders, is far more common than the law of averages would suggest. Shoulder pain related to either stress or injury frequently involves one of these Small Intestine points. When the problem is chronic, often the entire shoulder area is so tight that the muscles feel like a series of hard lumps, or a mass of tangled knots. This band of tension across the back of the shoulders gradually becomes a ring of tension, as compensating blockages develop in the front [in the #30 and #3 areas]. Points #23, 33 and 19: SI are renowned trigger points for releasing the entire shoulder area.

According to traditional acupressure theory, imbalance of the Small Intestine Meridian can correlate with severe pain in the shoulders or arms—with shoulder pain so intense that it feels as if someone were pulling the bone out of joint, or with arm pain as if the arm were broken. (Of course, one wants to be sure that the shoulder isn't in fact out of joint, nor the arm broken.) Release of this meridian is also useful when there is difficulty in raising or bending the arm, and when the arm joints are rigid or weak. Blockages of this meridian can also clamp down the jaw, obstruct movement of the neck from side to side, and affect the throat and ears.

Small Intestine Meridian

Points of the Small Intestine Meridian

Source point—On the outside of the hand, feel the depression between the base of the fifth metacarpal bone and the wrist (trigonal) bone. Press up into this depression, toward the knuckles.
["Wrist Bone"—SI 4]

JSD #23—On the back of the shoulder joint, measure about 1 *chon* below the bony ridge (acromion), and then press up toward it.
["Shoulder Blade Associated Point"*—SI 10]

JSD #33—This point is in the center of the shoulder blade (or, about 2 *chon* below the scapular spine) where pain is felt upon pressure.
["Heavenly Ancestor"—SI 11]

JSD #19: SI—Feel for the tense or sore place inside of and below JSD #19.** (Or, measure 3 *chon* outside of the second thoracic vertebra.)
["Outside Shoulder Associated Point"—SI 14]

JSD #2: SI—Directly down from the outer corner of the eye, feel the depression below the arch of the cheekbone (zygomatic bone). Press up toward the cheekbone.
["Cheek Bone"—SI 18]

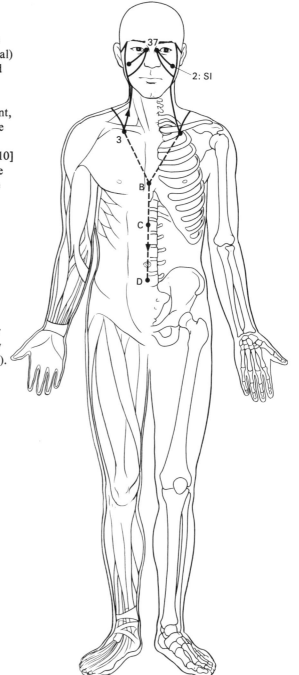

---

* *Small Intestine Associated Point*—see Chapter 8 for explanation of associated points.
** See Triple Warmer Meridian.

Examples of Local-Distal Point Combinations

Local point		Distal point
23	+	33, S., 3
19: SI	+	S., "H," 2: SI
15	+	31, 12,*** S.

S.=Source Point

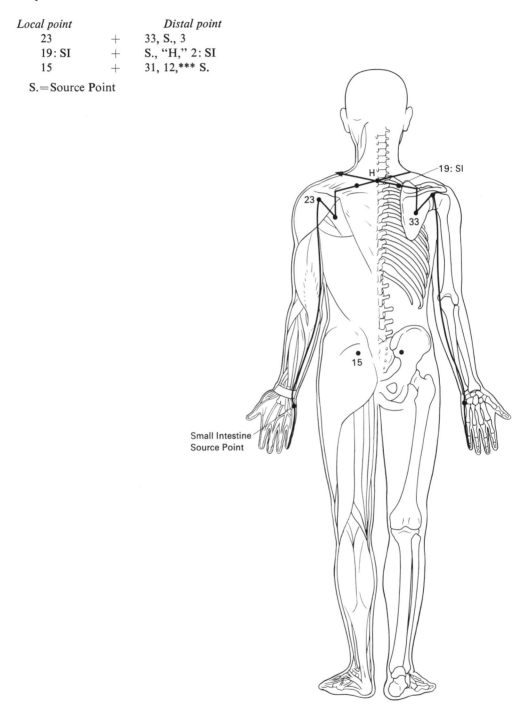

19: SI

H

23

33

15

Small Intestine
Source Point

*** #31 and #12 help release any of the associated points. (See the Bladder Meridian, Chapter 8.)
Hold the #21:B before the #22s afterward, in the ending neck release. (See the last part of
Chapter 1, "The Whole Session.")

Abdominal distension, digestive problems, diarrhea or constipation are other possible symptoms of imbalance in this meridian, which has an important influence on the abdominal area. Often the abdomen will relax as Small Intestine points in the shoulder are held with various distal points, even if no points in the abdominal area are pressed. As the abdomen relaxes, it may feel like the intestines are unknotting, and it is quite common to hear gurgling noises. It is also quite common that clients apologize for these noises, as though they are violations of some social code. On the contrary, such gurgles are the music of relaxation!

The Small Intestine is a "yang" organ—that is, an organ which transports and digests food and liquids, or transmits and excretes waste products. In general, the psychological associations of the yang organ meridians are parallel to their physical functions. They have to do with processing food so the body gets the nutrients and energy it needs, and they have to do with processing mental and emotional events, so the psyche gets the information it needs. Tension at yang meridian points can be related to defensive attitudes which inhibit the growthful processing of thoughts and feelings. Often these defensive attitudes are unconscious; frequently, they in some way oppose our conscious attitudes. In other words, there may be old tapes playing in the background of the mind. We can become conscious of them as the related tensions are released.

Let's first think about the physical function of the small intestines, and then look at parallel psychological associations. The function of the small intestine can be described in a word as assimilation. The small intestine receives partly digested food from the stomach, and adds its own digestive juices along with those of the pancreas and liver.* The enzymes in these digestive juices break complex food molecules down into smaller absorbable ones, and then the end products of digestion are absorbed into the bloodstream through the lining of the intestine. *Assimilation* refers to the whole process of changing food into a usable form and absorbing it into the body.

The classics call the small intestine the controller of the transformation of matter, who "creates changes of the physical substance" and is "entrusted with riches."[1] The Small Intestine is in charge of separating the "pure" from the "impure." Not only food, but also thoughts and information, feelings and emotions, sights and sounds need to be sorted, so that which is valuable or "pure" can be used, and that which is useless or "impure" can be discarded. Imbalance of the Small Intestine Meridian can correlate with assimilative problems, on the physical or psychological level.

What happens then is rather like what happens when we don't sort things out in our homes. After a while we may stop noticing the piles of unsorted things, because they're tucked away somewhere, or because we are so used to seeing them that it's like we don't see them. Similarly, when we can't sort out thoughts and feelings, we learn to disregard those we don't want to deal with. Unlike piles of things, some thoughts and feelings that we ignore may just go away. Others stay and

---

* The stomach ends in a narrow outlet, the pylorus, which widens into the intestine. Pancreatic juice and bile from the liver and gall bladder are secreted into the first part of the small intestine (the duodenum), which is about ten inches long. The remaining twenty or so feet of intestines (the jejunum and ileum) are draped back and forth across the center of the abdomen, and finally enter the large intestine.

turn into mental messes. One way to handle unassimilated psychic stuff is to try to be very patient; an opposite way is to be restlessly active, finding one thing after another to do. Both may be ways to avoid unconscious sources of psychic stress.

Stimulating the Small Intestine Meridian, and so the assimilative function, can aid recovery from physical or emotional stress. Disordered assimilation can result in under-nourishment and decreased bodymind vitality, so that stressors are more impactful and stress more easily turns into *dis*tress.

All stressors ultimately impact on the Small Intestine's partner meridian, the Heart, because the heart is the residence of Shen. Just as too much unassimilated food clogs up the intestines and weighs on the body, so too many unassimilated thoughts and feelings burden the spirit. Just as a large meal puts stress on the digestive system and makes us feel tired, so an overload of psychological stimuli is stressful and fatiguing to Shen. For the heart to be at peace, the "ten thousand things" need to be sorted out and assimilated. In carrying out this psychic function, the Small Intestine is rather like Shen's personal computer, clarifying information for use by the Self. When the inner computer is not doing its job, Shen may be confused by a stressful overload of unfiled or unassimilated information.

The close relationship between the Small Intestine and Heart Meridians can also be seen segmentally. Imbalance of the Small Intestine Meridian creates muscular snarls in the shoulders. When there is tension throughout the shoulder segment, the upper ribs become raised and immobilized, constricting the chest. This limits breathing and restricts the heart's openness, so that heartfelt feelings don't easily rise to conscious attention. The shoulder segment is the intermediary between the head and the heart. When the shoulders are relaxed, the messages of the heart can reach the head.

> "The heart acts as bolt of the door to the storehouse; the small intestines act as messengers; therefore one says that the small intestines are the place where the disease becomes manifest."[6]

Armoring in the shoulder segment stands guard over the emotional storehouse in the chest. When the Small Intestine and other shoulder meridians are tense and hyperactive, they are like restless guards, who will neither allow necessary information to go through the gates, nor allow vital messages to go out. It is fatiguing to be so constantly on guard against our own heartfelt feelings, and fatigue makes the shoulder muscles even tighter. There is less and less movement of energy through these tense muscles, so the meridians eventually become hypoactive. Then they are rather like stressed-out and tired guards, who can no longer distinguish between riches and dross.

Free to Fly

When the heart is free and joyful, it seems to soar. This is such a universal feeling that images of winged creatures like butterflies and birds are archetypal symbols for the free spirit. The image of wings is also quite common to release of tension at Small Intestine points around the shoulder blades, for these bodily parts resemble wings. In effect, tension here binds our wings, so that our hearts can't soar or fly free. For example, Heather said the feeling of these tensions was about "not being able to fly, or not knowing where to fly." At the time, she was trying to leave her parental womb and enter the "real world."

In a later session, asked to picture what tension at #19: SI looked like or reminded her of, Heather replied, "It's really a feeling more than an image—of all the violent, hateful things and my reaction to them." Assimilating the real world, along with its history, is a difficult, stressful and sometimes shocking process. To mature, or to become adult, is to encounter a vast array of things that we don't want to assimilate, or even to consider. Yet there they are. Heather, who would have greatly preferred a *nice* world, felt overloaded by all the media input about violence and destruction throughout the world. Trying to ignore the world's shadow (and her own personal shadow) was not working, but she was not yet able to take it all in and assimilate it.

At the next session, Heather said the feeling of the shoulder/neck tension (along the Small Intestine Meridian) was "like gripping, as though to hang on." To hang on . . . to what? "To MYSELF!" She had the image of a boat, and of herself gripping the boat as though to keep her balance until she got her "sea legs"—that is, until she was comfortable in the "real world." She was trying to be patient, but the winds of change kept knocking her off balance.

The antidote to gripping or hanging on is getting one's balance. The center of gravity or inner balance-point is the "hara" in the lower abdomen—the center of generative force and vitality. The strength and balance that comes with awareness of the "hara" allows us to move through life with more energy and with more inner peace.

When Heather said she felt the energy becoming very strong in her head, I asked her to put her awareness into the lower abdomen, suggesting that this area might be energically deprived because so much energy had been locked up in her tense shoulders and neck. I put Heather's hands over the "D" area, while I held Small Intestine and Gall Bladder points in the lower segments and legs, to help bring the excess energy down. After breathing into the "hara" for a while, Heather said she felt grounded and balanced. I asked her to experiment with sending the energy back up to the neck and head. She said that didn't feel very good, then used abdominal breathing to bring the energy back down into the hara. Enjoying the feeling, she repeated the experiment, and concluded that the "hara breathing" was calming and stabilizing.*

After this experience, Heather began to use hara breathing as a tool for relaxing and centering after stressful events. As she began to feel her own vital energy, she began to "own" her power. Feelings of empowerment, along with deep relaxation, are common effects of hara breathing. One of my favorite images of this inner power was a ferocious-looking lion with twinkling eyes, who made his appearance during another client's work with hara breathing and Small Intestine release. What would it be like to let this lion out more? "I'd withhold my growls less," he said. "I'd let go of my 'good boy' image, but keep the childlike curiosity—the bright, twinkling eyes." Part of Heather's task, similarly, was letting go of her 'nice girl' image so that she could be her whole Self, in the "real world."

---

* "Hara breathing" is described in detail in Chapter 12, Part 1, "Synergic State of Chih." Heather's journey is continued there and in Chapter 10, Part 2.

Boulders on Our Shoulders ———————————————

A boulder is another common image for shoulder tensions. One woman said the tension at Small Intestine points in the shoulders felt like something heavy and thick, then exclaimed "SISYPHUS! It reminds me of Sisyphus, who had to keep pushing the heavy boulder to the top of the hill." In Greek mythology, Sisyphus was the wise but greedy king of Corinth who barbarously murdered all travelers who came into his realm, by hurtling them down on rocks. For his crimes, the head god Zeus condemned Sisyphus to a sunless abyss called Tartarus, where he had to roll a big, round stone up a steep hill. As soon as the boulder reached the summit, it rolled down again, so that the labor was unceasing. Sisyphus' incessant toil is supposed to be a symbol of human endeavor.

Getting the boulder to the top is elating, but then it always rolls down again—that is, there's more work to do. Thinking about the work that remains to be done is like carrying the boulder all the time, on one's shoulders. Thinking about the task up ahead can be telling the muscles to tense in preparation for the effort. The task of picking up or pushing heavy things involves all the muscles along the Small Intestine Meridian, in the arms, shoulders and neck. Feeling the knots of tension in these muscles, my client said, "Maybe Sisyphus learned to really enjoy the spaces *between* having reached the top, and then having to roll the boulder up the hill again! Maybe he learned to stop thinking about the next round of work, and to really enjoy the free feeling of lightness as he stood on top of the hill and then walked down. Maybe that's what I need to learn."

After enjoying the image for a while she said, "I still feel energy blocked in my head, although my shoulders feel lighter." I asked her to feel whether some part of her body was deprived of energy, and to put her hands over that part. She put one hand over the heart center ["B"] and the other over the solar plexus ["C" area]— two points along the internal flow of the Small Intestine Meridian. She then moved her hand over the diaphragm segment, feeling a blockage going from "C" around to the back [#17 area]. "The front feels vulnerable, and the back feels the opposite— protective."

Breathing through the diaphragm and into the solar plexus ["C" area] she said, "This feels like the center of all energies. It's like a portal, or doorway. Beyond it is the desert, and the big blue sky." The solar plexus is the midpoint between the chest and the lower abdomen, or between the heart and the guts. It is the meeting point between Shen and Chih—between the heart center and the hara center (which influences reserve energy and sexual energy). Opening this doorway allows energic movement between the heart and the "lower centers," and so reveals a vast expanse of energy—which can be channeled into work and play, rather than blocked in the shoulders.

On a cold and cloudy November day, as I wrote this Sisyphus analogy, it began to sleet and I recalled that the corral needed to be shoveled, unless I wanted to clean up a big mess a few weeks later. While exercising my shoulder and arm muscles with the shovel I thought: "A never-ending job! A good illustration of unceasing human toil! At least, it's easy to enjoy the spaces in between the corral cleanings—the riding. And even if there's a lot of horse-shit, cleaning it isn't really so bad, once I get down to it. Although I like focusing on my hara while riding more than moving from my hara while shoveling." A distinctive "Plop!" sound interrupted my reflections. My horse was reminding me that there will always be more shit to shovel.

There's always more dishes and there's always more dirt. You get the laundry done, and by the time it's put away, the hamper is half full again. You get the desk cleaned off and almost overnight it's covered with piles of letters and bills, books and notes. We have to keep dealing with the "stuff" of life, like Sisyphus had to keep rolling the boulder up the hill. But in the pauses between the busy-ness, we can remember to look around, listen, feel, smell and taste life. We can stop running downhill towards the next task, and start enjoying being where we are. We can take time to stretch the body, close the eyes, breathe deeply, and feel the wonderful vital energy which is inside each of us. Then maybe we can dissolve the muscular boulders in our shoulders.

The Right to Be

Tense and stooped shoulders look like they are carrying the weight of the world; there is a sense of being overburdened by life, or of carrying more responsibilities than one is really able to. This might be due to actually having taken on too many responsibilities, or because an old tape says "you are responsible for everything; it's all on your shoulders." Julie, for example, had felt responsible for her twin sister since she was a toddler. If anything happened to her twin, her parents always said it was her fault, so Julie felt like she was the "bad one."

When she first walked into my office, she wouldn't look at me, and her eyes looked glazed and lusterless. As she talked, she reminded me of a caged creature shifting its gaze in search of escape hatches. She laid down and I palpated major points, finding spasms and knottiness in the shoulder, chest and lower back muscles. After I had been working with these areas for about ten minutes, Julie blurted out, "I feel like I shouldn't be here. There must be a lot of people who need you more. I'm just taking up your time." I asked her if she always had difficulty allowing herself pleasure. She recalled being surprised by feeling happiness while skating—and looking up and saying, "Take me now, while I'm happy!"

As I focused on Small Intestine points to release the shoulder area, Julie said she had almost never felt free just to *be*. She had never felt that she had a right to pleasure, or even to life. "My mother often said, 'If you hadn't been born. . . .' " Before she could finish the sentence, the shoulder points, which had been releasing nicely, were suddenly and painfully in spasm again. Julie also felt tension in the segmentally-related ♯30s; while I was holding them, she suddenly curled up into a fetal position and started crying.

"When you touched me in the chest area, I didn't understand what was happening," she said later. "It felt as though you had plugged in there; it was a pulling sensation. I remember asking you if you were mad that I was there, because I felt like the energy you were touching was so negative. You said, 'Is the energy that goes through an electric wire good energy or bad energy?' I said, 'Good energy, because it gives us light.' You said, 'Yes, but it could also cause fires. Energy is just energy—

not good or bad. We choose to use it in positive or negative ways.' This was significant for me because I had felt I was intrinsically bad.

"I remember also feeling like I was about four years old, scared and wanting my dog to be there. You had me picture that he was right there with me. I started feeling good, like a little bunny! You encouraged me to feel my 'bunniness,' which was pleasant and comforting." I also asked her if bunnies and dogs have a *right to be*. Julie began to see that she too had a right to be, and to be *with pleasure*. Her shoulders relaxed deeply and her chest opened up. After the session, her body looked very different. Her eyes were sparkly and she looked at me directly. It was hard to believe that this was the same young woman who had seemed totally lacking in confidence and vitality just an hour and a half ago.

At a later session, Julie wanted to focus on the shoulders again, for they had been tense since having carried a heavy backpack. During release of the Small Intestine, Lung and Kidney Meridians, she had the image of cobwebs, and then of herself and her sister crossing the snow. "She said she couldn't take another step. I remember pulling her up out of the snow and dragging her out of the park. I was scared that she was just going to lay down and die." Was there some part of Julie that identified with the desire to give up? "Yes, sometimes when I'm skating and fall, I don't want to get up," she said. "I think there's a rigidity in my body that I need to surrender, a brittleness that needs to let go. But when I start to let go, I feel an irrational fear."

Gradually, Julie began to understand her fear, and to see that some of it was anxiety about letting go to pleasure. Sometime later, she complained that she had been feeling discomfort in the hara area. She breathed into the discomfort while Small Intestine points were held, and said it felt "like a rock with tentacles." She felt frightened. Her reconciling insight was that she needed to build a "strength from the inside" which could counter the fear.

In a session focusing on the Kidney Meridian, Julie visualized her inner strength as being like dragon flames. "A flame can get snuffed out if you cover it, but not so with dragon flames!" she said. "I feel like a playful dragon. I'm imagining going to board meetings and using my dragon fire unpredictably, like by lighting old men's cigars!" She was trying to breathe through her whole body, but said her legs felt cut off. After several minutes of hara breathing, she felt sensation in her legs. "Then I heard music and imagined myself on a funeral pyre all aflame," she said later. "A bed of flowers. Peaceful floating. Death felt good. I'm not a big bad terrible person! Letting go of that; surrendering to *me*. The pyre turned into me, reborn." When Julie "came back" from this image, she felt relaxed and peaceful, and more able not only to be herself, but also to be *with pleasure*.

The Strength to Be Free

Profound release experiences can occur when we are ready to listen to the body and give in to the urges of the Self. The following account, shared by a colleague, describes a deeply moving session which began as an impromptu shoulder release, while we were sitting on the floor, listening to a lecture. "I first remember some powerful work on Small Intestine points: #33 and #23 with the source points and

By Reika Yoshikawa

other distal points. During the energizing of the Small Intestine points, an image began to stay and get clearer, although I didn't think to speak of it for a while. I remember some brief work on #16s, and I recall that the #18s helped greatly to mobilize the energy into release.

"The image began to take shape first as a square corral, set in a clearing, behind which was a dense forest. Rising above the dense forest could be seen the tall snow-covered peaks of a mountain range. The scene was like a still photograph—very brilliant color, nothing moving. Then, after a while, I realized that a horse was restlessly pacing around inside the corral.

"This horse is myself. I know this. I feel this, unmistakably. I am a golden color, a palomino, with a blonde mane and tail. Now I observe that the corral is a blonde color also. It is new, fresh, unweathered wood. The corral has no gate. This is important, somehow; I felt charged to realize that. There is no way out. But, also, how did I get in there?

"My main concern, however, is *getting out*. I am desperate. I long to be free and go home. Where is home? I get a feeling that it is in the *high country*. Higher than where I am now. Where the forest is less dense. Where exquisite rock shapes jut into the sky. Where the sky is closer. Where nothing is between myself and the sky—the endless, all-accepting blue.

"I feel my body filling with tension. I feel my body becoming a horse's body. I see my horse, in my image, rearing, pawing the air. I feel my hands feeling like hoofs, hard and strong. I want to paw the air. Energy is filling my legs. I begin to feel that I have haunches. My legs are getting larger and more energized. I start to know that I can leap over the fencing of this corral. I know that my horse is strong enough to leap straight up in the air. My body knows it must jump. I feel a sound coming. I start to cry, but so much energy is welling up that I know I have to release it through a sound. I know I must go through with it or waste the value of this treatment. There is a moment when I start to censor myself, thinking not to make too much noise, not to get carried away. But I know too much the value of this release, so I allow myself to follow my body urge.

"I hear my sound come out as a high-pitched neighing. It comes in waves. My back arches. I feel enormous strength in my legs. I feel myself stiffen and flip to my right side as my high-pitched squealing throws my head back. I truly feel horse-like. I see my horse rising easily up—floating upwards like a bubble. There I stay, suspended, hovering above the corral. I wait to see where I will go galloping off to. But I notice I really don't want to go anywhere. It is good enough to be out. I know I can do it. *I know I have the strength to free myself.* That seems to be enough.

"Next, a very interesting phenomenon takes places. As I relax into the aftermath of the intensity of energy that has passed through my body, my legs start to shake. Uncontrollable streams of energy are moving down my legs—uncontrollable trembling. It feels marvelous. I don't want it to stop. I feel light. I feel strong. *I feel free!* The energy is streaming from my pelvis into my legs. This interests me, because there was no direct work on my pelvis. Releasing the shoulders and chest released my pelvis and legs.

"I laid on the floor for a while, barely feeling my body weight. When I stood up, I felt so light on my feet—as though I were floating. My legs moved effortlessly. I felt taller, higher off the ground.

"I have often felt trapped in my life. Trapped in situations. Trapped in relationships. Trapped in my body. This session was a significant experience, because I created a deep sense of being able to lift out of entrapment. No struggle; no process. Just my own strength to make a leap. It is very graphic and very cellular."*

* Printed with permission of Camille Bertolet.

6. Stomach Meridian

The *Nei Ching* says "the stomach acts as the official of the public granaries and grants the five tastes."[1] Its yin partner, the Spleen-Pancreas, is like the official in charge of energy transportation. Together, these two officials govern bodymind nourishment. The stomach is the controller of "rotting and ripening," or of decomposing food into a digestible gruel called chyme, and passing it on to the intestines. There, the secretions of the pancreas come into play, to further digest all classes of foods.

The spleen and pancreas are both nourished by the same meridian. The spleen-pancreas and stomach are very closely related, physiologically and functionally. Acupressure theory explains their interrelationship on an energy level, saying that the *ku chi*, or energy of the food, is released in the Stomach, and then distributed by the Spleen. This meridian travels through the stomach and up into the lungs "to unify the ch'i of the food and air." If the Stomach does not hold and digest the food, the Spleen-Pancreas cannot transform it and transport its essence. Together, they are Earth within us; they are how the fruits of the earth are transformed, or used to form us.

Our lives depend on a continual supply of nourishment from outside ourselves. Because the stomach is in charge of receiving nourishing foodstuffs and liquids, it is called the "sea of nourishment." Digestion begins the process of transforming this nourishment into energy. Because the Stomach governs digestion, it is called the "sea of energy" for the five *tsangs* (yin organs) and six *fous* (yang organs). The stomach is central, physically and functionally. Since every part of the bodymind needs nourishment, an imbalance in the Stomach quickly affects other organs and reflects in other meridians.

We take in nourishment not only through the mouth and stomach, but through all the sense organs and energy centers. The Stomach Meridian passes through or close to all the sense organs: the eyes, nose, mouth and ears. It is also related to the internal energy centers, through its connection with the "Penetrating Channel,"[2] so it influences the "digestion" of information, sensation, feeling and emotion as well as food.

In short, the Stomach represents the digestive function—regarding mental, emotional and spiritual "foods" as well as physical foods. Releasing the Stomach Meridian is helpful for psychological indigestion or anxiety, as well as for digestive problems on the physical level. Stomach-related problems may arise from the need to take in something unpalatable—something we are not able to digest. We say, "I

Stomach Meridian

Points of the Stomach Meridian

JSD #2—Below the cheekbone and directly down from the center of the eye, feel for a little hollow and press upward, toward the cheekbone.
["Great Cheekbone"—St 3]

Jaw point—Clench your teeth and feel where the muscle bulges in the jaws. Relax and let your teeth part, and feel the tension that remains. The point is in the masseter muscle, inside of and above the edge of the jaw bone (mandibular angle), where a hollow is felt when the mouth is slightly open.
["Jaw Chariot"—St 6]

JSD #3—Below the middle of the collarbone (clavicle), feel for a knot of muscular tension. The point is 4 *chon* out from the midline of the chest.
["Ch'i Door"—St 13]

JSD #4—Directly down from #3, and one rib space above the nipples, press into the space between the ribs (the third intercostal space).
["Breast Window"—St 16]

JSD #5: St—About 1 *chon* inside of and higher than JSD #5,* press up into a small depression at the bottom of the rib cage. The point is 2 *chon* out from the midline of the abdomen.
["No Admittance"—St 19]

JSD #38: St—The point is 2 *chon* directly outside the navel (on rectus abdominis muscle).
["Heavenly Pivot"—St 25]

JSD #39—Press down onto the outside top of the pubic bone. The point is about 2 *chon* out from the midline of the abdomen.
["Rushing Ch'i"—St 30]

JSD #40 ("Sanri")—With the leg straight, measure 3 *chon* down from the bottom of the kneecap (patella), and one finger's breadth out from the shinbone (tibia). With the foot flexed, the point is at the prominence of the tibialis anterior muscle. Avoid on children under 12 and on pregnant women.
["Leg Three Miles"—St 36]

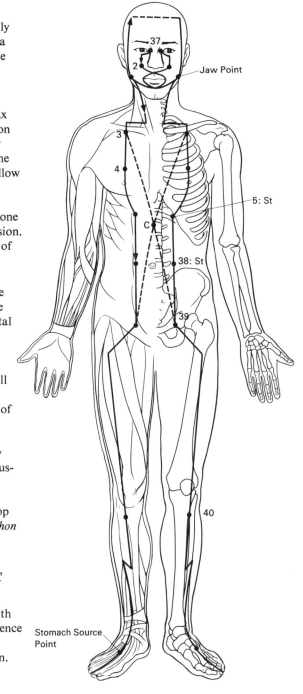

Jaw Point

5: St

38: St

Stomach Source Point

---

* See Liver Meridian, Chapter 13.

Source point—Trace up from between the second and third toes, to the highest point at the top of the foot, feeling for a sensitive spot. The point is above the junction of the second and third metatarsals. ["Rushing Yang"—St 42]

Examples of Local-Distal Point Combinations

Local point		Distal point
Jaw	+	2, 3, 22**
3	+	2, 4, S.
5: St	+	16 area,** 40, first three toes
39	+	40, S., 3

S. = Source Point

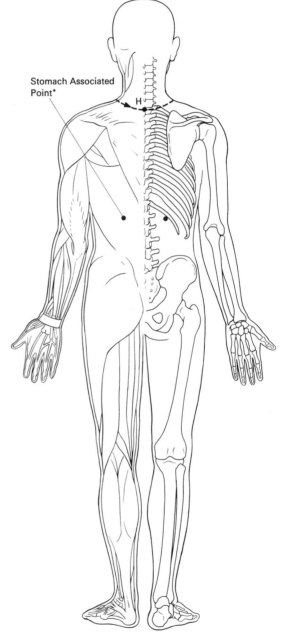

Stomach Associated Point*

---

* *Stomach Associated Point*—see Chapter 8 for explanation of the associated points.
** Notice the use of points in the front and back of the segments (as discussed in the first part of Chapter 4).

can't stomach it," meaning that I can't take it in, or I don't want to. "It hit me in the gut" means that it impacted and distressed me. Then maybe "it stuck in my craw," because I couldn't digest it, or convert it into usable form.

The stomach is easily affected by stress. A common sign of stress is a knotted feeling or gnawing sensation in the stomach area. Ulcers and other kinds of gastric (stomach) distress are frequently stress-related. Tension along the route of the Stomach Meridian is a more subtle barometer of stress and distress. For example, a significant amount of tension and soreness in the #3 area often correlates with extensive tightness throughout the entire neck and shoulders, which can indicate excessive worrying, or a conflict between thoughts and feelings. This tension can be a sign of living up in the head—going over and over problems, while neglecting the needs of the body.

Imbalance of the Stomach Meridian can also *increase* susceptibility to stressors. If food is not well digested, we don't benefit fully from what we take in. Less energy is derived from the food, and there may be feelings of lethargy and muscular weakness. Energy depletion may lead to feeling like you just can't bear the problems and difficulties of life, and so to becoming reclusive. Hypochondriacal thoughts are another possibility. At the least, the hard things in life are harder to stomach if you feel malnourished. "This is a self-imposed tension," one man said of the Stomach Meridian. "It has to do with not taking care of myself in the busy times—not nourishing myself, and not giving myself enough space. The result is a lot of worry and anxiety."

Do you deserve to be nourished? This is an important question. Do you feel that you deserve nourishment, emotionally as well as physically? If not, it may be hard to perceive nourishment when it *is* available, from other people and from Nature. Unconsciously, one may choose less nourishing foodstuffs as well, or in the extreme refuse nourishment (as in *anorexia nervosa*) or induce vomiting rather than letting the body make use of food (as in *bulimia*).

Feeling the body, and its connection with the earth and with others, depends especially on well-functioning in the land of I'. Tension along the Stomach Meridian can close off awareness of the chest and breast, the stomach and solar plexus, the abdomen and guts, the pelvis and sexual organs, and the legs and feet. These areas are related to some of the most primal instincts, including the drive for physical nourishment, and sensual and sexual impulses. Points of the Stomach Meridian include some of the most highly erogenous zones of the body, like the nipples and the oral and genital areas.

Stomach Mania

A good way to feel like you are going nuts is to live up in the head, and not let the body out to play. Traditional associations of Stomach imbalance include becoming anti-social, feeling restless, and being easily startled by noise. There may also be violent shuddering, as if the whole body were chilled. The trembling or shuddering may be the body's way of trying to shake off tension and release muscular blockages.

With irregular changes of this meridian, traditional theory says that the person likes to climb hills and sing a lot, or strip and run about naked. "When the disease is serious, the patient hates other people, is alarmed when hearing the sound of leaves rustling, has palpitations, and wishes to close the doors and windows and live by himself in the house. In severe cases, he may ascend to high places and sing, take off his clothes and run away," says Felix Mann.[3] The tendency sounds like social phobia—anxiety in and defensive avoidance of social situations. Social withdrawal can also be a compensation for low energy or hypersensitivity. We are cyclically more and less sensitive. This sensitivity needs to be respected and protected, like by escaping to the soothing world of nature. It also needs to be balanced, by getting grounded in the physical world, or else we may feel and even appear "nuts."

Does the "mania" associated with Stomach disharmony have anything to do with "schizophrenia"? Some parallel symptoms include withdrawal from the external world, preoccupation with egocentric and illogical fantasies, loosening of ego boundaries, and hypersensitivity to sound, smell and sight. But the word "schizophrenia" means "split or divided mind." *Schizophrenia* is a mental disorder characterized by a fragmented thinking process and psychotic symptoms: delusions, hallucinations, disturbed psychomotor behavior or bizarre loosening of word associations, resulting in incomprehensible speech.

Letting oneself act a little "nuts" can be therapeutic. The same symptoms that can indicate Stomach imbalance may also accompany its release. Sometimes, after release of armoring along the Stomach meridian, people *do* spontaneously sing or have the urge to run—through the woods or on city sidewalks. These urges can be antidotes to our civilized over-emphasis on the mind and analytical thought. Over-thinking, over-concern and over-involvement with the affairs of the head can mean under-involvement with Nature. At an extreme, this is "robot-man," living up in his head, alienated from his body and the earth.

Most people today are so immersed in the social world, with its rules and conventions, that taking off one's clothes and running naked through the woods, singing, sounds like a ridiculous fantasy or a wonderful but impossible release. One such individual was a social worker in his mid-forties, married, with three children. Clark complained of pain in his neck whenever he breathed fully through his chest. I focused mainly on the Stomach and Spleen Meridians. In the first session, besides holding chest points like #3 and #4, I focused on tense points in the neck area, along the Small Intestine, Triple Warmer and Large Intestine Meridians. There was some reduction of the pain on respiration.

During the second session, I held points to sedate the Stomach. All the main points of this meridian were sensitive or sore. Clark had the image of a man running naked in a field. "He feels good to be alive! He knows how to *be*. He's just watching and enjoying and appreciating." Clark thought he spent too much time thinking, being overly concerned about others and worrying about problems, to the detriment of his joy in life. "It's all to do with positive intentions, but it has taken over my being." He thought that men tend to be less in touch with their feelings than women, but he feared being *governed* by his feelings.

In the third session, I first held the #30s with Lung distal points and encouraged full chest breathing. There was no neck pain! "I feel as though something is stopping my breath here," Clark said, putting his hands over the solar plexus area. There was a great tightness and a knotted feeling at "C" (the Stomach "alarm" point), so I asked Clark to breathe into the blockage while I held it and then held points for diaphragm release [#17 with #42, and the Spleen-Stomach "associated" points in the back with #10 and the source points]. "There's something ugly in there," he said. Or maybe it's just something primitive?

Tension in the solar plexus and diaphragm can relate to the suppression of primal urges which seem ugly to the civilized mind. It can reflect withholding gut feelings, which likewise seem ugly or at least not worthy of attention. But it puts a lid on one's personal power at the same time.

"It's not ugly, is it?" Clark asked wonderingly, after perhaps half an hour of energy surges, with tingling and trembling throughout his body. "*It's just real powerful!*" The silence had been punctuated by occasional grunts, groans and animalistic sounds. There were twitching movements in his arms and legs, and then wavelike movements of his body with his breathing, in a visible freeing of sexual tension. Then he felt energy coming up from his legs into his pelvis. He looked strong and beautiful. Not being quite in touch with the usual "reality," he relaxed and walked around for some time, until he felt grounded enough to leave. There was little anxiety about his powerful experience, because Clark welcomed feeling his body anew and responding to life more spontaneously. This intense release happened partly because Jin Shin Do is a powerful tool, and also because Clark was ready to let go to his own energy.

Can You Stomach It?

During a session focusing on the Stomach and Spleen Meridians, Sam felt his gastric distress leave. "And I mean, completely! After, I was left with a very peaceful and calm feeling in my abdominal area, which is something I rarely feel. This was remarkable, because it was the first time I had gotten such complete relief of a gastric upset. I had always just let the upset go on, not wanting to take medication for it. Usually, it would gradually go away on its own." Sam hypothesized that the gastric upset was emotional in origin.

In the prior session, there was a dramatic deep release of the chest [including at #s 3–4 and in the #30 area]. Afterwards, Sam was able to take a deep breath without the pain he'd been accustomed to for fifteen years, since a fall from a bridge in which he'd broken several ribs. Though he looked calm, he said that memories and feelings about the accident kept coming up for days. "I remembered what it was like to be taken to the hospital and treated by people who didn't care if I was a person or a sack of potatoes. I vividly remembered the X-ray lady, who was in a big hurry and got upset with me when I couldn't move into position for the X-ray faster. Her boyfriend was waiting, and I was merely an object in her way. I also remembered something else. The day after the accident, my mother left to go meet my father, who was coming back from the war. This left me alone for about a week. I suppose what I felt was abandoned. I was fifteen years old at the time, so I thought it was stupid to feel like I needed attention. It wasn't as though I couldn't take care of myself. Still, the feeling of being left alone kept drifting into my mind."

The pain and the feelings of neediness and abandonment were too much to stomach all at once. He could neither digest it all, nor let it go at once. Later, he tended to think that his feelings were unimportant or invalid, especially if they were needy emotions which might trouble or bother others. He also sometimes found it hard to empathize with powerful feelings when they were expressed by others, though the problem was *not* that he didn't care.

Like Sam, we might think that we *ought* to understand, and *shouldn't* need what we feel we need. We may think that we *should* be able to accept things and go right on, but we may go on with physical records of our needs. Sam's gastric problem and breathing difficulty were such records. Though he was able to take care of his physical needs after his fall, he was still in shock and needed emotional support. In the effort to be understanding, Sam always tried to figure out the how's and why's of things— and hesitated to trust his feelings and intuitions. He could be wonderfully under- standing, but being open with feelings triggered anxiety about being exposed and vulnerable. "I am trying my best not to be so darn analytical," he said later. "I don't want to stop being analytical altogether, but I have learned that it's also real important to be intuitive and spontaneous."

The Distorted Body Image

Eating disorders and distortions of body image often go together, and may be symptoms of an Earth imbalance, especially if over-concern and worry are accom- panying characteristics. Jana, for example, was overweight in adolescence and developed a "fat" self-image. The negative self-image did not disappear when she lost weight. In her early twenties and very skinny, Jana still saw herself as overweight. Her distorted body image and excessive anxiety about being obese sounded like anorexia nervosa. Her pulses reflected an imbalance in Earth (Stomach and Spleen/ Pancreas) and in the Gall Bladder Meridian. Her presenting problems included: headaches (since childhood but especially debilitating in recent years), menstrual pain and peptic ulcer.

Jana's hair was in a wild "punk" style, and her style of dress was a rebellion against conventional ideas of a proper appearance. She claimed to not care about others' opinions, but as we traced her problems back to adolescence, it seemed she actually had been over-concerned about others' opinions. Her rebellious appearance was partly a reversal of an old pattern of trying to please others—and partly a way to get approval and acceptance from her peers.

Jana's ulcer had been diagnosed a year earlier. She had then gotten into some drug abuse, supposedly because of the pain of the ulcer but also, perhaps, as part of a counter-script acting out. Before she came to see me, Jana had been concerned about a rapid heartbeat and a recurrent fluttery feeling in her chest. A cardiologist assured her that these symptoms were anxiety-related. Anxiety and emotional stress were also precipitating factors behind the peptic ulcer. To ease the symptoms, Jana was trying to eat smaller meals more frequently and to avoid foods which aggravated the ulcer (like spicy or fatty foods, alcohol and sugar). To lower her stress level, she also needed to make some changes in the way she dealt with stress and emotional conflict.

Jana's history included a "nervous breakdown" about eight years earlier, when she was in high school at a boarding school. Just before this she had gone through "an angry period." The real cause of the anger was the death of her mother and distance of her father, but the anger came out in her relationships at school. Others didn't like that, so Jana simply decided not to be angry. Popularity with her peers was particularly important because of her lack of parental nourishment. To be liked, she pretended to have only acceptable feelings. She became very involved in school activities, and was the editor of the school newspaper. Then she had a "nervous breakdown." For years afterwards, she felt somewhat depressed. Internalizing her anger had the predictable result of first creating internal havoc, and then depressing the body energy.

About two years before I met her, Jana had decided not to be depressed. She decided to be happy. She said this hadn't worked either. Nobody can feel happy *all* the time, so looking that way requires faking it, or repressing some feelings. Jana said she sometimes felt "blue" now, but thought it was positive to be able to feel let-downs, rather than just pretending to always be fine in every way. The hardest problem was feeling powerless about her headaches and ulcer. I assured Jana that she *could* have a better relationship with her body, and could alleviate those symptoms by using acu-points and considering dietary and emotional factors. As her sense of self became clearer and stronger, it would be easier to change other things.

To get in touch with her body, though, she might have to spend less time up in her head. "I spend a lot of time thinking about everything, working things out in my own mind, trying to figure out solutions, and then worrying about the solutions," Jana admitted. "So there's less time and energy for doing things. I'm gradually getting better, but I wish I had more motivation."

Sometimes Jana tried so hard to be tolerant and patient that she denied her own feelings in the process. She was trying to find a middle ground between the explosiveness of her early teens and the reactionary emotional repression. Her goal was to be open and self-expressive without incurring the wrath or scorn of others. "I am trying to learn to express myself without just freaking out and saying things that I really don't want to say, like I used to do. I am trying to express my feelings in a way that will help me get them out, and also help other people." The problem is, other people might be defensive even if they're being "helped." There is no way to have all of our words and actions always be appreciated.

Difficulty in nourishing herself was a general message behind Jana's peptic ulcer, weight problems, and distortion of body image. "I have a real fear of gaining weight back again and being really heavy," she said. "I've never been able to stay on a diet. The only way to lose weight is to make myself physically ill, so I'm afraid to get rid of the ulcer. I'm afraid I'd gain my weight back, and I can't do that." Jana's ulcer was acting up less frequently, though she couldn't tolerate spicy foods at all. Her body image was significantly distorted. "I know that visually I am distorting something, and I try to make it look different, but it doesn't!" Jana said. "For example, I have a friend who seems really, really thin. I asked her if I could wear a pair of her pants, but I didn't think they would fit me. They were *loose* on me! And it *still* seems to me that she's thinner than I am."

When she was about thirteen, Jana said she looked like she was sixteen. Her friends were several years older than she was. "I was basically able to get by on my looks then," she recalled. "I didn't have to think or do much for myself. It was nice. Then I got heavy, and I realized I couldn't get by on looks anymore. So I learned to think." She also learned to be very concerned about others' opinions. "I didn't want to be discriminated against because I was fat. And when I finally did get thin, I still didn't want to be judged by my looks. I really resented it when people did judge me by my appearance—kind of a reversed discrimination. It made me feel used. I don't know why. I don't like being treated that way anymore."

Jana craved being appreciated just for *herself*—not because of how she looked or what role she played. She said she didn't care what others thought, but then admitted that she didn't like it when she *did* care. She cared about having some sympathetic acceptance, and about the *quality* of her connection with others. She realized that if she wanted to be accepted by others just for who she was, she needed to appreciate and love herself.

Jana had spent a lot of time trying to control her feelings—first her anger and then her depression. There was anxiety with the discovery that she could not both express her feelings and have control. She could not expect to control others' reactions so that they always liked what she said. Yet she couldn't just let her feelings eat away at her inside. Jana learned to say "I feel" and then skip the stress of defending her feelings. As she learned to just say her truth *before* a lot of emotional tension built up (and despite anxiety about others' reactions) her ulcer improved. The earth meridians became more balanced, and her next menstrual period was normal. The headaches [related to both Stomach and Gall Bladder tensions] also disappeared.

Feeling improvement of her physical symptoms increased Jana's motivation to change her lifestyle. Her condition improved further after she moved into an apartment of her own, out of one she'd shared with roommates. "I learned some things about self-expression from living with them," Jana explained, "but it seemed like they didn't want to really communicate and work out problems. I was getting too stressed trying to avoid upsetting them." She learned acu-points for helping herself, and these points became like gauges, warning her of stress building up inside. [♯22, ♯30: Sp, ♯s3–4, ♯5 area, ♯6, ♯10]

Filling a Hole, Making a Whole

"I don't usually cry easily," said Charlotte, surprised that tears came up as I held a few points of the Stomach Meridian. The first time this happened, the tears followed images of her son, and of her dreams for him. She was sad that he wasn't fully using much that was available to him. She was also sad because of all the energy she'd directed his way for twenty years, while not doing some things she'd wanted to do in her own life. Charlotte was much better at giving sympathy and nourishment to others than to herself.

She didn't like being twenty pounds overweight, or having almost desperate urges to eat. "Is there some hole that you're wanting to fill?" I asked. Suddenly her foot cramped around ♯10; I held the cramped place with Spleen points in the chest. Much affect came up with the image of herself "running on a surface like Swiss cheese." She said this was the theme of an old recurrent dream, and the feeling with it was anxiety. In the dream, it felt like there was a vacuum under those holes, which might suck her down.

One week, Charlotte said that her upper abdomen felt really tense, and she'd been having digestive problems. As I held the ♯5: St and "C" with stomach distal points,

I asked her to breathe into the tension. What did it look like or remind her of? The image that came up was a black ball, in the area of "C." Where did this ball of tension come from? In her vision, pieces were splintering off the ball. It was a ball of suppressed energy! "It feels as though there's a tidal wave of energy inside there, which could engulf me," she said. "But maybe I can ride it now." As the tension released, she said, "I feel like there's a womb in my chest—maybe I don't know which end is up!" She felt anxious about all the energy that was beginning to move through her body. There were strangled, gurgling sounds, and her body twitched. She said it felt like a baby wanting to be born, like that baby was her inner Self, and like it would die if it didn't come out. Then there was peace with knowing that it *would* come out, as long as she valued her core, whole Self.

In another session, focusing on the Stomach and Spleen meridians, her image was of "a serpent tying me, or my feelings, up." The serpent became an umbilical cord, and then a penis. Charlotte had locked her feelings up first with the umbilical cord (to be a good girl), then with the penis (to be a good wife), and then again with the umbilical cord (to be a good mother). She was developing a relationship with herself, but sometimes would again get fused with her children and lose touch with her own needs. What would happen if she visualized the serpent leaving? "I would feel empty," she replied. The serpent was also a symbol for her own primal energy. Breathing into "C," she began to feel nauseous. The feeling dissipated as she visualized the bound-up energy extending through her whole body. Then she recalled a dream she'd had a few days earlier, in which she held the top of her head and felt energy moving down into the lower chakras and then throughout her being. The dream seemed to be saying that it was time to open up the centers of personal power.

A few weeks later, working with Stomach sedation after release of the Gall Bladder, Charlotte felt overwhelmed with feelings of vulnerability and helplessness. "I just couldn't understand people hurting others and not caring," she said. "So I withdrew and locked myself up, though really I'm a very feeling person." She felt her heart opening up. "My mother taught me to be very careful, like about men—that I would get hurt if I let them get close. I don't know why there was so much emphasis on the fear of getting hurt. What's so terrible? How can you avoid getting hurt and making mistakes?"

There had been plenty of hurts, and many that needed to be worked through. Charlotte had received little emotional nourishment from her mother, who herself wanted to be taken care of, and none from her father, who left when Charlotte was a baby. A poignant memory was watching the other children's fathers getting off the bus each night, and hoping that her dad would come home. She felt deprived and different, because she didn't have what everyone else had. Since the world didn't seem to like her neediness, she tried to hide it. But the old hole was still there—just covered up lest someone fall into it. Filling that old hole meant learning to nourish herself emotionally, intellectually and spiritually.

Falling into the old hole had been frightening when she couldn't understand what was happening. During one session, Charlotte was strongly impacted by really *feeling* the emotional place where she'd spent a lot of her childhood. It was a place of aloneness and helplessness. It was a place familiar to her adult self, too. As I held points to sedate the Gall Bladder and Stomach Meridians, Charlotte remembered always being expected to take care of her mother, and then recalled her first menstrual period when she was ten. Her mother said, "Now you're a woman," and sent her to the store to get Kotex. That evening, she was to stay overnight with two girlfriends. She went over there and said, "I can't play, or spend the night in the tent, but maybe I can have supper with you." The girls' mother asked what was happening. Charlotte thought that being a woman meant that she couldn't play like a child anymore.

"How sad! How pathetic!" she said. "That's how I grew up. There was usually *nobody there* when there was a big emotional impact. My mother showed no understanding for how I felt, I think because she was too concerned with how *she* felt." After quietly being with her feelings for a while she said, "This is the same feeling as I get when I feel like I'm 'in the pits' now! At those times, I feel so all alone. I think, how could anyone feel so alone? I feel the most needy when there is some big emotional impact, which is when I felt most unsupported as a child. I think there's nobody there, even if there is, because I've gone into this other place where I am just alone. It's like how I felt when I was five or ten."

Charlotte remembered feeling very insecure as a child, and yet also feeling somehow that she was much wiser than her mother. When she felt upset, she would talk to God, or just withdraw, from her feelings and from others, and ('gut it out.') "It was the only way I could live," she said, "and I thought I could handle anything. Later, when a friend suggested I see a psychologist, I remember saying to him, 'So I didn't have a father. So what?' I wasn't going to just sit there and cry or be passive about it. I wouldn't be a victim, like my mother. So for a long time I denied that there was any problem."

I was reminded of the Swiss cheese image in her old recurrent dream. It's like in life there *are* places where it feels fairly solid, and others where it doesn't. When there really is a hole of some sort and we *are* more needy, then we also feel the old childhood neediness, like a vacuum which threatens to suck us down. Charlotte said, "When there's a little, present hole—when I need something, maybe just support and understanding . . . then I feel in danger of falling into that big, old hole. And sometimes I do, feeling again so very, very alone and helpless."

She said the powerful part of this session was really *feeling* that old sense of total aloneness, rather than just remembering it. "The acupressure got me in touch with deep parts of myself that it's hard to reach by myself or in verbal therapy. My defenses were relaxed, so I could really let myself *feel*. As the blocked areas opened up, I experienced my feelings *at the level I felt them then*, as a child, when I really was alone, because there really was nobody to go to with my deep feelings. In my adult life, sometimes the feeling of total helplessness has seemed way out of proportion, because there *were* friends to call and people to talk to. After realizing that it's how I felt as a child, it's not as distressing now when I feel that way. I *know* that I'm not helpless now."

7. *Large Intestine Meridian*

The Chinese classics poetically refer to the large intestine as the "drainage ditch." Its primary function is elimination of waste materials, so if it is not functioning properly, toxic wastes can accumulate throughout the body. The large intestine, or colon, also reabsorbs fluids; if this conservation of liquids fails, the body's stores of salt and water can be quickly depleted. Although the colon secretes no digestive enzymes, its alkaline fluid helps complete the digestion begun in the small intestines and its bacterial action can synthesize vitamin K and some of the B vitamins.

The most common gastrointestinal problem is the "irritable colon," or *colitis*, with symptoms of lower abdominal pain and constipation alternating with diarrhea. Commonly, these symptoms are triggered by anxiety; they tend to flare up during periods of stress about social, family or occupational problems, and they tend to subside as the stressful situation is relieved. Somehow, our reaction to stress can induce changes in the motility pattern of the intestinal tract. Emotional distress seems to most strongly affect the transverse and descending parts of the colon.*

Constipation and diarrhea can occur on the mental and emotional level, as well as the physical. Colon dysfunction and the accumulation of toxic wastes not only causes physical discomfort, but also impairs the ability to think clearly. The Large Intestine Meridian has to do with the elimination of things that are toxic to the organism: both physical waste products and psychological garbage, like negative thoughts and toxic feelings which cause confusion, depression and obsession. "Old shit" is a common metaphor for uneliminated and tension-forming old thoughts and feelings, which are the vestigial remains of old trials and traumas. "Working through our old shit" means looking at and letting go of toxic, distressing thoughts/feelings/attitudes.

The classics call the Large Intestine the "Controller of the Drainage of Dregs"—a rather elaborate title for the bodymind garbage collector, whose job is eliminating the most undesirable stuff. Paradoxically, the lower intestines also "are like the officials who propagate the Right Way of Living, and they generate evolution and change."[1] To the Taoists, the "right way" of living had everything to do with *flowing* and almost nothing to do with man-made rules and regulations. "The more

---

* The colon is much wider than the small intestine and only about five feet long. The small intestine enters the colon through the ileocecal valve, just above the lower end of the colon (where the appendix is attached). The *ascending* colon goes up the right side of the lower abdomen. Under the liver, the colon bends and the *transverse* colon crosses to the spleen on the left. The *descending* colon goes down the left side of the lower abdomen and empties into the rectum, which exits as the anus.

Large Intestine Meridian ───────────

Points of the Large Intestine Meridian

JSD #35 (Source point: "Hoku")—In the webbing between the thumb and index finger, find the sensitive spot and press toward the hand. The point is about halfway between the junction of the first and second metacarpal bones and the end of the web of skin. IT IS FORBIDDEN FOR PREGNANT WOMEN.
["Joining of Valleys"—LI 4]

JSD #25—Bend the arm and press just below the outer end of the elbow crease. The point is in a large hollow that can be felt there.
["Crooked Pond"—LI 11]

JSD #24—At the lower end of the deltoid muscle, feel for the tense or sensitive place. Press directly in, toward the upper arm bone (humerus).
["Outer Bone of Arm"—LI 11]

JSD #34—Raise the arm above the head, and feel the depressions at the top of the joint between the arm and shoulder. The point is in the front-most (anterior) hollow. Lower the arm, and you will still feel this hollow, but it will be smaller.
["Shoulder Bone Associated Point"*—LI 15]

JSD #21: LI—From JSD #21,** go around to the side of the neck and feel the outer edge of the sternocleidomastoid muscle. Often there will be a very tense area in the back part of this muscle. Find the sore spot within the tension, at the level of the "Adam's apple." The point is between the sternal and clavicular heads of the sterno-cleidomastoid muscle, behind the visible blood vessel.
["Support and Rush"—LI 18]

JSD #2: LI—Inside JSD #2*** and just outside the nostrils, feel the hollow at the bottom of the cheekbone. Press upward, toward the cheekbone.
["Welcome Fragrance"—LI 20]

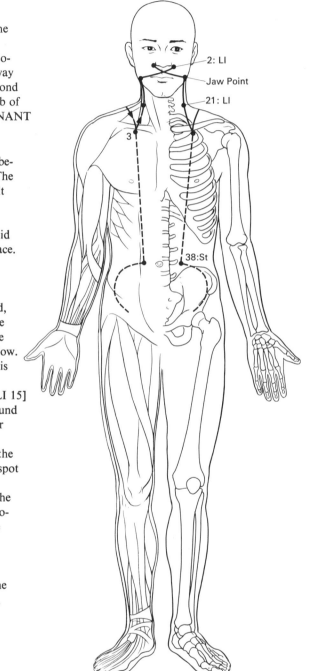

* *Large Intestine Associated Point*—see Chapter 8 for explanation of associated points.
** See Gall Bladder Meridian, Chapter 4.
*** See Stomach Meridian, Chapter 6.

Examples of Local-Distal Point Combinations

Local point		Distal point
21 : LI	+	3, 35, Jaw, 2: LI
34	+	24, 25, 35
38 : St†	+	35, 15 area, 3

If there is a problem in any area, that place may be taken as the "local point." *For example:*

25	+	35, 24, 34

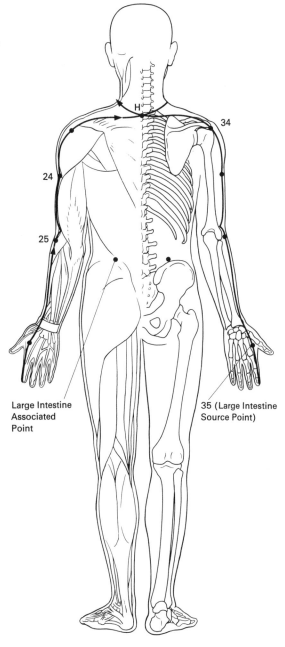

Large Intestine
Associated
Point

35 (Large Intestine
Source Point)

---

† *JSD #38: St*—see Chapter 6 on the Stomach Meridian. This point has a strong effect on the large intestines and may be used as a local point for colon problems.

laws and regulations are given," says Lao Tzu, "the more robbers and thieves there are."[2] The more restrictions there are, the greater is the likelihood of acting out against those restrictions. Evolution and change depend on flexibility—on being able to let go of the old in order to make room for the new. Rigidity leads to decay.

The psychological parallel of rigid intestines is rigid mindsets, which can't let go because of unwillingness to experience feelings which contradict introjected notions of what is Right. Resistance to "old shit" allows it to build up. When the bodymind garbage collector is on strike, or on vacation, the sewage accumulates and can become a health hazard. Some years ago, when I couldn't see a way to extricate myself from a pile of "old shit," I dreamed that it was hard to get in the door of my house because mud was accumulating all around it. A disaster was approaching; my home (or lifestyle) might get destroyed, because the sewage pipes under the house were blocking up. A wise old man appeared and told me to just get out!

Sometimes it *looks* like things have changed, but we are still hanging onto old toxic, life-limiting messages and unexpressed, stagnant feelings. These uneliminated psychic wastes may manifest in a generally negative attitude which resists real change. The yin version is a lack of positive thinking and a tendency to be easily disappointed; the yang version is holding things in rather than talking them out, and a perpetual sense of dissatisfaction. When we notice how self-sabotaging the inner negativity is, we may try to eradicate it by willing ourselves to "think positively." The predictable result is that the withheld shit *will* out, eventually, because the bodymind is programmed to eliminate that which is toxic.

Just pasting positive messages over the inner negativity does not work forever. Discovering that he had inherited the tendency to paint negative pictures of everything, Joe took a course in positive thinking and worked hard at holding a positive mental outlook, but found that those pesky negative thoughts and feelings kept popping up. "I have to eliminate negativity from my *being*, not just from my vocabulary," he said. "You can't just ignore it and skate around on the surface; you have to go *through* it." He complained that his parents and his wife had wanted him to perform and meet their expectations, not just to *be* who he was. "A person has to be whatever he's going to be! That's the whole idea in this life: to be yourself. Whatever that is, it's far better than these plans people have for you. Being yourself: isn't that an unalienable right? To know that you *can* be who you are—that's a good feeling!"

Thinking of all the negativity, or old shit, Joe exclaimed, "It's an albatross! I guess that was about the epitome of having to deal with something you didn't want to deal with. Remember that poem, *The Ancient Mariner*, where someone put an albatross around the guy's neck and he had to deal with it? You get so used to the albatross after a while that it seems like a natural way to live. And yet if somebody walked out into society with a dead albatross around his neck, you'd think 'Holy shit! That guy is really out of it!' Dead rotting albatross around the neck . . . and yet people walk around like that and other people think that's great. 'That's the way to be, Joe! So what if it smells; it's dead and rotting. Just look at how great you are, at how much you've accomplished!' I think that's sad, when someone has the potential to be something and doesn't become that. If you just give it your best effort and you don't, that's one thing. But when you let someone else put an albatross around your neck to stop you, that's piss-poor!"

Joe's albatross allusions are full of anger. Discharge of old withheld, toxic anger is one common correlative of Large Intestine release. This meridian not only nourishes the colon, but also goes through the powerful muscles which would be mobilized for attacking movements—those in the arms, shoulders, neck and jaws. At the primitive level, these are the muscles involved in seizing food and beating back enemies; they allow us to extend and bend the arm and forearm, make a fist, bend the head forward and sideways, and bite. Undischarged anger may tense these muscles, for the primitive urges have not been completely lost.

The arm, shoulder, neck and jaw muscles also influence self-expression. Relax for a moment and go back to your earliest memory of having your feelings ridiculed or criticized. Feel how you stopped yourself from crying or yelling or just saying something you thought was unacceptable. You probably learned that you could stop your feelings from showing by tensing the throat, clamping down the jaw, and clenching the fists. All these defensive maneuvers create tension along the Large Intestine Meridian. They are part of a very primitive defense mechanism: denial. The sophisticated version is defensive pride.

Abdominal tension also helps restrain emotional expression. Just as it can inhibit the peristaltic action of physical elimination, so this tension can hinder psychic elimination by blocking the wavelike body movement that naturally takes place with uninhibited sobbing. As little kids, we may have learned to tighten the abdomen, neck and jaw so as not to cry noisily—perhaps fearing more punishment, or not wanting to "give them the satisfaction of seeing how I feel." Tension release may bring awareness of an old pattern of emotional inhibition, which originated as a protection against anxiety-producing feelings or as a reaction to the wounding of the ego. Psychic elimination requires being able to *feel* that which needs to be let go.

Defensive Pride

Because they are so important in the defense against feeling, the tensions along the Large Intestine Meridian can reflect a generally defensive attitude. When asked to just feel this tension, and then describe what it feels like or reminds them of, clients have said: "Defensive pride, so I won't be submisive"; "Pride—thinking I have to perform"; "Self-righteousness and perfectionistic expectations of myself and others"; "Greed based on need, and fearing that things will be taken away"; "Stubbornness—worth is based on what you have and what you get"; and "Stoicism." One woman described the attitude of the tense #21: LI as, "I can take it; I don't need to express it!" Another said it felt like "a muzzle around my mouth and gauze in my throat." "It's a way to 'bite the bullet'," said a man, recalling that "big boys don't cry."

"Shut up!" is another common theme. "I don't want to hear it!" Okay, I'll shut up then; I'll just tense my jaw, purse my mouth, and tighten my throat when it feels like there's a lump in there. Years later, I might remember why and reverse the process. "What are you seeing?" I asked Bill, while working with #21: LI and the jaw area. "My father saying 'Shut up!' and then, if I asked why, saying 'Because I said so!'" We were working with the Large Intestine Meridian because of arm pain. "It hurts," he said, "but I won't let them get to me. I won't let them get me down. But I don't want the pain!" Feeling the area around #34 he said, "It's a defense against having lost so much before, and fear of losing it all over again." Bill said his "understanding front" was at the expense of "so many defenses that keep me from fully experiencing love and life. Feeling is really not as scary as *not feeling*."

Holding back feelings is accomplished partly by "stiff-neckedness," which requires tensing the sternocleidomastoid muscle [♯21: LI]. Being stiff-necked amounts to carrying an old emotional burden around, maybe because defensive pride makes it hard to face, feel and release it. "A wall" is a characteristic image of this tension— sometimes a steel wall, and sometimes just a dark one. In one client's image it was a brick wall, which turned into sandstone midway through the release and then crumbled. A wall is a defense, a structure which keeps some things in and others out. The wall in the throat is vital to keeping back unwanted tears, sobs, screams and words—including angry or assertive ones. The release of this wall affects the voice and opens up self-expression.

"These tensions are about *coping* rather than *creating*," said Charlotte, in a gravelly and broken-sounding voice. "It's the fear of letting myself be, and of my feelings," she said. "It's a block between my head and my feelings." As the tension released, she exploded into anger about "not being allowed to feel my feelings," pounding the table with her fists. A key memory was of her mother saying, after her grand- mother's death, that they were moving to another state. "I said I was happy, and my mother made me feel like that was bad and I was weird—like I shouldn't be happy about anything because of the death."

In another session, without knowing that I was focusing on the Large Intestine Meridian, Charlotte imaged these tensions as "old shit." "Let me out!" she shouted, and then, pausing as though listening to someone, she yelled, "You can't make me come out!" She said it felt like she'd gone way down inside herself, and then she'd seen her father bending over her crib and saying he was leaving. As she described her feeling of abandonment and her emotional withdrawal from an unaccepting world, she frequently interrupted her story with "I'm not saying it right." When I pointed this out, she remembered her mother saying, "Bite your tongue! Don't be conceited!" Conceit was hardly Charlotte's problem. "I think I developed a kind of false pride, as a defense against pity and self-pity," she said. "I felt like a victim. But what was not imposed on me, I imposed on myself. I locked myself up, by locking up my feelings."

"Do you need to defend against your feelings, or others' opinions of them, now?" I asked. This is a real question: we can let go of defense mechanisms when we no longer feel that we need them. Feeling good about our lives can open the door to feeling the inner strength that makes defensive pride obsolete. Sometimes letting go of "childish" feelings requires giving into them, but it may seem more mature to "grin and bear it," "keep a stiff upper lip" or "grit your teeth." Some people are even proud of the ability to "just set my jaw and grin, when they start to get to me." Dropping the defensive postures can bring a feeling of vulnerability, which can be delightful or anxiety-producing. When there's enough awareness of the core strength, the "grin and bear it" defense needs to be dropped because, like all originally survival- oriented defenses, it ultimately becomes growth-inhibiting.

"I'm okay and my feelings are okay." As Charlotte repeated this, she could feel the area around ♯21: LI wanting to tense. As she relaxed, she affirmed: "I'm not going to change who I am. I have something to say, and I'm going to say it. I have the right to feel what I feel, and to say it. I'm not going to judge myself for what I feel any more, and I'm not going to let others do it either." Her voice had become remarkably clearer and more even in tone, and her words no longer sounded like they were stuck in her throat.

While focusing on release of the lower back in the area of the Large Intestine associated point, another woman saw this tension as "a pile of shit on my back, so that I can't sit up straight." While I was holding points to sedate the Large Intestine Meridian, another felt an "angry defensiveness" and then had the image of her intestines being "stuffed with arrows and demons." She had been non-orgasmic for many years, and still sometimes felt angry and wanted to eat compulsively after sex. There was also anger at how long it had taken her to feel sexual pleasure—"all those years of pleasure deprivation." I asked where the arrows in her image were coming from. "My family," Jessica responded. "I grew up in a psychological war zone. Maybe I've digested some of that trauma, through therapy, and now I'm ready to shit it out!"

I asked Jessica to breathe into the lower abdomen—feeling the skin and muscles expanding as she inhaled and relaxing as she exhaled, feeling how good it felt to give her intestines some space, letting her abdomen open up from the inside. After about fifteen minutes of this "hara" breathing, she had the image of little red demons marching out her anus, and the pelvic tension released deeply [at #15 and the Large Intestine associated point, and in #6 and #39 in the front as well]. After the session, Jessica felt more in touch with her pelvis and legs. "I smiled and giggled a lot the next few days," she said later. "As I walked around I kept having the image of little red demons marching out of my anus—a whole bunch of them, like a tail!"

According to the pulses, the Lung and Kidney Meridians were deficient, so we worked a little with #30 and #16 as local points. That night, Jessica was able to relieve an allergy attack (from a close encounter with a cat) within a couple hours, rather than the usual dozen or so hours. She held points we'd used in the session as they "talked" to her, or felt tense.* She discovered that she needed to learn to be more gentle with herself and to give herself more emotional nourishment, instead of defending against pleasure as well as pain, and then overeating to get sensual gratification.

Another woman complained of an odd sensation down her arm, like it was asleep. As I held #21: LI she said it felt "like a boulder blocking the flow." As she got in touch with some withheld anger, she began punching into the air. She then felt tingling in her arms, as though the energy flow was unblocking. The vibratory movement increased until it felt like her whole body was vibrating. At the end of the session, her body felt "like a cross" with energy coming in from her hands. She held them in the air and felt them wonderingly. I asked her to put them over her "power center." Slowly, she put her hands over her lower abdomen, breathing into her "hara." I then held some points in the feet to help her feel grounded.

---

* #30 with #29: Lu, the source point and #36; the #18 area; #9 and the Kidney source point; #17 and #42.

TMJ: Nice People Get It

Symptoms of TMJ—jaw pain and teeth grinding—can come from chronically holding back the negative, in the interests of being nice. Often there is also muscular armoring around #21: LI, #21 and #22. What would happen if you expressed your real feelings? "Probably nothing," said Becky. "Maybe people wouldn't think I was so wonderful." After six hours of listening to a relative stranger's problems, she had awoken the next day with her whole left side bent like it was in spasm, and then her jaw had locked up. Busy being a good listener and comforter, had she put her own feelings on a shelf? I asked her to shout "bah!" but it came out "bah?" Surprised, she remembered yelling the day before, then suddenly losing her voice so the yell was softer than her normally soft voice. Maybe anxiety about losing control made her "stuff it"?

Jennifer's presenting problem was also TMJ (*tempo-mandibular joint syndrome*), but it took a while to find out what had been stuffed. There were dense tensions in the jaw and along the Large Intestine and the Gall Bladder Meridians, as well as throughout the chest segment. In her first session, she said the jaw and neck tension felt like "defensive pride." "That's all I had," she said, remembering how it felt to be "different" as a child. "I felt like it was bad to feel weak, so I held my head up high. Maybe now there's a different pride—an inner pride, and I can drop the Super-woman cape." Jennifer tended to talk *about* feelings and try to figure them out. When she got in touch with her anger, about some business dealings in particular and modern society in general, she was surprised to realize that she generally avoided that emotion. Her stubborn pride instead tightened her jaw and neck. It felt like the tension was saying "don't let them see they have power to hurt me" and "if I show anger I might lose them."

"I don't know what I'm feeling sometimes," she said. "It's hard to get down from the head and to not see feelings as distractions. I feel more alive than I have for a long time, and more aware of my feelings as forces, but I want to be more on the inside looking out." She was still grinding her teeth sometimes, but didn't have jaw pain. "I tell myself to stop, and then I try to feel what's going on," she said. "A lot of times it's anger. Why is it so hard to let go to anger?" Often her anger was to-wards men; not surprisingly, it went back to dear old dad. He was an alcoholic and had seemed weak, while her mother seemed strong and they "fought ugly." Jennifer either held her anger inside or let it out in passive-aggressive ways. "Thank God I couldn't repress all of me!" she said. To live up to her parents' (and her own) high expectations by succeeding socially, she continued to control her feelings and keep them from showing, so that they couldn't be used against her.

As the jaw tension subsided, Jennifer became more aware of her shoulder and chest tension. In an earlier session, she had realized that it was hard to breathe into the chest, and had correlated that with "lack of confidence, and some hurt," but it hadn't been a *feeling* realization. In Chapter 9, Jennifer's story will be continued with her journey into the land of Shen, in the chest. After working through some of her hurt and anger, she said, "What I got from my mom was *love*; from my dad I got *loss*. Both were necessary." There was also loss from her mother, for she had died shortly after Jennifer's marriage. "Why did she have to die then?" While I was holding Large Intestine points and directing Jennifer to breathe into her chest, she felt a desire to talk to her mother. "I always see her hugging me, then pulling away before I was ready to let go." It took a while to get a clear picture of her mother. Dialoguing with this image, Jennifer realized how much her mother had loved her, and felt more understood by her. Afterwards she had a sense of forgiveness and softness.

"Old Shit" and the Devil

Becky complained of constipation, lower back pain [♯s 15–16 area], and arm pain along the Large Intestine Meridian [♯s 24–25]. All these symptoms had begun a few days earlier, after a conversation with a "very judgmental" male colleague, in which she had felt "shut out" by his defenses. As we focused on release of Large Intestine points, Becky found herself thinking about a "very negative ten-year relationship" which had ended a couple of years earlier.

As I was holding ♯21: LI, Becky said the tension there felt like a steel wall. "What's behind the wall?" I asked. "Red," she replied, associating that color with rage. As I was holding ♯24 with Large Intestine distal points, Becky recalled how her right arm had suddenly become weak and powerless some years ago. She was living in a sub-zero climate and her husband would not allow her dog to sleep in the house, so she built a shelter for it. As soon as the doghouse was finished, she lost the use of her arm for several months. Becky saw this as a protection against her rage at her domineering husband—a rage so intense it had felt like the urge to kill. She could neither escape the situation nor find a way to let the anger out.

Since her lower abdomen was very tense, I massaged in the direction of the colon and then asked Becky to breathe into the abdomen as I held ♯38. At first only her chest moved; then continuous deep abdominal breathing brought up a convulsive sob. As I held ♯15 and ♯6 to help release the pelvic area, Becky compared these tensions to corks, and said that her sexual responses had for some time seemed superficial. She had the image of a mischievous Devil; then the Devil's face became expressionless, reminding her of her ex-husband. "When I would try to talk with him, his face would become blank, he'd shift his feet, and then he'd leave, saying sarcastically, 'I can't communicate; you do it so well.'" Recently, Becky had responded, "No, you're communicating very well—by the way you shift your feet, become expressionless, pick up your briefcase and stomp off. I just have trouble with that way of communicating!" After this she felt less bottled up inside, and her body seemed more responsive to deep release.

Then Becky dreamed that she drove through a guardrail, over the edge of the road and into a hole. "Not this again!" she thought. When she got out of the hole, half of her old and dented car was new-looking, and then it turned into a new car. On the psychological level, Becky had fallen into an old hole, but emerging from it was transformative. Suddenly, half the bodywork was done! A new vehicle could be interpreted as a new way of moving through the world.

At the next session, the Large Intestine was still excessive and the Lung deficient; also the Bladder was excessive and the Kidney deficient. I began with points to strengthen the Kidney Meridian. Suddenly Becky got the message her arm pain had been sending. "It has to do with holding back from wanting to reach out, to receive, to *contact* others," she said. As I moved into working with the pelvis [the Large Intestine associated point and ♯38], she began to feel jerking sensations in her arms, and then it felt like her arms were grabbing or clutching something. Finally her arms relaxed and opened wide, and there were tingling sensations. As I held more pelvic points [♯15 with Bladder distal points, and ♯6 with Spleen points in the legs and feet], the tingling increased until her whole body felt alive. She started laughing. "I just saw the Devil again," she replied, "but he was so funny! And I thought, 'Why take everything *so* seriously?' " After getting up, Becky said she felt more grounded: "There's a lot of feeling in my legs, and I'm really *feeling* my feet." There was no pain in her arm.

8. Bladder Meridian

The Bladder Meridian could be called the "great mediator." Its functions include not only regulating the bladder, but also moderating the entire energic balance of the body. The Bladder has a unique position in the body-mind energy system, because it is the only meridian with points that directly relate to *all* the main organs. These points are located on the back in the #18, #17, #16 and #15 areas. Their relationship to the organs is a segmental one; that is, the point related to a particular organ is in the same segment as that organ. Looking at the Bladder Meridian chart, notice that the points related to the lungs, heart and pericardium are in the back of the chest; the points related to the liver, gall bladder, spleen-pancreas and stomach are in the abdominal area; the point related to the kidneys is in the lower abdomen, and those related to the intestines and bladder are in the pelvic area.

If an associated point is particularly tense or sore, it is a good idea to work with the related meridian besides using Bladder distal points. For example, you might hold #16 together with distal points of the related Kidney Meridian, as well as with Bladder distal points like #31, #45, #12, and the Bladder source point. For another example, if the #18 is painful, you might hold it with distal points of both the Pericardium and Bladder Meridians; if the area just a little higher is also tight, you might add distal points of the Lung Meridian.

Because of their segmental relationship with the various organs and meridians, one or more of the "associated points" are commonly used in Jin Shin Do sessions. In many of the sessions described in preceding chapters, the relevant associated points were held at least briefly. For example, the Small Intestine associated point (in the #15 area) might have been held after working with the Small Intestine Meridian. In the next five chapters, the associated points are frequently mentioned in stories of sessions focusing on the yin meridians to release the chest and lower segments.

An example is a chest release experience which Karen described as "mind-blowing." I worked with the Lung Meridian and with the #18 area (using Pericardium and Heart distal points), then held #18, #17 and #16 with Bladder distal points. I asked Karen to breathe into the closed areas, being open to any feelings or images that might come up. She first remembered her elementary school, and feeling bored and anonymous, then thought of her childhood best friend, who had done everything "right" while Karen had rebelled. I wondered if part of her would have liked to have done everything "right." She denied this, but later said, "I could have 'shown them' from a place of power if I could have done what they wanted, and *then* scorned it."

Bladder Meridian ————————————

Points of the Bladder Meridian

JSD #37—Just inside and above the inner corner (canthus) of the eye, press up into the hollow.
["Eyes Bright"—B 1]

JSD #21: B—Feel for a tense or sensitive place about 1 *chon* below and slightly inside of #22.* The point is on the side of the trapezius muscle.
["Heavenly Pillar"—B 10]

JSD #18—Between the fourth and fifth ribs, on the muscular tension inside the shoulder blade
["Rich Vitals Correspondence"—B 38]

JSD #17—Between the ninth and tenth ribs, about 3 *chon* outside the spine. The point is about two rib spaces below the bottom of the scapula.
["Soul Gate"—B 42]

JSD #16—Approximately at the waist, this point is about 3 *chon* outside from the junction of the second and third lumbar vertebrae.
["Ambitious Room"—B 47]

JSD #15—This point is in the gluteus maximus muscle, at the most tense place outside the sacrum (at the level of the second sacral foramen).
["Womb & Vitals"—B 48]

JSD #14: B—In the center of the hamstrings, inside JSD #14* (or 6 *chon* down from the gluteal fold).
["Prosperous Gate"—B 51]

JSD #31—Bend the knee a little, and press into the middle of the crease behind the knee.
["Commanding Middle"—B 54]

JSD #45—Midway between #31 and the heel, press into the bottom of the gastrocnemius muscle.
["Mountain Receiving"—B 57]

JSD #12—Press into a little hollow about 1/2 *chon* directly below the outer anklebone (malleolus).
["Extended Meridian"—B 62]

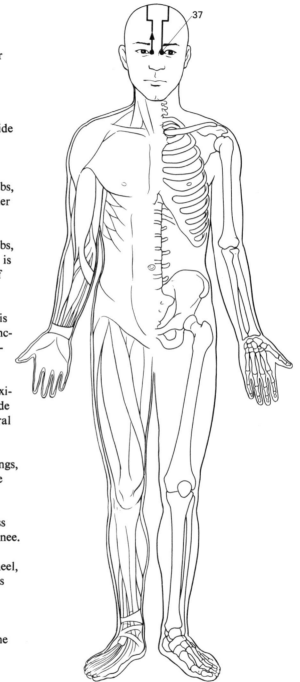

* See Gall Bladder Meridian, Chapter 4.

Source point—On the outside of the foot, in a hollow below the top of the fifth metatarsal bone.
["Capital Bone"—B 64]

*Associated Points***

♯*18 area:* Lung (B 37)
♯18   Pericardium (B 38), Heart (B 39)
♯*17 area:* Diaphragm (B 41)
♯17   Liver (B 42), Gall Bladder (B 43),
       Spleen-Pancreas (B 44)
♯*16 area:* Stomach (B 45), Triple Warmer
       (B 46)
♯16   Kidney (B 47)
♯*15 area:* Large Intestine (Extra point)
♯15   {Small Intestine
       {Bladder   (B 48)

Examples of Local-Distal Point Combinations

Local point		*Distal point*
any associated		
point	+	31, 12, S., 21: B***
45	+	12, S., 31

   S.=Source Point

How to hold back points on yourself and others is explained in the last part of Chapter 1 ("Pressure and Point Holding").

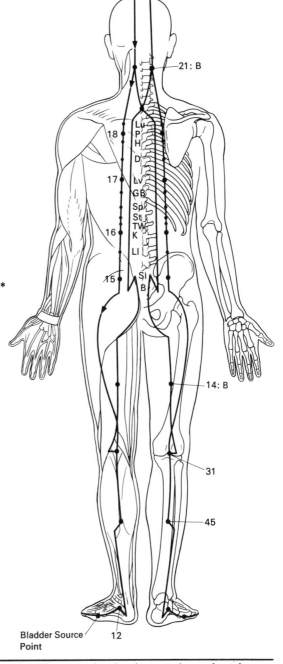

Bladder Source Point

** *The Associated Points:* The traditional "yu points," or associated points, are located on the inner Bladder Meridian. These are useful points, but I find that more people have more tension along the outer line of this meridian, in the ♯s18, 17, 16, and 15 areas. The adjacent points along the inner line of the Bladder Meridian have the same basic associations as the points shown here.
*** Or hold ♯21: B in the ending neck release. (See "The Whole Session" in the last part of Chapter 1.)

The #18s were particularly knotted. I asked Karen to feel into the tension, as though asking the muscles why they needed to be so tense. "It's because I haven't forgiven my parents," she said. I suggested it might be because she hadn't forgiven herself. "The moment I accepted this, my back fell open and I cried," she said later. "I had the image of my dad saying I had made my brother throw up by kicking him out of my room, and that he hoped I would throw up all over my room. I was never allowed in my brother's room, so this scene symbolized the double standard enforced in my family." Since this was an issue Karen had worked over in previous therapy, I suggested she could explore this image and free herself from it, or she could hold onto it. "I realized I was doing the latter. Because staying angry for the rest of my life was the only defense I had back then, I was still hurting myself with my anger. I was beating a dead horse. I wasn't being happy in a joyful world."

Towards the end of the session, Karen envisioned the trees around her cottage at night. Her lips started to tremble, then she bit her lip to stop it. I asked her to let her lips tremble and to breathe deeply. "I felt like I was biting down the good things I have," she said later. "It's all so beautiful, so welcoming! I realized how difficult it was for me to feel joy, and to express my feelings in my face and in the rest of the body. After the session, I laid down for half an hour. Finally I stretched one shoulder, then the other. I couldn't remember feeling such looseness. I let my body move as it wanted to, reveling in the movements, stretching my free shoulder blades.

"The next time I saw my chiropractor, he was astounded by the changes in my back, and reduced my visits from every other week to once every six weeks. There were big changes psychologically, too. I realized that it is extremely important for me to forgive myself, because this is the path to loving others. I also learned how quickly and dramatically a physical problem can disappear once its psychological root is exposed and accepted."

As Karen's session illustrates, the Bladder Meridian is important whenever there is a significant amount of tension in some part of the back. This meridian becomes the main focus of work if the entire back is tense, or if there are bladder problems—that is, if the "controller of the storage of fluid" is malfunctioning.

Sometimes there is a direct correlation between back tension and bladder problems. An example is a client who thought her problem with *cystitis* (bladder infection) was hereditary, because her mother and sister also had spells of it. Diet did not seem to be a factor at present, since she was macrobiotic and had already adjusted her liquid intake and choice of food. As the cords of tension along her back relaxed, her bladder problem coincidentally cleared up. About a month later, when she was stressed because of an upcoming musical performance, her back tensed up again—and the cystitis recurred. This time, we worked with her performance anxiety as well as with the Bladder Meridian. Again, her bladder improved as her back relaxed.

Putting Your Problems Behind You

Since the Bladder Meridian is located along the back of the body, understanding its psychological associations means understanding the functions of the back. The muscles of the back help us *do* a great many things, and they have a protective function. Imagine that you are about to be attacked, or that something is about to fall on you.

What would be your instinctive defensive response? You might protect the front of your body with your hands, and you might turn so that you took the impact on the back of your body—rather than in the face, breasts, solar plexus or genitals. In general, the front is the more vulnerable part, while the back is the more protective part.

The back is one of the most yang areas of the body. The big muscles along the back of the body are very active. They take the brunt of physical and emotional stress, and so are the sites of many common problems. For example, if you run or hike farther than you are used to, afterwards you are likely to feel tense or sore in the back of the legs. If you move to a new apartment, after packing and carrying all the boxes you are likely to feel some back strain (although bending your knees to pick up those boxes, rather than bending your back, would reduce the strain). If you bend over a low worktable too long, your back is likely to protest. If you just sit in your car or at your desk for hours without stretching, your neck and back may tell you this is unnatural. If you stand with your knees locked, and with your pelvis tilted forward, your back may let you know that this is not so good for you.

Similarly, if you are under a lot of emotional stress, the back is one of the first areas that will tell you about it. The back reacts to emotional stressors in much the same way as to physical stressors. If you are feeling attacked emotionally, instinctive protective mechanisms may make the back of your body tighten defensively, as it might if you were being attacked physically. If you are feeling emotionally burdened, your back may become bent and sore, as it might if you were carrying heavy physical burdens.

In short, back tension is "putting your problems behind you." With chronic back tension or pain, whatever the cause, there are likely to be some powerful suppressed feelings. For example, after a back injury, there may be fear and anger about the pain or disability. On the other hand, back tension can be a corollary of suppressing feelings that we don't want to notice and deal with. Surprisingly, these may include not only "negative" emotions like anger and fear, but also "positive" ones like love and joy.

When tension in the back muscles is chronic, it is as though the muscular tension rather than the spine is holding the person erect. If there are problems in the spine, like dislocated vertebrae or *scoliosis* (curvature of the spine), the back muscles *may* actually be holding the person erect. In this case, having the spine adjusted by a qualified chiropractor can reduce the strain on the muscles and make it easier to release the muscular tension. On the other hand, it may be that the tension in the back muscles is affecting the spine, and pulling the vertebrae out of place. Sometimes, after release of the muscular tensions, the spine will adjust by itself or with the help of some stretching.

To summarize, tension in the back can reflect physical or emotional strain. It can also function to prevent awareness of feelings that we don't want to face. A stiff-backed posture can help suppress pain and painful feelings, for a while. A rigid posture can help keep inner feelings and forces in line, but it also helps keep negative feelings *in*. The back becomes like a trash pile of suppressed feelings, or like a stock-pile of congested inner forces. Eventually the tension is again experienced as pain, which has to be dealt with or suppressed. On the physical level, we can try to block out the pain. Or we can try using some acu-points, gently stretching and breathing

142

through the tension and pain. The alternatives on the psychological level are similar.

Releasing points of the Bladder Meridian can help release all kinds of suppressed feelings, because back tension helps put a lid on all our feelings. Fear is the extreme emotion particularly related to Chih—to the Kidney and Bladder Meridians. Often, some kind of fear is lying behind other suppressed feelings—generating anger, accompanying hurt, stimulating worry, and keeping love down. It may be fear of intimacy, fear of loss, fear of failure, even fear of fear. It almost certainly is a fear of feeling, for lacking that fear we wouldn't need to tense up and try to protect ourselves against threatening feelings.

For example, Sylvia said she found herself *feeling* for the first time in days, as the Bladder Meridian source point was held. "I felt fear and ambivalence about my relationship. Then more and more fear came up, as though in waves, starting at my feet and coming up my whole body. This undulation was accompanied by crying that felt very deep and complete. I felt relief and wonder at the amount of feelings, as opposed to not feeling for days. I became clear about a lot of the feelings I'd been having about the people around me: paranoia and not belonging, inferiority and irritability. It felt wonderful, almost orgasmic.

"Some of my old fear began to lose importance. After the session, I had a sense of calmness and of being centered, as though I'd finally glimpsed the inner core of health. Feeling this transformation from fear to a peaceful strength helped me trust that I can walk through my fears, in my life in general." In a follow-up conversation several months later she said "I just keep walking through the fear." She was continuing to heal herself through self-acupressure, and by talking back to her old fears and resolutely putting her energy into creative pursuits.

A Safe, Secure Little Niche

In her mid-thirties, Janet ran a small business by herself and lived alone. Her presenting problem was back and neck pain. There was a thick "rope" of tension along the Bladder Meridian from the neck down to the pelvis. Her posture was a little stooped, and though she was quite athletic, her movements seemed somewhat awkward. Her hair was fine and broke easily, so that it was fairly short though uncut. The general impression was that she didn't much care about her appearance.

For several weeks, Janet was silent during most of her sessions. When she spoke of problems, she would often laugh nervously and make light of them. She realized that she felt burdened by the responsibility of her business and wanted to be less tied down by it, but talked little about her "private life." Alternately, she seemed resigned to a prolonged lack of intimate relationships, then sounded discontented but pessimistic about changing the situation.

In most of Janet's sessions, the Bladder Meridian was the focus. Also, I often worked with its partner, the Kidney Meridian, since blancing the Kidney Meridian helps the Bladder Meridian. Before working with the Bladder, I commonly held points of the Gall Bladder, Triple Warmer or Large Intestine Meridians to assist neck release, and sometimes worked with other meridians, notably the Lung. When working with the Bladder Meridian, usually I would hold segmentally related points in the front, at least briefly.

Though Janet began to stretch regularly and had chiropractic adjustments, the back releases weren't holding very well. Towards the end of her ninth session, Janet said she felt like she was in a dark tunnel, falling and feeling frightened. The next week she told me about a dream where she was with a friend, going down a glass tunnel in a place that looked like a new furniture warehouse. There was a "black blob" outside the tunnel. She woke up feeling afraid, went back to sleep, and again saw the scary black blob on the other side of the glass tunnel.

"If the black blob were a part of you," I asked, "what part would it be?" "Something unconscious," she replied. Perhaps there was a fear of falling into or being overwhelmed by unconscious feelings? Janet talked about her family's work ethic, and about how work had been the dominant part of her life, with little time for play. She needed to let her feelings out to play, but she didn't know how. She was strong and practical—and not very much in touch with the sensuous, feminine, weak part of herself. With the release of her body armoring, Janet began to relax her hold on things and allow her feelings and her life to flow more. As she got acquainted with the "weak" feminine self, she discovered that it was very strong in its own way. She began to see the world with wonder, excitement and a feeling of newness. "I think it has a lot to do with this Jin Shin Do stuff!" she said.

"I can't imagine being able to feel this way a year ago. Then I might have had thoughts about doing new things, but I wouldn't have been open to actually *doing* anything that was very different. I used to just pick a safe niche and stay there. I always felt that I was capable, but I didn't really *be* it. It was like I was strong *within* that safe, secure little niche. I think a lot of people are like that—just looking at the world in one way and not open to other ways." As she got more in touch with her feelings, they were leading her towards doing new things—getting an attractive haircut, taking unusual classes, and traveling. "I can find reasons why it's a good idea to go abroad," she said, "but it's like reasons are for other people. The reasons aren't why I'm going." Fear popped up here and there, but it didn't stop her in her tracks. Also, she didn't stop in her tracks long enough to have a session for several months.

That summer, Janet returned for more sessions because her back tension had recurred. She was generally more self-expressive, but it had not been so easy to stop tucking her problems away, out of sight. It also had not been so easy to stop being hyper-responsible. "I've been noticing that others often leave the responsibility to me, because I tend to get things done," she said. "I think it will be simple to take charge, but then it gets involved and I don't have enough time to do things just for myself. The responsibilities pile up, and I feel like escaping or withdrawing." The back tension was much more responsive to acupressure release than at our first sessions. After much of it had "melted" she said, "It's like the responsibilities are receding or dropping away. It's just things to do, not things to be!"

It is indeed tiring to feel like you have to take charge of everything and be strong for everyone. At her next session, Janet said she had suddenly been struck with self-pity, after feeling how fatigued she was from all her efforts. What did she want? "Someone to be real with—really myself with," she said. "Do you really have to be strong with everyone?" I asked. She replied, "I was raised to accept my lot—just do it and not complain. But I've been complaining more lately!" Janet had been raised to put "mind over body." I suggested that her stiff back might have something to do with this attitude. "I'm finding that people see me as being always centered, and never carried away by my emotions," she said. "But lately I've been forgetting to do things for other people. Maybe that's like saying. 'I'm human! I'm not a robot, and I don't want to be one!' But I'm still not being very open in my relationships." By the end of the session, she was feeling a lightness and warmth inside, and "a power all the way through me."

The next week, her back was much looser. "I'm learning that I can't depend on myself," she said. "I always thought I could depend on myself and not on others, like I'm a rock. Now the rock is melting, or crumbling away. I like it! I really can't do everything. I used to think that I should be able to. But heroes are a bitch to live with anyway!" Janet thought the recurrence of the back tension and pain had been related to her fear of losing control. "It's the fear that everything will fall apart if you stop controlling it all—but it doesn't!"

Then Janet had a couple of unsettling dreams. In both, an oppressive force reminiscent of the "black blob" seemed to be after her. First the oppressive force was covering a tiny little building in which she huddled, and she was trying to protect herself from it. Then, in the next dream, she was outside an unfinished pink house with doors that didn't lock. There were tracks going out to hills and a lake; the oppressive force was out there somewhere. "I knew I had to deal with it, but it wasn't as oppressive as in the first dream," she said. "Maybe it's something I once had but lost—something I have to fight *for*." I asked her to visualize the oppressive force. She said it was hollow and dark. I suggested she ask the force, "what are you?" After a few minutes she said, "It's myself." "What part of yourself?" I asked. "It's the dark side of me." After the session she said, "I feel like I've awakened from something—but I don't know from what!" I suggested she do some journal-writing to explore the "oppressive force."

The next week Janet reported on a couple of great insights produced by her journal-writing: "It's not evil: it's primeval" and "it's not outside, but inside." Because of these insights, the oppressive force felt less threatening. Maybe fear of the dark side is, in a way, fear of life? "YES!" she said, "because the dark side is a big part of life!" In this session we had focused on the Bladder Meridian [especially #16] and worked with Gall Bladder and Large Intestine release. During the final neck release, she said, "I feel like I'm a bubble on a stream, just flowing along and adjusting to what's happening."

After not having sessions for many months, Janet returned for some "maintenance work." She was surprised and happy about a new love relationship. Asked what she wanted to focus on, Janet said she'd had some strange fear/anxiety attacks, but wasn't sure that she was ready to deal with that. While I held Bladder and Kidney points, she described one such episode, which had happened at a party. Her lover and some other friends were there, and her father joined them. She said, "It felt like a welling up from my lower abdomen. It sucked me in until it seemed like everything around me just shut down. It was painful—like I wanted to black out, but not really. I felt like I needed to just be away from everything, from all of them. But I felt trapped. I can't remember much of what happened." She thought the attack was related to a fear of being rejected by her lover, but said there was no real basis for that fear. She was happy to be getting some affection and sexual pleasure—and afraid of having it taken away.

Feeling a lot of love can bring up fear of loss. Relationships may trigger old fears of rejection or abandonment, or a subliminal fear of death. Somehow we have to face the fact that those we love will someday be taken away from us, or we from them. By avoiding intimate relationships, Janet had largely avoided the fear of losing love, so perhaps this fear now felt overwhelming. However, it was interesting that the fear/anxiety attack occurred after her father appeared on the scene.

I asked about her childhood relationship with her father, wondering if this might be at the root of both the acute fear and the old fear of intimacy. Janet remembered family dinners at which her father would get angry and shout, and her mother would cry. She never saw them resolve their conflicts, or display warmth and affection towards each other. She remembered the feeling of "hiding out" as being like an animal instinct. "You feel hurt, so you just go away—to come back or not."

The next week, we worked intensely with the Bladder Meridian, beginning with the #21: B and then moving successively into the #18, 17, 16 and 15 areas while holding distal points on the legs [and briefly holding segmentally-related points in the front]. There had been no anxiety attacks since the last session. Remembering the last one, Janet realized that the desire to hide was a common theme in her childhood. The scared child inside wanted to run away, to avoid disapproval and punishment.

"As a kid, I remember wanting someone to find me, hug me, say they loved me," she said. "But I usually had to go back on my own—and often I'd be in trouble." She saw herself sitting in the corner of her playhouse, feeling scared, and then saw her father coming in and grabbing her. "I remember he would say I had no reason to cry, and if I didn't stop he'd give me one!" She was silent and her face was expressionless. Finally I asked, "Where are you?" "Out of touch with everything," she replied. "Numbness . . . it's spreading . . . cold . . . I feel stuck." "Like the world is a very scary place, and maybe like being in a glass tunnel?" I asked, reminding her of the dream where the black blob was outside the glass tunnel, and she was inside.

After the numb feeling passed she said, "I spent a lot of time watching things happen, and not wanting to be out in them. Now that I am out in them, the old fear sometimes comes up, and then it feels like someone else has taken over." Maybe the back tension had been like a shell, behind which she could hide? I asked Janet to try to feel the little child hiding inside. After a few minutes she said, "I never really felt accepted by Dad." Then she remembered a Halloween pumpkin she had carved as a child. "The expression on its face reminds me of a wolf crying, or the wind howling," she said. "It feels real cold . . . . My mother told me I was cold even as a baby."

I asked Janet to breathe deeply, and to visualize her Dad. Then I suggested she tell him that the pumpkin is her—its cold foreboding face is hers. "He wouldn't listen or take me seriously," she said. I asked her to try it anyway. After a few minutes she said, "I'm trying to get myself to tell him that. *That's* the hard part!" After she did tell him, in her image he hugged her. Then she had a feeling that was "warm, spreading, lightening." It began behind her eyes—a warmth "like a bubble brusting," spreading through her body. She sighed and said she felt like crumpling. In her Dad's hug, she had felt warmth and an unexpected acceptance. "Now I can see some little ways in which he's tried to show me acceptance and care lately," she said. "I feel real warm inside."

I asked Janet to express her childhood resolution about a world that felt scary. She said, "If my Dad won't accept me, who will? It's hard to even accept yourself then." All of her life she'd seen everything as a struggle, and felt she had to fight her way through things. I asked how she could transform that. "I can keep this euphoric sense of warmness in my relationships," she said. "And just with yourself," I added. "I have to remember this self-acceptance," she said. "As a child I went away, either by hiding out, or like to some other plane of reality. And I made my body like a shell. There's a connection between the hardness, the coldness, and not accepting myself."

Janet said her back felt dreamy and softer than usual, and her hands felt tingly. I suggested that she didn't need to protect so much now, and that she could let herself feel warmth and acceptance from others. She didn't need to be so afraid of losing it, because it was coming from inside herself and not just from others. In my mind I saw Janet as she had looked a couple of years earlier, with her slightly stooped posture. It reminded me of ducking, and it was like being stiff with fear. I pointed out how different her body and her face looked now. She said her face had been drawn back "like a scared rabbit." Sometimes that feeling came back, but generally she felt and looked much happier, lighter and more attractive.

At the end of this session Janet felt very tired. "It's like I'm feeling how all that struggle made me feel," she said. "It's so good to let go of that struggle! But my body is tired from it." For some time now, Janet had arranged her life so that she hadn't needed to struggle on the external level, but she had still been struggling on an internal level. It was wonderfully freeing to have confronted and made peace with her old fear, and to feel that she didn't need to hide from her own feelings.

In the next couple of weeks, Janet cried a lot, both by herself and with her friends and lover. She shared her feelings with them, telling them about her big need to cry. "I cried as a baby, maybe because I needed more attention," she said. "I think I didn't get it, so I just shut it all off. I felt like I had thirty years of crying!" She also reported feeling good with her father—accepted, not disapproved. "He's a different person now!"

"Because I'm accepting myself, I'm accepting others too, so I'm not so irritable. I realized that I shut people off most when I feel they're controlling me. And I got in touch with a lot of anger about not having learned to express my feelings as a child— not having had the space to do that. In later relationships I didn't really express what I was feeling because I just couldn't, even when I had the space to. Now I'm expressing myself more, and it feels like I'm responding more, instead of just reacting. I'm not feeling so threatened, and the old fears aren't welling up. So I'm not wanting to shut things and people out. It's like all the pieces have been falling into place. I've been a pompous ass with delusions of perfection!"

9. The Land of Shen Revisited —Heart and Pericardium Meridians

Part 1. SYNERGIC STATE OF SHEN: joy, happiness, self-confidence, compassion

"With all its sham, drudgery and broken dreams, it is still a beautiful world," says the *Desiderata*.[1] "Be careful. Strive to be happy." Can we be happy by striving to be? Striving or struggling seem like the opposite of happiness, since difficulties and hassles usually bring feelings of unhappiness as they run their course. Later, though, these same hardships may seem to have been an indispensable part of our journey, because they made us grow—kicking our feet all the way, perhaps. The strife produced not only moments of unhappiness, but also, eventually, a new happiness— if we didn't give up on ourselves. It's like the stories of all the troubles we had camping, or how the dog got away and what it did on the loose, or the time when we got lost on the way to the mountains. It didn't seem so funny at the time. But now that we've seen the whole movie, we might chuckle at the mental reruns.

Life is a constant moving on. Is happiness the goal of that movement? What *is* happiness? Is it something to strive for? Happiness is a feeling of good fortune, or the sense that we are thriving; it is a state of well-being and a feeling of contentment or pleasurable satisfaction. Happiness must then have to do with the ability to experience pleasure and contentment.

> "Happiness is like a butterfly.
> The more you chase it, the more it will elude you.
> But if you turn your attention to other things,
> It comes and sits softly on your shoulder."
>
> —R. Lessor

Whether or not we should strive to be happy, *chasing* after happiness doesn't work well at all. Why not? Because the *idea* of happiness is not *happiness*. We just create an illusion when we define happiness as that which will result when we finish school, find a job, get married, have a child, are promoted, or whatever. Chasing after symbols of happiness is like running towards a mirage—ignoring the lovely little stream by our feet to pursue the dramatically beautiful oasis on the horizon. Chasing after illusory ideas of happiness wears us out through the discouragement of failure. Instead, turning our attention to the things at hand brings happiness. This much-sought feeling naturally appears as we focus energy on projects, relationships, and inner processes. Happiness is somehow related to fruitful activity.

Dr. Alexander Lowen gives a simple definition of happiness: it is the "consciousness of growth."[2] Lao Tzu also implies that happiness is related to the endeavor to be self-aware. Contentment is related to staying on the course that is right for oneself, which Don Juan called "the path with heart."

Heart Meridian

Points of the Heart Meridian

Axilla point—This point is located at the center of the armpit (axilla). Press lightly.
["Extreme Spring"—H 1]
JSD #28: H—With the arm bent, the point is at the end of the crease on the inside of the elbow (inside from JSD #28).
["Lesser Sea"—H3]
Source point—At the flexure of the wrist on the little finger (ulnar) side, press under the tendon (of the muscle flexor carpi ulnaris).
["Spirit Door"—H 7]

Emergency point—Just a little (0.1 *chon*!) below the inner corner of the base of the little fingernail.
["Lesser Rushing"—H 9]

Examples of Local-Distal Point Combinations

Local point		Distal point
18 area	+	29, 27,* "B"
Axilla	+	28: H, S., "B"

S. = Source Point

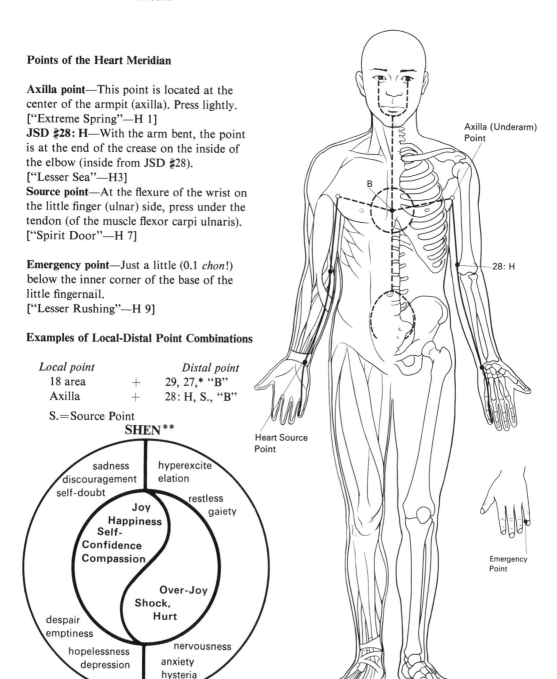

* Points of the Pericardium also benefit the Heart, and are frequently used to facilitate opening the Heart center.

** For explanation of this drawing, see "The Emotional Kaleidoscope" in the last part of Chapter 2, which describes five emotional spectra, each of which correlates with one (or, in the case of Shen, two) of the yin organ meridians.

Pericardium Meridian

Points of the Pericardium Meridian

JSD ♯29—On the inside of the arm, find the pain point between the heads of the biceps muscle. Two *chon* below the fold of skin in front of the underarm (anterior axillary fold). ["Heavenly Fountain"—P 2]

JSD ♯28—With the arm bent, feel the tendon (of the muscle biceps brachii). The point is inside (on the ulnar side) of this tendon, at the crease. ["Crooked Marsh"—P 3]

JSD ♯27—Measure 2 *chon* above the wrist, and press between the bones of the forearm (the ulna and radius), and between the tendons. (Moderate pressure). ["Inner Frontier Gate"—P 6]

Source point—In the middle of the crease at the inside of the wrist, press between the tendons. ["Big Mound"—P 7]

Palm point—In the middle of the palm, press between the third and fourth metacarpal bones. ["Labor Palace"—P 8]

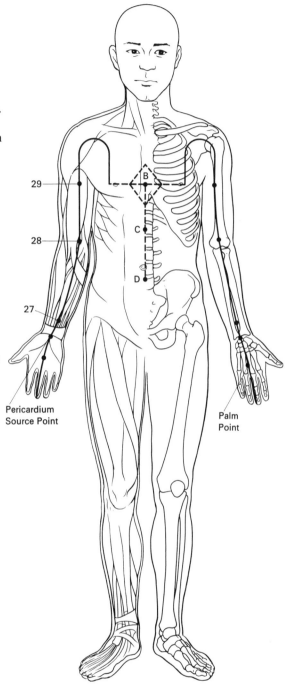

29
28
27

Pericardium
Source Point

Palm
Point

Heart and Pericardium Meridians———————

Examples of Local-Distal Point Combinations

Local point		*Distal point*
18	+	29, 28, 27
"B"	+	27, S., Palm

S.=Source Point

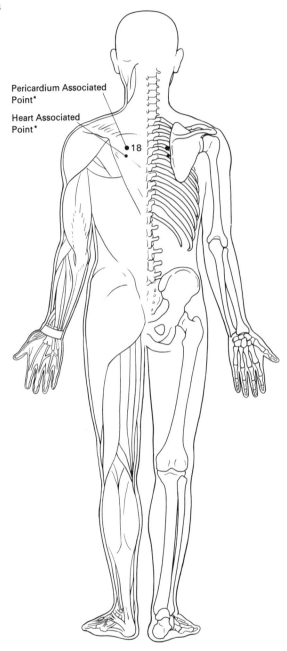

Pericardium Associated
Point*

Heart Associated
Point*

• 18

---

* *Heart and Pericardium Associated Points*—see Chapter 8 for explanation of associated points.

"He who knows others is wise;
He who knows himself is enlightened.
He who conquers others is strong;
He who conquers himself is mighty.
He who knows contentment is rich.
He who keeps on his course with energy has will.
He cannot deviate from his place,
  because he becomes one with all things."[3]

First we must know who we are. If we are following a path that is right for our *ideas* of who we are, but not right for who we *really* are, how can we be contented? Relationship problems, for example, may indicate that the two people need to follow separate paths, or that they need to clear upset feelings and open their hearts to each other again. Without knowing ourselves and our real needs, we may stay in unhealthy relationships, depriving ourselves of happiness, or we may flee from viable ones, chasing after illusory ideas of happiness. When relationships fail, often the reason is not so much that we misjudged the other person as that we didn't really know ourselves and so couldn't accurately gauge our own needs or listen to our own feelings. In 20/20 hindsight, we can usually see that the relationship we called a "failure" helped develop some aspect of ourself, but was not satisfying to our *whole* Self. As we come to know ourselves more completely, we can increasingly perceive our experiences for what they are, as they are happening.

Distress inevitably results from trying to turn a thing into what it *is not*. The enjoyment quotient is higher when we can appreciate a thing for what it is, or a person for who s/he is. This is easier when we have developed enough self-esteem to be inner-directed, rather than being dependent on external things for our happiness. The bigger the inner hole (or lack of self-esteem), the more we try to turn things into what they just are not. As we persist in getting acquainted with our real selves, the inner hole gets filled with self-appreciation and self-esteem. Then we can more easily perceive *what is* in another person and in the surrounding environment, and we can enjoy things as they are, rather than through the lens of illusions and delusions. Thus the search for self-awareness brings happiness in its wake, though it may entail following a course that is contradictory to our *ideas* about happiness.

Like happiness, joy is a state of pleasure generally evoked in the presence of self-esteem, but *joy* implies a deeper and more rapturous emotional experience. Like love, joy is a feeling of appreciative amazement at the beauty of life. Perhaps a feeling of well-being *is* happiness and *allows* joy. Joy is the expansive emotion that arises as Shen fulfills its inherent nature—as we creatively extend ourselves into the world and become "that self which we truly are." Acu-therapists Lawson-Wood say, "Joy represents the feeling of *Inspiration and versatility of the Spiritual (psychic) faculties* which becomes possible to living creatures only when the Human stage has been reached, with the Symbol forming and interpretive faculty."[4] Existential psychologist Rollo May defines joy in a similar way:

"Joy is the affect which comes when we use our powers. Joy, rather than happiness, is the goal of life, for joy is the emotion which accompanies our fulfilling our natures as human beings. It is based on the experience of one's identity as a being of worth and dignity, who is able to affirm his being, if need be, against all other beings and the whole inorganic world . . . . But we do not wish to imply such joy is only for the heroic and the outstanding; it is present qualitatively in anyone's act, no matter how inconspicuous, which is done as an honest and responsible expression of his own powers . . . if a man does not fulfill his potentialities as a person, he becomes to that extent constricted and ill."[5]

Joy and happiness equate with less distress, but not with an absence of stress. Alternating cycles of stress and relaxation, pain and pleasure, are characteristic of life. Joy is not found by seeking continuous tension-free living, nor by trying to maintain a mood of pleasantness and contentment. We don't get to choose to feel just one emotion, not even joy. And yet, in some way, we do *choose* joy. The fact that a task, or a relationship, is currently stressful need not mean that joy has vanished. On the contrary, joyful and loving feelings come with *doing* the task or *completing* the communication. Neither displeasure nor hurt need mean that our joy is altogether gone. Perhaps it is just about to be born, as we learn and grow from our struggles.

Joy comes with opening the heart center, and contacting the inner Self, or Shen. Sometimes images of fountains, waterfalls or springs arise with release of chest tension related to the Heart and Pericardium Meridians. Perhaps joy is like an underground stream, which pops up in springs here and there, and which we can learn to tap. Maybe the source of that underground stream is our inner nature, and its name is Joy. Maybe that is why there is simply a *joy of feeling* besides the joy of doing.

And maybe that explains a paradoxical phenomenon: there can be joy *and* all the other emotions—fear and anger, grief and worry, and the rest. There can be joy, as there can be love, in or through it all. Nothing makes us exempt from the human condition, but nothing need totally rob us of our joy, either. There is a joyfulness that can pervade all the dark spots. It is the joy of inner freedom, increasing feeling awareness, and deepening appreciation of life. This joy is like the sun, cyclically eliminating the darkness and bringing some light even through the darkest clouds. Or maybe it is like the moon, always shining, though the darkness is cyclically there too. Compassion and love are the natural radiation of this inner light into the world.

Joy is in the whole process. Joy is the inner and whole Self dancing. Balanced joy is rejuvenating; enjoyment is energizing. Enjoyment of the task at hand stimulates increased production of hormones which affect energy output. In a natural or free state, joy is a spontaneous reaction to life—to its little pleasures as well as its great delights. When Shen is encased in a tense muscular breastplate, there is less energy available for *feeling* joy. Circulation and respiration are inhibited; the resulting low energy level decreases self-confidence and increases susceptibility to anxiety. Release of defensive chest armoring (along the Heart and Pericardium Meridians, and in the related ♯18 area) mobilizes the energy and can lead to an intensely pleasurable heart opening experience. Experiencing the *core* of oneself yields feelings of joy and self-confidence, for beauty and strength lie there.

For an example of the emotional transformation which can accompany chest release, let's look in on a session with Carol. She complained of feeling pain in her chest and upper back for ten years, but had no heart problems evident to Western medicine. The Heart, Pericardium and Kidney Meridians were deficient, and the Gall

Bladder excessive. It was hard for Carol to receive or express love, and she'd never really felt self-confident. "I always try to meet the challenges and weather the storms, but it feels like whatever I do is not enough." After some neck and shoulder release, as she focused on chest breathing, she said, "When I was really little, it was like I shrunk myself, trying to disappear." As the upper back [#18] tension began to release she said, "When I think of my mother I feel cold, and when I think of my father I feel warm." "Where?" I asked. "In here," she said, putting her hands over her heart center ["B"]. "I feel like hugging myself," Carol said. And she did.

I directed Carol to breathe into her heart center, visualizing light and lightness filling the chest as she breathed "from the inside out." She began to feel the #18s expand as she inhaled and relax as she exhaled. As the tension there released more deeply, I asked if she felt herself getting bigger. "Yes!" she replied, "and I feel my body. I feel full. I feel myself, and know that I *can* let myself expand into the world. I guess it's a feeling of confidence!"

Suddenly she chuckled. "What was that?" I asked. "When I shrunk myself, keeping quiet and making myself small, it was for acceptance," she responded. "Acceptance of *whom*? Whatever self might then have been accepted was not my Real or Whole Self. That Self couldn't be accepted, because it wasn't even present—or at least it wasn't revealed! That Self was not even *regarded*. It was not *considered* by my mother or by society." After feeling her beautiful core Self for a while, with a new sense of self-love Carol said, "I don't feel empty or alone now. And I don't feel pain in my back! I feel like I'm radiating! It seems that the more I am my intentions, the less pain I have."

The Inner Child

Typical of chest release is the feeling of vitality, freshness and childlike joy—of somehow being reborn. This is often symbolized by images of a fetus, birth, a baby, or some little being. Charles, for example, saw himself as a child, while I was holding the #18 [with Pericardium and Heart distal points]. What came up was "feeling like I'm not worthy to play; I have to be a good boy." What happens then? "Nothing." Charles said he wasn't hugged as a child; his hand wasn't held; there was almost no physical contact. He felt unloved and unloveable. He learned to avoid being noticed, so as not to call attention to his unworthy self. In the next couple sessions, the image of himself as a child led Charles into contacting his sadness and anger about all the years of emotional deprivation and self-suppression. After allowing those feelings, he began laughing. Asked what had come up, he replied, "Joy!"

Still, Charles often felt a barrier between himself and others, and there were undercurrents of anxiety. "I'm afraid that if I let anybody in again, they'll hurt me," he said. After some continuous chest breathing, while I held #18 with Pericardium and Heart points, he had the image of a black ball inside his heart. What was inside the black ball? "Me," he said. "It's like a baby that hasn't been born yet . . . it's a little baby, but it's still me." I asked if it was ready to be born. After a while he said, "It turned into a little guy with a black top hat, tails and a cane! The black ball became transparent, and there was this little guy running around, saying 'Let me out, you jerk!' " At the end of the session, chuckling and laughing, he said, "I'm still liking that little guy!'' Remembering that image helped him get in touch with his playful and joyful inner Self.

Joyfulness has to do with rediscovering childlikeness or innocence. As we experience the disappointments and disillusionments that are part of maturing, we may leave joy by the wayside like a forgotten toy of childhood. As pain comes cyclically, and sometimes intensely, we may become embittered. We may begin to feel very old, because of our joylessness. As the Sunshine Company sang in the sixties:

> "Children could help us find the way
> Back to our world of yesterday
> Where a cow can fly
> And nobody wonders why."

Childlikeness is the way out of adult skepticism and pessimism, back to joyful amazement at life. At a point when I had largely forgotten the way to joy, I was greatly impacted by finding a journal I had written at nineteen. It talked about "the child's ability to enter freely the world of the beautiful, and to communicate on planes which adults seem to have barred themselves from, while caught up in their love of numbers and appearances." My younger self said it is necessary "to daily rejuvenate our energies so we can actively love life." The opposite is saying to some- one or to the world: "drown out my dissatisfactions and give me something to con- tinuously look forward to, so that I need not see into the void of meaning in the midst of which stands my rickety construction of a self-image." My journal continued:

> "We must stop, understand, listen to ourselves. Then the 'negative' feelings will change, and we can go on in the flow of life—no longer trying to *stop that flow*. Not being content where we are may be useful, as long as it facilitates the process of 'exploring that which is unknown *in* us by that which is unknown *to* us.' But we must also experience contentment, so that our wanderings are not just because of discontent but of, say, joy for life. At least a part of inner contentment is being able to love: to give one's heart and to lose time over something or someone."

Recently psychologists have mapped adult life as a series of growth phases much like those of child development. Longer "stable periods" alternate with shorter "transition times," many of which coincide with the change of the first digit of our age—like the "Age 30 Transition" and the "Mid-Life Transition" around age 40. In these transition periods, our task is to question our lives and explore new possibilities, so we can actualize parts of ourselves that have been dormant. As life goes on, often what we need to rediscover is the childlike inner Self. As my teenage self put it:

> "We must get back to the values of the heart. Those who are spontaneous and free *live* their essence. They are not bounded in by rules and pasts; they are continually open to new understandings. To be really alive is to be tuned in with your whole being. Perhaps the best secret is whatever tunes you in to unity with the world of nature, people, and spirit. Beauty is of the heart, but if the eyes of perception are blind, so is the heart. It is necessary, therefore, to search—always, and with your *whole being*."

Choosing Joy

Disharmony of Shen has to do with being tuned out, or with some form of uncon-sciousness—even the physical unconsciousness of heart failure. Imbalance of the Heart Meridian can correlate with muddled thinking, inappropriate crying or laugh-ing, insomnia, and in the extreme, hysterical fits. Clarity of Shen brings a feeling of being tuned in—to our inner beauty and strength, and to the beauty of life. Harmony of Shen implies emotional harmony, for Shen controls the emotional nature. The classics say that when Shen is weak, or distracted by physical imbalances and social mores, negative emotions can gain dominance and begin to rule our being. "In man, with his highly developed nervous system, emotional stimuli are in fact the most common stressors," says Selye.[6] When a negative emotion is intense, it makes a strong demand on the body's adaptive capacity. When a negative emotion is chronic or habitual, this demand becomes excessive and thus damaging. The emotional stress has turned into emotional *dis*tress.

When Shen is strong, negative emotions can be heeded and then transformed into positive ones like joy, love, and compassion. We become conditioned to avoid that which stimulates negative emotions. However, when we live within the limits set by such conditioning, we evade positive emotions without being exempt from negative ones. For example, it has been my experience that speaking in front of groups is anxiety-producing. Had I therefore avoided such situations, I would have avoided _____ would also have missed out on a lot of joy. _____ know that positive emotions come not with _____ her through a personal integrity that allows _____ e life paths. As Selye points out, instincts _____ ic and intelligence are used "only to verify _____ ce of an emotionally selected aim."[6] The way _____ hy, openness and other "positive emotions"— _____ e these feelings, not one which attempts to

_____ ds feelings of peace, love and joy. There is _____ the land of Shen, and the sense of well-being _____ of enjoyment—of being *in joy*. One manifesta-_____ presses bodymind well-being and appreciation _____ ardium tensions and breathing fully through _____ ut unlocking the feeling Self involves release _____ area in the upper back to #30 and #3-4 in the _____ defenses against feeling must melt. Since many _____ ns of the "yang" meridians in the neck and _____ s a "heart opening" experience. Opening the heart means, quite simply, being in touch with Shen—the wellspring of joy.

To illustrate the process of releasing chest armoring and experiencing the joyful inner Self, I would like to present Sue's account of an inner journey that took place during six Jin Shin Do sessions. She felt blissful after her first session, which focused on the head and neck segments (with Gall Bladder points). "When I opened my eyes, I was perceiving all the different people and objects very acutely. The quality of the light in the evening seemed very special, almost poetic. People said I looked radiant, and I felt like it too."

156

The next two sessions also began with neck release. Sadness and anger came up as Sue thought about her boyfriend and the baby she'd lost a year ago. I held points in the chest and diaphragm to facilitate her catharsis of grief and anger. What was she told when she got angry as a child? "To be a good girl." The message was: "When you're angry with a person, it means you're not loving that person." Sue said, "It was not okay to express my anger, and I got the impression that I was not accepted *as I was*." When our feelings are rejected, some part of ourselves is rejected. If we take this to heart (and it is hard not to), we try to limit what we show of ourselves in order to get accepted. Contacting our feelings is contacting our Selves. After these sessions Sue said, "There arose in me a strong desire to *live*—to express my anger and my love fully."

The next session again focused on the neck and shoulders (the Large Intestine and Gall Bladder Meridians). When the #20 was pressed, Sue's head spontaneously started shaking from right to left. The obvious message was "No!" "No" to what? Asked if something was bothering her, Sue replied, "Nothing that I am aware of at the moment." But then she thought of her boyfriend, who was in another state, and her desire to phone him. "I was fighting with my head, my reason, against this desire to phone him. My feelings said to do it, but my head argued against it. My feelings were saying 'No!' to being controlled by my head."

Encouraged to trust her feelings, Sue began to feel some release in her neck. But then she felt tension building up at the #22s. As these points released Sue said, "I've been putting a lid not only on my anger, but on all my emotions—joy, love, tenderness .... The main cause of this neck tension, for example, was trying to control a deep joy I had experienced, with a group of friends, before the session. My joy was so great that I tried to control it, being afraid that it would disturb the session!" When she allowed the joy to surface, the tension at the #22s released completely. "I started to feel my womanship," Sue said later. "I felt attractive, beautiful, sensual. Afterwards my shoulders felt so good that it seemed like very big rocks had fallen from them. There was a nice warmth in my upper back, which stayed for a couple days."

In the next session, Sue had a powerful heart opening experience. The feeling of the open heart center is indescribable, except by words like lightness and brightness. It is a feeling which may arise from looking at the grandeurs of nature, or from being with children, a lover, or close friends. Often there are tears and laughter, ooooo's and aaahhhh's. There is a sense of lightness in the chest and light-heartedness. Sue was en route to this experience when she felt a need to control her great joy before the last session. In this session, the #22s were held first, because she was feeling "a very big tension" there. She began seeing trees that looked like redwoods, but were much taller. Looking at their branches and leaves, far away from her, Sue felt a poignant pain in her chest as she became aware of a strong desire to be among the branches. The feeling was loneliness, sadness. She started crying.

"Then I could feel the softness of the branches, as though they were caressing my heart," she said. "It felt so good. I looked further and saw a chain of very high mountains. They were so beautiful. The same intense desire to be on them made my heart feel like it was breaking again, because I felt that I could not. I started crying again. Then I described my images out loud, and suddenly, I *was* on the mountains. I enjoyed the feeling, until I saw the highest peak. The same thing happened. I wanted to be on that peak but thought I could not, and my heart started hurting again. I expressed what was happening, and suddenly I *was* on that peak! It was such a joy to realize that I was where I deeply desired to be, but thought I could not be.

"On the peak of the mountain I felt the presence of a luminous being. I wanted very much to be with her, and again came the heart pain and the tears. My therapist said to let this being enter into my being, and then it was like light pouring out, and I felt my heart chakra taking on gigantic dimensions. The light in my heart moved up to my third eye. I had a sudden headache, and asked with all my strength for the grace to see. My hands were trembling and I held them up above my head. I felt like light was streaming through them into my body. Then I saw the light of the third eye, and my whole body started shivering. Afterwards, I was in bliss. I couldn't talk or move for some time. I felt like I was loving the whole universe."

In the next session, the focus was on the abdomen and pelvis. I began with a short neck release, and asked Sue what her neck and throat tensions reminded her of. She saw many trees with a sun behind them, and said it was beautiful, but the circulating energy was giving her uncomfortable sensations. Could she let the sun shine more? She was afraid to, because she thought it would be hard to stay grounded. I asked her to just let the sun grow and tell me if she had trouble remaining grounded. "Immediately the sun started shining more," Sue said later. "One or two trees fell down, and the sun took more and more space. It went up to my throat and started to enter my forehead." As I held the ♯37s and "J," the light penetrated her "third eye" and started to circulate in the top of her head.

As I put one hand on her heart chakra and the other on ♯30, Sue started crying. After a while she said, "The sadness is coming from my joy to feel like I am 'back home' inside myself, and from the hurt of not having allowed myself to be here for such a long time, because I felt like I had to do or be certain things." I asked Sue to let the light come down into her lower energy centers. She felt a little afraid of losing contact with the "high" feeling. "To my greatest surprise, I felt a very big warmth, like a sun, in my solar plexus," she said. "It was thrilling to feel so much light there, instead of heaviness and darkness. The light went down into my abdomen. It felt like electricity running through my legs. My hara felt very warm, like there was much space inside. I had the image of a big little man in there, sitting in lotus position. He was full of laughter. I felt like love and light were circulating through all of my being. The little man seemed to be inviting me to let the energy circulate in all the parts of my body. I laughed when I got that message. I used to think the Eastern masters were interested only in the higher chakras, but now I knew this wasn't true, at least for this little man.

"At the end of the session, I felt a soft warmth circulating in my neck, which remained for a couple days. I was especially happy because I had been able to be in contact with many different emotions, going through them, but not being trapped in them. When I started to feel uncentered or overcome by one emotion, I could move through it (or let it move) into other feelings, by centering my attention on the third eye and hara at the same time." Focusing on the energy centers of the forehead and lower abdomen *at the same time* means contacting the whole inner Self or energic core—not only from the heart upward into the spiritual centers, but also downward into the primal centers.

It is significant that Sue's deep release of heartfelt feelings came as she communicated her experience in words and gestures. It seems that deeper *experiencing* of the Self comes with *self-expression*. *Speech* is related to the Heart Meridian, and this can be interpreted as a general "Communication Sense" including all symbolic as well as verbal communication.[4] Communication, in all its forms, is necessary for continuing clarity of Shen. If self-expressive communication—through words, symbols, gestures and acts—is restrained, then Shen feels constricted and joy is limited.

Love and the Pericardium Meridian

The connection between the heart and love has long been celebrated in poetry and song. Like joy, love is a heartfelt emotion. The gratification of love is felt in the chest as a lightness and expansiveness which radiates through the body and into the world. The frustration or loss of love is called "heartache" or "heartbreak," and registers in the body as a heaviness or aching in the chest. If the shock of lost love is too painful, we may try to shut down our feelings, by tensing up and by suppressing respiration, but we will probably still feel "heartsick" (unless we are "heartless"). The longing for love needs to be satisfied, through relationships and by learning to *love life*.

Tension in the Pericardium-related breast and upper back [#18] areas is an important part of the unconscious defense against heartfelt feelings. This tension can reflect a conflict between the desire for love and the fear of letting go to love. It can originate as a defense against not feeling loved, and then function to prevent letting love in. It can reflect difficulty in loving oneself, as well as dissonances in love relationships. The Pericardium Meridian is related to the circulatory system and to emotional warmth. It is also related to sexual responsiveness, as indicated by its alternate name: "Circulation-Sex Meridian." The main meridian goes from the heart and pericardium through arm muscles which allow us to reach out and embrace. The internal part penetrates the diaphragm to connect the heart center with the lower energy centers which empower sexual responsiveness.

In the firey and passionate land of Shen, the heart is the "supreme controller," while the pericardium is the "protector of the heart." Physically, the pericardium is a membranous sac surrounding the heart and enclosing a lubricated membrane, which allows the heart to beat with almost no friction. "The Pericardium is the walled palace of the heart," says the *Su Wen*. "Since the heart is the king of all the other organs, evil must not be allowed to approach it. The evils of the heart are, therefore, borne by the pericardium." Just as the pericardium to some extent bears the stresses of the physical heartbeat, so emotional stress tends to affect the Pericardium Meridian first.

As long as our feelings keep circulating, we will get back to the love and joy which open the heart center, but the fear of being vulnerable and getting hurt can make us armor against really feeling love. Feeling the physical constriction of the chest can bring awareness of correlative emotional constrictions. When there is empathetic support, vivid memories may come up, sometimes with cathartic release of the pain which was bound into the body tensions. To work through the fear of hurt is to accept the alternation of pain and pleasure. This increases the joy of feeling in the present, and in a sense it can change the past—insofar as our memory is distorted by tunnel vision. By releasing the defensive postures which keep us from really letting love into our lives, we can renew our ability to love and to feel joy.

"Don't beat me any more! No more!" This outburst occurred while I was holding Linda's #18 [with Pericardium distal points], after we had worked together for about a year. (Earlier in this session, Linda had complained that her cheeks and forehead felt tense, so I had focused on facial tensions that were acting like a mask, concealing her feelings. Her presenting problems included periodic anxiety-related heart palpitations, pain on full respiration, and feelings of worthlessness.) "Stop beating me! No, no!" I asked Linda how old she was. "Real little . . . a baby . . . I'm afraid. . . . They're throwing me around. They're beating me." Who are they? "My parents . . . my father." This image vividly illustrated how it had felt to be repeatedly beaten in childhood, sometimes with a whip, and to have that abuse compounded later by being approached sexually by her father. Suppressed hurt and anger, and a lot of fear, lay behind Linda's dependent and avoidant personality style.*

As a child Linda craved to be hugged and told she was loved. As an adult, she stayed at home waiting for the demonstrations of love that she had missed as a child, and tended to project her childhood needs onto her friends. When she spoke of feeling hurt by a parent or friend, Linda often would feel a sudden pain in the #18 area. "My mother keeps criticizing me and telling me I'll give her a heart attack. I wanted to answer her back but instead I held it in and got terrible chest pains. Oh, screw everyone!"

It was hard for Linda to accept her conflicting feelings of love and hate for her parents. Resolving this emotional paradox required many confrontations with the old hurt and anger, but gradually she began to accept her feelings, and so herself. In another session focusing on the Pericardium, Linda saw a man and woman tossing a baby, like a ball, over a net. With distress, she watched this mad game. Finally, she caught and hugged the baby, associating this with loving her battered child-self. By contrast, in an earlier session when a similar image came up, Linda could not bring herself to hug that lonely little girl. For a long time she could not see herself as lovable. The abuse of her childhood had stunted the growth of her self-esteem.

Choosing to recover means having the courage to choose in favor of life, rather than succumbing to helplessness. Linda's hurt and anger were not *just* the result of her childhood traumas. These emotions were also saying "Get out of your traps! Be your own person!" Inner healing requires facing *what is* and loving oneself, or treating oneself like a friend. As one of Linda's images (from a Pericardium release) illustrates, healing oneself also requires learning to play and enjoying oneself.

> "I see a park where children are laughing and playing. Some are sailing little boats on a pond. On one of the benches I see an old lady—a 'bag lady.' As I approach her, something strange happens. She looks so familiar. She says, 'Look at me closely. I am you fifty years from now. This can be your future. Do you like what you see?' She looks very lonely. I ask her what I should do. 'Learn how to play. Enjoy your life. Be a child once in a while, and be happy. If you need to talk, come to this park bench and I'll be here. I love you and care about you.' She takes me by the shoulders and says she'll be my guide. I feel grateful to her."

---

* Linda's story continues in Chapters 12 (Part 2) and 13 (Part 3).

Reflecting on this image Linda said, "It's incredible how the unconscious mind works!" The images that arise during bodywork can indeed be incredibly precise in pointing the way to recovery and wholeness.

The pericardium is "the official of the center who guides the subjects in their joys and pleasures," says the *Nei Ching*.[7] If the pericardium is strong, there is a dynamism about carrying out the wishes of Shen, the most basic of which is *being free to feel and to be that Self which one truly is*. Keeping the heart open, and letting love flow, is the gateway to an increased energy for life. It is also an important part of finding *the joy of feeling*.

The Joy of Touching

There are three main channels for communicating heartfelt feelings to the world, corresponding to the three branches of the Heart Meridian (and the two branches of the Pericardium Meridian). These channels of communication are: the throat and voice, the genitals, and the arms and hands. The latter is the most basic form of communication: *touch*. Babies feel loved and cared for by the way they are touched, and they communicate love through touching. Young children learn most easily by *touching*, and they spontaneously demonstrate affection by touching and antipathy by hitting. Gradually, their behavior is conditioned according to whether it receives approval and "strokes," or disapproval and reprimands.

Touching is an instinctive activity and need. *How* and *how much* we are touched is important, for the child in us still feels loved according to how s/he is touched. The heart is lightened by the touch, stroke or embrace which says "I care." Through touching we can fulfill a large share of our human needs and bring happiness to ourselves and others. Through touching we can affirm friendship and love, and promote physical and emotional health.

Enjoying the power of touch is one of the easiest ways to feel that solid contentment and state of well-being called *happiness*, and that expansive, rapturous, liquid state called *joy*. Touching is one of the simplest ways to convey and receive the feeling of warm regard, for our intentions are conveyed through the quality of our touch. The spirits are lifted by such simple acts as a pat on the back, a friendly hug, a cordial handshake, a heartfelt clasp or a warm embrace. Self-confidence involves feeling the right to touch and be touched, rather than avoiding touch out of fear of rejection.

To touch or to feel "touched" is to feel care, contact, closeness, love. To be "in touch" is to be aware. Jin Shin Do® Acupressure is a continuous experience of being touched, with a slow-paced and firm but gentle pressure, in a way that evokes the experience of being held and safe. The feeling of being touched is enhanced by the precision of the acupressure system, which allows us to put our fingers on tensions at their core. A strong trust bond is elicited by this caring touch, which searches for muscular and energic blocks and then encourages their release. This supportive interaction makes it *safe to feel*—to relax self-control and freely explore the whole Self.

With any form of bodywork, it is necessary to consider the basic implications of touching, and to realize that some people are resistant to touch. When touch is highly anxiety-provoking, a person may need verbal psychotherapy before s/he can tolerate bodywork. The "taboo" against touching derives partly from the sexual implications that society has attached to touching. In Jin Shin Do, the recipient usually remains clothed, which makes it easier to let go of defenses against touching. The absence of undressing makes it clear that Jin Shin Do is about therapeutic, not sexual, touch.

We cannot eliminate the connection between touching and sexuality, however— nor should we. Acupressure theory says that sexuality, like love, is a *reflection of the whole being*. As we feel better, we tend to radiate more love and sexual vitality. Sharing Jin Shin Do within a love relationship can increase sexual responsiveness, because enhanced feeling awareness and enhanced sexual satisfaction go hand in hand. Love and sexual feelings are a natural part of our whole physical/emotional response to other human beings. Therefore, it is normal to feel love and sexual attraction towards more than one person; these feelings can be enjoyed rather than promiscuously acted out.

Overcoming the *taboo against touching* is an important step on the road to well-being. Touching and being touched allows us to be more in touch with each other, and with ourselves. Jin Shin Do is a simple and non-threatening way of overcoming the taboo against and deprivation of physical contact, which often goes back to infancy. Under all the defenses, most people do want to be touched and held. The therapeutic touching of Jin Shin Do is a way to begin satisfying that need. It is a way to the *joy of feeling*. Receiving Jin Shin Do is receiving *care*, for you cannot so continuously touch another person without caring. Care nourishes the Spirit; it is like fuel for the inner flame.

> "Moving in touch with my free and adventurous inner spirit (Shen) is the story of my continuing experiences with Jin Shin Do. This art is an incredible vehicle for sharing, caring and opening with others. I am still completely in awe of the magic I experience and participate in by receiving and giving Jin Shin Do acupressure."

As I write this student's comment, a woman calls to find out more about Jin Shin Do. She says it's helped her recover from being "really sick" three years ago, and tells me of trying it with her eight-year-old son when he had trouble breathing due to a cold. As the boy felt better he said, "That's magic, mom!" and later, "Will you do some more magic with me?" Jin Shin Do helps the body to balance and regulate itself, and there is magic in its tremendous capacities for self-healing. Jin Shin Do helps you to feel yourself, and there is magic in you. Joy is magic. Magic is love.

Part 2. "EVIL" OR EXTREME EMOTIONS OF SHEN

In this and the following chapters, as we explore the "evil" emotions, it is important to remember that in the Chinese language "evil" meant *extreme*, not bad. When prolonged, these emotions can be debilitating, but they also serve as warning mechanisms and release valves. Traditional acupressure theory says that when an emotion is expressed consistently, the related organ first becomes hyperactive and then breaks down into pathological disorder. On the other hand, since the emotions guide and move the body is its activities, excessive emotional restraint causes the energy to become blocked in the related organ and then, in a domino-like effect, in other parts of the bodymind system. Because Shen rules the emotional nature, any emotional stress affects the heart.[8]

Extreme Emotion	Effect on Consciousness and on the Energy (CH'I)	Related "Yin Organ"	Aspect of The Psyche	Related Synergic Feeling
Anger	Ascends or rushes up and becomes strong in the head, neck and shoulders.	Liver	HUN	Self-Assertion
Grief	Is dispersed, leaving the body weak.	Lungs	P'O	Openness
Fear	Descends to the bowels and lower extremities.	Kidneys	CHIH	Resolution
Over-Concern or Anxiety	Becomes coagulated or stagnated, in effect paralyzing the body.	Spleen-Pancreas or Lungs	I' or P'O	Empathy or Openness
Reminiscence (regret)	Becomes concentrated in the brain; feels stuck or knotted.	Spleen-Pancreas	I'	Empathy
Shock (hurt)	Is disturbed; becomes chaotic.	Heart & Pericardium	SHEN	Joy
Over-Joy (excitement)	Becomes suspended at the point of inhalation, then slow and scattered.	Heart & Pericardium	SHEN	Joy

(Compare this table with the Emotional Kaleidoscope diagram in Chapter 2.)

Any extreme emotion may also be a "dominant emotion," or one that is expressed consistently and tends to arise in reaction to a wide variety of stressors. For one person, the first reaction to any problem is fear; another person usually gets angry first; another is a worrier. Looking at the extreme emotions listed in the accompanying table, ask yourself which are *your* dominant emotions. Press some points of the related organ meridian; are they tense or sensitive? Reflect on the related aspect of the psyche, and on the related synergic feeling. Learning to appropriately release the extreme emotions, and transform them into synergic ones, is part of the challenge of personal growth.

Extreme Emotions of Shen: Over-Joy and Shock —————————

The classics say that two seemingly opposite emotional stresses directly affect Shen, or the heart: shock and over-joy. At first glance, shock or hurt may seem inherently negative, while it may not be so obvious that "over-joy" is an "evil" or extreme emotion. The classics say that both are strong passions which can reduce the body-mind energy. Modern stress theory also says that both sudden hurt and sudden joy are stressors, for both make an intense demand on the bodymind to adjust to a new situation. Yet stress is a normal and unavoidable part of life. By stimulating adaptation to change, stress can stimulate growth.

"Over-joy" basically means *excitement*, which can be addicting—so much so that many people make it a goal, confusing it with joy. The media encourages the search for excitement, because excitement sells. It sells television shows, movies, records and all kinds of products. Notice how many advertisements imply that this car, or toothpaste, or even floor cleaner, will make life more exciting. The prevasive chase after excitement has also manifested in a widespread use of drugs which produce temporary physical and mental excitation.

Real joy emanates from an open heart. Over-joy comes from a sudden "change for the better" which in effect bursts the heart open, or else is a compensation for the closed heart which cannot feel real joy. Chest tension not only defends against pain, but also blocks off the door to joy. "But my life has been generally very fortunate," said Jennifer, feeling how locked her chest was. "What would have hurt me so much that I closed down my heart?" Jennifer thought she didn't have a right to feel hurt about anything, because she was quite "well off." To close down the heart, a grievous trauma or big loss is not necessary; a series of unresolved "little" losses, disappointments, and disillusionments will do the job just as well.

Jennifer had been feeling excited because of a big promotion. As the higher energy charge tried to move through her system, she felt how bound up her chest was. I held the #18s with Pericardium and Heart distal points, and asked her to breathe into the tense chest points. After a few breaths, her chest stopped moving. I pointed that out, and she took a few more full breaths, then stopped again. "It feels like I can't get my breath!" What was happening when her chest was closing down? After a while, her mouth started trembling. What was she feeling? "Sadness," she replied. "I was thinking about an acquaintance who was murdered because of his heavy involvement with cocaine traffic."

"He was so gifted, yet so adrift," she said tearfully. He never got to really *be* who he was! He got sidetracked, and not just by the drugs, but by the values they represent. The value isn't on what's *real*, and really important, like people and feelings and growth—but rather on *things* and status. People mistake excitement for joy, and drugs provide instant excitement. Instant highs . . . instant relief." Maybe what is sought is relief from pain, and from a sense of inner emptiness. Maybe what's missing is feeling the power of the inner Self, the joy of being, and the magic of love.

"It's not just him," Jennifer continued. "He's a symbol of our times. In some ways, all of us are him. We all want instant relief, easy gaiety, pseudo-tranquility." We all participate in the escape from feelings, emotions, and spirit. We numb ourselves with drugs and alcohol, or we lose ourselves in our work and acquisitions, or even in our religions and philosophies. "Our armoring protects our numbness, while

164

our world goes mad." Jennifer's tears turned into sobs as she thought of the planetary dis-ease: nuclear issues, ecological problems, war. "I was listening to the news the other night, thinking they were talking about a revolution I'd just heard about. I was dismayed to discover it was a battle in yet another country!"

As her sobs subsided, I asked if she had cried about this before. "No," she said. "You know when I cried last week? It was when I was watching this Indian doing a war dance, at the half-time of a football game!" More tears came as she recalled the Indian's dance. "Even though it was modernized, it was *so* beautiful," she said. "Did it feel triumphant?" I asked. "Oh, yes, and there was a power, a bravery." By crying in response to the Indian's dance, Jennifer was also crying for the loss of that dance. Being impacted by the symbolic Indian was a way of regaining contact with her own heroic spirit.

The Indians lived at the mercy of natural forces, facing all kinds of dangers. The symbolic Indian represents a courage that we need for facing the equally intense dangers and challenges of modern life. The Indians *celebrated stress*—in war dances and fertility rites, songs and dances of grief and joy, and rituals for important life passages like attaining wo/manhood. They allowed time to prepare emotionally for events; they made spaces for processing and recovering from both pleasant and unpleasant life events.

Modern Stress Theory and the Extreme Emotions of Shen

Modern stress theory says that both pleasant and unpleasant changes, both sudden changes "for the better" and sudden changes "for the worse," are stressors. Hans Selye, a pioneer of scientific research into the effects of stress, says that extreme joy is as much of a stressor as is a hurtful shock:

> "From the point of view of its stress-producing or stressor activity, *it is immaterial whether the agent or situation we face is pleasant or unpleasant*; all that counts is the intensity of the demand for readjustment or adaptation. The mother who is suddenly told that her only son died in battle suffers a terrible mental shock; if years later it turns out that the news was false and the son unexpectedly walks into her room alive and well, she experiences extreme joy. The specific results of the two events, sorrow and joy, are completely different, in fact, opposite to each other, yet their stressor effect— the nonspecific demand to readjust herself to an entirely new situation—may be the same."[9]

Selye calls this reaction to stress the "general adaptation syndrome" and outlines three stages of "G.A.S.": *alarm, resistance,* and the final stage of *exhaustion.* Studies of stress reactions have shown that "the body's adaptability, or *adaptation energy,* is finite," says Selye. Eventually exhaustion sets in. "We still do not know precisely just what is lost, except that it is not merely caloric energy, since food intake is normal during the stage of resistance."[9] Traditional acupressure theory also talks about "adaptation energy," calling it *ching ch'i.* (Since this energy has a particularly strong relationship with the Kidneys, we'll discuss it further in Chapter 12.)

Stages of Reaction to Stress

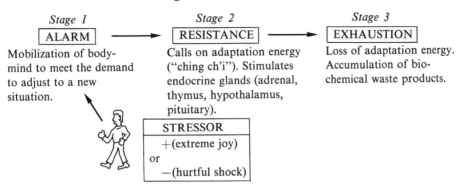

Stage 1
ALARM →
Mobilization of body-mind to meet the demand to adjust to a new situation.

Stage 2
RESISTANCE →
Calls on adaptation energy ("ching ch'i"). Stimulates endocrine glands (adrenal, thymus, hypothalamus, pituitary).

Stage 3
EXHAUSTION
Loss of adaptation energy. Accumulation of bio-chemical waste products.

STRESSOR
+(extreme joy)
or
−(hurtful shock)

Adaptation to stress involves the entire bodymind system, but the role of Shen is especially important. The heart and circulatory system are directly affected by the exhaustion phase of the stress response, which is characterized by an accumulation of biochemical waste products, resulting in diminishing elasticity of the connective tissue and progressive hardening of the arteries. Hypertension (high blood pressure) and predisposition to cardiovascular emergencies are common results. Additionally, the endocrine glands related to Shen, the thymus and hypothalamus, are involved in the many chemical processes required for adaptation to life's stressor demands.

"Stress is not something to be avoided," says Selye, because "no matter what you do or what happens to you, there arises a demand for the necessary energy required to maintain life, to resist aggression and to adapt to constantly changing external influences."[9] Stress simply makes a demand upon the adaptive energy. *Dis*tress can result from intense stress, or from inappropriate or excessive reactions to stress, which increase the energy drain. For example, we can use a lot of energy in excited tales of woe or in agitated self-defense. Hair-trigger emotional reactions often indicate that some unresolved emotional conflict is overloading the adaptation circuits.

Fear is a common culprit behind exaggerated stress levels, because it stimulates release of adrenal hormones which raise the blood pressure and stimulate heart activity, increasing the feeling of excitement. The adrenal hormones release extra energy for emergency responses, but at the expense of normal body activities like nourishment. Thus chronic adrenal overstimulation results in energic depletion. Acupressure theory relates fear and the adrenal glands to the Kidney Meridian, and emphasizes the relationship between the Kidney and Heart Meridians. Deficiency of the Kidney Meridian and of the adaptive energy sets the stage for being more easily frightened and more likely to experience pathological changes due to shock or stress. In other words, fear causes "over-nervousness of Shen."[8]

All the organs and aspects of the psyche are interrelated, and Shen is the master of them all. Therefore, the entire bodymind is affected by the condition of the Heart Meridian, and the Heart is affected by stress in any organ or part of the psyche. Shen is the ruler of the bodymind. Yet the classics also say that the Shen which resides in the Heart is "the *minister* of the monarch who excels through insight and understanding."[10] How can Shen be both monarch and minister? The Shen of the heart is the bodymind ruler, yet it is subject to the Shen of the "third eye." This vital energy center is related to the pituitary gland, which plays a cardinal role in the stress response because it governs the activities of the other endocrine glands.

Also related to the "third eye" is the pineal gland, which contains vestiges of optic tissue and is thought to be evolved from a primitive central eye. Experiments show that nerve impulses arise in the pineal in response to stimulation by light. Perhaps the pineal gland also responds to a feeling of inner lightness, for people commonly report seeing a beautiful purple or gold light in the "third eye" during states of deep relaxation. The Taoist classics say the "third eye" is the residence of "Yuan Shen"—the primal, "heavenly" or guiding spirit which directs all energic activities. The more earthly aspect of Shen, called "Shih Shen," resides in the heart, and has to do with the passions or heartfelt feelings. *Yuan Shen*, the original or spiritual Self, is like an inner *witness* which watches the play of life and sees the unity of it all. *Shih Shen* is the emotional Self—the part that loves the movement of passionate feelings. Excessive emotional movement and excitation make it difficult to hear the voice (or see the light) of Yuan Shen, because this original inner spirit loves stillness.

In the Taoist view, joy depends on the freedom of both Shih Shen and Yuan Shen, or the harmony of the emotional and the spiritual Self. The idea is not to "rise above" our emotional nature, but rather to ground spiritual awareness in acceptance of our emotional nature. In other words, the heart must be considered and nurtured. "The heart is the root of life and causes the versatility of the spiritual faculties," says the *Nei Ching*.[10] The condition of the heart, or of Shih Shen, is reflected in the condition of P'o, Hun, I' and Chih, which together are called the "spiritual resources." "Thus when the Heart is joyful, energy flows throughout the body and the organs are balanced. If, however, joy becomes frenzied excitement, then the energy of the Heart is exhausted and this affects all other functions."[8]

Dr. Selye says that an abundance of positive emotions like happiness and joy depends on *allowing energic cycles to be completed.* Unless each cycle is allowed to run its full course, an excess of waste products accumulates. How can we relieve our stress when some cycle of activity *cannot* immediately be completed? Selye recommends a change of activity, pointing out that "the body is not built to take too much stress always on the same part." If mental work, like problem solving, is interrupted by a lack of resources or by fatigue, the resultant mental stress can be relaxed by physical activity. Muscular stress gives the brain a rest. "In other words, stress on one system helps to relax another. Actually, when completion becomes temporarily impossible, a diversion into a substitute activity not only simulates completion, but it does so quite efficiently and usually provides its own satisfaction."[11]

It is late in the day as I write this. I want the satisfaction of completing this section, at least, before closing up my writing shack for the day. (Yes, it's really a shack, looking out at a stream running through the forest.) The subject of my writing encourages me to stay tuned into my bodymind feelings as much as possible. I have to grant that fatigue is diminishing my ability to concentrate. Maybe it is time to put stress on the physical system and see if that changes the mental fatigue? . . . It is amazing how a little physical exercise can transform a weary being into an energized one!

To avoid turning stress into distress, and to recover from stress, Selye recommends satisfying the urge for self-expression. One way to do this is to find a purpose in life—for example, a suitable kind of work. Another solution is finding that the purpose of life is just *to be*—or to be *aware*. Urges for self-expression come from all parts of ourselves. Joy comes with finding suitable outlets for them all—by learning new ways to play as well as by developing new skills. The satisfaction of thus *living fully* yields an *"attitude of gratitude,"* which Selye says is the best insurance against excessive stress. An appreciative attitude tends to create goodwill in others, and so "abolishes the clash between our selfish and selfless tendencies."[12]

The Bodymind Effects of Shock

The classics say, "During shock, there is no home for the Shen."[8] Shock is a disturbance that penetrates to the core, so that both the body energy and the spirit become chaotic. If the Heart is weak, or if Shen has been traumatically disturbed, even a brief occurrence of shock can produce dis-ease. Often, as a client remembers back to the onset of a physical problem, we find that there were traumatic or shocking events around that time, or that it was a stressful period of many big changes.

A state of shock can range from a mild but upsetting disturbance of consciousness (for example, being startled by a loud noise) to the bodymind distress of life-endangering trauma. For example, the shock of a near-miss on the freeway can produce a sudden lurching feeling in the chest, as though the heart has jumped. For another example, an elderly lady crossing a Los Angeles street was so shocked by seeing a car rapidly entering the intersection near her that she had a heart attack. In these cases, obviously fear is part of the emotional reaction; in fact, the extreme emotion of shock is sometimes translated as "fright." But this is not the only kind of shock associated with the heart. After an accident or the death of a loved one, we may be "in shock"—emotionally numb and not in full possession of our mental and physical faculties.

Shock can also be a serious and possibly life-endangering medical emergency—the "clinical shock syndrome," which requires careful treatment. In this extreme form of shock, the peripheral blood flow is not returning enough oxygen to the heart for normal functioning, so transportation of oxygen to the organs and tissues is decreased. The symptoms of this shock syndrome correspond to traditional associations of imbalance in the Heart Meridian: marked paleness; expressionless face and lack-luster, staring eyes; weak and rapid pulse; decreased or unobtainable blood pressure, often extreme thirst; occasionally restlessness or excitation, and disinterest in surroundings (if the person is conscious).

Western medicine says that such shock can result from emotional stress and excessive fear, joy, anger or grief, as well as from a variety of physical problems and overdoses of various drugs. Some degree of shock accompanies all injuries; it is called "traumatic shock," and should be treated promptly along with the injuries. First aid for shock involves keeping the person comfortably warm, with the body flat or the lower extremities slightly elevated to maintain circulation. Unnecessary noises or questions should be avoided, and fluids should be given sparingly. If symptoms of clinical shock syndrome are present, a physician should be called at once; the person may need to be moved to an emergency room if the shock does not respond at once to treatment.

Acupressure is a useful adjunct to medical treatment for shock, and can be sufficient to bring a person out of shock. Although it would be foolhardy to ignore available help from Western medicine, acupressure can sometimes be very effective for reversing the effects even of severe shock—as this anecdote from a doctor demonstrates:

"A patient was brought to our Intensive Care Unit from another hospital emergency room, where he had been given 100 milligrams of thorazine (an anti-psychotic drug) intramuscularly. Thorazine has a faster and greater effect when injected than when taken orally, but it also has a greater chance of lowering the blood pressure. This man had been given a very high dosage—and they hadn't noticed that he was drunk. You *never* mix alcohol and major anti-psychotics, because they are additive in effect.

"When the patient arrived, the medication was just taking effect. He went under before the eyes of the admitting personnel, becoming less responsive and groggy, then turning gray. When I arrived, his pulse was so weak that I couldn't feel it, and the blood pressure was 40/0—which indicates a coronary arrest with the imminent danger of croaking. By the time we got him into a room, he was totally unresponsive and just whitish gray, like a person looks just before dying due to lack of oxygen.

"I put my knuckle into his sternum and dug in hard to elicit a pain reflex and stimulate adrenalin release, which sometimes can revive a person. Nothing. I didn't have the necessary medical equipment to do some of the things that Western medicine can do, because this was a psychiatric unit. Here I was, looking at a guy who was going to have a cardiac arrest at any moment. I could stand by and watch him die, or I could do something— anything. I suddenly remembered from your lecture that #43 is a primary revival point, and the most important one for loss of consciousness. So I pulled the patient's shoes off and, without explaining to the nurses what I was doing, proceeded to put my thumbs almost through his feet at these points.

"It took about two minutes—three at the most. He started moving around a bit at first and then moaning a little. By the end of those few minutes, he had sat up in his chair and was talking to us. He had a strong pulse and a blood pressure of 90/40. There was an amazed look on the nurses' faces as they asked what I had done. I said I had worked with acupressure points to mobilize the reserve energy. I don't know if that made any sense to them, but they were amazed and happy that the patient was alive. Meanwhile, by the way, a priority code ambulance—with sirens and lights and the whole bit—was on its way to pick up a supposedly dying patient."

Points for Shock and Loss of Consciousness

• #43—disperses the reserve energy, or adaptation energy, into the entire bodymind system. This point is located on the Kidney Meridian, which according to acupressure theory is the "controller" of the Heart Meridian.

• Heart emergency points—may also be used for heart failure; strong stimulation, like with the fingernails, is recommended (along with calling the doctor or paramedics).

• Heart source point and #27—helps to balance the Heart, quiet the spirit, and reduce anxiety and hysteria.

- #18 and "B"—help to increase circulation and release tension in the chest. #30—may be added to stimulate respiration.

- #22—to reduce shock by relaxing the system.

What is "Over-Joy"?

Joy is having a spring to one's step; over-joy is like walking on air. Joy is a feeling of lightness; over-joy is like being too "up." Most people prefer feeling "up" to feeling "down," so how is this a problem? For one thing, "extravagant joy" wastes energy. Another difficulty is the crash which naturally follows the high. The classics say extreme joy suspends consciousness at the point of inhalation; the feeling is like that of inhaling deeply and then holding the breath. Just as it is not possible to hold the breath forever, so it is not possible to be constantly over-excited. The overall effect is a slowing down of the circulatory and respiratory functions.[8]

Strong joy or excitement accompanies major life events like falling in love, getting married, graduating from school, moving, buying or building a house, finding a job or getting a promotion. In addition to all this powerful real stuff, there are also excitations spun of hopes and fantasies. The wonderful powers of our imagination let us live through many events in our minds, besides the ones that "really" occur. These imagined events are real emotionally, for they can stimulate the same emotional excitement as the actual event would. Over-joy can come from expectations as much as from actual events.

When we hope for something, not only do we create it in our imagination, but also we often project it onto the real world. For example, we hope for love, perhaps imagining it as an unconditional acceptance which will make all our problems vanish. When we meet someone who embodies many of the qualities we have imagined, we begin to hope that this is "it." We start imagining what life together will be like, emphasizing the pleasurable possibilities. These lovely pictures call forth an over-joy which seeks to circumvent the passage of time that is required to find out if what we are feeling is really love.

Like the Taoists, existential philosopher Jean-Paul Sartre distinguishes between joy as a balanced state and "over-joy," or a kind of joy which is "characterized by a certain impatience." Speaking of the latter, Sartre says:

> "Joy is a magical behavior which tends by incantation to realize the possession of the desired object as instantaneous totality. This behavior is accompanied by the certainty that the possession will be realized sooner or later, but it seeks to anticipate this possession. . . . To dance and sing for joy represent symbolically approximate behavior, incantations. By means of these the object, which one could really possess only by prudent and, in spite of everything, difficult behavior, is possessed at one swoop— symbolically."[13]

A superficial and hyper-excited enthusiasm creates muscular hypertension and it opens the doors to depression, if the high hopes don't "come true." The backside of exaggerated hope is an equally intense feeling of hopelessness. "Blind hope" can arise as a compensation for low self-esteem. It can also be like a thread of optimism leading us through life's rough spots. The problem with blind hope is precisely that it is blind: it sees only one side of things, and is fixated on one imagined outcome. Blind hope insists that the real world match the wonderful world of imagination, and so it resists seeing the whole picture. This resistance adds to the distress (or damaging stress) of life—especially when the hopeful imaginings are thwarted.

There is another kind of hope which is not fixated on particular external objects or events, but which is much like a non-specific faith. This kind of hope exists alongside acceptance of life's stress/relaxation and pleasure/pain cycles. It is a generally optimistic outlook born of the trust that there *is* a growthful purpose to it all. It is a confidence that we will find joy and satisfaction in life. This means that we need not blindly hope that someone or something else will make us happy. Real hope is transformative. It reduces stress, because it reduces the hyper-excited emotional states produced by object-specific hopes and imaginings.

As an example of physical problems related to crushed expectations, and of an ensuing psychological transformation, I am reminded of Melanie. An attractive woman about 45 years of age, Melanie described herself as a "Type A Personality," because she felt always driven by something, or driving herself towards something, with a high level of anxiety. Her presenting problem was pain in her right shoulder [#18 area and #19: SI]. After two sessions focusing on this area and on her tight neck [#s20, 21, 22], she had no pain for a month.

After the Christmas holidays, which brought up relationship issues, her shoulder began to hurt again. As I held the #18 she said, "I first remember feeling this tension about ten years ago. It felt like it was about the size of a quarter." Ten years ago, Melanie had been shocked by the hurtful breakup of her first marriage, and then by the disillusioning discovery that her boyfriend was bisexual. What did the tension feel like now? "It's like a metal cylinder." After the #18 area had released somewhat, she said, "Now it feels smaller, like it's squashed." What did the increasing openness of her chest feel like? "Like being *out there* in the world, with no excuses."

As the deeper chest armoring released, what came up was the stress of going from past "success" and relative wealth to a present indebtedness and lack of material things. Melanie needed to affirm her new values, so that she could consistently measure "success" by self-awareness and growth, rather than by old materialistic yardsticks. As long as her life was lived in the shadow of introjected values, she was prone to the stress of unfulfilled expectations, or of not "measuring up" to societal opinions. In a session focusing on chest release [#18 with Pericardium and Heart distal points, and #30], Melanie had the image of running through meadows, feeling peaceful, free and light. "There's no anxiety," she said. "God has me where he wants me." She was finding self-confidence and joy in simply being herself.

In her fifteenth and last session, a real change of perspective was apparent. Melanie talked about living with no bullshit and no clutter, with humor, taking one day at a time. "If you stop comparisons, stop the right/wrong syndrome, *life flows,*" she said. "Even if I were successful financially, I would complain about something—like not having enough satisfaction. *I have to find the joy and satisfaction in each day. There has to be time for feeling, and for my body.*" Her intermittent doubts had been debilitating, as had her tendency to invest money, time and energy in others instead of in herself. Fixing her hopes on others had continuously resulted in disillusionment. She needed to invest her self-esteem squarely in herself. "The satisfaction and the joy is there," she said, "and when it's not, just accept that! I've always tried to control things. If I didn't have control, I was afraid that I'd be the loser. I'm tired of being nervous and anxious! It wears you out! You end up in the human scrap pile. To have been born with such a great body, and to have messed it up so much with my mind!"

Melanie was increasingly valuing what she called "this spaceship—my body," and she was enjoying feeling the connection between her body and psyche. "I really want to feel, know and love myself," she said, giving in these few words a fair definition of self-esteem. "I don't want to need somebody else to reassure me about myself. I want to learn that 'alone' doesn't mean 'lonely.' I don't want to live without joy. I want more of it! Joylessness is *not* okay. And I think for me joy has to do with freedom." I commented that freedom is a dynamic business. Melanie replied, "The thing is, the more freedom you have, the less control you have! *That* is a great insight! Trying to control things is not the way to spontaneity and flow. Freedom is just letting myself, and others, BE. And that's when there's joy—when I'm investing in myself and creating my own life—when life flows!"

Part 3. HYPOACTIVE SHEN: sadness, discouragement, self-doubt, despair, emptiness, hopelessness, depression

Deficiency of Shen is a lack of fire or warmth. The complexion may be pale or lusterless, with poor circulation, cold extremities, or increased susceptibility to chest problems. A lack of emotional warmth implies difficulty in reaching out and low initiative in friendship and sexuality. It is a contracted, cool state. The opposite, warming state is affection, as Lowen describes:

> "Affection is a reaching out to others and the world from an excited state of pleasurable anticipation. It represents an expansive reaction in the body. It is based on a flow of blood to the surface of the body resulting from the dilation of the peripheral blood system. This flow of blood to the surface creates a sensation of physical warmth. Affectionate feelings are characterized by their warmth. . . . The musculature is soft and relaxed, the heartbeat is slow, the pupils are contracted, and so on.
>
> "The warmth of affection is mainly in the skin, which is strongly suffused with blood. This produces a desire for some physical contact with the person who is the object of these feelings—a clasp of the hands, an embrace, or a kiss."[14]

A deficiency of Shen does not mean that one has no affections, but there may be difficulty in *experiencing* and *demonstrating* affection. This can be the effect of transient low spirits, or of low self-esteem and lack of self-love.

A simple form of Shen deficiency is sadness. Whereas grief is the extreme emotion evoked by loss, sadness is the lack of a positive emotion. It is the absence of joy. Sadness is like a slow little brook, while grief is like a big and sometimes angry river. Sadness can bring tears, or it can be like a tear that doesn't need to cry, but just to be quietly felt. Trying to escape the sadness (for example, by a restless search for excitement) is like putting a wall around the heart. Walled-off hearts tend to feel empty and cold.

Experiencing the sadness melts the wall and brings softness. The *Nei Ching* says the heart grants the capacity for sadness "in times of excitement and change."[15] Sadness gives witness to the phenomena of meeting and parting, coming and going. It is a response to times when it is as though we can see and feel past and future almost simultaneously with the present—when we feel ourselves suspended amidst the forces that move our lives. Sadness is deeply feeling the fundamentally poignant nature of human life.

To feel our sadness is to feel our humanness; it is to feel alive. Depression, by contrast, is an avoidance of feeling and an unresponsiveness to life that makes us feel dead inside. By trying to escape feelings like sadness, we are acting in the interests of non-feeling and so of depression. It is, therefore, rather amazing that we so often persist in defensive patterns calculated to reduce our feeling awareness. Without the capacity for feeling sadness, we also lose the capacity for feeling joy. As Lowen puts it, if we can't let go to sadness, we can't let go to gladness.

"We cannot recover the capacity for joy without reexperiencing our sorrow. And we cannot feel pleasure without going through the pain of rebirth. And we are reborn again when we have the courage to face the pains of our lives without recourse to illusion. There is a dual aspect to pain. Although it is a danger signal and represents a threat to the integrity of the organism, it also represents the body's attempt to repair the effect of an injury and to restore integrity to the organism."[16]

Fear of pain and fear of pleasure ("pleasure anxiety") are intertwined. Without the capacity for facing pain, we feel threatened by pleasure unless its perpetuation is guaranteed. There are no such guarantees, but balancing the fact that loss of pleasure can bring sadness or pain, there is also the fact that release of pain brings pleasure. Because it heightens awareness of Self and appreciation of life, sadness can open the door to feeling, and so to joy. Being able to feel pleasure is a criterion of emotional health; being able to tolerate sadness is a prerequisite.

This account of a chest release experience beautifully describes the way that feeling one's sadness can be a transformative experience:

"The nurturing, supportive touch helped create a safe space, where I could get in touch with myself and even become lost in myself. I was feeling more and more relaxed as the chest points released. Then, to my utter amazement, I actually felt an emotion. I *felt* sad—it wasn't just knowing I was sad, but *experiencing* it. Though it may seem strange, it was overwhelmingly beautiful to feel and experience this emotion of sadness that had been stored up in my chest.

"As the upper back points were held, I saw my scapulae as wings bound up. I had the image of my Spirit as Pegasus, a white horse, with its wings bound to a barren hard ground, preventing any movement. As I struggled against the binds, they became more painfully buried in my wings and more securely fastened to the rocky surface. I began feeling a tremendous sadness, and then cried. As I let go to my feelings, I felt the bonds begin to loosen. My 'wings' felt like they were opening up. It felt like my spirit was unbound, soaring exuberantly free, a Pegasus stretching its wings and sailing with the wind. It was an exhilarating experience, reaching into the depths of myself and awakening sleepy, forgotten and frozen feelings I had tucked carefully away in hidden crevices of my body. I felt *alive*, and in touch with life like I was newborn."

Variations on a Blues Theme

Discouragement and self-doubt can be born of physical or psychological weariness, or can follow a round of "low blows." When the chest caves in depressively, and the back slumps and the head sinks, it's like the body is curling over the heart. The child, which lives in the heart, wants to be protected. It feels most hurt when it is alone in its hurt. There is protection in the love of others, but the ultimate protection is getting in touch with the spark of joy and vitality hiding inside, which moves us to keep experiencing life.

To never feel discouraged would require being highly favored by fate, or having unfailing ego-strength. Being able to accept feelings of discouragement is a kind of courage, which helps ensure that the discouragement will be transient. On the other hand, chronic discouragement and self-doubt amount to faintheartedness. Self-esteem is low and depression is on the horizon. The loss of inner resiliency can manifest in forgetfulness and contradictory or incoherent speech. The eyes are lackluster. The inner lights are off; nobody is at home, or at least they're not admitting it. There is a loss of contact with the consciousness of Shen—the awareness that shines from our eyes when we are truly awake.

Beyond discouragement lies despair—the abandoning of hope and acceptance of defeat as inevitable. "There's nothing I can do about it anyway" so "what's the use?" Despair is giving up. It is feeling powerless, or unable to find pleasure and satisfaction in life. Self-confidence has been drastically eroded. How do we get into this devastated, despairing place? Kierkegaard explains:

> "Despair is never ultimately over the external object but always over ourselves. A girl loses her sweetheart and she despairs. It is not over the lost sweetheart, but over herself-without-the-sweetheart. And so it is with all cases of loss whether it be of money, power, or social rank. The unbearable loss is not really in itself unbearable. What we cannot bear is in being stripped of the external object, we stand denuded and see the intolerable abyss of ourselves."[17]

A feeling of emptiness comes from being deprived of external sources of joy, or of hope for their attainment, being thrown back on our own resources—and finding them atrophied through prolonged neglect. Zweig describes the "experience of inner emptiness" as "the frightening feeling that at some level of existence I'm nobody, that my identity has collapsed and deep down, no one's there."[18] Stripped of the familiar self-image, and the things that sustain it, we stand face-to-face with the inner Self, which may feel like an "inner void." The real solace lies not in renewing our dependence on external sources of happiness, but rather in connecting with our inner resources.

What about ecological and nuclear despair? The loss of the earth would be the loss of *all* external sources of joy—and internal ones too, excepting those of disembodied spirits. If the earth were covered with atomic or chemical waste beyond "tolerance levels," then we might suddenly see into the great abyss, not just the internal one. It is easy to feel fainthearted at such thoughts. How can we depend on our inner resources in the face of possible global disaster? Perhaps by connecting with the power of the earth, and of its creatures. One of our inner resources is being able to consciously connect with other beings and with nature, and so to feel supported and strengthened.

If we cannot find a way to move through despair and back to joy, we begin to feel depleted and empty. The feeling of emptiness is one of the most common modern psychological complaints. Emptied *of what*? And why does this emptiness feel bad? Having empty spaces—with no responsibilities or inner agendas to fulfill—can be wonderfully relaxing. The Taoists say that being empty like an infant is the source of tranquility. This kind of emptiness gets filled with joy. Being emptied *of a sense of self,* on the other hand, brings psychic stagnation and depression. There is no "joie de vivre," no zest for life.

"The human being is not empty in a static sense, as though he were a storage battery which needs charging," Rollo May points out. It is not that there is no Self inside, nor that this Self has been diminished, but rather that he has lost touch with the inner spirit and its power. It is not the *fact,* but the *experience* of emptiness, which comes from feeling powerless to do anything to change his life or his world.

> "Thus he gets the deep sense of despair and futility which so many people in our day have. And soon, since what he wants and what he feels can make no real difference, he gives up wanting and feeling. . . . The great danger of this situation of vacuity and powerlessness is that it leads sooner or later to painful anxiety and despair, and ultimately, if it is not corrected, to futility and the blocking off of the most precious qualities of the human being."[19]

To the psychotherapist, lack of feeling is a danger sign, indicating the possibility of depression. Other symptoms include low energy, loss of appetite, loss of sexual desire, sleep disturbances, lack of interest in normal activities, slowed thinking, passivity and apathy. There is a sense of emptiness, or of being heavy-hearted or weighed down. Depression is the "helpless-hopeless syndrome." It is the opposite of aliveness—even literally, for suicide is a possibility.*

People loosely use the word "depression" to refer to various "down" feelings, so "I feel depressed" may translate as "I feel sad, discouraged, disheartened, or just plain tired." If the chin or lip is trembling, or there is a tear in the eye, and you say, "You look sad," the person may suddenly realize that s/he *does* feel that, and tears may come. Just recognizing feelings like sadness often lifts a depressed mood.

Feeling is precisely the way to break the depressive spell. Almost any kind of emotion will do, but the depressed person is often much closer to sadness than to happiness. S/he may also be sitting on anger. Depression can be part of a grief reaction, so to avoid falling back into the depressive bog may require working through unresolved grief. (For an example, see the story of Mandy, in the discussions of grief and anger in Chapters 11 and 13.)

Charles, whom we met in the first chapter (through his submarine and armoring dreams), had suffered from chronic depression. A loner since early adolescence, he had almost no social activities. His conscious stance was that of being "calm, cool and collected," but when he sought therapy in his early thirties, he was severely withdrawn and depressed. He felt unable to go anywhere by himself, even to a movie. At each weekly session, he complained of how boring and empty his life was, and of how he could not make it better.

At our fourth session, Charles said that our relationship was "the only one where I talk about me." He resisted exercises for emotional release (like pounding a pillow or shadow boxing), saying they were "silly." He described his childhood home as being "just neutral." No feelings had been expressed—not anger, not fear, nor even love. Growing up in this "blah" environment, Charles hadn't learned how to com-

---

* Seek professional help if the depression is severe or if there are suicidal thoughts—especially if there is the means to carry them out.

municate feelings. "That's just not right!" he said angrily. "Parents should help their kids learn how to do that."

A recurrent dream was of being chased by a vague animal being, having a gun in his hand, and being powerless to pull the trigger. What was this psychic impotency? Charles was powerless to deal on an emotional level. He had always retreated from strong feelings—from love as well as from anger. Gradually he learned to acknowledge anger—first at me, for insisting that he share his feelings and that he do something (anything!) different each week, and then at his parents, for helping him learn not to feel.

A dominant childhood memory was of a nightmare he had at age twelve, after moving to a new neighborhood. Soldiers fighting an unseen enemy were getting slaughtered—then reviving and fighting some more, minus arms or legs and with bleeding holes from cannon balls. He woke up scared, went down the dark hall to his parents' room, and woke his mother up, crying and saying he'd had a bad dream. She said, "You're too old for that," and went back to sleep. A couple years later, after another move, she again informed him that he was too old to be afraid and cry. He hadn't cried since; instead he had pushed his feelings down and withdrawn into himself. As he learned to acknowledge and accept daily emotional changes, Charles began to feel less depressed. After about three months, Charles again dreamed of being chased by a shadowy figure. This time he chased the figure and, after trying several types of guns, managed to pull the trigger of an "energy gun." The creature vanished.

Another dream helped Charles contact the strong, vital, adventurous part of himself. Sean Connery was leading soldiers in Civil War uniforms on an expedition to the North Pole. A storm arose, but all the cavalry made it across a rough river—except for Connery's horse. "Without his horse he's nothing," so he went back to get it—into a cave which led into smaller and smaller rooms. Charles got more and more frightened, while "Connery turned into me!" I asked if he was on any kind of journey. "Just this," he said, referring to our work. At first therapy is like looking into smaller and smaller internal rooms; this can be scary if these rooms were long avoided. Charles' "civil war" was a struggle between the depressive tendency to shut down, and the desire to grow and embrace more of life. I asked if he'd like to finish the dream. He saw himself going on, and the rooms getting larger. Then he was attacked by "mutated human beings." What were they? "They've cut off some aspect of themselves—as I have." After defeating them, he found his horse, or the power to move, then went to an opaque window and broke out. With interest in what lay ahead, he rode off towards a city on the horizon.

Charles was a sensitive and intelligent man who thought he had to be a charming, witty extravert to be liked. As he learned to value his introverted qualities, like being a good listener, he felt less anxious in social situations, but still had trouble meeting people. "It feels like a wall goes up," he said. After we began doing bodywork, he noticed that the wall was related to his chest armoring. While working with #18 and #30, he had the image of big steel doors shutting. He said, "It's the despairing part of myself. It wins too much!" What would happen if he opened the doors? "I would feel sad, angry, afraid, and other stuff like that, for a while." After this session, he began having mood swings that at first felt uncomfortable, but he realized that changing moods was a healthier state than a frozen neutral stance.

In the first part of this chapter, I described the image Charles had as his deeper chest armoring released: the dancing little guy with the top hat and tails, which helped him connect with a joyful inner Self he hadn't known existed. A month later, he complained of feeling pain and tension at the #18s. "I've been feeling depressed and weighed down," he said. By what? "By myself, obviously," he said with exasperation. He was having trouble letting the "playful little guy" out. His predictable old ways, while boring, were safe.

As I held #18 with Pericardium and Heart distal points, and #30 with Lung points, Charles saw himself entangled in barbed wire. I asked him to look around and see if there was a way out. He saw several paths, but in tearful frustration said, "I don't know which one to follow." I suggested he follow the one that attracted him most. "It's a dead-end," he said, discouraged. He found another path, then said, "There's something here I want, but I can't have it." Why not? "Because I'm not good enough." Why not? "Because I can't be honest with my feelings." At last, he was relating his unworthiness to something he *could* change. "The something I want is a part of myself, that should be within myself, but I can't get to it." I couldn't see any movement with his breathing, so I asked him to breathe fully and be actively receptive. Suddenly his body jerked. "What was that?" I asked. "The part of myself that cares about me and about other people," he replied. "It feels like whatever is outside, is inside. . . . Whatever I find was already there; I already knew."

What was already there was an interesting inner Self that had been waiting for a chance to come out and play. In another session, while I was holding neck points [#21: LI and #21: B], Charles allowed himself to make some sounds. After working with chest, diaphragm and pelvic tensions, he felt a strong tingling throughout his body, and then had a numb, sick feeling. He realized it was a reaction to getting afraid of the tingling sensation. As I encouraged him to allow the sensations, he said it felt like lava from some kind of inner volcano. It was the unleashed energy of the suppressed parts of himself—the repressed feelings and emotions of the oppressed inner child.

In the next session, sadness and anger came up about his move at age twelve, from a friendly neighborhood to a "better" one where the families didn't socialize. Charles recalled, for the first time, how he had felt before that move. With pleasure, he remembered a child-self who hadn't been afraid of rejection. That little boy had played with other children and visited neighboring families. He hadn't minded being asked to go home, because he had felt accepted and acceptable. After this session, the introjected voice that said "you're no good" was much fainter. The next week was Christmas—a time which usually deepened his depression. But the "holiday blues" didn't arrive! With the help of his child-self, Charles was learning that "it's actually easier and more fun to move into life, than to run away from it."

The depressive avoidance of feeling is a way of avoiding contact with oneself. Learning to allow and express feelings means learning to be true to oneself, and this helps produce a cheerfulness that doesn't depend on the world doing what we want it to. Being real with feelings is a way of being *present*.

Feeling the body is a shortcut to the present, which is where the joy is. Depression is a loss of contact with the body as well as with the emotions, as can be seen by symptoms like decreased appetite, energy and sexuality. The general unreality of the depressive attitude includes being unaware of the muscular tensions which are

178

preventing spontaneous self-expression. Being in touch with the body is the opposite of depression. Lowen says bluntly:

> "The person who is in touch with his body doesn't get depressed. He knows that pleasure and joy depend on the proper functioning of his body. He is aware of his bodily tensions, and he knows what causes them. Thus he can take appropriate measures to restore his bodily good feelings. He has no delusions about himself and no illusions about life. He accepts his feelings as expressions of his personality, and he has no difficulty in voicing them. When a patient gets fully in touch with his body, the depressive tendency is eliminated."[20]

Someday It Will All Be Different . . .

The genesis of depressive feelings can be illusions and expectations which originally arose as compensations for childhood pain and lack of confidence. Early blows to the self-esteem can lead to an all-consuming focus on symbols of success, so that a person loses sight of the simple joys of *being*, which exist only in the present. Dreaming about making it big brings a mental excitation that substitutes for a present lack of joy. Such fantasies can be a way of surviving when the present is bleak, but losing sight of their origin allows them to become the very meaning of life. There is no longer any knowing of oneself except as the person who must achieve the fantasy. The main illusion is that happiness will come when the fantasy is fulfilled. This alternates with a depressive hopelessness, if the dreams don't manifest with all imagined splendor.

A seeming recovery from depression can be but a return to the hope that things will be different *this time*—especially if there is a sudden mood swing towards elated hyperactivity. If the future not only does not reverse the past, but actually *repeats* it, the illusory foundations of life are rocked and an emotional crash may be immanent. Repeatedly broken dreams can crush the spirit, when life is founded on illusions. Even if the dreams are realistic, investing self-esteem in them is not. Focusing on external symbols of success makes it more difficult to withstand adversity. The *I Ching* says:

> "Times of adversity are the reverse of success, but they can lead to success if they befall the right man. When a strong man meets with adversity, he remains cheerful despite all danger, and this cheerfulness is the source of later successes; it is that stability which is stronger than fate. He who lets his spirit be broken by exhaustion certainly has no success. But if adversity only bends a man, it creates in him a power to react that is bound in time to manifest itself. . . . Therefore in times of adversity . . . there is nothing a man can do but acquiesce in his fate and remain true to himself. This concerns the deepest stratum of his being, for this alone is superior to all fate."[21]

Getting in touch with this "deepest stratum" of being is the best antidote to discouragement or depression. At the core, if we can but get in touch with it, is a stability that makes it possible to meet adversity with strength, instead of seeing adversity as the defeater of hope and the robber of joy. We can confidently invest our self-esteem in ourselves by contacting the wisdom and power of our core spirit. Feeling this inner power to react, and knowing that it is certain to manifest, if one is but true to oneself—in modern terms, this is strong self-esteem.

James, an artist who cyclically felt depressed and anxious, had a series of Superman images during work with his low back pain. (See Chapter 12, Part 2.) James' Super-self was all-powerful and never missed his target. The Superman image seemed to be a compensation for James' frequent feelings of inadequacy. Similarly, his dreams of "making it" compensated for his dissatisfaction with just "getting by." James' dreams were not unrealistic. Though sometimes embroidered with fantasies of fame and fortune, they basically involved getting the commissions he wanted and being financially comfortable.

The problem was that his self-esteem was invested in the dreams, not in himself. A strong introjected message was, "Worth is based on what you achieve." The repeated fall of the hope of recognition brought discouragement, despair, and feelings of worthlessness, which dampened his creativity. As long as his feeling of worthiness was attached to external recognition, James could not seem to find the time to paint just for the joy of it. He was not really manifesting his artistic talents, and not just because of the lack of commissions.

Then came a session in which the focus was tonifying the Pericardium and Heart Meridians. The Superman image arose again, but this time the omnipotence was gone. Superman was doing things that were part of James' normal life—painting and practicing a martial art. When he threw rings at buildings, some made it and some didn't. Further, this Superman was embracing people, not exerting power over them. Afterwards, James said, "A Super Man is one who is in full possession and command of his power—who is aware of, and feels free to use, his entire Self." This means manifesting inner potentialities and creative talents, whether or not there is external recognition for doing so.

James' hopeful illusion-building had this theme: "Someday everything will be different. I'll be recognized and I'll have plenty of money. Then people (and I) will see that my professional struggle was worthwhile—that my talent (and my self) is worthwhile." After another glowing hope of recognition and remuneration faded away, it would be: "After all these years, I'm still not succeeding—maybe I'm just no good and it's selfish for me to want to be an artist." Yet James could not imagine enjoying any other kind of work. Art was his calling: without this creative self-expression life felt empty.

To accept the innate worthiness of his talent and of himself, James had some old business to resolve. Some of the sense of worthlessness came from feeling unsuccessful by comparison with the standards his father had set. He had loved painting as a hobby, but had encouraged James towards a business career. While his pursuit of business contacts was important, it was interesting that sometimes James could find time for nothing but the *business* of art, for months at a stretch. To be more artistically productive, perhaps he needed permission to be an artist—from his father or his internalized father. Accepting his calling as real and valuable meant accepting his core Self as intrinsically valuable, for it was this Self that was issuing the calling. Cyclic depression came from instead hoping that recognition and fame would validate his chosen profession in the world's eyes, and so by reflection in his own.

At the beginning of one session, James was having throat problems and complained of neck tension [at #21: LI]. Asked what this tension was about, and directed to tell me the first thing that came up, James said "lack of confidence." I wondered if defensive pride was blocking awareness of his inner power. He said, "I also use over-thinking as a way to stay out of touch with my power."* His obsession with external expectations had again thrown James into despair, because professional recognition seemed to be around yet another corner. As I was holding #18 with Pericardium and Heart distal points, I asked "Why did you become an artist?" "Because I fell in love with art," he said. "It was not a rational decision." "Art is not a rational thing," I replied.

"Also I thought I would make money at it," James continued. I observed that sometimes he thought not making a lot of money *means* he's no good. The image of his father came up. "Did your father disapprove of your career choice?" I asked. "He did at first," James replied, "and I always thought he was disappointed in me because of it. But now that I think about it, before he died he helped me get my career established on a more business-like level. I can remember him being quite enthusiastic about some of the work I was doing."

I asked James to call up the image of his father, and see if there was anything he wanted to ask now. "What do you think of my choice of a profession?" he asked. It sounded like he was also asking, "What do you think of me?" "You are part of a chain of spirit made to make art in the world," was the response from his internalized father. "Your art, and your awareness, give my life meaning." James saw his father's life as one of struggling for his rights. He saw that his own parallel struggle for his rights as an artist sometimes interfered with *being* an artist. The longer he didn't paint, the more he questioned his talent, and the less confident he felt. Valuing his talent meant remembering the joy of painting, and of expressing his feelings through his art. It meant claiming the freedom to create.

"The need for self-expression underlies all creative activity and is the source of our greatest pleasure," says Lowen. "The self is experienced through self-expression, and the self fades away when the avenues of self-expression are closed. The self is fundamentally a bodily phenomenon, and self-expression therefore means the expression of FEELING. The deepest feeling is love, but all feelings are part of the self. . . ."[22] Love—of others, self, nature and life—can be expressed just in the eyes, face and voice, by body movements and through touch. Feelings are also expressed in creative activities—like painting, drawing, writing, making things, playing music, doing acupressure. And feelings are expressed in our dreams.

Just as our sleeping dreams are often spun from unresolved or unexpressed feelings, so our waking dreams too are expressions of feelings. We need our dreams—our visions of what *can* be. The process of manifesting our dreams is part of Self-transformation. A *dream* is something we want to do, something that feels meaningful and satisfying. An *illusion* is thinking *everything will be perfect when* the dream comes true. We are all right NOW and there is happiness NOW, when we stay in touch with body, feelings and Self. The inner Self wants to grow and expand, so it dreams

---

* Over-thinking and obsessive tendencies can correlate with an excess of I' or earth, which was frequently reflected in James' pulses.

of what it wants to experience. Like feelings, dreams arise to lead us on in becoming all of our whole Selves.

What is an illusion and what is a dream? What is impossible, and what is possible? This book, for example, has sometimes seemed like an illusion, for completing it has seemed impossible. Yet this book is a dream which can be manifested—given enough time, persistence and flexibility. What are your dreams? What would you like to be, do or experience? Self-esteem cannot be invested in our dreams, yet doing our dreams enhances self-esteem. A dream need not be impressive to be important. It might be about making or achieving something or about changing one's physical appearance, moving to a new place, learning something, having a party. Manifesting a dream won't change everything, but finding that we are able to manifest some of our dreams *can* change how we feel about ourselves.

Part 4. HYPERACTIVE SHEN: hyper-excite, elation, restless gaiety, nervousness, anxiety, hysteria

Hyperactivity of Shen is being "all fired up." The hyper-excitement may be fun, but when it feels exaggerated, the "high hopes" are like hot air which is carrying the bodymind balloon up, up and away. Illusions are the fuel behind this burst of hot air. The illusions generally find their origin in the hope that the past can be reversed. The present is not enough unless it vindicates us by totally reversing past hurts and failures. Not only must love be found, but it must be the best love(r) ever. Not only must satisfying work be found, but there must be greater success than ever before. Not only must status be recovered, but there must be more prestige than in the past.

"Hyper-excité" is a state of excitation beyond that warranted by the actual event, derived from "reading something into it." Not only have you met an interesting and attractive wo/man, but you have found your true love and s/he is perfect! Not only have you gotten the job you wanted, but you are on the road to fame and fortune. Now *everything* will be great! But elation leads to deflation. Soon, not only have you had business problems, but now *everything* will be terrible. Not only has your new love disappointed you, but that means it is not a true love. So the restless chase after illusions of happiness goes on, with new excitement about the image on the horizon.

An addiction to excitation means being devoted to illusory values and looking to external sources for happiness. To maintain and intensify the excitation, we may paint castles in the air, idealize other people, or interpret events as the fulfillment of ego-aggrandizing goals. Looking to others to make things right, we risk disappointment, despair and depression. As long as the illusions rule, we are prone to mood swings between elation and deflation, anxiety and despair, or "manic" hyperactivity and depression. Swaying from one extreme to the other, we bypass the inner center— the source of real joy.

Energy devoted to the pursuit of illusions is energy diverted from simple enjoyment of being. Investing happiness and self-esteem in other persons or things ignores the real foundation of these psychic states: self-awareness and personal growth. Being other-directed rather than inner-directed is an unstable condition. It is like a business corporation that invests all its profits in other companies, neglecting its own needs. Its directors can argue that these financial diversions are good investments, likely to turn a profit. Likewise, the individual can find many reasons why excitement over a particular person, thing or event is justified—becoming increasingly elated as s/he does so. Distinguishing between illusions and dreams is not always easy, but one guideline is that the latter are founded on real Self-felt abilities. Manifesting our dreams may test our abilities and stretch our limits, but manifesting illusions would require changing the nature of reality.

Elation is an intense and thrilling from of hyper-excité, which can short-circuit our connection with reality. The word derives from the Latin "elatus," which means "elevated." Elation may be a lifting of the spirit, but more often is an inflating of the ego. We paint an ego-aggrandizing picture of reality, and feel elated by the picture. Sometimes the "high spirits" are not at all in accord with actual circumstances; the picture is a total illusion and the hyper-excité just mimics happiness. To maintain the high we paint increasingly rosy pictures, which have a decreasing resemblance to reality. *Euphoria* is another word for this exaggerated and often unaccountable feeling of high spirits. Euphoria and elation are rushes towards joy, which may be generated less by real events than by projecting onto them the fulfillment of our greatest hopes. These feelings are especially addictive when long bouts with adversity or low self-esteem have made us impatient about having pleasure.

Gaiety is a simple kind of hyper-excité. Like humor, gaiety can have two faces. There is the joyful laughter of organismic well-being and there is humor as a defense. There is the gaiety of simple fun, and there is the frenetic pleasure hunt which seeks to escape feelings of emptiness. It also escapes feelings of joy, because hyperactivity of the periphery is deprivation of the core from which real joy emanates. Inappropriate laughter, a perpetually smiling mask, or a restless search for gaiety is likely to be a cover-up for the lack of joy, rather than its reflection.

The *Nei Ching* says that "extravagant joy" is injurious to the Heart and spirit. "Violent joy is hurtful to Yang," or to the capacity for activity, because it is energically draining.[23] Dianne Connelly explains:

> "The desire for permanent joy is an impossible thirst, and if sought after inordinately through work or play can put too much stress on the Fire Element causing something to *give*. Often the symptom of high blood pressure is the bodymind's way of saying, *Take it easy or I'll succumb to this pressure*. Heart attacks are often the final straw, a desperate attempt of the bodymind to alert us to the excessive striving, hence the actual deficiency of the emotion joy. Within this stress there is often a great deal of sexual frustration. An imbalance in the emotion of Fire almost always revolves around relationship in a person's life."[24]

Happiness is a Figment of Your Imagination ────────────────

Joan married at age 18 and had one child, a year later. After her divorce at age 21, she tried to support herself, but then gave up and let herself be supported by a "sugar daddy." She gravitated toward exciting people and places. In her late thirties, she didn't yet feel strong enough to be alone, though she had been supporting herself for several years. When she first came to see me, she said even the office building intimidated her. Her boyfriend had encouraged her fears, so she would look to him for comfort and protection. "But my own anxieties and insecurities allowed that," she said.

Joan had somehow hurt her left shoulder, and had pain going from the left ♯18 up through the ♯19 and ♯20. She remembered having felt pain in this area when, as a teenager, she was returned to the "very restrictive environment" of her parental home. A main issue was wanting to break up with her boyfriend. The relationship had been exciting at first, but now his antisocial behavior frightened her. Still, she felt lonely and anxious when he threatened to leave.

During work with the Heart-Pericardium [♯18] and Lung [♯30] in the fourth session, Joan said, "I'm in a crib all alone. My mother is upstairs . . . the basement is dark and there are burglars around . . . alligators. A snake is coiled at the bottom of my crib." Joan's resolution of being left alone had been, "There's something wrong with me; I am bad." Her mother was "upstairs"—distant from Joan, physically and emotionally. Her love was so often whimsically taken away that Joan could not depend on it at all. When Joan was six, her mother went into a psychiatric hospital for six years, and Joan was sent to another city to live with her grandparents. Their home was also short on love and emotional nurturance, "but at least I had some freedom of movement."

What about the snake in the crib? Was it a literal memory or a symbol? Joan had recurrent dreams of snakes and a phobic fear of them. She remembered other children tormenting her by putting snakes down her blouse, when she was four or five. Asked for associations to the snake in the crib, Joan said she felt threatened by her mother's energy, her mother felt threatened by Joan's energy, and she was afraid of her own power. The snake has long been a symbol for strong energy or power. In yoga, the guiding energy which must be aroused to actualize the Self is called the "Kundalini." It may manifest as strong energy rushes through the body, and is symbolized by a serpent or a dragon. Jung described the Kundalini as the spirit of adventure that makes life livable—the guiding spark or incentive that forces us on.

At another session, Joan was anxious about getting disentangled from a woman she had been studying with. I asked her to follow her feelings back in time, while focusing on chest release. As I held #30, Joan remembered a plastic rose given her by a loving woman who took care of her before she was sent to her grandparents. "It was all I had of her," she said, "and my mother made me give it away. She put my toys in the attic, and pulled up the ladder so I couldn't get to them. Later my grandmother just took my toys and gave them away." This deprivation of loved objects also symbolized a deprivation of "love objects," in the sense of other human beings.

As the chest release continued with #18, Joan remembered sitting in the basement with her grandfather, watching the sunset, while her grandmother paced upstairs, swearing. "He was the only one I could talk to," Joan said. "My grandmother had a crazy side to her, like my mother. She was jealous and suspicious." Whenever she didn't approve of Joan, she made her sit on a chair in the corner. Joan felt sad a lot, and anxious. She also developed a pain in her chest. "They said I was a nervous child." Recalling her anxiety about breaking off with the teacher, Joan said, "It's like if I upset her, she might get crazy, and in some way my 'toys' will be taken away. I can never do enough. But I always have to keep trying, to get my toys back."

A few weeks later, I was working with the #16s and then the ocular segment. Joan was breathing into her "hara" and feeling very relaxed. In her mind she saw white clouds in a blue sky, and then her mother's frowning face superimposed on the pastel scene. What was her mother saying? "*You can't be happy. Be miserable with me. Happiness is a figment of your imagination!*" Joan's determined pursuit of pleasure in her twenties could be seen as an attempt to negate the message that "you can't be happy." It was an over-compensation for a deep-rooted fear of being like her mother. Her refusal to be miserable was certainly healthy, but putting her hopes for happiness onto others (usually men) led to dependency, disillusionment and desperation.

In another session, during deep release of the chest [#18], Joan saw a young "dapper daddy dressed in a suit." Then her mother came into the picture, yelling, and daddy brushed Joan's arm off his sleeve. She remembered him explaining later that he had to be undemonstrative to Joan, or her mother would "get crazy." In this impactful session, Joan realized that her "strong program of needing a man" stemmed not only from cultural messages, but also from a childhood deprivation of closeness with her father.

Joan's conflicts about the masculine or yang part of her own psyche were illustrated by a dream a few nights later. "I was in a pool with a woman and a man who was a spy. I shot the man, then had to hide. He found me hiding in a conservative home and he had my car keys. I felt he would kill me. In a devil-may-care mood, I went walking on a dark road. He followed me, and I was afraid. But then we fell in love and went off together!" If the spy were some part of her, what would it be? "The unconventional part. I really do feel I am unique. I used to deny it. Now I'm not hiding it so much." The spy in her dream reminded me of the serpent in her earlier image: she can't kill it, and it doesn't kill her, but rather enlivens her. The dream marriage to the spy symbolized the need for merger of the feminine and masculine within herself.

Insights notwithstanding, Joan was still having trouble letting go of her boyfriend, though he had become abusive. It was hard to accept the fall of illusions. She had hoped to find a sense of wholeness through her relationship with him; it seemed much harder to find it within herself. After he left, she felt depressed and "curled up a lot." Her hurt and pain had much to do with anxiety about being alone and feeling empty. It was the same feeling that had led her into dependency relationships with "sugar daddies" earlier in her life. She had repetitively escaped the feeling of emptiness by latching onto a man; the last one was just a psychological dependency rather than a financial one. Low self-esteem had led her to make choices she was now embarrassed about, and this made her feel she couldn't trust her judgment. I asked Joan what she had wanted in a man before. "That he had two legs," she said. "I was just happy if a man I was attracted to reciprocated."

Learning not to judge NOW by THEN involved "learning to love myself and let it flow." As her heart opened, she felt increasing confidence, contentment and joy. But she also felt increased hurt for a while. It was as though the pain held in by the old chest armoring was coming out in waves. Facing the old negative messages and feeling the old pain, Joan felt like she was "wallowing in self-pity." She saw that for many years she had avoided her real feelings, though it didn't look that way on the surface. There had been a sense that something was missing.

There was not only hurt, but also anger over hurt, and over the loss of love. Joan's diaphragm tension was reflective of an inner anger and frustration; it was also a *source* of frustration, for sometimes a sudden diaphragm contraction caused her to start hiccuping during sex. In sessions focusing on diaphragm release (with Liver, Gall Bladder and Spleen points), anger about her parents and her ex-boyfriend came up cyclically. The resolution of her anger problem required knowing that her Self was worth expressing, and tolerating the anxiety that came with asserting herself more fully. "I can be assertive without getting angry over it!" Joan learned. "It's easier to say what's on my mind than to keep it in and let it boil. It's really okay to 'start shit,' if that's how it's taken. I don't want to play with, or be friends with, people who won't talk feelings." She had discovered a core frustration just at not being real with her feelings.

Joan saw that she had used men as a defense against contact with the core of herself. She had chosen those men because of some very real needs. She learned to have compassion for the needy person who had so chosen, rather than staying in old snares of self-blame and feeling unworthy. "I decided I don't need to be so hard on myself," she said. "Just because I picked men with problems, I don't need to take them all on myself!" The excitement of these relationships had bolstered her shaky self-esteem. Where joy was not, gaiety would suffice. She *would not* be miserable. Learning to tap the inner sources of joy was the essence of Joan's therapeutic journey. In a follow-up conversation several months later, Joan described herself as "creating a wonderful reality for myself!"

Anxiety and Stagefright

The classics say that excess joy can cause a "shaking of the heart"—in other words, *anxiety*. The anxiety related to the Heart Meridian can be defined as *repressed excitement*. Psychologist Fritz Perls describes this kind of anxiety. He says that the human being has a basic energy or excitement—an "èlan vital"—which wants to be expressed, either on the public or on the private stage. We went to play some role, or interact with others in some way, but we don't quite dare. The excitement is anxiety-producing, so we try to hold it back.

> "Any disturbance of this excitement metabolism will diminish your vitality. If these excitements cannot be transformed into their specific activities but are stagnated, then we have the state called anxiety, which is a tremendous excitement held up, bottled up. *Angoustia* is the Latin word for narrowness. You narrow the chest, to go through the narrow path; the heart speeds up in order to supply the oxygen needed for the excitement, and so on. If excitement cannot flow into activity through the motoric system, then we try to desensitize the sensoric system to reduce this excitement."[25]

The word anxiety derives from the Latin *angere*, which means "to strangle," or "to pain by pushing together." One way to reduce the feeling of excitement is to suppress the breath by constricting the chest and throat. This has a numbing or desensitizing effect, but a temporary one. Restricting respiration is like strangling ourselves. Soon there is a new anxiety: it is the body asking, "where is my oxygen?" Also, the mounting excitement has already generated energy; the higher energy level begins to feel like anxiety if it is bottled up. The only real solution is to breathe through the anxiety and *use* the energy. The only place the energy can be used is in the present. Perls says:

> "My definition of anxiety is the gap between the now and the later. Whenever you leave the sure basis of the now and become preoccupied with the future, you experience anxiety. And if the future represents a performance, then this anxiety is nothing but stage fright. . . ."[26]

Stage fright is hyper-excité coming from expectations about terrible or wonderful things that may happen in the future. James, the artist we met in part three of this chapter, discovered that his cyclic anxiety was actually stage fright. Feeling the constriction in his throat and chest, he said, "There's a fear that I won't be able to come through—that I don't have the talent or energy." After trying to breathe into his chest, he said, "I can't relax, because I'm holding onto all these thoughts about upcoming events—like if I let go, something would go bad. There's always this fear that I won't be able to do the job right when I get it." After focusing on chest breathing for a while, he said: "I'm getting sick of this anxiety about not being able to deliver the goods! It's pissing me off! It's not appropriate, and it's a real block in a lot of things." Tensing to meet the future meant blocking off awareness of his body and feelings, and so damning up the sources of creativity. As James relaxed, he discovered that his anxiety was rooted in an old fear of disapproval, not in a present lack of ability.

Stage fright results from trying to control something that only works when it is a flow. Anxiety arises with thoughts about upcoming meetings, discussions, projects, jobs, lectures or performances. Yet these often "come off" precisely when we let go of self-consciousness and just tune in to the situation, moment by moment. The phenomenon of anxiety boils down to a lack of Self-confidence. Not trusting ourselves, we feel anxious about being able to respond appropriately to new situations. Our compensating attempts at control are reflected in crunchy neck and shoulder tensions. The alternative is to persistently channel our energy as dictated by *present* needs and realities. Perls says:

> "If you are in the now, you can't be anxious, because the excitement flows immediately into ongoing spontaneous activity. If you are in the now, you are creative, you are inventive. If you have your senses ready, if you have your eyes and ears open, like every small child, you find a solution . . . the meaning of life is that it is to be lived. . . . "[27]

Anxiety at first stimulates hyperactivity, but the after-effect is energic depletion. When we get excited, we use up energy in restless physical and mental activity. We also tend to talk a lot, and "forget" to breath. Charlotte, for example, felt anxious about being asked to chair an activity for a club she had recently joined. I pointed out that she had been holding her breath. "I'm tempted to call them and say, 'I've had a lot of pressures in my life, with my children and everything, and I don't want any more pressure.' . . . That sounds silly." Her upper back muscles [#18] had tensed. I asked if there was anything about the project that she couldn't handle. Like the "writer's block" she often complained of, Charlotte's anxiety about the project sounded like stage fright. She wanted to pull back because of fear of failure and inability to sustain the excitement. "I don't need to do that," she said. "I can just say 'no' if people expect me to do more than I can." The simplicity of this solution made her laugh. To tolerate the excitement, she tried breathing through it instead of shutting it down. As her chest and neck relaxed, her arms and legs jerked and trembled. "It feels like rushes or jolts of energy!" She saw how that energy could be put to work, by extending it into whatever was at hand.

A certain amount of anxiety can stimulate purposeful action, but excessive anxiety has the opposite effect, and interferes with effective functioning. Anxiety is a distressing uneasiness of mind, with muscular tension, or discomfort in the "pit of the stomach," a high resting pulse rate and feelings of being "on edge," impatient or unable to relax. Muscular aches and fatigability are the yin backlash of bottled-up excitement. There may also be symptoms like those classically associated with the

Heart Meridian: being easily startled, restlessness, insomnia, racing or pounding heart, sweating, dry mouth, light-headedness or dizziness, cold clammy hands and flushing. An *anxiety attack* is the most distressing case, for with symptoms like palpitations and chest pain, it can mimic a heart attack (which possibility needs to be considered). There may also be trembling and cold or sweaty extremities, indigestion, and a bandlike pressure around the head.

A high level of motor tension characterizes anxiety, as can be seen by symptoms like jitteriness, shakiness, trembling, jumpiness and fidgeting. The trembling and shaking, which can also occur in therapy, can be interpreted as the body's attempt to break down muscular tensions and ego defenses. "It is a therapeutic reaction, an attempt on the part of the body to shake itself loose from the rigidities that limit its motility and inhibit the expression of feeling," says Lowen. Pleasure anxiety is "fear of the pain that inevitably develops when an outward-flowing, expansive impulse meets a contracted and bound area of the body."[28] The trembling or jerking comes from the body trying to expand, and encountering the pain or resistance of muscular tension. There may be a fear of "falling apart," but it is just the *rigidities* that are starting to fall apart. If the trembling and breakdown of muscular tension is allowed, feelings of relief and pleasure may evoke tears of joy.

What is the difference between anxiety and fear? Both mobilize the sympathetic nervous system in a fight or flight reaction, stimulating heart activity and respiration, and causing a rise in blood pressure. Acupressure theory correlates fear with the Kidney Meridian, and anxiety more with the Heart and Lungs, and with general systemic hyperactivity.* A common psychological distinction is that anxiety is vague and indirect, while fear is object-specific. Fear is the anticipation of a particular painful experience, while anxiety almost begs to be attached to something, and so actively looks for signs of impending misfortune. In other words, fear is aroused by actual dangers, while the causes of anxiety are often unconscious. Anxiety can be the fear of losing control over emotional drives (like sexual, assertive, and love or relationship needs) which are unconscious sources of conflict.

The anxiety-producing value of a problem can be way out of proportion to real dangers. For example, anxiety about a relationship may be stimulated by anything which triggers old fears of abandonment; there need be no actual threat of lost love. Anxiety is a rehearsal for calamity, often stimulated not by an actual impending threat, but by a *symbol* of that threat. For example, anxiety about signs of aging (receding hairlines, wrinkles, menopause) arises if these are taken as symbols of decreasing attractiveness. Anxiety over job or sexual performance is intensified if these are seen as symbols for personal worth. In other words, anxiety often comes from the stories we tell ourselves—especially the ones with tragic titles, which have the moral that "*this means* something terrible!"

"More often than not, anxiety is generated from a change in our sense of self, rather than a change in the environment," says Gaylin.[29] Anxiety comes from anything which stimulates questions about our ability to cope with change, because this rocks our sense of self-value and self-esteem. The nature of life is insecurity: we know that everything will change, but we don't know how. To tolerate the lack of sureness about *what will be*, and even about how to interpret *what is*, it is necessary

---

* For more on anxiety, see Chapter 10, Part 4, and Chapter 11, Part 2.

to have some sureness about *who I am*. If I can't know what will be, I need to know that I can get through it—whatever "it" may be. In other words, I need to know my core Self.

Kierkegaard called anxiety "the dizziness of freedom." Some new possibility is opening up, bringing a confrontation with our own potentialities, and perhaps a radical change of self-image. Anxiety is the tension of imagining *then* as a situation we might not be able to cope with. "There are few people who can stand this tension," says Perls, "so they have to fill the gap with rehearsing, planning, 'making sure,' making sure that they don't have a future. They try to hold onto the sameness, and this of course will prevent any possibility of growth or spontaneity."[30]

Some More and Less Functional Ways of Handling Anxiety

• Convert anxiety into a physical symptom like high blood pressure, chest or shoulder pain, or heart palpitations. This somatization produces a vicious cycle, because the symptoms themselves are anxiety-producing.

• Rationalize or universalize the anxiety; find a cause for the anxiety, and see it as normal under the circumstances. If the anxiety is just displaced onto something irrelevant, this defense won't work for long.

• *Do something* release the pent-up excitement. Almost anything will work, if it helps your self-esteem and counters questions about being able to cope. Talk with friends, get involved in a service activity, clean the house, exercise, go to a concert, take care of business, fix something or make something. Make love, if it brings the feeling of being loved and therefore lovable.

• Hold some points—#27, Heart source point, "B," "G" and "H"—and breathe!

• Take time to feel, and to connect with your capable core Self, like through meditation, movement, time out in nature—and by receiving Jin Shin Do!

"You are Being Hysterical, My Dear . . ."

"Hysteria," in common usage, means intense excitation caused by unmanageable anxiety or fear. In this sense, anyone may become hysterical under conditions of extreme stress. A "hysterical reaction" may be just a release of nervous tension, or it may amount to temporarily "losing it." The antidote is staying conscious of the psychic center—Shen. (The Heart source point is easily accessible and has a calming effect.)

Chronic psychological stress makes hysterical reactions more likely. Similarly, after a long habit of withholding emotions, an eventual release of feelings may look hysterical. When someone begins trying to communicate rather than suppress feelings, s/he may bounce back and forth between the extremes of avoidance and dramatics. A fund of pent-up emotional excitation can supercharge whatever first gets expressed, so that feelings seem disproportionate to the situation. The agitation and anxiety arise because emotional honesty seems risky—that's why it was avoided for so long.

"Hysterical" can also refer to a dramatic personality style. A great need to gain others' esteem and admiration makes for attention-seeking and manipulative behavior.* Because of periodic emotional outbursts, the appearance is of being very emotional, but there is "the feeling that the whole person is not participating in these effects and expressions."[31] The hysterical outbursts are not "owned," but feel rather like whirlwinds that have passed through. They are just releases of emotional excitation within a context of a general shrinking from emotionality. There is as much discomfort with *felt* emotions as in the opposite, avoidant personality style.

Hysterical tendencies that are classical indications of Heart Meridian imbalance include being easily surprised or embarrassed, blushing or giggling abruptly, talking constantly and being mentally over-excited. "Hysterical" can also refer to a thought process dominated by that which is vivid, colorful and emotionally charged. The hysterical thought process is romantic, impressionistic, and distractible, so there is often a quick movement from one fashionable thing to the next. "Hysterical attention, in other words, is easily captured," says Shapiro.[32] Getting fired up by each new wave of excitement allows escape from a mundane or painful reality. It also tends to fire others up, because enthusiasm sparks interest and excitement is contagious.

Under a superficial or theatrical warmth, there may be an inner coldness which protects against hurt or loss of love. Often, this defense goes back to a deprivation of maternal love. For example, one client suddenly curled into a fetal position, because it "felt safe," then saw herself as a child, sobbing, not wanting to go through more pain. "I feel cold, really cold," she said, recalling being hit as a child and being "absolutely powerless to do anything about it, wanting to leave but not being able to." Gradually, as she got more in touch with her body, she felt "a warmth flooding through me." She hadn't realized how closed-down her heart was. As Heart and Spleen points in the chest released, she said her hands felt like they were coming alive after a long sleep. She began making moaning sounds and then started crying. "It sounds like a child crying," she said. "It's the cry of freedom!"

---

* When the need for approval or affection is overwhelming, the hysterical personality may even threaten suicide to make an impact on others. Such threats need to be taken seriously: unfortunately, gestures can make a person just as dead as a genuine wish to die.

10. The Land of I' Revisited —Spleen-Pancreas Meridian

Part 1. SYNERGIC STATE OF I': empathy, sympathy, consideration, recollection

> "Therefore come with me
> To the palace of Nowhere
> Where all the many things are One. . . ."

"Show me where the Tao is found," a student demanded. "There is nowhere it is not to be found," Chuang Tzu replied. But the student insisted on an example. "It is in the ant," said Chuang. "Is it in some lesser being?" the student wondered. Chuang replied that the Tao is in the weeds . . . in a piece of tile . . . in a turd. At that, the student was speechless. "Why look for Tao by going 'down the scale of being' as if that which we call 'least' had less of Tao?" Chuang Tzu asked. "Tao is Great in all things, Complete in all, Universal in all, Whole in all . . . the Reality is One."[1]

The *oneness of all things* is the basic perception which infuses Taoist writings with a feeling of acceptant tranquility. A feeling of oneness also characterizes the synergic state of I'. A musician is in this synergic state when s/he is so "into" the music that it seems to permeate every pore. S/he is one with the nuances of sound, and the listener too can be transported into a state of synergic bliss. Love is perhaps the most sought-after feeling of unity. Romantic love is a satisfying resonance of two hearts, spirits and bodies. In the harmony of love-making, time stops its march and two people feel like one. Lovers are (some of the time) *empathetic*, or deeply in tune with each other.

The Taoists tell many stories of craftsmen who are similarly "in tune," or at one, with their work. The enlightened carpenter is in touch with the Tao of the wood; he empathizes with the wood, feeling into its essence. Working with the grain of the wood, his role is helping the wood to manifest its hidden potential. An example is the woodworker Ch'ing, who carved a bell stand for the Prince of Lu. Everyone marveled at its beauty, saying it seemed like the work of spirits. The Prince asked Ch'ing what his secret was.

> "I am only a craftsman, so how would I have any secret? There is one thing, however. When I am going to make a bell stand, I never let it wear out my energy. I guard my spirit, and do not expend it on trifles that are not to the point. I fast to still my mind and set my heart at rest."

This is the "fasting of the heart," which brings a feeling of inner unity. The fasting of the heart is emptying the psyche—doing without preconceptions, and getting free from limitations and preoccupations.

Spleen-Pancreas Meridian

Points of the Spleen-Pancreas Meridian

Source point—On the inside of the foot, press into the hollow above the joint of the big toe (head of the first metatarsal bone).
["Supreme Whiteness—Sp 3]

JSD #10—In the arch of the foot, find the depression below the upper joint of the first metatarsal. Press into the muscle and toward the bone.
["Grandfather Grandson"—Sp 4]

JSD #41—Measure 3 *chon* above the tip of the inner anklebone (malleolus), and press into the back edge of the inner leg bone (tibia) at the pain point. **IT IS FORBIDDEN FOR PREGNANT WOMEN.**
["3 Yin Crossing—Sp 6]

JSD #8—On the inside of the leg, feel the hollow below the head of the tibia, and press up toward this protrusion.
["Yin Mound Spring"—Sp 9]

JSD #7—With the leg straight, measure 2 *chon* above the top of the knee, and press into the middle of the bulge of the vastus medialis muscle.
["Sea of Blood"—Sp 10]

I'

mental
fatigue
lack of
concentration
over-
thinking
brooding
worry

forget-
fulness

Empathy
Sympathy
Consideration
Recollection
Over-
Concern
Over-Sympathy
(Pity)
Reminiscence

difficulty
giving &
receiving
sympathy

indifference
alienation
anxiety
obsessiveness
obsessions

30: Sp

B

Grand Lo

5: Sp

38

6

7

8

41

10

Spleen Source Point

JSD #6—This point is in the lower abdomen, just above the groin line (inguinal groove). It is about 1 *chon* higher than the top of the pubic bone, and 4 *chon* out from the midline of the abdomen.
["Home of the High Official"—Sp 13]

JSD #38—Find the intersection of the navel line and the nipple line, or measure 4 *chon* out from the navel.
["Great Horizontal"—Sp 15]

JSD #5: Sp—This point is 3 *chon* directly above #38, and just below the bottom of the the rib cage.
["Abdomen Sorrow"—Sp 16]

JSD #30: Sp—These two points are directly below #30**, in the second and third intercostal spaces. Press into the pectoralis major muscle, toward the rib cage.
["Encircling Glory"—Sp 20, "Chest Village" —Sp 19]

Grand Lo—Directly down from the underarm (axilla), on the side of the rib cage in the sixth intercostal space (or, two rib spaces below the level of the nipple).
["Big Enveloping"—Sp 21]

Examples of Local-Distal Point Combinations

Local point		*Distal point*
30: Sp	+	Grand Lo, 10, S.
38	+	5: SP, 8, S., 17
		area***
6	+	7, 41, 10

S.=Source Point

If there is a problem in any area, that place may be taken as the "local point."
For example:

8	+	10, S., 7

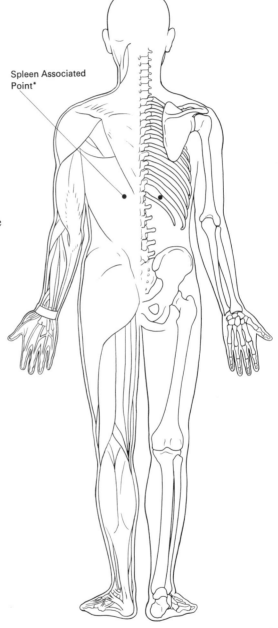

Spleen Associated Point*

---

* *Spleen-Pancreas Associated Point*—see Chapter 8 for explanation of the associated points.

** See Lung Meridian, Chapter 11.

*** Or, while you hold the other points, hold this back point with an acu-releaser (see "Pressure and Point Holding" in the last part of Chapter 1).

194

"After three days, I have forgotten gain, success and rewards. After five days, I have forgotten praise and blame or criticism. After seven days, I have forgotten form, and all thought of your highness and the court has faded away. After that, I go into the mountain forest and examine the Heavenly nature of the trees. If I find one of superlative form and I can see a bell stand there, I put my hand to the job of carving; if not, I let it go. If I had not met this particular tree, there would have been no bell stand. What happened was that my own collected thought encountered the hidden potential in the wood. From this live encounter came the work which you ascribe to spirits."[2]

Ch'ing says his carving of the marvelous bell stand began after a "live encounter" with the "Heavenly nature" of a tree. To him, the essence of the tree is a reality that can be felt. This is a state of empathy—being able to feel into and understand things and people. The word "empathy" derives from the Greek word for feeling, "pathos," and literally means being one *in feeling* with something or, more often, someone. Looking at dictionary definitions of empathy, however, I am struck by the implication that empathy is a *projection* of one's personality or an *attribution* of one's own emotions to something or someone. Was Ch'ing projecting the qualities of a bell stand onto the tree? Or was he really feeling into the nature of that tree, seeing the bell stand as a hidden potential that needed only to be realized?

And is it important whether Ch'ing was perceiving or projecting? Does it matter if the tree only *appeared* to Ch'ing to be infused with certain qualities? I think perhaps it *is* important. Seeing empathy as a projection comes from the common Western view that things and beings are innately separate. From this analytical viewpoint, a feeling of oneness is an illusion. To the Taoists, it is this perspective which is *the* great illusion, from which we need to awaken. All life is *really* one whole—all things are manifestations of a universal energy or spirit. From this integrative viewpoint, it is not only possible but natural to feel empathy for, or be one in feeling with, things and beings.

When combined with acceptance or "unconditional positive regard," empathy is a powerful healing force, in the words of Carl Rogers. To have empathy for someone is to be sensitive to the changing felt meanings of their words and behavior. Empathy, in therapy and as a way of being with another person, means entering the other person's perceptual world, being at home in it, and accepting its polarities or contradictions. Empathy is understanding. If we can be understood, we belong. We are one with others. We feel released, and confirmed in our being.

Sympathy, which has long been a favorite on most lists of virtues, is a slightly different phenomenon. It is a wonderful feeling—something we all need sometimes—but in excess it can be distracting. Sympathy implies more attachment than empathy; literally, it means *feeling-together.* It is a kinship of feeling that goes beyond empathetic understanding. "I *feel for you*"—this is sympathy. It is a togetherness of feeling which can come from or give rise to mutual liking.

The parts of a system have a "sympathetic" relationship with each other, because a change in one part affects the other parts. The body is a system in which a dis-

* From the Greek, "syn"—together and "pathos"—feeling.

order or pain in one part induces a compensating effect in another. The bodymind is a system, in which the wellness or dis-ease of the body affects the psyche, and vice versa. Families or social groups are systems, in which a change in one person can affect others. Sympathy is a harmony of feeling and action, which enables the various parts of a system to work together. But it also makes for a mutual or parallel susceptibility, because whatever affects one part or person affects the others. A common solution to this problem is to just shut down or cut off feelings.

While we were focusing on the Spleen Meridian, Jesse had an image which suggested a happier solution to being overly affected by other people's thoughts and feelings. He saw self-societal interactions as being like a pinball game. "People's comments can just serve as rubber bumpers, if I let them," he said. "I don't need to let them push me off balance. I can just bounce off them." He began to feel less scattered and more centered. As his breathing became deeper and slower, I asked Jesse to focus his attention inside his abdomen. "*It's so powerful!*" he said after a while. "It's almost too much! I don't know if I can sustain the energy . . . it's wonderful! I can feel blocks, but they're like porous dams now. I feel I can let go of even the more sensitive ones fairly easily . . . I don't need to *do* anything in particular with this energy. Instead of wanting to manifest it in this or that, I feel like I can just take it into the general world. *I know oneness now!*"

In the next couple sessions we again worked with the Spleen, focusing on the pelvic area. Jesse said, "Grounding is breathing." He made purring sounds, then said, "Everything feels like sunlight. . . . I can feel how you can have energy and take it wherever you want to take it—into a sexual place, or an intellectual or emotional one. . . . Can we put this into a bottle and put it in a knapsack? Because I want it! I'm so over-flowing with energy! I am really feeling marvelous! It feels like energy is just pouring into my abdomen."

After being silent for a while, Jesse said, "It feels like ecstasy. I can't believe it." He reached out his hands like he was cradling something. "This feeling of complete oneness, or whatever you would call it—this session has doubled my life quota of that feeling! It's the kind of comfort you want but you never seem to get. People can't give it to you. It has to come from the Mother in the sky. It's a kind of blissfulness. I think one reason life is so stressful is that we don't remember where we came from. We just have to feel our way into everything. It takes an enormous amount of time.

"Civilization and spontaneity . . . all paradoxes can be solved, because there's nothing new. You can have both; you can have the whole thing. Anything which seems like opposites, I can put together if I really spend time with it. It goes beyond my reason . . . I'm going to be it all. I'm not going to cut off my feelings. I feel strong. . . . If I let everything in my body go where it wants to go, that would be the opposite of holding! *That* is a great insight!" After a long, hearty laugh, Jesse concluded, "I can do it without gritting my teeth. I'm not going to live by denying, but by accepting. I'm not going to do it the old way anymore. It doesn't make my body feel good. It doesn't make anything feel good. . . . I think what really hurts is the resistance!"

The next week, the subject was love. "Boy, last night when I came home, my chest was absolutely locked," Jesse said. "I worked with it, breathed into it, and got it all washed out. I never even used to recognize the feeling of being blocked there." Sometimes we close the chest down because intense positive emotions are threatening. "Love can be alarming, because there's not too many places for love in this world," Jesse said. Suffering can also be hard to take. "To look the suffering in the eye and say, 'I'm not going to run from you anymore'—that feels good! If I can accept it without ducking, then I can feel the love. I'm not really afraid of love—just of having no place to take it. I want to be accepted, that's all. Sometimes it seems like nobody is there when you want them. But I would like to be there for myself."

Paradigms of Oneness

There is a saying that when we are "in the Tao," what we really need will be at hand. When we accept that what we need may not be what we had imagined, we can be *present* to life. We can see and hear and feel what *is*. We are "in the now," which is about the same place as "in the Tao." A lot of interesting things happen in the now. For example, we think about someone—and then we get a letter, or they call or come by. Is this just coincidence? Similarly, sometimes for no reason we become very concerned about someone, then find out that s/he indeed is having difficulties. Such synchronistic experiences suggest that there might be some invisible connection between persons physically distant from each other. What could that connection be, if not the energy or consciousness which, in its universal form, can be called the "Tao"? We can always get the support and sympathy we need, not only from others, but also from this larger force. Jesse called it "the comfort from the Mother in the sky."

Lao Tzu said, "I value seeking sustenance from the Mother." He described this "Mother" as a primordial nourishing and unifying force:

> "There is a thing inherent and natural,
> Which existed before heaven and earth.
> Motionless and fathomless,
> It stands alone and never changes;
> It pervades everywhere and never becomes exhausted.
> It may be regarded as the Mother of the Universe.
> I do not know its name.
> If I am forced to give it a name,
> I call it Tao, and I name it as supreme."[3]

Recently in the West, there has been a proliferation of paradigms for describing a universal energy or consciousness. Carl Jung theorized about a "collective unconscious," evidenced by the spontaneous arising of the same primordial images in people of differing backgrounds and varying cultures. Similarly, some psychologists remarked on the fact that the same invention or philosophy often arises spontaneously in different parts of the world, without any direct connection between, say, the various inventors of the steam engine. They said it is as though there is some kind of "time spirit" or "Zeitgeist." Perhaps this force which seems to move us in certain directions, at certain times, is the unified consciousness of humanity. Recently, Rupert Sheldrake has described the unity of consciousness between individuals of a species as "morphic resonance," observing that after a number of people (or rats) learn to do something, other people (or rats)—even in different parts of the world—spontaneously start doing that same thing, or can learn to do it more easily.

Similarly, modern physicists say that even the tiny electrons act like they know what the rest of the universe is doing—like they are in total agreement and harmony with everything else. Physicists started out dividing matter into smaller and smaller particles, looking for the "basic building blocks" of matter. Instead, like the Oriental mystics, what they found was a basic unity throughout the universe. Relativity theory showed that matter is a form of energy. The mass of a particle is equal to a certain amount of energy, and energy is a dynamic quality which is associated with activity or process. Therefore, particles of matter are dynamic patterns or processes, not static solid objects. And since its essence is energy, matter is mutable. Particles can be transmuted into other particles; they can be created from energy and can vanish into energy. Besides all that, the observer influences the observed, and so is a part of the process.

In short, "the whole universe appears as a dynamic web of inseparable energy patterns," or "an interconnected web of physical and mental relations whose parts are defined only through their connections to the whole," says physicist Fritjof Capra.[4] The concept of a "quantum field" is used to explain the unity and inter-relationship of all things. "The quantum field is seen as the fundamental physical entity: a continuous medium which is present everywhere in space. Particles are merely local condensations of the field; concentrations of energy which come and go, thereby losing their individual character and dissolving into the underlying field."[5]

To the Taoists, of course, the Tao was the fundamental reality. "The Tao is ever inactive, and yet there is nothing that it does not do," says Lao Tzu. The Tao is empty and formless, yet it is the source of all forms. It is like a great forcefield; its energy is called "ch'i." The ch'i condenses to form the ten thousand things; when the ch'i disperses, the material forms dissolve, or rejoin the Tao. Like the quantum field, the ch'i is a continuous medium which is present throughout space and which concentrates to form material objects.

All life hangs together in the Tao, and is nurtured by the Mother of the Universe. We are sustained not only by the fruits of the earth and the empathetic support of other people, but also by the ch'i or universal energy which surrounds and embraces us. We can experience this vital life energy, which permeates all things, just by sitting down and "forgetting." By forgetting judgments and thoughts for a time, we can sense our identity with the "Great Thoroughfare" or flow of life. Feeling a one-ness with all life is a peak experience of empathy. It leaves us feeling filled and energized, yet peaceful.

Perhaps the easiest way to feel this oneness would be to close this book and take a walk. Go to a park and wander through the trees. Go to a beach or stream, and look at the water. Go to the mountains and hike into the wilderness. If you live in the mountains, get out of that cozy cabin and explore a new part of Nature's wonder-land. As you walk through the woods, over rocks or by the water, if you listen, perhaps you will hear the music of nature, which Chuang Tzu describes as a power "blowing on a thousand different holes."

Mother Earth and Grounding

Heaven, earth and man are manifestations of one power—the Tao. Lao Tzu says, "Man follows the laws of earth, earth follows the laws of heaven, heaven follows the laws of Tao, and Tao follows the laws of its intrinsic nature."[6] Tao is the Mother of the Universe.

The earth is the mother of human and other live beings. "Mother Earth," we call her. Ancient cultures worshiped the earth mother, who was also the goddess of fertility. (Revering the heavenly father came later, as a package deal with patriarchal society structures.) The earth, which supports and feeds us, is our most direct connection with the universe. We can see and touch this foundation of our physical being and source of our bodily nourishment.

The earth is where we start from, so feeling our unity with the earth is a basic part of tuning into the Tao. When we connect with Mother Earth, she connects us with the universe. That is why walking, hiking, riding or skiing can be forms of meditation. It is also why ancient Chinese landscape paintings have such a mystical, spiritual feeling. Like the Chinese poets, these painters were seeing the universe in a tree; they were feeling the Tao in the stream, the mist and the mountains.

"Everything that is created by the Universe meets in the center and is absorbed by the Earth," says the *Nei Ching*.[7] The earth is the source of life for all plant and animal creatures. Thus the most ancient drawing of the "five elements" shows the earth in the center of the other elements. Likewise, the earth organs—the Stomach and Spleen/Pancreas—are called the "center within the body" because of their central position in the body and their central importance in the process of transforming food into energy.

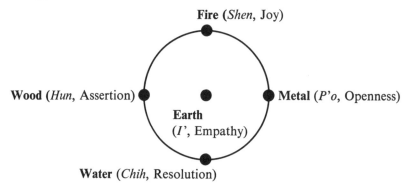

Fire (*Shen*, Joy)

Wood (*Hun*, Assertion)　　　　Metal (*P'o*, Openness)

Earth
(*I'*, Empathy)

Water (*Chih*, Resolution)

Similarly, earth has a central place in the psychological picture. Feeling a oneness with the earth, and with other beings on the earth, is nourishing and energizing, and yields a more joyful attitude towards life. Coming down to earth and feeling grounded is encouraged by balancing the earth meridians. As the earth is the center of our lives, so feeling in balance with the earth forces brings a feeling of being centered within ourselves. Centering is contacting the essential natural self which wants to dance and play on planet Earth. This basic self never loses touch with the ground of its being.

Wait a minute—isn't Shen the essential Self? Yes, but in another sense the part of the psyche called I' is the essential self; it is the bodily, earthly part of ourself, with all its instinctive needs for contact with other human beings. Its wellness has a lot to do with the wellness of Shen, the inner spirit; thus release of the Spleen-Pancreas and

Stomach meridians, especially in the chest area, often facilitates opening the heart. Armoring at points like #30: Sp and #s3–4 helps to constrict the breathing to suppress feelings of hurt, anxiety or even pleasurable excitement. These tensions in the pectoral muscles are part of the primary defense against feelings.

To get back to earth, here is a good description of what it means to have a balanced "earth element," from Dianne Connelly:

> "Being *grounded* is an existential experience of who we are in relationship
> to the Earth, that is, balanced and stable among the forces of the world . . .
> Equanimity and equilibrium stem from our connection with the Earth.
> Being connected, feeling ourselves to be an integral part of the life within
> and around us has to do with the Earth. Having a centre from which we
> operate, a kind of order and harmony emanating from within, rather than
> chaotic desperate energy, is a description of Earth within us. Being at home
> with one's self, integrated, unobsessed and at ease wherever we are is a
> description of Earth. We are balanced and centered within, interacting and
> connected without."[8]

Being "down-to-earth" means being practical and in touch with life's essential realities. To be "earthy" is to be simple and natural. An earthy person radiates vitality and sensuality, and has a hearty and practical attitude that "calls a spade a spade." The Taoists, for all their spirituality, were earthy. (For example, consider Chuang Tzu's statement that the Tao is in a turd. . . .) They were centered within and one with what is without. They found simplicity in oneness. Of such a one, Chuang Tzu says:

> "The ten thousand things may all be capsizing and turning over at the same
> time right in front of him and it can't get at him and affect what's inside—
> so where could he go and not be at ease?"[9]

It is said that growth and development depend to a large extent on the proper functioning of the earth organs, the Spleen-Pancreas and Stomach. The Spleen-Pancreas is "the official who distributes nourishment."[10] When we absorb the fruits of the earth, they first go to the stomach. Then the powerful pancreatic juice is secreted (into the small intestine) and plays a leading role in digesting all kinds of food—starches, proteins and fats. The pancreas also secretes insulin, which is crucial for carbohydrate metabolism. A concentrated intake of simple sugars stimulates the production of insulin—and over time can lead to hypersensitivity of the pancreas and problems with the blood sugar level (as we will discuss in part four of this chapter).

The Spleen-Pancreas is also called the "official of energy transport," who distributes energy throughout the bodymind system. To me, this is illustrated by the energizing and balancing feeling which often follows from holding various Spleen points, like #10 and the "grand lo." The classics also say the Spleen "unifies the blood." Its points are used for blood excreting problems, including all kinds of menstrual difficulties.* (The lymph tissue of the spleen does influence the blood by filtering spent red cells and foreign substances from the blood.) The Spleen Meridian also influences the transformation of liquids; edema and diarrhea may be symptoms of its imbalance.

* The Kidney and Liver Meridians may also be important (see Chapters 12 and 13).

Decreased ability to derive nourishment from food, energy depletion and lethargy can indicate weakness of the earth element. The nourishment and wellness of body and mind, and the day-to-day energy level, depends on its well-functioning. A strong need for emotional nourishment and support can, likewise, indicate weakness or imbalance in the land of I'. Not feeling grounded and strong within, we seek support from without, craving the sympathy of others. At an extreme, we can't even function without others' support and approval, because we can't nourish ourselves. We seem to always be saying or thinking, "I need." Perhaps what we really want and need is for someone to pay attention to us in a way that will help us to get grounded and feel our own centers.

Not to overlook the obvious, a person who intensely craves support and sympathy may really need it, but a perpetual craving for sympathy usually has roots in the past. It may feel like there is a hole inside—like the craving for sympathy is so deep that there is despair about ever satisfying it. Sometimes the emotional craving turns into a craving for food, to compensate for the lack of emotional nourishment.

In short, if mommie didn't hold and love us, if daddy didn't support us, if neither understood us, or if we had few friends, we missed out on lots of good stuff. Later we might want to make up for lost time—or lost love. To fill the old hole, we need to get supported, understood and sympathized with. To get sympathy, we need to be able to give it, and to ask for it by communicating feelings and needs. Also we need to find our inner centers and learn to nourish ourselves. That is like having sympathy for all the aspects of ourselves.

Thought and Mental Monarchy

The *Nei Ching* says "the mysterious powers of the earth" are related to "contemplation," and "of the emotions they create consideration and sympathy." I' is the "seat of thought" and "directs recollection." I', or the "spiritual resource" related to the Spleen, "controls the ideas and thoughts."[11] Why is this? Basically, it just is. Partly, perhaps, it is because energy is required for mental as well as physical processes, and the Spleen is "the official of energy transport." The Spleen, or the energy it distributes, nourishes the muscles and so influences physical movement. It also nourishes the mind and so influences thought, contemplation and memory. Balancing the Spleen Meridian can help improve concentration, the ability to synthesize, and memory.

However, spending an excessive amount of time up in the head can be a way of avoiding the body and the feelings. This way of posturing oneself in the world is imbalanced, because it is top-heavy; the head is energized and the body is deprived. To move out of the head and back into the body, points of the earth meridians can be helpful. Here theory merges with personal reality, for in the midst of this heady work called writing I have often found myself holding the "grand lo" points, when feeling mentally blocked or ungrounded.

Being so up in the head that we are out of touch with the body just doesn't feel good. "A marionette!" said one woman, during release of the Spleen [focusing on the #6]. "I get an image of a marionette with strings attached. The strings are pulling the legs and moving the body," she said with anger. Being "up in the head" is like being a puppet, moved by mental impulses, unable to move as a whole. As she breathed into the blocked places, the image changed. "First I saw the separation of the parts, the individuality of each part, and then I saw the parts fitting together into a whole."

I'll let Jesse make the final comments on the problem of mental monarchy. "The most beautiful parts of myself I'm sacrificing to a rational god which has to be appeased!" he said. "I'm realizing that everything will be okay, just being what it is, without all this judging. It's *so* unnecessary! It's like a crazy notion that I'm supposed to somehow make it all right—like there's some rational sense which has to be appeased by making huge sacrifices to this big rational center. Judging is one component of living, but it's got too much control. It's got me doing all these exercises—like staying after school and writing on the blackboard, 'I shall not be a bad boy.' Ylch! I mean, I don't *need* to do that after school. There are lots of other things to do! I wish I had a computer that would transform judging into *accepting*. Or some formula—stamp three times, whirl around, say five Oms, and suddenly you're in an acceptant place!" After breathing into his chest for a while he said in an 'aha!' voice, "The key is love! Not just regular love, but really letting people be. Not just people, but events and things."

Part 2. EXTREME EMOTIONS OF I':
over sympathy, over-concern, or pity

The *Nei Ching* says "extreme sympathy" is injurious to the stomach and spleen-pancreas.[11] What is "extreme sympathy"? It is being so concerned about the needs of others that our own needs don't get met, or trying to please others to the point of being obsequious. Such extreme devotion to others may seem like a Christian virtue, but what Christ said was to love others *as* yourself. Nourish others *as*, not instead of, yourself. The best way to serve others is to also take care of ourselves. In fact, we have to be able to take care of ourselves in order to be able to take care of others.

The capacity to feel sympathy for someone is a measure of our caring attachment to that person. Concern arises within sympathetic relationships. We feel concern when we sense that a loved one is troubled, or feel that our relationship with that person is threatened. Concern can arise to call our attention to something that needs to be dealt with. "Over-concern" is being too plugged into something or someone. Over-concern is also a natural response to perplexing problems. It is an attempt at doing something about the problems but, ironically, excessive concern can actually *create* problems.

When the excessive concern is continual, "worry" is a good word for the distressed feeling.* The classics say that worry causes the consciousness and energy to coagulate and become stagnant, in effect paralyzing the body.[12] Over-concern is a yang or active state, but in the chronic case it causes energic blockage, muscular tension, and physical and mental fatigue.

Over-concern and over-sympathy can be smothering to others, as well as paralyzing to oneself. It's rather like what happens if you are so concerned about your house plants that you water and fertilize them too much. The result is about the same as if you'd just neglected to water them. A balanced concern for your plants means observing them and being responsive to their needs. Similarly, a balanced sympathy towards other people means paying attention to their needs, but not suffocating them with excessive (and probably unwanted) concern.

Do you tend to get caught up in "over-sympathy" and "over-concern"? Do you spend a lot of time thinking about others' feelings, needs, words and actions? Do you tend to take others' feelings personally, or too often wonder what they meant by this or that? Do you concern yourself a lot about pleasing others? Do you take on their problems and try to fix things for them? Or maybe do you also try to fix *them*? And do you spend as much or more time worrying about the future, or thinking about the past, as you do focusing on the present? If your answer to one or more of these questions is "yes," it is likely that you are familiar with "over-sympathy" and "over-concern."

Excessive concern is a habit, usually learned from our childhood caretakers. Heather, for example, often expressed concern about others' opinions or problems,

---

* "Worry" is also sometimes related to the Lung Meridian, but "worry" can be a loose translation of "anxiety." The Lung and Spleen are closely related in "Five Elements" theory, so the condition of one affects the other. Both meridians are important for release of the chest.

though she was frustrated at her mother's constant concerns, which limited her independence. Heather's Spleen points were very blocked; during her menstruation and accompanying bouts of cramps, the #6 and #38 were especially tense. While focusing on release of these areas, I asked Heather to rate her tendency to be concerned about others' feelings, on a scale from one to ten. "Ten!" she exclaimed. "That's my whole problem!"

Then she had the image of herself walking a long ways, past her father's room, then her brother's room, then her mother's room, en route to the kitchen and her own room. She took a similar walk in her mind, as she concerned herself about everybody else's welfare and worried about their reactions to everything, before she got around to the kitchen—or, to nourishing herself. Her challenge seemed to be getting past each "room" without emotional interference.

"But how can I avoid feeling the emotions of others as though they were my own?" Heather asked. I asked if she could recall feeling just plain indifferent. She remembered feeling like she "just didn't care," after getting "really angry" at her parents. According to the *Nei Ching* (and common experience) "anger counteracts sympathy."[11] Self-assertion also controls sympathy; i.e., asserting our own needs keeps sympathy from turning into over-concern about others' needs. However, to be constantly angry or assertive is a rather yang way of handling concern—and might produce more concerns! The other necessary antidote is taking care of our own needs and nourishing ourselves—with appropriate foods and supportive relationships, by treating ourselves to fun and relaxation, through doing things that bring joy, and by noticing the beauty in each day—just in simple things like clouds, trees and sunsets.

During the following month, Heather was "doing better about not plugging into others," but the old habit of over-concern kept trying to take over. One week, because of digestive problems, I asked her to focus on the "C" area, breathe into it, and get an image of the tension there (which felt like a tight knot to my fingers). "It's like a ball," she replied. "It's like I've compressed everything into a small, hard ball so that I can get on with my life." Could she visualize that ball evaporating? "I'm afraid it would get messy." Because she was afraid to spontaneously express herself, Heather often hid her concerns behind a nice smile and inside a knotted abdomen.* After looking at several problems that seemed to be stuck in her guts, she realized that "a lot of it has to do with taking on other people's concerns, rather than just letting them be and insisting on the same courtesy for myself!"

Sympathy, or feeling for others, requires energy. That's why sympathy can be an "evil emotion," when it is extreme or prolonged. In the *Nei Ching*, another translation for "extreme sympathy" is "pity," which can be like an acute attack of sympathy, or taking others' problems upon ourselves.[13] Pity is feeling sorry for someone who is suffering, and whom we perceive as weak or unfortunate. In this sense, we might pity handicapped, retarded, destitute, grief-stricken or ill persons. Pity can also imply a slight contempt. In this sense, we might "pity" a person who is so mixed-up, immature, narrow-minded, fearful or bitter that s/he seems bent on misery or self-destruction. Here, the pity is perverted by anger, but nonetheless the emotional involvement shows concern. If the anger can be released, sympathy may remain, and the beginnings of understanding may replace the scorn. To catalyze the transforma-

* See Chapter 12, Part 1, for her discovery of how to transform fear into resolution.

tion of pity into empathy or sympathy, we can consider the ways that we too have been (and are) weak, mixed-up, immature, narrow-minded, fearful or bitter. Sympathy and empathy can be expressed by helping or just *hearing* others, and by the general process of moving along our paths in life with as much integrity as possible—staying in touch with our own essence and tuning into the essences of others.

Reminiscence

Reminiscing about old times can be a lot of fun. To talk and laugh about the past, with friends or family, is one of life's pleasures. How can reminiscence be an "evil" emotion? By being extreme, of course. Reminiscence is a backward-looking emotion. Prolonged psychic journeys into the past can interfere with balance and grounding in the present. I think we sense this possibility even while we are enjoying the act of reminiscing. In a way, we have re-entered an old world, by recalling past events, sights and feelings—and perhaps even the sounds, smells and flavor of former times. After a while, usually, we want to get back to the here and now.

Remembering the past may be a necessary part of self-reflection, and of considering problems and contemplating the most appropriate courses of action to take. But excessive reminiscence creates imbalance by concentrating energy and consciousness in the brain. Thinking about the past leads to thoughts about what might have been. Thinking about what might have happened, or not happened, "if only I had done things differently" brings regret about the past. Prolonged reminiscence generates "stuckness" and stirs up distressed feelings. It is a fixation on the past which restrains movement through the present. Kok Yuen Leung explains:

> "Reminiscence is an emotion which concentrates the consciousness to consider problems. Before the Will changes direction (alters its emphasis), the spirit considers past lessons through the process of reminiscing. However, too much reminiscing, or brooding fruitlessly over the past, can cause changes in the Spleen and Heart (Shen). The energy concentrates to consider and recollect, but this can soon change to coagulation" (of P'o).[12]

Excessive reminiscing also brings a *feeling* of being coagulated or stuck, as I discovered about fifteen years ago, after moving to Los Angeles. Feeling lonely and uprooted, I comforted myself by reminiscing, which soon turned into "brooding fruitlessly" over what could have been. I felt like I was stuck in slow motion or half asleep. My thoughts seemed like "muggy, sticky, slow, yin, egocentric blurs." My journal from that time sounds like it was written by two people—one insisting "I *must* be my own person," and the other busy being concerned about living up to the doctrines of others. I wanted to write, but I couldn't concentrate or synthesize my ideas. My physical symptoms were likewise characteristic of Spleen Meridian imbalance—an obsession with food, amenorrhea, and periodic indigestion.

I was impressed that acupuncture and acupressure not only helped my physical symptoms, but also seemed to make me feel more energetic. After a while, I complained that "it gives me *too much* energy—I don't know what to do with it and just get more uptight physically and mentally." I needed to find channels for the unbound energy. "I feel looser," says a later journal entry. "I feel like I am coming home. . . . The process is simply listening to my body and my feelings, and learning to do *what is* for me, now, knowing that *what is* always changes." That journal ended abruptly, for I started to instead write articles (most of them unpublished). The last entry of the journal was:

> "The house was lonely and empty, and I was afraid.
> Then it was peopled with my imagination, and with the story-article
>   emerging from my brain and from the ether."

Re-connecting with the body (like through acupressure and exercise) helps to transform reminiscence, because being in touch with the body is being *in the present*. The feeling is like "coming home," or really *being here*. It's like all the senses are awake, and there is a deliciousness to ordinary life—just to the sight, sound, smell, taste and touch of things. For this delightful feeling to become a way of life, the whole bodymind has to wake up. Releasing and balancing the Spleen Meridian can be an effective alarm clock.

Reminiscence can be transmuted "into the self correctional exercise of learning from experience," says Leung.[12] Talking with friends is a way to "vent the spleen," and it can be a way of learning from experience, because others' responses can help put our thoughts and feelings into perspective. Writing, drawing, singing or playing music are a few other ways to let out feelings about "old stuff," and to learn from experience. One of the simplest exercises in self-reflection is journal writing-just sitting down with a blank book and a pen, and writing whatever comes into your mind. Basically, this is "free association"—allowing one thought, feeling or image to lead to another. It is a way to learn from ourselves by "working through" disturbing thoughts, feelings and attitudes until we uncover their sources.

Reminiscence and the Psychotherapeutic Process

Free association is basic to the Western psychotherapy process. The client is encouraged to just let thoughts and feelings come up. S/he is also encouraged to remember the past, so as to uncover childhood traumas or introjected attitudes underlying present conflicts. In other words, the client is encouraged to reminisce! This sounds regurgitative—and it can be. It can also be transformative, when the mental recall and understanding are charged with strong feeling. Insight, catharsis and *just feeling understood* are some elements that can make this process therapeutic, and keep it from being prolonged reminiscence. The emerging of intense feelings and the unbinding of long-suppressed energy can be anxiety-producing, but the eventual result is a lower anxiety level, a higher self-esteem level and being more at peace with oneself.

The Eastern meditative process seems to be just the opposite. Stilling the mind is basic to all the Eastern forms of meditation. Instead of letting the mind go wherever it will, the emphasis is fixing the mind on something—for example, on the breath, the inner energy centers, or a mantra. This sounds repressive—and it can be. It can also be transformative. Just by letting go of each passing thought that drifts through the mind, there comes a gradual sinking into the core of oneself, and an increased self-awareness. Here, too, the unbinding of stagnant energy, the arising of new sensations and the discovery of new levels of reality can be anxiety-producing. The overall effect is relaxation and increased tranquility.

Jin Shin Do is a synthesis of these approaches, and in a way, so was Taoist meditation. *The Secret of the Golden Flower* says it is important to fix attention on the inner centers, like on "the point which lies exactly between the eyes," because then "the light streams of its own accord." The circulation of the light is the circulation of energy and consciousness. The *Golden Flower* also says that "the light is contemplation," and that contemplation (or self-reflection) is part of meditation.

> "[While meditating] one must not stay sitting rigidly if worldly thoughts come up, but one must examine where the thought is, where it began, and where it fades out. Nothing is gained by pushing reflection further. One must be content to see where the thought arose, and not seek beyond the point of origin. . . . Together we want to bring the states of the heart to rest, that is true contemplation. . . . When the flight of the thoughts keeps extending further, one should stop and begin contemplating. Let one contemplate and then start fixating [meditating on the circulation of energy] again."[14]

In Jin Shin Do, the first emphasis is relaxing the body. That may require lulling the conscious mind to sleep. Relaxing the neck and face, and balancing the earth meridians, may help quiet down the hyperactive movement of the mind from one concern to another. The client is encouraged to *focus attention on the tension* and breathe through it. As the tensions are releasing, if feelings or memories come up they are taken as messages from the inner Self—to be looked at, listened to or contemplated. Just *being with* any feelings or images that come up often leads us to their origin in past experiences and in old introjected messages.

Being open to images or emotions that come up, while focusing on bodymind feelings, can allow upsetting memories and suppressed feelings to emerge. For example, the memory of a traumatic sexual experience or of old negative messages about sexuality may come up during a focus on release of #6, in the groin. In a sense this is "free association," but it is also just listening to the body. It is not only that the groin area carries sexual associations, but also that the tensions there were originally developed to defend against pain or distress, or to suppress conflictual urges. On the body level, that defense is still operating.

The emergence of feelings and memories related to certain body tensions may be "reminiscence," but it is also self-reflection. Whatever has been generating tension and influencing bodymind feelings is *present*, even if it stems from the past and is largely unconscious. To become conscious of such underlying feelings or attitudes, focus your attention on a tense or sore place, while holding it, and try asking yourself: "Why does this need to be tight? What does this tension feel like, or remind me of? How would it feel to let go of this?" As the tension relaxes, let your breath take you down inside yourself, down to the spiritual and energic core where you will find synergic feelings like empathy, sympathy and love.

If upsetting memories arise while you are doing Jin Shin Do with someone, it helps to remember that the kaleidoscopic shifting of emotions and feelings is natural. People will most likely get to a more peaceful and happy place by just accepting and following feelings through their natural cycle. If tears, sobs or angry sounds come up, people may need your assurance that it's okay to feel what they're feeling, and to feel it in your presence. If you are empathetic—if your inner spirit reaches out to and touches the spirit of the other—that in itself can make it safe to feel. If you say, "It's okay," just that can be enough, if you really *know* that it *is* okay to let go to your feelings. Other people usually doesn't want you to fix up their feelings or their lives. They just want you to be there for them, fully present to them.

Part 3.   HYPOACTIVE I': lack of concentration, forgetfulness, absent-minded, indifference, alienation, difficulty-giving/receiving sympathy

Hypoactivity of I' can correlate with physical and mental fatigue, muscular weakness or lack of tone, poor appetite and digestion, and abdominal tautness or slight pain. The general feeling is of being under-nourished, physically and emotionally. The person may sleep without getting rested, and may be tired in the morning or all day. There may be difficulty in giving sympathy, and in receiving it, so that the appearance is of not caring about others, or not having much sympathy for their needs. However, only sociopathic personalities are truly lacking in sympathy and concern for others.* The feeling of just not caring can be due to physical, mental or emotional fatigue, or not having the *energy* to care. Apparent unconcern can also be a defensive cover-up, designed to hide the fact of caring to reduce anxiety-provoking feelings of vulnerability. When the feeling of indifference and non-relatedness is prolonged, the phenomenon is called "alienation."

In the past several decades, social psychologists have expressed concern about how widespread the feeling of alienation is in our society. Several have related it to what Erich Fromm called the "thing orientation"—the emphasis on possessing, and the equation of personal worth with *how much* one is worth. In the fifties, Fromm saw the "alienated personality" as the product of a society in which affluence was the aim and "automaton conformity" the means. Social movements of the sixties countered this materialistic orientation and brought humanistic values back in fashion. Widespread protest against conformity to the "establishment" centered on basic issues like racial integration, the end of a futile and unjust war, and equality of the sexes. Social attitudes became freer.

The seventies brought a focus on personal growth and communication—on inner and outer relatedness. Now, in the eighties, "property consciousness" is also becoming popular, and the after-tax dollar has again been proclaimed by many as the measure of success (though with more ecological and psychological awareness than in the fifties). A sad side-effect is that many people think they are nothing, and feel left out and alienated, if they are not materially successful.

Materialistic orientations tend to get balanced by more spiritual or wholistic orientations. Things keep changing, as we explore various extremes on our way to finding the whole. With any extreme there is the sense that something is missing. Often we rush to embrace the opposite extreme, hoping that what is missing will be found there. In a sense it can be so, because seeing another aspect of ourselves and of life is seeing more of the whole. Ultimately, however, what's missing is a sense of inner and outer wholeness—awareness of the whole Self and of the basic wholeness of all Nature.

As Fromm pointed out, part of what's missing in the "thing orientation" is a concern for what really matters, like love, beauty, life itself—and the life of the Self.

---

* A sociopathic or antisocial personality disorder may involve a rather severe imbalance of I' and Hun. Symptoms include antisocial behavior, low frustration tolerance, impulsivity and lying. The person may be very charming, but is incapable of loyalty, of long-term caring, and of feeling guilt.

Experiencing oneself as a commodity is the opposite of experiencing *oneself*. Paradoxically an antidote to alienation is having *a sense of self*, because that is what
allows the experience of relatedness to others and to nature. "The alienated person
is out of touch with himself as he is out of touch with any other person," said
Fromm.[15]

Being in touch with oneself means feeling the bodymind unity and acknowledging
all the changing aspects of one's Self. This brings the discovery of having *something*
in common with everyone, and so increases the feeling of relatedness to others.
Experiencing all of oneself involves getting acquainted with the wild part of ourselves,
which wants to freely move, feel and relate to others. This part protests our alienation from our bodies, each other and Nature. It craves just to hear the wind blowing
through the trees, to listen to the birds and watch the animals playing, to run and
laugh and sing.

Indifference is a lack of feeling towards someone or something; alienation is a lack
of feeling relatedness towards others in general. Indifference and alienation are parallels to a physical symptom of Spleen Meridian deficiency—lack of skin sensation or
numbness of feeling. A numbness of feeling towards others is often a defense against
the risks of real relatedness, or the anxiety of exposing real feelings. Such indifference
may be cultivated to better get on with the business of obtaining things and succeeding in life, or because focusing on things seems safer than investing in relationships.
When the assumed indifference stops being self-protective, there may be a gradual
awareness of a deep sense of aloneness, or of not having felt loved and appreciated.

A Force Field of Indifference

In her late twenties, married and very involved with her husband's business and
children, Eve did not appear to be alone or alienated. Yet she complained of sometimes feeling an indifference that was "like being encapsulated under layers and
layers of protection." At an unconscious level she felt very much separate from
others. During work with her deficient earth meridians, Eve saw herself as a little
girl, with jam all over her pink dress. "I would always get everything all over those
nice little dresses," she said. She associated this image with "feeling expectancies from
other people" and remembered knowing, as a child, that getting pleasure from others
depended on having certain expressions or acting certain ways. "Now I'm aware that
I start to tense up when I feel such expectations. I used to give the impression that I
didn't give a shit about what others thought. I really tried to keep up an outer
crust."

Eve said that her energy had been low, she had been forgetful, and she'd had
difficulty with concentration in the past few months. Her menstruation was irregular
and difficult, and supposedly she couldn't conceive, due to an "infantile uterus."
She'd been feeling "like everyone's notepad" and was tired of taking care of all the
details. "When I feel this way, I withdraw my energy and make a force field around
myself," she said. "I cloak myself in indifference. I finally figured out that it's the
indifference that upsets people so!" The indifference was a defense that had originated in childhood needs to protect herself—from others, and from her own anger.
When Eve cloaked herself in this protective indifference, other people got frustrated
at not being able to connect with her. Their angry or insensitive words and acts

would "prove" to Eve (or to the little child inside) that they didn't really care about her, so that her indifference was right.

After a few minutes of silence, Eve said she was feeling a lot of intense energy built up inside herself. Where in her body did she feel this? Eve put her hands over the solar plexus [♯5 and "C" areas]. "It's like a huge, gray monster, that can be real concentrated," Eve said, crying. "I've been trying to kill some part of myself, but I can't do that anymore. . . . It's like being in a rocket, somehow encapsulated under layers and layers. . . . When it started, it seemed like it was okay—just a little bit of armoring, to maintain some sort of balance, so I wouldn't be completely crushed. It *was* all right then; it had a function. But now the protection is what's crushing me! But I'm so scared of being tender." With that, more tears came up.

Eve told me about an image she'd had in childhood. It was of herself as a woman, walking down a corridor in some busy place, with people all around her. "Somehow I'd kind of stand out. I'd be walking assertively, like I was really going somewhere. There was this power field or force field around me, and when I got to where I was going, people would be listening to me, respecting me. It was like there was a quiet, peaceful power inside me—and because of *that* people were around me, and we would confer about things. But to be that woman, I'd have to open up *so much*, and trust *so much!*" In this image, Eve's "force field" emanated from a quiet inner power, which *attracted* people to her; it was not just a defensive mechanism. It was a "power field"—an extension of her core energy. Perhaps this image was saying that Eve needed to contact her inner power and let her energy radiate out into the world, instead of using it to shield herself from the world.

Some of the psychic layers, which Eve described as somehow encapsulating herself, were composed of suppressed anger. She said it felt like a hurricane or a volcano inside. Pain in the diaphragm area [♯5 and ♯17] was a long-standing problem. Eve associated this tension with the old anger, and with just "keeping on keeping on," doing what others and society expected of her, rather than really manifesting her power. "I'm afraid that my power is not okay," she said, "or I get anxious when I feel it. Maybe because of all the anger. For so long I just kept getting stabbed. It's like all of that, inside me, is saying 'no, no, no!' "

Feeling anger is often anxiety-producing, perhaps because of an old fear that we will be punished for any expression of anger. Feeling our personal power can also be anxiety-producing, perhaps because its intensity can feel similar to that of anger. In fact, assertive power and anger *are* directly related; anger is the more extreme form of the *motivation to do*. Anger needs to be released through activity and assertiveness. When anger is not expressed and transformed, it can decrease sympathy and produce feelings of indifference. [Anger creates hyperactivity of Hun, which "over-controls" and eventually weakens I'.] The more energy is used to suppress anger, the less energy is available for sympathetic concern. To reverse her indifference, Eve needed to vent her suppressed angers. At first this brought anxiety, but as she accepted her anger, she also gradually became more comfortable with her assertive power.

During a session focusing on release of the ♯6 area, Eve began to cry. After a few minutes, I asked, "Where are you?" Haltingly she replied, "My brother . . . my father. . . ." Hitting the table with her fists, she exclaimed, "So much stuff about what girls *should* do! From all of society—school, teachers, principals, the neighborhood kids, my parents talking about what people will think. . . . Stop!" Sobbing, she continued, "When my brothers would hit me, and I'd be trying to tell them to stop, they'd tell me to stop breathing so funny. They'd try to make me breathe the right way, and I'd tell them, 'I can't, I can't.'"

"This is the same feeling as when my father would hit me—all kind of tingly all over," Eve said after a while. "It's a spacey feeling, *like I'm not here*. It's like I can't find my arms." She was crying and gasping. After breathing slowly and visualizing energy going into her arms, she pounded the table, saying "I asked him to stop, but he wouldn't stop!" She stopped talking. Her body became immobile, as the old defenses took over. I held the #30: Sp points with the "grand lo," #10 and the source point. After a while Eve said, "It felt like all the muscles around my ribs were crunching me, closing in. It was the same as when my father would hit me—my whole upper body would tingle and then be numb. . . . Then if I sobbed and 'breathed funny,' he would hit me more. I'd try to control the sobs by holding my breath, but I couldn't instantly stop it. He would hit me, saying 'Stop breathing that way! There's no reason for you to breathe that way!'" She was crying, and I was crying too, imagining how it would feel to be hit because you were crying. After a while Eve said, "I just want to stand up straight without *hate* again. When I would get hurt, I would apologize. Whatever I did. I'd tell him I didn't mean it, and he'd tell me that I talked funny. Oh-h-h. And I would think, doesn't he love me?'"

It wasn't hard to understand why Eve had developed a defensive force field of indifference. A couple weeks later, trying to breathe through a sudden pain in the #17 area, she noticed herself automatically holding her breath upon feeling pain, and realized that this happened with emotional pain as well. As a child Eve had learned to suppress her breathing, to hold back hurt feelings that wanted to sob out their pain. An appearance of indifference was accomplished with the help of chest and diaphragm armoring [including at Spleen, Lung and Liver points]. As it began to release, Eve felt "a beautiful tenderness."

But there was a conflict about letting go to it. "My experience for a long time was that if I would be tender, I would be crushed," she said. "I felt ostracized by my family and pushed away. When I was sick and weak, my mom would say, 'Eve, you're so difficult—why don't you just stay away from people when you're sick.'" Sobbing, Eve remembered her mother often saying "You're so difficult!" Just allowing herself to feel the hurt and anger gradually brought Eve in touch with a powerful inner energy. "When I let myself get into this energy, and just be it, when I let myself gain access to it and let it flow, it feels so good! After so long!"

While we were focusing on release of mid-back tension, Eve remembered a grade school teacher who had accused her of things she hadn't done, and then told her parents that Eve hadn't handed in her work and was doing poorly. Not believing Eve's statements to the contrary, they made her stay home and do the work over. It turned out that Eve's papers, along with those of some other children, had not been filed, but this was discovered later. "For months my mother believed her, and told me it was just my damned negative energy that didn't let things come out right. Finally I cried in the principal's office, and the teacher said I was crazy. My mother took me for psychiatric evaluation. They gave me a bunch of physical tests including a spinal tap."

A sudden pain in the middle of her back [#17 area] reminded Eve of the pain she'd had after that spinal tap. "The doctor told me I'd feel a little pin prick as she ap-

212

proached my spine. I was afraid it would be a lot more than a pin prick, so my muscles tightened up. I couldn't relax. The doctor said, 'I can't believe how tight her muscles are. It's like going through a brick wall.' Then she told me, 'You're going to have to relax, or I'll have to go through your muscles.' She shoved the needle in, and after that I couldn't walk for two or three months." Eve took pain-killers and muscle relaxants, but the muscle spasms in her back were excruciating. "It was like I was in a fog," Eve said. "Sometimes I was delirious with pain. When I was conscious, I felt humiliated that my *father* had to carry me to the bathroom."

One day Eve's mother accused her of being purposefully manipulative, self-destructive and rejecting of attention, even as a child. "I didn't shrink away from her words this time," Eve said. "I'm not willing to be her victim, like when I was a child—nor her rescuer, like when I was older. She asked what I had ever done for myself. I said 'nearly everything!'" In a sense Eve had gotten where she was by herself, and she needed to acknowledge herself for that. Yet she was *not* by herself now. Anger had given her the strength to leave home, and later to leave other abusive situations. But now she was less motivated by anger and more by feeling sympathetic connections with others. The anger was still dominant towards her mother; anger at parents is often the first to come and the last to go. Some of this anger may be saying, "See who I am! Acknowledge me! I need your sympathy and understanding."

Eve's armoring was by now significantly decreased, and she was increasingly aware of her physical reactions to emotional stress. During a painful menstrual period, Eve felt a connection between her pelvic tension [♯15 and ♯6] and diaphragm armoring. "I held points like ♯6 and ♯7, and did hara breathing for the pain," she reported. "I became aware that my jaw was clenched and my diaphragm felt like a tight fist. Finally I threw up. It felt like I had to, because of the energic chaos. Afterwards my diaphragm felt looser and my pelvis was less tight." While I was holding ♯6 with Spleen distal points, Eve's legs began to feel shaky. Memories of childhood conflicts about sexuality came up. She recalled feeling shame and embarrassment at age ten, because of not having a shirt on. Memories of being sexually approached, and having a man exhibit his penis to her, brought up the remembered feeling that her body was bad. "No wonder it has taken so much work to feel good about myself!"

"At the bottomline, I just want to be open and free of all this garbage," Eve said. "I want to be able to have my magic. I'm sick of cutting myself off—from all of myself, from my feelings. I'm tired of staying up in my head, trying to figure it all out. Just breathing barely down there, in my chest, just to exist. But not enough to live." Crying, Eve exclaimed, "I don't want to be afraid to be my own self anymore, or to be afraid of my own family any more. I don't care what my parents did or didn't do. I mean, I'm not living with them anymore! I just want to get rid of the old shit. I want to be me."

Eve felt anxious about letting others see her whole Self, yet angry when she suppressed herself. The "force field" of indifference was a protection against being misunderstood and hurt. The facade of "not giving a shit" shielded a sensitive person who did care, very much, about others, and about being accepted *for herself*. To drop the shield and freely *be* herself, she had to reject old introjected thoughts about being unlovable and "too much for anyone to handle." (The story of her journey, to accepting and loving herself, is continued in the next part of this chapter.)

Real relatedness is being present with others where they are, and being honest about where you are—but not forcing it on others. Empathy is being involved, yet also in a sense standing back and witnessing the flow of things. There is freedom and power in this feeling of empathetic *presence*. Eve said it felt like "core level changes" inside herself. "Sometimes now I just watch my environment responding, and I feel this ebb and flow of energy and feeling between myself and others. I feel this connection, this oneness. Instead of feeling always dissatisfied, I have a new sense that it's okay inside me, that *I* am okay. There's a feeling of deep appreciation and deep satisfaction." There was an increased feeling connection with her body, too, and a coincidental improvement in her menstrual cycle. (Her uterus was diagnosed as normal, and she had a healthy baby a year later.)

The Absent-Minded Professor, the Space Cadet, and the Martyr

The "absent-minded professor" is a stereotypic example of one version of the hypoactive I' syndrome. Being "absent-minded" means being so lost in thought as to not pay attention to what is going on around oneself. Habitual and often hilarious forgetfulness has made the absent-minded professor the subject of countless cartoons. He is also a good illustration of the polar nature of the psyche. Why does the absent-minded professor forget about practical things? Why does his mind wander away from the immediate situation? Often it is because he is preoccupied with other things—obsessed with his research project, perhaps, or engrossed in thought about the book he is writing.

Sitting on the other side of the classroom is the dreamy-eyed "space cadet," who dwells in an imaginary world, wandering through the exotic mental spaces of some alternate reality. S/he escapes from boredom by "spacing out" and being "nowhere," or at least nowhere near the "real" world of the classroom (or wherever). "Jim. Jim! Did you hear me?" Finally the voice penetrates and Jim "comes back" with a start. "Peru? What about Peru?" he says, having tuned out somewhere in the middle of Argentina. Maybe Jim feels embarrassed. Or maybe he can laugh, knowing that the ability to "space out," or enter a different mental space, is not without stress-relieving value.

Tonification of the Spleen-Pancreas Meridian may be indicated when the attention wanders easily, memory is poor or it is hard to concentrate. Lack of concentration makes it difficult to grasp details, create ideas, and synthesize information so as to form conclusions. This makes for suggestibility and a general lack of persistence and morale.

Low morale can also come from an unsatisfied need for sympathy, or from the feeling that "nobody really cares." A deep craving for sympathy can lead to an unconscious exaggeration of problems, aimed at getting attention. The "I need" may be so pronounced that the person seems inconsiderate of others' needs, and they may turn away from what feel like demands. When a person is not well or not happy, the "I need . . ." naturally is pronounced. The focus of attention is on personal needs and, because these feel urgent, it *is* hard to concentrate on the needs of others. The need for sympathetic support is amplified.

"The *I need*. . . , the craving sympathy says that the Earth [I'] is imbalanced in the same way someone craving sweets is signalling an Earth imbalance," says Diane

Connelly. "Health is a balance of needs and emotions."[16] To maintain this balance, basic physical and emotional needs must somehow be satisfied. A chronic craving for sweets or for sweet sympathy may reflect an actual present or past lack of body-mind nourishment—or an inability to take in available nourishment.

The craving for sympathy can also pop up in compensation for a long period of over-concern about others' needs and feelings, and denial of self-felt needs. At an extreme, this is the "martyr syndrome." The longer the denial, the more likely we are to feel overwhelmed by needs when they become conscious—and then to react in a way that seems childish or "out of character." An example, from a country song, is the wife who spends twenty years serving her family and catering to her husband, without complaining about his inattention to her needs—and then suddenly takes off, after the children are grown, leaving a note that she's gone in search of the love and caring that she so badly needs. A less extreme reaction can follow just from long weeks or days of working hard and putting out a lot of energy towards others.

It can be hard to ask for sympathy, or even to acknowledge that you need it, if that contradicts your self-image or conditioning. "I never let anyone give to me unless I am so physically wiped out that I have no alternative but to receive," said Vicki. Of a powerful session focusing on the Spleen and Stomach Meridians, she said later, "Old hurt from the past poured out like oil from a leaky valve. All my life I had been conditioned to be compassionate towards others but to watch out for people who tried to 'work on my sympathies' to manipulate me. I recalled so many times from childhood on when I was punished for feeling hurt or wanting sympathy." That sounds like a recipe for making a martyr, or at least for producing a self-sacrificing attitude. "Deep-seated anger that was not 'nice' to express came up, and I felt it in the pit of my stomach, in my guts, where there are no 'shoulds,' " Vicki continued. "I was always told how grateful I should be. When you told me my story was sad— I had never heard that. It is okay to have some self-sympathy! This inner realization opened up my stomach.

"For five years I have been dealing with a weight problem caused by shoving down my anger, sadness, and grief. After this memorable session, I have stopped burying and hiding my emotions (to the best of my conscious ability)—and I don't have excess weight. I have been deserving to be treated fairly, and to be more honest in my personal relationships. When I don't let my honest feelings out, my body tells me about it!"

Some time later, Vicki had such a bad cold that she couldn't drive to her appointment. She called me, and we carried on a session over the telephone. She said her eyes were half closed, her face was puffy and she had a throbbing headache. She had felt sexually indifferent towards her husband for some time, and had recently discovered "an anger inside me" about his past insensitive behavior. I asked if she had cried about it. "No, we talked, then I fell asleep!" she said. "The next night I went out, pretending to be fine, and got such a bad headache and earache that I felt like vomiting, and *then* I cried because I felt so terrible. I realized that I couldn't imagine being without him." After this Vicki thought everything should be better, and felt angry at herself for not being "over it." She said, "I *should* be getting back to loving." I suggested that communicating might not *instantly* change everything. "But it does on T.V. and in the movies!" she laughed. "I really felt frustrated because I couldn't respond as I thought I should. But I suspected that this 'head cold' was from being too much up in my head!"

Vicki complained that her sinuses and nose were congested (as was apparent from her voice). I suggested that she could hold the most sensitive points around her nose [in the area between ♯37 and ♯2: LI]. As she did so, her nose and sinuses began opening up. Earlier, holding tense neck and shoulder points [♯21, 20 and 23], she had gotten in touch with a lot of confusion, "not knowing what to do with my knowledge—when to do something and when not to." When she touched the "grand lo" the day before, it was "so painful that I went into orbit." The ♯30: Sp area was also very sore, and all the Spleen points were sensitive to touch. Also, her abdomen was bloated. I asked her to hold and breathe into the tight and sore places, closing her eyes. She saw a "yucky reddish color" that changed to purple and pink. Her nose continued to open up.

There was gurgling in her abdomen, and then she felt hardness in the ♯6s. As she focused on this area and breathed into her abdomen, she remembered a couple interesting things. One was her husband reminding her of her statement years ago that sex wasn't as important as communication, caring and affection. Another was vowing, after the hurtful break-up of her first marriage, "not to let someone get that close to me again." As she talked about this, Vicki felt her abdomen tensing into a painful knot again. Freely and honestly expressing feelings brought up anxiety, especially if the communication was about things that seemed to threaten her relationship. Her abdomen relaxed as she repeated: "It's safe for me to be close to someone now. Communication, caring, affection *and* sex are important." At the end of the session, Vicki said with amazement that her face was less puffy and her ears and head no longer hurt. "I just feel a little dizzy." I suggested she relax for a while, holding the ♯22s and any other points that "talked to" her, and allowing sensations to move through her body. Afterwards she feel asleep. "I normally can never fall asleep in the day," she said later. "When I awoke I felt much better—no headache, no sore throat, and my head felt clearer."

The next day she went to work, and came home with a headache, sinus congestion and some coughing. She lay down and held ♯37s, ♯22s and the Spleen points in the ♯30 area. "I knew I needed to cry, but I felt no emotions of sorrow. Something in me got me off the couch, and I grabbed for my old college yearbook. Swelling with memories, I began to cry buckets of tears—first while looking at pictures of men I had loved, or had wanted to love, and then looking at pictures of my professors, and remembering the openness we shared before I learned to play the 'maturity game.' It took another week until my coughing stopped, but my head had cleared afterwards and I felt good." Self-acupressure and following feelings as they arise can be a very powerful form of treatment.

Part 4. HYPERACTIVE I': over-thinking, brooding, worry, anxiety, obsessions, obsessiveness

"Over-thinking" characterizes the hyperactive state of I'—and much of modern life. It comes with the territory of academia—for the student studying for exams, the professor preparing a lecture, the researcher writing a report and the author writing a book (present company not excepted). Over-thinking is an occupational hazard in the legal and business worlds, and it pervades the social services as well. Often, more time is spent thinking about and filling out triplicated forms than performing the functions they describe.

Over-thinking can also can be a way of life. The chronic over-thinker is always trying to figure things out. S/he analyzes the dynamics of problems from every angle possible, and often ruminates about why s/he and others did this and said that. All these things are part of self-reflection but, as a habit, over-thinking gets in the way of *being*. There is a noticeable lack of spontaneity. Not only does the person think before s/he speaks or acts, but s/he thinks and thinks and thinks. Once the situation has been so thoroughly thought over, trying to finally address the problem is like studying ancient history.

John, a research scientist in his mid-forties, complained that he had been thoroughly trained in the art of thinking, but not at all in the art of feeling. "Now you say I not only have to get in touch with my feelings, but also with my body," he exclaimed. "That's a lot, speaking for my head! It's like triloguing!" When sciatic pain had claimed his attention, John had not been much in touch with his body tensions. As we worked, he became aware of an extreme tightness throughout much of his body. As his body armoring began to dissolve, he felt soreness at points in his neck as well as in his pelvis. "I've gotten comfortable with these blocks!" he exclaimed. "What are you—am I—doing?" But the blocks were obviously not completely comfortable. For one thing, the low back pain was interfering with his jogging. "Besides wanting to run freely again, I know that there's just much more to feel— much more joy—once I can release these stuck places," John said, "and I know that I have to get out of my concept blocks in order to release the stuck energy. I really want to be able to *feel*."

During a session focusing on Spleen sedation and chest release [and including Lung sedation, and Kidney intercostal points], I directed John in breathing first into his chest and then into his abdomen. "I have the feeling there's a whole part of myself that I'm not into," he said after a while. "One reason is that I escape from my body into my head. I just had the image of suck-holes in river rafting. Thoughts are like suck-holes: some of them are keepers!"

"My head is just too busy," he said at our next session, which also focused on Spleen sedation. [To prevent a recurrence of the sciatica, we also worked briefly with #16, #15 and #32, with Kidney, Bladder and Gall Bladder distal points, respectively.] "A case of *zippy head*, that's what it is!" he said. "It feels like I can't slow it down." The zippy head was sometimes busy with judgments and critical analyses, and sometimes with fantasies. "For example, in relationships, I tend to jump from the here-and-now into a preoccupation with the future, or worries about the relation-ship not working out. The critical, judgmental part of me can be so strong that my feelings get negated. I'm so concerned with what I think should or might be happen-ing that I don't get around to really enjoying what *is* happening!"

In another session, I asked John to focus his attention on his armored abdomen [especially ♯5: Sp, "C," and the Spleen associated point on the back]. John said, "It feels like a tight band. It's like I'm bent over something there—protecting un-wanted feelings. I want to reach out and be open!" After the abdominal tensions had relaxed a great deal, John impulsively reached out to touch my arm and said, "I just realized how much I block what is coming towards me by blocking what I am giving out! What a powerful realization!"

Again focusing on the abdominal area ["C" & ♯38], John had images of being with children. When I asked "how do you feel?" he responded, "How do I *feel*? What does that *mean*?" After several minutes of abdominal breathing, he said, "*It's just the feeling.*" Childlikeness is being able to just feel, without needing to know what everything means. A relaxing calmness followed this insight. John said afterwards, "That tension in my guts had a lot to do with messages I got, and intro-jected, about what I *should* be, what I should and shouldn't feel, what's acceptable and what's unacceptable."

While concentrating on the pelvic tensions during another session, John saw the armoring in the ♯6 area as being "like metal," and later had the image of the metal melting. He said, "It has to do with pleasing others, or performing." The image of a metal chastity belt came to mind. "There's like a circuit between here and my head, and my head takes energy away from my groin." Excessive mental activity uses energy, and it is the centers of the physical life which thereby become energically deprived. An inordinate amount of intellectual activity can be a way of sublimating sexual desires. Romanticism, or idealizing others, can also be a way of controlling gut reactions—sexual and otherwise. "Romanticism gets in the way of people relating to me, and me to them," John explained. After the release of ♯6, he felt "like there's a space that I can breathe into, that wasn't there before."

John had often spoken of his desire for spiritual growth. I suggested that spiritual development might include more and more feeling, seeing, hearing, sensing—not just meetings with God and mental raptures. "My head wants to tell me it can take me there," he said. "My head says, 'I've taken you this far, so trust me; I can figure it out.'" The head seems "higher" than the body, so it is easy to see the head as the way to spiritual heights. Spiritual development, to the Taoists, was not an escape from the body, and certainly not an escape into the head, but rather a movement into an aware relationship with the whole bodymind and with nature. "On the way here today, I had the thought, 'I'm a man of the *earth*, not a man of God,'" John said. "I want to be here, now!" Maybe being a man of the earth, being grounded, is a shortcut to heaven. Or maybe really feeling HERE, NOW *is* heaven!

After about six months without low back pain, John had a recurrence of sciatica on the left side. He was able to largely heal himself by meditating on points which felt painful or blocked and consciously releasing the tension. At his session, the focus he requested was on ♯15 and the Large Intestine associated point (above the sacro-iliac joint); I used mainly Bladder distal points, also working briefly with the dia-phragm [♯17] and neck [♯21], while directing John to breathe into his lower abdomen.

The following week, I focused on #6: Sp and #15 [with Spleen and Bladder distal points], along with the Central Channel.

While I was holding #6, John felt like there was a band around his pelvis. "It's as though my head put it there," he said, groaning as he struggled against the tension. "It's a way to control the body and its feelings." I commented on his tone of voice, and John thought I'd said vice. "An interesting slip?" he asked, mentioning he'd been celibate for some months. Gradually he felt the band of tension getting thinner and dissolving. At the end of the session, he had the image of a bird rising from the ocean and flying away, and said the feeling was freedom. A bird is a free spirit; the ocean can be a symbol for the unconscious, or for the universal energy or spirit of life. The next week, John reported being pain-free, as well as psychologically freer.

In telling John's story, I have, of course, omitted a lot of details, for it would take a whole book to relate all the particulars of even one person's journey to bodymind awareness. More importantly, I have left out the *silent places*. John's words brilliantly describe "head-tripping" and its effects on the body. But as he observed, "Talking *about* feelings isn't *it*! It can be just another way of being clever. As Erhart said, 'Understanding is the booby prize!' " Or maybe understanding is the door prize. Really getting in touch with one's feelings and one's body is, if not the grand prize, at least a wonderful surprise. In Jin Shin Do sessions, much of this experience takes place in the silent places between the words, when the body takes over, and what's important is the world of sensations, sounds, movements and feelings.

Worry, Worry, Worry . . . ───────────────

Hyperactivity of the Spleen Meridian is typical of the general stress reaction. Physical symptoms can include indigestion, muscular tension, appetite imbalance, weight problems, abdominal pain or menstrual difficulties. The person may be "running on nervous energy," but is easily fatigued. There may be a heavy and aching feeling in the body. Over-thinking and worry are usual psychic symptoms. The simple question, "have you been worried about something?" may be enough to set off a lengthy tale of woe, the telling of which can bring relief. However, when worry is a habit, the relief of talking about particular concerns is limited—because there are always more.

Worry is a distressed, troubled or uneasy state of mind that comes from clinging to concerns, going over and over them. Worry is using our mental teeth to bite and tear at a problem like a dog worrying a bone. Chronic worry is a self-imposed mental harassment; it is pondering the problems of life until it seems like life *is* problems. That's a good way to increase the stress level! Pondering over concerns is like lifting heavy mental weights. (The word in fact derives from the Latin word for weight—"pondus.")

Brooding is almost synonymous; it implies continuously thinking about or pondering something in a troubled way. To "brood" also means to hatch, like a bird sitting on its eggs. Our worries can be like eggs; our brooding over them can be a way of protecting our problems and hatching more. Brooding over the past can hatch regret and other morbid feelings. Such a continuous concentration of thought also automatically takes us out of the present, so that we can't really see, hear and feel what's going on *now*.

Brooding and pondering are yang conditions, since they are characterized by excessive mental activity. However, the backside of chronic worry is depletion of the body energy, physical weakness, and perhaps even feeling unable to move. Continuous worry results in stagnation of the ch'i, and perhaps a disturbance of the body's ability to transform food into nourishment, with symptoms like abdominal distention, poor digestion or appetite problems.

Considering that worrying basically isn't a lot of fun, it is amazing what a common psychic addiction it is. Chuang Tzu comments on this phenomenon:

> "Is there such a thing as supreme happiness in the world or isn't there? . . . This is what the world honors: wealth, eminence, long life, a good name. This is what the world finds happiness in: a life of ease, rich food, fine clothes, beautiful sights, sweet sounds. This is what it looks down on: poverty, meanness, early death, a bad name. This is what it finds bitter: a life that knows no rest, a mouth that gets no rich food, no fine clothes for the body, no beautiful sights for the eye, no sweet sounds for the ear.
>
> "People who can't get these things fret a great deal and are afraid [or anxious]—this is a stupid way to treat the body. People who are rich wear themselves out rushing around on business, piling up more wealth than they could ever use—this is a superficial way to treat the body. People who are eminent spend night and day scheming and wondering if they are doing right—this is a shoddy way to treat the body. Man lives his life in company with worry, and if he lives a long while, till he's dull and doddering, then he has spent that much time worrying instead of dying, a bitter lot indeed! This is a callous way to treat the body."[17]

It is easy to see that worrying is doing other people no good. It may be harder to see that our own concerns are excessive, and that we could just let self, others and life *be*. As one client put it, "What I want is obviously right and necessary, so I have a right to be worried if things aren't working out the way I think they should!" When we have a problem, one thing we can always do is *worry about it*. Worrying is somehow comforting—perhaps because it feels like we are *doing* something about our problems when we worry about them. Worrying provides the illusion of useful activity.

Worry can also be a job that the unconscious mind thinks it has to perform, as I discovered one day while drying my hair. I remember standing in my room at my college dormitory, and suddenly realizing that I wasn't worrying about anything. Immediately, out of habit, I searched around in my mind for something to worry about—and then laughed at myself. I was worrying about not having anything to worry about! As though I might be forgetting something that needed to be worried about! The classics called worry a "low emotion." Yet it certainly is a common emotional habit or hobby.

Worry "makes a mountain out of a molehill." If the object of the worry is the body, the result may be a hypochondriacal exaggeration of symptoms and imagining of diseases. Similarly, worry can lead to an exaggeration of distressed feelings. As we think something over, and over, and over, we can find all kinds of new problems to worry about, and the worrisome thoughts can generate all kinds of emotional distress —regret, resentment, guilt, jealousy, self-pity, mistrust and fearfulness, to name a few possibilities. Worry is like an itch. Just as itching (another symptom of Spleen hyper-activity) is an irritation of the skin, so worry is an irritation of the psyche. It produces negative thoughts and distressed feelings which, so to speak, ask to be scratched.

Worry causes energy to become concentrated in the neck and forehead, and blocked in the abdomen [around "C"] and chest [♯30 area]. This constricts the breathing and paves the way for an escape up to the head. There, we can avoid feeling our gut reactions and confronting our underlying fears and anxieties. Instead, we can occupy ourselves with worrying about and brooding over things.

Worry as a Defense Against Anxiety

Habitual worry correlates with a high anxiety level, and may be a defense against anxiety. In other words, worry is one of the things that we do with anxiety. Anxiety seeks an object. Worry can be the attempt to find some object, or cause, that the anxiety can be hooked onto. Anxiety is less disconcerting if it is associated with some real problem, rather than experienced as a general and nonspecific distress.

There are many situations which are almost inherently anxiety-producing, unless your self-esteem is very solid or you have developed a totally acceptant attitude towards life's changes. For instance, what if your boss or an associate calls to say s/he's received critical feedback on your work? Or what if your spouse or boy/girl-friend calls to say, "Something has been on my mind a lot, and I need some time to discuss it with you tonight." Rare is the person who would receive such news with absolute equanimity—without anxiety and without worry about a string of nega-tive possibilities. Taoistically, this rare person might say, "Things will be as they will be, so why waste my energy worrying about it? There is what I want, and there is what I need, and I don't always know which is which. Why worry that the news will be bad, when it may not be, and when I don't even know for sure what *is* bad?"

Most of us will, however, feel some anxiety in response to such a call. We will begin to anxiously imagine what might be said or worry about what might be wrong. We might experience the anxiety as a nervousness throughout the body, a rapid heartbeat, clammy hands, an uncomfortable dryness in the mouth, abdominal pain or gas, or "a knot in the pit of the stomach." Adaptive responses include breathing slowly into the lower abdomen, and channeling the energy behind the anxiety into activity. If negative thoughts keep coming to mind and bringing up anxiety, talking with someone or depositing the worries onto paper can help order the mind and bring the focus back to the here-and-now. Acu-points which can help to calm a wor-risome mind include ♯10, the Spleen source point, the ♯30: Sp area, the readily accessible "great connecting point" (the last point of the Spleen Meridian), and any of the neck points.

Being at ease with ourselves depends on being *present to ourselves*—to our body-mind selves. This allows us to be present to others, too: able to connect and em-pathize with them, without getting fused with them. Fusion with others is one factor which can greatly increase our anxiety levels. Fusion with others means seeing them as indispensable to our existence, or using them as our primary source of self-esteem. The result is a lot of anxiety about how they are feeling or what they are thinking, or worries about whether their words or actions mean they no longer care. At an extreme, this may amount to an obsession with their condition, their feelings, their opinions, or just their very presence in our lives.

"Not feeling secure in one's self and depending on the presence of someone else as a measure of existence may be a cry of help from Earth," says Connelly.[18] It also may be a cry for help from "Water" (the Kidney Meridian), since fear or inadequacy feelings often underlie our anxious attachments to others. With chronic fear, the adrenal glands are responding as though to continuous danger. The nourishing functions have taken a back seat to the defense functions, and there is a continuous demand on the energy reserves. The eventual result is energic depletion, with "nervous energy" replacing real energy. [The Kidney Meridian is deficient, and the Spleen Meridian becomes excessive to compensate for the energy shortage.]

Low energy makes us more susceptible to anxiety, and a lack of reserve energy is, in itself, anxiety-producing to the body. The lack of *a sense of self* is similarly anxiety-producing to the psyche. Experiencing oneself as a *thing* to be manipulated, by oneself and others, amounts to lacking a *sense of self*—and so lacking a place from which to relate to others. The result is both feelings of alienation and increased anxiety, as Fromm explains:

> "This lack of self creates deep anxiety. The anxiety engendered by confronting [the inner] abyss of nothingness is more terrifying than even the tortures of hell. In the vision of hell, *I* am punished and tortured—in the vision of nothingness I am driven to the border of madness—because I cannot say 'I' any more. If the modern age has been rightly called the age of anxiety, it is primarily because of this anxiety engendered by the lack of self. Inasmuch as 'I am as you desire me'—I am *not*; I am anxious, dependent on approval of others, constantly trying to please."[19]

The popular pastime of worry can keep us so busy that we don't have to face our underlying anxieties. In the act of "worrying," we are calling several defense mechanisms into effect. These are some of the things that we are doing when we worry:

1. *Rationalizing*—trying to prove that our anxiety and our behavior are justifiable, and thus that we are worthy of approval.
2. *Intellectualizing*—analyzing the anxiety-producing situations, in order to cut off their emotional charge.
3. *Universalizing*—saying that anyone would feel anxious or worried under the same circumstances.
4. *Projecting*—blaming others for our problems and attributing undesirable thoughts and feelings to them.

Western psychology explains how different patterns of these and other defense mechanisms employed against anxiety produce different "neurotic" symptoms. Anxiety is seen as the *core* of neurotic symptoms. Whether or not it is the core of psychic distress, anxiety *can* be related to distress in any of the five emotional spectra. In the last chapter, I discussed anxiety as repressed excitement, related to hyperactivity of Shen. Imbalance of Chih, or feelings of fearfulness and apprehension, can increase the anxiety level. Imbalance of Hun can also stimulate anxiety, for anger and assertiveness can be experienced as anxiety-producing. The involvement of P'o, or the Lungs, is more direct; suppression of respiration is both a response to acute anxiety and a cause of chronic low-level anxiety. Restricting the breathing is an immediate, automatic defense against anxiety, whereas worry, or the mental hyperactivity related to I', is a more secondary defense.

Anxiety and Low Blood Sugar

Traditional associations of hyperactivity in the Spleen-Pancreas Meridian include anxiety symptoms like restlessness and a disordered, desperate kind of energy which makes it hard to relax. Anxiety can in fact be related to imbalance in the regulation of insulin by the *islets of Langerhans* in the pancreas. Insulin is essential for the metabolism of sugar. Secretion of too much insulin results in *hypoglycemia* or low blood sugar, with symptoms like weakness, shakiness, restlessness and irritability. Hypoglycemia creates a predisposition to anxiety. Anxiety in turn can cause hyperfunction of the pancreas and hypoglycemic reactions, because a common reaction to anxiety is consuming sweets.

Let us look more closely at this example of the bodymind connection. Eating simple carbohydrates, like white sugar, amounts to flooding the system with sugar. When we eat complex carbohydrates, like whole grains, sugar is released more slowly because the starch chains must be broken down gradually. Even when we eat sweets, if the liver is healthy it can store excess sugar or "glucose" and release it to the bloodstream as needed; if insulin secretion is well-regulated, appropriate amounts will be released to control the blood sugar. However, simple sugars strain this regulatory system; they are rapidly absorbed by the body and so can make the blood sugar level soar.

When a flood of insulin is secreted in response to the flood of sugar, so much glucose is removed from the blood that the blood sugar level drops abruptly. The brain needs a steady supply of blood sugar to function. A sudden drop in blood sugar is therefore "interpreted as a danger signal, and the adrenal glands usually respond by secreting adrenalin," explains Rudolph Ballentine, M.D. "This helps mobilize stored glucose from the liver, but it also sets off a general alarm, alerting the whole body as for emergency action." Persons with hypoglycemia tend to have high levels of adrenalin. "They are repeatedly responding as though to danger. The result can be an overall feeling tone similar to what we call 'anxiety.'" This "internal stress" provokes or aggravates external stress.[20]

Persons with hypoglycemia may be prone to acute anxiety attacks during stressful situations, or may suffer from chronic anxiety, being unable to control anxiety even over things that others would take for granted. This is because hypoglycemia can cause the adrenaline level to rise dramatically within minutes, producing feelings of apprehension and anxiety. In other words, the hormonal roller coaster creates an emotional roller coaster. The mood may alternate between being calm and easygoing, then anxiously testy or "impossible." The person may or may not be aware of being anxious, but is likely to complain of weakness and shakiness. There may be trembling, rapid heartbeat, rapid and shallow breathing, sweaty hands, staggering or double vision and, in the extreme case, even coma.

For persons prone to hypoglycemic reactions, regulating the diet is clearly an important part of the treatment of anxiety. However, a change of diet involves a change in the whole emotional/physical pattern of response. To make such a change, it may be necessary to uncover maladaptive defenses against anxiety, like the tendency to displace anxiety-producing feelings rather than dealing directly with situations and persons who arouse them. When anxiety is displaced onto the body, there may be bodily complaints for which no physical disorder can be identified.

Another way to displace anxiety is through obsessions or compulsions. An obsession is a recurrent, persistent and seemingly involuntary thought, image or impulse; a common example is an excessive concern with cleanliness and order. A compulsion is a repetitive behavior which seems purposeful but is performed in a stereotypic manner—a classic example is Lady Macbeth's ritualistic hand-washing. Such actions are supposed to expiate some repugnant deed or defend against something that one is unconsciously afraid of doing. For example, compulsive overeating could be a defense against underlying sexual urges.

What is commonly called "obsessive" is not as extreme as an "obsession." When someone says "I am obsessive about checking to see if all the doors are locked—twice!—before I leave home" or "I am obsessing on my studies (or work)," s/he is describing an extreme or intense *preoccupation* with certain thoughts or activities. Obsessiveness is a form of obstinacy. The classics say that the capacity to be obstinate is related to the Spleen-Pancreas and Stomach.[11] This capacity can help us to get things done, but in the extreme, obstinacy can amount to having a lot of fixed ideas and rigid thought processes. In this case, the conscious mind is being largely directed by the unconscious mind.

Unconscious Obsessions

When old introjected thoughts and unresolved feelings are alive in the unconscious, in a sense we are obsessed with them. Though we may not be consciously aware of the obsession, it comes out in our attitudes and in our anxiety levels. Often the unconscious mind is obsessed with an idea which is a direct blow to self-esteem, like "I'm not lovable" or "I'm really bad (or weak) inside." For example, after working through a lot of childhood trauma, Eve said she got in touch with its origin one night when her husband held a few points for her mid-back pain. "It was the feeling that I wasn't lovable, that it wasn't okay for me to love or be loved," she said. "There was a lot of confusion about that. It felt awful that I gotten that message so long ago.

"But the deep, deep part of the spirit that everybody has to drawn on—that wasn't crushed. I just tightened up here and there, from the fear that I wasn't lovable and from not understanding why I wasn't loved. I just tightened up to survive. A few months ago I would have hated my family because of that realization. Now I ask, 'How? How could they have been so blind?' I lost so much. I felt like a caged animal—a leopard! I cut off the feeling of love, because if I felt love and then got hit or hurt, I'd be worse off. It felt like a hurricane inside me. I tried to please so I'd be treated better, but the punishment never seemed to end."

While I was holding #10 in the arch of the foot [with the "grand lo"], I asked Eve, "Is this where you grab on and try to stand your ground?" Focusing on her feet Eve said, "I keep hearing my mother telling me it's wrong to feel weak. . . . That's why I don't usually ask for help. But then I end up feeling like a martyr . . . My feet are like panic buttons. Tighten up more and more and more and then curl my toes, and then I'm walking on my tiptoes and I don't know where in the heck I am. I'm just teetering along. Afraid to be real." Afterwards, as Eve practiced unlocking her knees and feeling the stability in her feet, she said it felt surprisingly intimidating and amazingly good.

She often expressed anxiety about being "too intense" and "threatening" to other people. As we focused on the Spleen/Pancreas Meridian, she had the image of people giving her injections so she'd behave with decorum. "I'm saying, 'Wait, wait! I just want to be all of me!' And they're laughing, saying an eighth of me is too much, saying 'if you're going to be all of you, please don't be it around us.' It's too real!"

As I held some tense neck points, Eve said, "My neck likes to trick me. It likes to keep me away from true, wonderful, powerful stuff. I'm smart, and I used to use my intellect as a defense. In fact, I was an intellectual snob for a while. My whole family was like that. But because of my 'electric head,' I'm missing out on so much of the richness of how people and life really are. Right now, my life is telling me that I've got to yield to something, and it might as well be to my real self."

When she relaxed, Eve felt the most resistance in her stomach or solar plexus area. "There's something about holding my stomach so tight," she said. "It feels scary to go in there. I feel like I'm going to crumble or something." I asked Eve if she didn't trust that deep, deep core of herself not to crumble. I asked her to go into the tightness in her upper abdomen. "I feel like I'm a prisoner in my own body," she said. "It feels so heavy in there . . . I'm so tired of being so locked up. It's like I'm scared to death in there—or really anxious, anyway." About what? "I'm scared that I'm really bad," she responded. "It's still there, the thought that I might be a bad person." Why do you keep it there? "I don't know . . . Maybe because I still believe my parents and all the people who didn't believe in me. . . . But there's not the feeling that I have to fight back, like I used to. It's more like I need to just slide through all that, and stop suppressing my energy."

In her mind, Eve saw all the people who had helped her think that she was unlovable or bad. I asked her to separate herself from them, suggesting that she could later connect with them in a different way, if she wanted to. "I feel like I don't have access to my legs, so I have to use my arms to pull myself away," she said. "Now I'm on the banks of a canal. I don't understand why it's so scary to leave the old stuff behind! It's like a trap—my own little trap." I asked Eve to visualize herself being free from all the old negative opinions of herself. She had the image of getting into a balloon, but felt a strong pull to stay with the people on the ground. "Maybe parts of me still don't want to be okay," she said. Then she saw herself flying away, over the canal and people. "Does that feel good?" I asked. "Yes and no," Eve replied. "It feels pretty insecure." Insecurity is another word for freedom; tolerating feelings of insecurity is part of staying free. Erich Fromm asks:

"How can a sensitive and alive person ever feel secure? Because of the very conditions of our existence, we cannot feel secure about anything. Our thoughts and insights are at best partial truths, mixed with a great deal of error, not to speak of the unnecessary misinformation about life and society to which we are exposed almost from the day of birth. . . . We can never be certain of the outcome of our best efforts. The result always depends on many factors which transcend our capacity for control. Just as a sensitive and alive person cannot avoid being sad, he cannot avoid feeling insecure. The psychic task which a person can and must set for himself, *is not to feel secure, but to be able to tolerate insecurity, without panic and undue fear . . . Free man is by necessity insecure; thinking man by necessity uncertain.*"[19]

11. The Land of P'O Revisited —Lung Meridian

Part 1. SYNERGIC STATE OF P'O: openness, receptivity, non-attachment

Just let things come and let things go? How can we do that? What would we have then, if we stopped grabbing things and holding onto them? Maybe we would have simpler lives, with more openness and more space for joyfulness. Modern wo/man often acts as though there is only so much stuff in the world, and to succeed s/he must grab as much of that stuff as possible, before someone else does. When s/he can hold onto a whole bunch of that stuff, then s/he is successful. Successful at what, and to whom? How does s/he know that it is even important to grab the golden rings while riding the fame-and-fortune merry-go-round? Lao Tzu asks:

> "Fame or your person, which is nearer to you?
> Your person or wealth, which is dearer to you?
> Gain or loss, which brings more evil to you?
> Over-love of anything will lead to wasteful spending;
> Amassed riches will be followed by heavy plundering.
> Therefore, he who knows contentment can never be humiliated;
> He who knows where to stop can never be perishable;
> He will long endure."[1]

How can we stop, while the clock ticks on? How can we know when to stop with the pressure of deadlines and appointments and meetings and classes and . . . Sometimes it seems there just isn't enough time for everything, or for settling into anything. So how can we stop? Yet if we live hurrying forward lest we be left behind, then *consciousness* has stopped and we are left with only its facsimile. Lacking awareness of present feelings and energies, we are just marking time—not *living* it. We are marching toward deadlines. We can stop holding onto these *dead* lines that we have painted onto the future, and just let things unfold, doing what is needed in each moment. When we are really *present*—to another person, to our work, to ourselves—then time seems pregnant with possibilities rather than hedged in by limitations. Perhaps this is because letting go of deadlines is letting go *to* ourselves. It is accepting and working within *what is*, in each changing moment.

If change is a universal law, then it's just plain silly to hold onto everything and everyone. It's also tension-forming. Imagine that you are holding onto something or someone with your hands, and then that you are pulling that object towards you. Now imagine that what you are holding onto is moving, and you are trying to make it stay put. Feel the muscles in the inner arms and chest that are tensing in this effort. Notice how the line of muscular tension follows the route of the Lung Meridian? Letting go is the opposite of holding on; let go of your imaginary object and let your

Lung Meridian

Points of the Lung Meridian

JSD #30—On the outside of the rib cage, at the level of the second rib, press into the muscular tension and toward the rib cage. The point is about 2 *chon* below the collarbone (clavicle).
["Middle Palace"—Lu 1]

JSD #29: Lu—On the upper arm, feel for a sore or tense spot in between JSD #29 and #24, and a little lower than both.* The point is on the outside of the biceps muscle, 3 *chon* below the fold of skin in front of the underarm (anterior axillary fold).
["Heavenly Mansion"—Lu 3]

Source point—On the crease at the inside of the wrist, press lightly in the depression below the thumb. At this point, the pulse of the radial artery can be felt.
["Bigger Abyss"—Lu 9]

JSD #36—This is a pain point in the middle of the muscular part of the palm below the knuckle of the thumb. The point is in the middle of the first metacarpal bone, pressing toward it.
["Fish Border"—Lu 10]

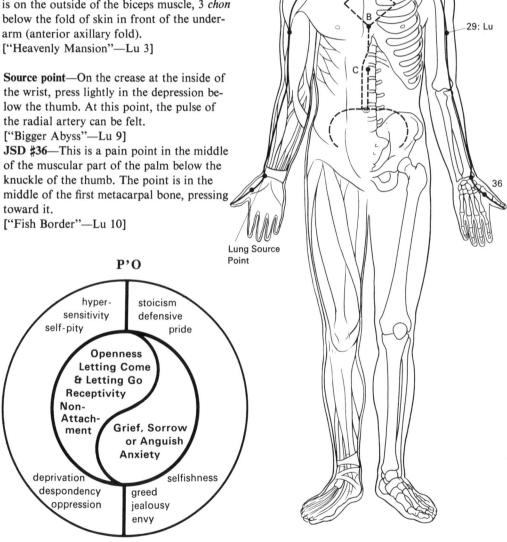

Lung Source Point

P'O

- hypersensitivity
- self-pity
- stoicism
- defensive pride

Openness Letting Come & Letting Go Receptivity Non-Attachment

Grief, Sorrow or Anguish Anxiety

- deprivation
- despondency
- oppression
- selfishness
- greed
- jealousy
- envy

---

* *Lung Associated Point*—see Chapter 8 for explanation of the associated points.

Examples of Local-Distal Point Combinations

Local point		*Distal point*
30	+	29: Lu, S., 36
"B"	+	18 area, S., "G"

S.=Source Point

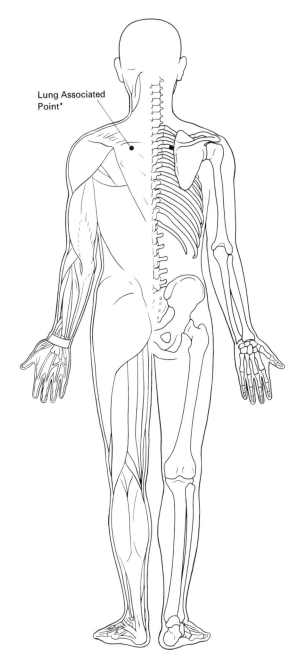

Lung Associated Point*

---

† *Liver Associated Point*—see Chapter 8 for explanation of the associated points.

hands drop, relaxing your arms. Feel lighter? To enhance this feeling, try holding the ♯30s while breathing out to these points, letting the chest expand and relax fully with each breath.

Trying to hold onto everything, as though we could thereby bodily prevent or force change, is as ridiculous as throwing people and things away. Just let it, and yourself, *be*. There are cycles to how things work: there are hellos as well as good-byes, meetings as well as partings. The law of change is both severe and merciful: what is not needed is taken away, and what is needed comes. The Tao of Heaven is to reduce excesses and fill voids. The Tao of Heaven supersedes the way of man—which often is to take from the insufficient and give to the redundant. In other words, there is plenty of stuff in the world. We get it, or what we need of it, not by a forced march towards it, but rather by creating or allowing voids. We get what we need by being open so we can perceive it and empty so we can receive it. Recalling the ancient saying, "Be humble and you will remain entire," Lao Tzu added:

> "Be bent, and you will remain straight.
> Be vacant, and you will remain full.
> Be worn, and you will remain new.
> He who has little will receive.
> He who has much will be embarrassed."[2]

I am reminded of a lady who learned a lot about letting go by moving to the mountains. Moving necessarily involves letting go of familiar scenes. For Lillian, it also involved letting go of a materially comfortable life-style, and accepting a simple and physically demanding one. This change was the more difficult because she hadn't imagined the hardships of living in the country, while dreaming of how much happier life would be amidst the beauties of nature. Through meditation, she had once felt a joy and harmony so complete that hurtful emotions were "just like gnats, pricking a little." It was hard to maintain this ideal, however, when her husband's illness and ensuing emotional instability obliged Lillian to care for him, besides providing the family income, for several years. Joyful walks in the forest and along the creek with her dog helped to temper feelings of deprivation and oppression, but these and other "negative" feelings kept coming up, while she kept trying to suppress them "to avoid setting my husband off." Eventually Lillian became very sick herself. Suddenly she had to let go of all external concerns, because she literally didn't have the energy or strength to move her body.

"Suddenly I had the alarming experience of feeling *nothing*," she said. "People used to say I was too sensitive, and I used to wish not to feel so much. Suddenly I wanted that same sensitivity back! I just wanted to feel—anything." Even "negative" emotions didn't seem as bad as *not feeling*. "Because I wanted harmony so much, I had tried not to have negative feelings. I held it all in, until my body couldn't take it any more. Then I had to just let go, and I started seeing things from a new perspective. I stopped holding myself back to avoid threatening my husband's ego. After I got well I started doing things that *I* thought would work—and they did! I have what I need. It just took longer than I expected."

Voids do get filled. Therefore the Taoists say not to strive for more than we need, wasting our energy, and not to strive against what is natural. So-called "negative" feelings and emotions *are* natural. There's no point in aiming at a constant harmony that excludes the negative. The "negative" cannot be evaded; along with the "posi-tive." it is part of the whole. The negative cannot be totally eliminated, yet it must be constantly eliminated. Toxic, destructive thoughts and feelings must be encountered and let go to make room for healing, creative thoughts and feelings. Openness is being able to see and feel what *is*. Staying open is the key to being awake and aware, to growth, and hence to joy.

> "The Sage will not allow his person to be the instrument of matter, nor to permit his peace to be disturbed by desire. Thus, when he rejoices, it is not with boisterous hilarity. When he sorrows, he will not suffer his nature to be wounded. Circumstances ever change and vary; there is nothing stable about life's conditions. The Tao-man, alone, lives triumphantly (or cherishes the magnanimous point), abandoning worthless things. He keeps step with the Tao. Therefore he has the wherewith to find his true nature."[3]

Illness can be a sudden awakening to what is important. It can be a sudden return to really feeling love for Self, Other, and Nature. Illness can make it very important to let go of that which is destructive and let in that which is creative. A less dramatic way of letting go is by breaking self-imposed limitations, even silly and harmless ones. Routines dull the senses; programming our lives is a way of going unconscious. Doing something—almost anything—a little differently is a way of waking up. A trip is a good example. In a new place, surrounded by new sights, sounds, smells and feelings, there is a change in self-perception too. Taking a new route to work, wearing something unusual, trying bodywork or a new sport, taking a class or workshop—such things can be like little trips, helping us see and feel with new openness, and so waking up dormant parts of ourselves.

The challenge is to stay awake. Then as new feelings, sights, sounds, thoughts and sensations come in and become our focus, less energy will be invested in the old stuff. As the old is let go, more energy will be available for the new. Openness is this continuous letting go and letting come. It is letting go of grief and hurt, and of dead-ening attitudes and petrified mindsets. It is also letting go of day-to-day disappoint-ments and tiny psychic "blind spots." And it is letting in a new awareness of inner feelings and outer realities—letting the light in or enlightenment. A moment of deep openness is a moment of enlightenment—whether it is really *hearing* music, really *experiencing* love or any other emotion, really *feeling* what an acu-point or tension is, or really *seeing* anything. Openness is letting thoughts and feelings flow, letting energy move through the bodymind, letting people move into and out of our lives.

Letting Go and Letting Come

Letting go and letting come are essential not just for consciousness, but for life itself. *The body and the psyche are designed to move. Where movement is not, dis-ease is.* Flexibility is life; rigidity is death, or at least stagnation. Tension blocks the flow of energy through the body, and it blocks the flow of feelings through the psyche. Tension is *resistance* to letting things flow, or letting go. Of all the organs, the lungs and large intestines most symbolize letting go. The lungs expand to take in oxygen, and contract to expel carbon dioxide; they continually receive air and then eliminate the unusuable parts of the air. The large intestine, somewhat similarly, accepts the residue of the digestive process, then eliminates the waste products, or the unusable parts of foodstuffs.

These physiological processes have psychological parallels. We continuously take in the psychic equivalents of food and air—"food for thought" and winds, or whirlwinds, of feelings and emotions. We also need to continuously eliminate the toxic aspects of our thoughts and feelings. We need to let go of limiting self-images and conflict-making introjected messages. We need to release distressing feelings and encourage their transformation into peaceful synergic feelings, like openness and joy. This is facilitated by release of chest tensions, especially at the "letting-go point par excellence"—♯30.

Difficulty in letting go can manifest in depressed breathing and respiratory problems,* or in problems of the colon (the Lung's partner organ). Constipation, taken literally, is holding onto old shit; it can correlate with abdominal tensions designed to hold back hurtful feelings. Even the common cold may be the body's way of saying, "now you must stop and take the time to feel." The sore throat and mucus build-up which herald a cold will sometimes magically dissolve with the tears that release a coincidental emotional build-up.

Lung-related tensions [like at ♯30 and the associated point in the ♯18 area] tighten up or close down the chest area. Oppression is the feeling of the closed-down chest; suppressed breathing, fatigue and susceptibility to respiratory problems are results. Abdominal tightness related to the Lung and Large Intestine Meridians also restricts breathing and limits the ability to feel, while tension along these meridians in the arms, throat and face limits the discharge of energy through expressive gestures, words, sounds, and tears. As less energy is discharged, there develops an unconscious desire to limit the *intake* of energy too, like by suppressing respiration.

The Secret of the Golden Flower says that P'o surrounds and "adheres to consciousness, in order to affect it." Physically, P'o is the lungs, which do surround and affect the heart, the "residence" of the conscious spirit. P'o is also described as "the substance of consciousness" which begets "changes of form."[4] Yet the *Nei Ching* calls P'o the seat of "the inferior, animal spirits."[5] P'o has to do with instinctive desires and sensuous impulses, which in a way are the substance of which consciousness is made. The instincts and desires give rise to somatic messages, called feelings, which tell consciousness that the organism doesn't have something it needs. The effect is to stimulate movement towards that which attracts and away from that which repels, or feels toxic. P'o "directs the physical energies"[5] because of the energizing function of instinctive desires, as well as because breathing is basic to physical energy.

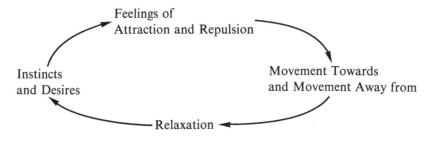

---

* Including asthma, which can be related also to deficiency of the Kidney Meridian.

It is, I think, obvious that breathing energizes the bodymind, and that deep breathing techniques can relax us. Like the Indian yogis, the Taoists masters claimed additionally that the internal organs could be influenced through the practice of meditative breathing techniques. Breathing is involuntary, yet it is also under voluntary control. We can consciously control the rate and depth of our breathing, and yet breathing fortunately goes on without our conscious attention. The autonomic nervous system influences the lungs, along with the heart and all the other internal organs and glands. Perhaps because all the autonomic functions are intimately connected, breathing techniques can, to an extent, control the state of the entire bodymind system. Full chest breathing can stimulate the sympathetic nervous system, to give us energy for activity. Deep, slow abdominal breathing, or "hara breathing," helps stimulate the parasympathetic nervous system to relax the bodymind. The *quality* of the breathing also has an effect. As a meditation technique, the Taoists advised listening to the breath until it has "no tone," or is very light and quiet. The *Golden Flower* describes how such breathing affects the heart, the residence of Shen.

> "If the heart is light, the breathing is light, for every movement of the heart affects breath-energy. If breathing is light, the heart is light, for every movement of breath-energy affects the heart. In order to steady the heart, one begins by taking care of the breath-energy. The heart cannot be influenced directly. Therefore the breath-energy is used as a handle, and this is what is called maintenance of the concentrated breath-energy. . . . The five senses order themselves according to the heart, and the spirit must have recourse to breath-energy so that heart and breath are harmonized."[6]

There is not only the question of *how* to breathe, but also that of *whether* to breathe. We cannot completely stop breathing, but we can have significant success at suppressing breathing. This reduces the general energy level, and so limits the energy that is available for feeling. We discover this at a very young age: by limiting breathing we can limit feeling. Can you recall having your feelings rejected, feeling unloved, being embarrassed or humiliated for showing emotion, and being determined not to cry—not to let them see that they "got to you"? Most likely you learned that holding your breath helped to shut down your feelings, so that you didn't feel the hurt in your heart so much. Some children also learn that this defense can be used offensively: by holding their breath until they become pale or blue, or faint. With increasing sophistication, there is the discovery of other little things that help to keep feelings from showing: tightening the throat, gritting the teeth, clenching the jaw, tensing the belly, making a painfully tight fist.

Interestingly, all these common defensive maneuvers involve muscles related to the Lung and Large Intestine Meridians. Such defense mechanisms are largely unconscious by adulthood; neither is a child really *conscious* of how they work. It becomes "second nature" to tense certain muscles and suppress breathing in order to restrain negative feelings. Therefore, many people are surprised at feeling how closed they are, and at feeling withheld old hurt, unresolved grief, self-pity, and so on, as they "move into" the chest with awareness. The happy part of the surprise is finding that the unconscious attempt to protect against pain also had the effect of unnecessarily limiting the pleasure and joy of deep feeling awareness.

234

Climbing off a Cross of Suffering ————————————

"You don't surrender easily, do you?" For some time I had been holding the left #30 alternately with the Lung associated point in the #18 area [together, and with distals including Lung points], without appreciable effect. Ruth said she felt an intense pain begin to pierce her left chest. "Good God, it's still more grief for my dead dog," she said. Tears were welling up. "What's the feeling?" I asked. "Waves of loneliness . . . immense loneliness," Ruth said. "No human being ever gave me that kind of unconditional love. No one." I encouraged her to follow the feeling, and to breathe through the chest tensions, out to the #30. Ruth let go to some sobs, but with embarrassment. She looked relieved when her sobs subsided.

I moved to her right side, beginning with the #30. "The pain felt like sharp knives," she said later. "To my astonishment, all my stuffed, gagged rage and grief about my childhood welled up. It wasn't stuff I would have expected, like my father raging around the house. Instead I went back to those war years when we were newly arrived, dirt-poor Jewish refugees from Europe. I went back to the weekly reunions where the ragged crew of refugees would talk and weep and look at each other with despairing eyes. The only child there, I would watch in silence as the women choked on their tears and the men sat with clenched jaws. I hated them for surrounding me with their unceasing grief—yet how could I dare to hate those who had suffered such horrendous injustice? I felt like their packing mule, condemned to carry their sorrows forever and ever. As these feelings welled up, I was stunned that they were still there, and I could feel how they were buried in all those bands of tension, as you moved your fingers back and forth across them. I felt ashamed, too, to be so old and so full of sorrow and sadness. Then you showed me how, now that I'd let some of it surface, there was less pain. Yes, those points were looser. *I* was looser.

"At the end you placed your hand over my heart ["B"] and suddenly my aunt Beth appeared. Her image was radiant and surrounded in a bright white sunlight. Again I was stunned. I knew I loved Aunt Beth very deeply. I'd said I carried her around in my heart, but I thought that was only a metaphor. I was wrong. I really had her in my heart, an image like the sun, radiating out at me. Thank God, there was something inside besides grief! Aunt Beth had suffered like a son of a bitch, more than the rest of us because she'd lived through the war in Europe. But she had loved like a champ, and had taught me more about love than the whole pack of them. What a gift to have her in my heart! As her image faded, I felt strangely quiet inside . . . and vulnerable. Open and tentative, I was also somewhat exhausted."

For Ruth this was a start to climbing off a cross of suffering. Her next major release occurred during work with the Large Intestine Meridian, after work with the Lung Meridian [#30 with #29 area, source, #36 and #18 area]. As the chest tensions began to release deeply, and after she had been breathing fully and easily for several minutes, Ruth suddenly looked like she was having trouble breathing. As I applied pressure to #21: LI and the jaw, she began to gag, as if she were struggling to release something vocally, and her body began to arch. I encouraged Ruth to make sounds as she exhaled, loudly saying "aaaahhh" with her so that she wouldn't feel embarrassed. As the sounds became longer and deeper, her throat and jaw tensions started to soften. To Ruth, the sounds seemed like "bloodcurdling screams." An almost unbearable burden of old suppressed hurt was wedged in her throat. This deep hurt was the source of her many defenses against feeling, and against showing feeling.

Ruth had previously described a "bitter fear of strangers" that sometimes made her seem anti-social. She began to see how the old unexpressed pain had caused her to hold back and pull away from others, to hold things in and refuse to share. She began to be willing to let all that melt away. She felt forgiveness for her younger self's impulsive and sometimes desperate attempts to get at least the semblance of love through sexual gratification, and for her attachments to "disdainful and un-attainable men." As she forgave herself for her confusion and mistakes, the hardness peeled off her face and revealed a radiance that reminded me of her image of Aunt Beth. Ruth said she felt much freer, and that the old themes of worthlessness were being replaced by the thought, "Maybe now I'll be able to let some joy into my life."

The Rhythmic Order of Desire and Discharge

Even within the so-called undiscriminating will of P'o, there is order. The classical teachings say that the yin organ of P'o, the Lungs, are the "officials of rhythmic order" who are "in charge of regulation of conduct."[8] In a balanced state, we breathe in and out fully and continuously, and this gives us energy. Likewise, our instincts and desires give us energy, if we are not *controlled by* our attractions and repulsions. Just as holding or suppressing the breath obstructs the rhythm of respiration, so excessive attachments obstruct the rhythmic discharge of desires.

A desire creates organismic tension and energic charge which, naturally, seeks discharge; discharge is followed by relaxation. For example, hunger is discharged by eating, and sexual desire by making love. Many desires pressing for satisfaction create many tensions. Being human means dealing with the various desires of our multi-faceted psyche, as well as with biological urges. The tensions created by this multitude of desires need to be discharged through exercise, work, self-expression, meditation, creativity and caring activity. Confusion about our real desires can lead to ineffective attempts at tension discharge. For example, promiscuity would be an ineffective way to discharging tension if the real yearning was for love, and eating binges would be ineffective if the real desire was for emotional nourishment.

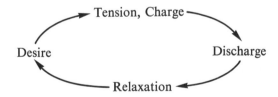

Attachments tie our desires and needs to particular external objects. Without this person, we think, the need for love cannot be satisfied; without this position or job, the desire for acceptance and approval cannot be satisfied. Such attachments obvi-ously limit the potential for satisfying the real underlying desire. If we cannot have this *particular* thing or person, and we cannot be open to the alternatives that life presents, then the tension created by the desire cannot be easily released. When the charge isn't followed by discharge and relaxation, the tension becomes chronic—and so do feelings of self-pity, and of envy towards those who seem to have what we desire. When the real underlying desire is perceived, then the desperation of attachment is replaced by the receptivity of openness. Being open to life usually yields perception of an appropriate way to discharge the tension by satisfying the real desire.

Illusory desires and excessive attachments make life very busy. The *Golden Flower* says that the life energies are wasted by attachments to external things. If our energies are continuously directed towards external things, then Shen becomes energically deprived, and the true desires of the inner spirit are obscured. The Taoists therefore recommended conserving the bodymind energy by reducing entanglements in the world, and letting go of attachments to things being a specific way. Richard Wilhelm, translator of *The Secret of the Golden Flower*, says this "liberation from external things" allows "an inner, ascending circulation of energies" to take place, so that an independent life-centre called "shen" is created.[7] In other words, increased openness allows an energic movement which liberates Shen, or gets us in touch with the inner Self and its real desires—one of which is "returning to the Tao." Seeing our attachments as just preferences is one way to start letting things go and letting life flow.

Learning to Stay Open

Sheila said that she often felt cold and her neck was always tight. "A lid on feelings," I thought, as I felt how extensively blocked her chest points [including #30] were. "I don't open up to others easily," she said. "But when I do, I become really attached. My last relationship ended two years ago, and I'm still not really over it." While we were working with sedation of the Large Intestine Meridian and tonification of the Lung Meridian, Sheila saw herself standing on the edge of a black hole, which seemed to symbolize old feelings of emotional deprivation. She knew that her romantic attachments had been attempts to fill this old hole, and that the loss of love relationships had restimulated the pain of childhood losses. I asked her to look into the hole, and to just watch and breathe. She saw a rope ladder, then went down it. "It's dark, but not pitch-dark," Sheila said. "It's like a maze." She laughed, seeing "a funny-looking old man," who guided her a ways.

Then she saw her grandmother, her mother who had committed suicide, and her father who had died of cancer. What was she feeling? "Sorrow . . . grief." The sorrow dissolved into tears, which brought up anger at her grandmother, for not letting her go to her mother's funeral. I suggested that Sheila could ask the grandmother-image about that. "She says she was trying to protect herself." A long silence. "She says she cared about me, but she couldn't show it." I asked if she could let her grandmother's love into her heart now. "Anger wells up," she said. "I can't get myself to trust her." I suggested that she didn't need to trust her grandmother's personality in order to feel the essence of her love.

Sheila was breathing continuously through her chest now. Because the upper back muscles were like gnarly, thick ropes, I was working with #18 and Pericardium/Heart distal points. "There's a lot of self-protection here," I said. "Maybe you *are* your grandmother in your closed-down chest and heart center." Psychoanalysis had shown Sheila that her own reserve was, in some ways, a repeat of her grandmother's inability to show feelings and be openly affectionate. "My head knows that, but my body doesn't," she said. "I don't want to close down, but I don't know how to stay open, unless there could be some kind of insurance against being hurt and deprived again." I asked Sheila to think of something that gave her joy, and then to take that feeling into her chest, breathing into it. As she did so, she felt lighter and lighter, until she looked positively radiant. Tears of joy replaced the tears of sorrowful deprivation. "I have never felt so in touch with my feelings, and with my Self," she said in a deeper and more resonant tone of voice. Sheila had been taught that openness was risky. Now she was discovering the big reward of being and staying open—contacting and feeling her inner Self.

As a postscript, I would like to mention a simple image of openness which is one of my favorites. During Lung tonification and Large Intestine sedation, a client first saw—of all things—an oil well. Her association to this image was that it was hard to go down—down into her feelings. It was also hard to breathe down into her abdomen, or fully through her chest. After release of tension in the neck and at the ♯30s, her breathing became fuller and freer, and she had the image of a bird with its beak opening. Her association to this was "a free and open spirit, willing to receive." By the end of the session, the image had changed, and the bird was just sitting lightly on her chest. She *felt* lighter, too—"rather like a free spirit, in fact!"

Part 2. EXTREME EMOTIONS OF P'O: grief, sorrow or anguish

The initial response to loss may be relief, if the loss was long foreseen, but often it is shock and disbelief. Sooner or later the shock wears off, and is followed by tears of sorrow, grief or anguish. "Sorrow" implies a sense of loss and suffering. "Grief" is like acute sorrow, or a more intense emotional suffering caused by loss, and "anguish" suggests torturing grief. The suffering is not just emotional. The pain of grief is an aching in the chest, and the pain of anguish can feel stabbing. Not only the psyche, but also the body feels tortured. The torture is the pain of separation.

In times of grief, or acute pain of loss, P'o gives rise to "the ability to weep and to wail."[8] What does the word "weeping" bring to mind? A common association is "weakness." Yet weeping and wailing, crying and sobbing, are inherently yang or active states of the bodymind. They *activate* the breathing to *mobilize* emotional release, when there has been a heartfelt or gut-felt loss. Only in the *aftermath* is there weakness, for grieving is tiring. As the classics put it, grief disperses the energy and consciousness, and leaves the body weak.

In primitive societies, the natural reaction to the death of a loved one was uninhibited weeping and wailing. The march of civilization brought increasing self-consciousness to the grieving process, until it began to seem almost unnatural to let go with intense emotion. This was brilliantly illustrated in the 1984 movie, "Greystoke: The Legend of Tarzan, Lord of the Apes." While he is living with the apes, before encountering other white men, Tarzan's ape mother is speared by African hunters. As he kneels by her side, crooning to her, her body suddenly goes limp. Tarzan keeps crooning to her, beseechingly. He brings her arm around his shoulders, as it would be if she were hugging him. But there is no life in her; never again will she hug him. His grief and anger rise up into blood-curdling yells and sounds that seem to come from the primal wellsprings of life. The intensity of emotion is evident in his whole body. His grief is so impressive that the hunters run off.

By contrast, later, after Tarzan has partly adapted to British ideas of what is proper, his human grandfather dies. Tarzan, now "Lord Greystoke," makes the same crooning sounds and puts the grandfather's arm around his shoulder in the same way he had with his ape mother. He shows the same despair, but he does not let go to his grief as he did when he was just a "wild man." Instead, he picks up his grandfather and carries him off, with the lords and ladies watching. Then he has a "grief reaction"; he becomes morose, depressed and irritable. It looks like he might just have an abiding sorrow from all his losses and disillusionments. One night, all the grief and anger breaks loose, and he vents it while driving a team of horses at a gallop around the estate, making loud guttural sounds, then jumping onto the back of one and yelling into the skies. The scene is as impressive as the one of his ape mother's death—but because of his partial adaptation to "society," it has taken Tarzan much longer to get to his feelings and let them out. He comes back to the manor looking like himself again, though quite disheveled, and feeling at peace with *both* the civilized and the wild parts of himself.

Grief is a natural response to loss. Grief is how we disperse the energy that was bound up in love, or in an emotional attachment to a being who is now lost to us. There is an emotional attachment to any being who helps satisfy our instinctive physical and psychological needs. The loss of this "significant other" can leave a big hole, for suddenly our love or desire has no object. The attachment is like an energic or emotional cord connecting us with the "love object." If that beloved other is lost, through death or another form of separation, it is like the energic cord has been severed. The energy that went into the emotional connection needs to be dissipated. The natural channels for this are tears of sorrow or grievous weeping and wailing. This emotional catharsis leaves the body temporarily weak, but also *unbound*. The eventual aftermath is a redirection of our emotional energy, or a feeling of non-attachment.

The Problem of Attachments

The more extreme the loss, the more extreme the letting go. Extreme dependence on another being, combined with low self-esteem, can produce prolonged suffering or abiding sorrow. But even when self-esteem is intact, grieving may take some time. Grieving has as much to do with rebirth as with letting go, because letting go of that which is lost means letting new feelings and relationships in. To do so, it may be necessary to resolve the problem of attachments—the problem of needing loving relationships with others, but having no guarantee against being hurt by being left. The guarantee is just the opposite: the other person ultimately *will* leave us by death, or we them. The *I Ching* points out another problem with attachments: man's tendency to perceive the beloved others as the source of his strength, and so to become subject to a lot of mood changes.

> "If his center of gravity depends on them, he is inevitably tossed to and fro between joy and sorrow. Rejoicing to high heaven, then sad unto death—this is the fate of those who depend on an inner accord with other persons whom they love. Here we have only the statement of the law that this is so. Whether this condition is felt to be an affliction or the supreme happiness of love, is left to the subjective verdict of the person concerned."[9]

Some passages in Taoist texts speak of freedom as a state with no room for grief or joy. "With one glance," the free wo/man "takes in past and present, without sorrow for the past or impatience with the present," because s/he knows that "all is in movement." Flowing with the movement of life means not carrying on sorrow *for the past*, and it means reacting appropriately *in the presence of loss*. Life is alternating fullness and emptiness, and "the game is never over," not even with death of the physical body. If "birth and death are even," then success and failure are even too. Therefore the free wo/man "does not rejoice in success or lament in failure," says Chuang Tzu.[10] Yet the "superior man" *does* rejoice in life and lament loss. "In bereavement emotion means more to him than ceremoniousness," says the *I Ching*.[11] The guideline seems to be what modern psychology calls "appropriate affect." It is not appropriate to greet worldly failures with the same intensity of lament that would be accorded the death of a loved one. Yet even death is not final, and so its grieving need not be excessively prolonged.

When one "perceives the true reality and is not affected by external appearances," then emotional responses are appropriate in dimension and duration. When one "lets things change naturally," then there is a balance of happiness and unhappiness, a moderation in both pleasure and suffering. Chuang Tzu says, "Death and life are important, yet they do not affect" this person.[12] In other words, sorrow and grief need not affect the inner spirit, or the core of oneself. *Letting things follow their natural course* means feeling what is appropriate and then letting the feeling go. There is a time for grief, and a time for letting go of sorrow.

> "For we were born because it was time, and we die in accordance with nature. If we are content with whatever happens and follow the flow, joy and sorrow cannot affect us. This is what the ancients called freedom from bondage. There are those who cannot free themselves because they are bound by material existence."[13]

Grieving, or letting go of that which has been lost, initiates an emotional transformation. The natural direction is back towards the synergic state of P'o—openness, and receptivity to internal feelings and external reality. An old Taoist story describes such a movement from grief and pain, through letting go of attachments, back to openness. This story claims to record what happened when Hui Tzu came to visit Chuang Tzu one day, and found him sitting in his yard, beating on a drum and singing.

"Come now," said Hui Tzu. "I know you are a respected sage and teacher. But your wife whom you lived with and loved, who took care of you these many years and brought up your children, has just died! And here you are, beating on a drum and singing! Isn't this going a bit too far?" Chuang Tzu answered, "When my wife first died, do you not think I grieved for her like all other men? But then, after some time of that, I looked back. I thought about who she was before she was a woman, and who she was before she was a girl, and who she was before she was a baby, and before she was born, and even before she had a spirit—and how can I grieve anymore? It is a wonderful mystery that a change took place in the infinite, and suddenly she had a spirit. Another change took place and she had a body, and then was born. Another change took place when she died. It's just like the changes of the four seasons. If I were to try to follow her to the void with my bawling and crying, that would show no understanding of fate. So I stopped."[14]

When the emotional catharsis of grief seems to go on longer or with more intensity than that warranted by the immediate loss, the reason may be that the crying and sobbing has opened the psychological vents to earlier, uncatharted griefs. The hyperactive breathing may have released tensions that were suppressing the old hurts. In this way, grief over a present loss may be a catalyst for the dissipation of old sorrow as well. Whether the loss is recent or long past, talking about it can help to "get it off your chest," but a deeper release often comes simply with claiming the space and time to breathe and feel.

Respiratory Suppression and Reluctance to Feel ——————————

Suppression of respiration is a primary defense against threatening emotions, like anxiety or grief. It is also the most basic form of the most basic defense mechanism: denial. We learn to limit our breathing to defend against our feelings long before we learn to use the verbal form of denial, and well before we learn sophisticated defenses like rationalization and sublimation. Limiting the breathing is a bodily form of denial. It is a way of disappearing, a way of shrinking, by not revealing who we are and what we feel. Acupressure release helps us *go through* grief, partly by freeing the respiratory system so that we can *breathe through* the pain and tension.

The problem with respiratory suppression as a defense mechanism is that we feel less because we have less energy—for feeling or for anything else. We may have pushed away the storm clouds of grief and hurt, but a fog-like heavy, oppressive feeling has settled on us instead. The repressive process is so unconscious that we may not even be aware of having held back our feelings after an emotional shock, trauma or stress. Tension in the chest muscles records the repressive act, because chest tension is the mechanism for suppressing the breathing and inhibiting the grievous feelings. Feeling the chest tensions can help us to become conscious of the emotional repression. But our defenses are so good at what they do that we often are not aware of the accompanying physical tensions, especially when they are chronic—unless they speak to us through pain, or unless bodywork heightens our awareness.

"I was really surprised by my reluctance to feel," said Zelda, after a session focusing on chest release. "What was also interesting was that as I left your office my eyes began to itch beyond belief. After I had walked home, my eyes were fine. Later that night I was able to grieve in the arms of a friend, and it was a liberating experience." Zelda was afraid of "losing her cool," but her eyes were saying it was time to melt an old block of icy grief. As the child of alcoholic parents, she had "learned to not feel, not express, and not trust." During release of chest armoring [#30 with Lung distal points; #18 area], Zelda was confronted with old abandonment and intimacy issues. Her grief was not for loss of her parents, but for a real lack of parenting. Instead of feeling loved and protected by her parents, Zelda had developed a pattern of trying to protect them, which later became her modus operandi in relationships. Often, she felt she lost herself in the bargain. One question which emerged was "have I served enough?" A broader question, and one that is central to openness, was "do I deserve to receive?"

The old feelings of hurt and grief were still so impactful because, as a child, Zelda had lacked any support for expressing her hurt while it was happening. The repeated hurt of the childhood abuse and neglect gradually lowered her self-esteem, and made it feel unsafe to be open about feelings. Now, the fear of openness was keeping Zelda out of the Tao, which is the now—the only place where she could receive the love and support she needed.

Zelda felt that a real change happened when she got in touch with the old grief, and was able to let go to it in a supportive situation. She said, "The important thing was that I had the chance to express my feelings while I was having them, rather than explaining them later when they were under control." Without this kind of experience, when strong feelings arise so do our habitual defenses. Before we know it, the breath has become shallow, or is being held, and we find ourselves becoming silent and withdrawing, or else rationalizing and explaining our feelings. The conscious intention may be to breathe fully, or to share feelings openly and not hold onto them, but only the process of doing so establishes a new bodymind operating program.

It may be easier to let go of old griefs if we can see some positive function of the situations which caused our hurtful feelings. For example, Zelda discovered that a certain competence, especially in intellectual areas, had developed as a survival mechanism. She saw that this, like most defenses, was a two-edged sword: it had brought her much satisfaction and fulfillment, yet her very competence served to isolate her from others, if she did not balance it with the ability to let go into play. The lack of play and lightness was itself cause for sorrow.

There was also sorrow with feeling how much she had withheld her feelings and so herself. This was a healing sorrow, for it pointed to a real change of heart. "Withholding my feelings was lying," Zelda realized. "I am responsible for my own abandonment, because I withdrew first. Not on the external level—there I am ever so faithful—but on the level of sharing my feelings and what is going on with me. I have a reluctance to share 'shadowy' thoughts and feelings with the persons I care about. I must now affirm that it is safe to let go, and to tell the emotional truth to people I love."

Chronic chest tension is usually accompanied by diaphragm tension, which usually reflects internal anger or frustration. Zelda was no exception; her tension pattern was saying not only "I hurt" and "I don't dare let go to my feelings," but also "screw you!" Anger can be a defensive response to hurt. There is anger over being hurt, and simply over not being heard and understood. Zelda's reaction to her parents' emotional neglect was a common one. "Okay, fine, I just won't feel then." But it's not okay, not at all fine. Not showing feelings and not communicating is passive aggression, as well as a defense against more hurt. The ego will not risk another blow. The ego unleashes defensive pride, saying, "If I can't have power over my environment, I can at least have power over my feelings." Defensive pride dictates non-expression of feelings; muscular tensions, especially those related to the Large Intestine and Lung Meridians, enforce this dictate. But the child within, the inner Self, still feels neglected, misunderstood, or unloved.

Anger is a Part of Grieving

Anger accompanies grief. It is a normal part of the emotional reaction to loss, though frequently an unacknowledged part. The anger may not be acknowledged because it doesn't feel safe to express it, or because low self-esteem has led us to internalize anger in the self-destructive conclusion that somehow "I am to blame." When the loss is by death, anger often doesn't seem like an appropriate response; we may feel guilty about the anger or just not notice it. How can we be angry at someone for dying? The general assumption seems to be that we should cry with sorrowful restraint or be brave, and that we should not have "ill feelings" towards the dead. Anger may seem like an ill feeling. Yet, death is the ultimate abandonment. Anger, while an intense emotion, is not necessarily an "ill" one. On the contrary, anger can be a healthy response, and depression can be the result of stopping, or not letting go to, feelings like anger and grief.

The word "grief" derives from the Latin "gravis," meaning grave or heavy. Feelings of hurt, and of anger over hurt, testify to the graveness or importance of the loss. Burying these feelings is going back to square one: denial. Not letting go to grief is denying that the loss was important. The result is an internal feeling of heaviness, or of being oppressed and weighed down. This feeling is symptomatic of a *grief reaction*; other indications are easy fatigability, hollow or empty feelings in the chest or abdomen, and feeling like there is a lump in the throat. There may be anxiety symptoms like agitation, insomnia and autonomic nervous system hyper-activity. Depression is likely. Anorexia is also a possible effect; as part of a grief reaction, it is an extreme of the typical depressive weight loss.

Grief reactions may well last for over a year, especially if the loss cannot be easily replaced. If the work of grieving is not done, the related symptoms can go on for years. An example is Mandy, who in her mid-twenties came for psychotherapy mainly because she desperately wanted to have a child and her temper tantrums were endangering her marriage. Beside the anger problem, her list of presenting problems included: anxiety "as though something is tearing me apart," withdrawal from people, bulimia (induced vomiting of food), feelings of self-pity, low self-worth, drug abuse (of several substances, which she had largely withdrawn from before beginning therapy), and depression.* Gradually, I discovered that all of these seemingly senseless symptoms, which Mandy saw as evidence that she was bad, had begun within a year after her father's death, when she was twelve.

We had begun with verbal psychotherapy. The third week, Mandy came to a session despite the fact that she had laryngitis. Since she could not talk, the natural conclusion was that it was time to try some bodywork. I decided immediately that the throat problem would not be my main focus; as I checked main points to find her primary tension areas, Mandy whispered, "don't worry about the laryngitis— just do whatever is most important." Yet the throat would be benefited by a focus on the neck and on Lung-related tensions, which along with work on diaphragm armoring was indicated by her body tensions and her psychological symptoms. Maybe the laryngitis was saying that she needed to dissolve the old lump in her throat by letting go to emotional expression.

During this session, which included work with the #30 and #17 and #5 areas, Mandy remembered her father's death. Tears of grief arose, followed by anger. Mandy first said that she felt angry at her mother "for not letting me go to my father's funeral," and then that "the way she carried on and on, crying and crying, made me mad." Mandy felt not only abandoned, but suddenly deprived of all understanding and emotional support. She had felt understood by her father spiritually, intellectually and emotionally—and not at all understood by her mother. Was she angry at her father for dying? Mandy had never acknowledged this feeling, thinking that it was bad or wrong. Nor had she really mourned her father's death at the time. Years

---

* Assessing the severity of depression includes assessing the risk of suicide. With Mandy, I found no "suicidal ideation." Professional help should be sought when there are thoughts of suicide and the means to do it. You can also say that you would feel hurt if the person committed suicide, and ask for an agreement that s/he won't "do it" without calling you or someone, and that s/he will take reasonable steps toward self-care.

later, grieving over the deaths of a couple of friends, she had gotten in touch with a little of the grief. As she felt the grief and the anger now, with intensity and accompanied by vivid images, Mandy let go to her feelings with tears and body movements (like reaching her hands up into the air and shaking them at the ceiling). Meanwhile, her physical tensions were letting go and her voice was coming back.

To complete the grieving, Mandy had to learn to tolerate the feeling of weakness, because "grief disperses the energy and leaves the body weak." She saw that she had scorned her mother's weakness after her father's death because it left nobody there to support her own need to mourn. She would *not* be like her mother. Therefore, she would *not* be weak. Mandy had equated grief or tears with not only *feeling* but also *being* weak, and being weak with being bad. To recover from grieving, Mandy had to learn to nourish herself, and to see herself as deserving nourishment; this was also the message behind and cure for her bulimia.*

Death and grieving are followed by birth and rejoicing, but this may not be instantaneous. Mandy had to learn how to deal with the world without her habitual defenses. She had to learn new ways of dealing with her anger when it arose at home, besides expressing it in therapy. She had to learn new ways to relax and enjoy life without drugs. Discovering what had been tearing her apart inside gave Mandy a big impetus in a growthful direction. Her self-esteem was instantly enhanced by seeing that her seemingly senseless symptoms had been successive reactions to the childhood loss of her father. Not being able to cathart her grief and anger at the time had resulted in a *grief reaction*. At age twelve, she had tried to jump from loss to acceptance without going through the pain of really *experiencing* the loss, and we don't get to do that.

It is natural, and sometimes even commendable, to leap towards acceptance-like when we have to support others through a crisis. It can be astonishing to discover later how much we held back our feelings. After the crisis is past, just releasing #30 may reveal a lot of inner aching that had not been penetrating our conscious awareness. After the tension along the Lung Meridian releases, it can feel "as though a cloud had suddenly lifted, one that I didn't even know was there." Or it can feel like "I've come back to myself." By the way, releasing the #30s and balancing the Lung Meridian is also indicated after the shock of near-loss. Grievous feelings and anxiety can arise not only from loss, but also from the threat of loss, and even from an illusory loss—like the loss of an illusion about how things are, or about what certain people represent.

Extreme Emotion of P'o: Anxiety

Anxiety can stem from the fear of loss, or from not accepting the flow of change and experiencing change as a hindrance. Existential anxiety is "*the experience of the threat of imminent non-being.*"[15] Change means rebirth, and also death. Changes bring new ways of being, but this means letting go of old and familiar ways. At first there may be just the sense that something new is coming, and that some new way of being

---

* The angry part of Mandy's story is presented further in Chapter 13, Part 2, "The Extreme Emotion of Hun."

is unfolding. Until we are midstream between the old and the new, we may not know exactly what will be different. When some potentiality is being opened up, or some new lifestyle embraced, the self-image has to change. Anxiety comes from not knowing just who *I* will be if I no longer have the familiar person, house, self-image, job, lifestyle, attitude, and so on. How will I be different? Will I like being different? Will things work out if I act or live differently? Anxiety is a response to the *threat of change*. It is an alternative to trusting what is happening. Rollo May explains:

> "Anxiety occurs at the point where some emerging potentiality or possibility faces the individual, some possibility of fulfilling his existence; but this very possibility involves the destroying of present security, which thereupon gives rise to the tendency to deny the new potentiality. . . . If there were not some possibility opening up, some potentiality crying to be 'born,' we would not experience anxiety. This is why anxiety is so profoundly connected with the problem of freedom."[15]

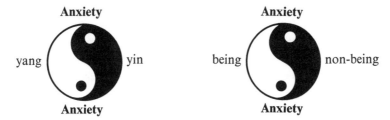

The anxiety related to P'o has to do with the basic insecurity of life—the fact that everything changes. This "existential anxiety" is like clinching when the yin changes to yang, or vice versa. It arises from an inner conflict about being and non-being—about being in new ways and not being in old ways, about being more or different and not being what we are used to. It arises when things slow down professionally or when personal relationships stagnate, and also when things speed up professionally or when there is a new relationship, or a new intensity within an old relationship. The most primary defense against anxiety is suppressing the breathing.

A vicious cycle can be created by anxiety about *symptoms* of anxiety, like difficult breathing, choking or smothering sensations, chest pain or discomfort, tingling in the hands or feet, feelings of unreality, sweating, hot and cold flashes, dizziness or unsteadiness, faintness, trembling or shaking.* The feeling of being out of control can make a person fear going crazy or even dying. Thus anxiety symptoms can create the fear of imminent, literal "non-being."

The stronger our self-esteem, the more likely we are to trust that we will be okay, come whatever may. The weaker our self-esteem, the weaker is our resiliency, or ability to flow with life's continual changes. Low self-esteem increases the likelihood of experiencing anxiety at the change points, and of having the anxiety overwhelm the sense of Self. New possibilities are opening up, and this is energizing—but it would be easier if someone would just explain what is happening and what to do about it—and guarantee that things will work out fine. Thinking and feeling out the individually right choice means accepting the responsibility of freedom. This is

---

* These symptoms are related to Shen as well as P'o; refer to the discussion of anxiety in Part 4 of Chapter 9, "Hyperactive Shen."

likely to be anxiety-producing and so people, individually and collectively, try to *escape from freedom*.[16] We surrender to dogmas and introject the opinions of others in the hope that we will thereby get rid of the anxiety.

Anxiety can arise to alert us of the need to be ready, to prepare ourselves for some new thing. It also can be a conditioned response, or one related to old unresolved fears. Such "neurotic" anxiety is the likelihood when one *always* feels extremely anxious in a certain situation—for example, in a social situation, or in the face of increasing intimacy. But even without such specific "hang-ups," anything new and different may feel risky, and so may provoke anxiety. Why not just avoid risks and live within safe, albeit narrow, bounds? Because taking risks is invigorating; a renewed sense of Self comes with doing something different and making it through. Boredom is the penalty for trying to avoid all anxiety by never "rocking the boat"—never taking the risk of doing things differently or experiencing new things.

This reminds me of some experiences in the wilderness, and in particular of one horse ride in the high desert, when half the sky was suddenly covered by an impressive dark cloud. Leaving the trail, we rode towards the sun, not suspecting we were riding minutes ahead of an unseasonal snow storm that would pursue us all the way home. The wind became intense, and raindrops were teasing our backs. My physical discomfort and my anxiety began to increase logarithmically. Though the experience *was* invigorating, I was anxious about rough-riding through unknown country over hills covered with cactus, and apprehensive because of a story my riding partner had told me earlier in the day—about cowboys getting lost there and fatally injuring a horse getting out of the canyon. In the wilderness, mushrooming anxiety has the potential of being life-threatening. Just keep breathing, and keep moving. (And hold a few acu-points!)

Deep breathing is a useful tool for anxiety control. It is possible to breathe through rather than suppress the anxiety, to go through the feeling to the other side rather than trying to escape it. Anxiety is a high energetic charge, which must be tolerated in times of change. Holding the Lung and Heart source points, the #30s and #3s (or any points which "speak up") can make it easier to slowly breathe through the anxious feelings, tolerate their excitation and let it pass. It will pass more quickly if the mind can be stilled and focused on the present. Imagining possible good and bad outcomes of a stressful situation is like fertilizing the soil in which anxiety grows. The simplest means of anxiety control is staying in the present—focusing energy on the task or person at hand, and on here-and-now actions and interactions.

> "Each of us is the architect of his own future, and if we use our best personal building materials we have nothing to fear. Merely being on the road to the discovery of one's best self lowers anxiety. The rest is work and time. Everyone moves at his own pace and in his own way.
>
> "No one can create your life for you. No one is supposed to. Others may point the way, help define your goals, but the work, the burden, the responsibility—and therefore the joy—are yours alone."[17]

Part 3. HYPOACTIVE P'O: hypersensitivity, deprivation, self-pity, dejection, despondency, oppression

What is "hypersensitivity"? Obviously it is "excessive or abnormal sensitivity"—but what *that* is can be guaged only by comparison with what is "normal," and psychological norms are rather elusive at best. The Taoist perspective is that responding to life with emotion is normal, but that emotional sensitivity needs to be balanced by the ability to be tranquil and so to hear the voice of the inner Self, which speaks in stillness.

How can we differentiate between normal *sensitivity* and *hypersensitivity*? Sensitivity means being able to feel sadness and sorrow, as well as being open to pleasure and joy. Hypersensitivity is getting your feelings hurt a lot, because of taking things too personally or too seriously. A parallel physical symptom is being easily susceptible to colds and respiratory inflammations, because of deficient defense energy. The Lung Meridian is in charge of the defense energies, and of the separation of that which is outside from that which is inside. A healthy separation between the two is necessary for tranquility; an inability to separate the outside from the inside is hypersensitivity.

For example, a friend calls to invite you to his party, but there is a flat sound to his voice. Taking that personally, you think, "He doesn't really want me to come; he's just asking me because he thinks he should." You feel hurt. An old introjected message assures you that nobody really likes you. You feel dejected. Maybe you decide not to go to the party. You feel deprived. You think "maybe he's not really a friend," and you feel despondent. Maybe you also think "I don't really *have* any good friends," and you feel sorry for yourself. In reality, your friend might have "*good feelings*" about you coming to his party, and "*bad feelings*" about something else. A quick reality check is in order. Perhaps you say, "Your voice sounds weak—is everything okay?" And he replies, "Basically, but I've really been having problems at work." By checking out your feelings, you have learned that you were being *sensitive* in noticing his tone of voice, and then *hypersensitive* in imagining it was because he didn't really like you. You have circumvented the downward spiral that might easily have resulted from withholding your feelings and just withdrawing. You might even have saved yourself from sinking into a depressive state.

Hypersensitivity can stimulate movement into the "hypoactive P'o syndrome," which is all about being *down*. One way we sink into low spirits is by "taking things personally"—distorting what's happening, inventing slights and insults where none were intended, and taking good-natured humor as ridicule. How can we tell when we are being "perceptive" and when "oversensitive"? Partly by our *quickness of defense*. Defensiveness usually comes up because one of our "buttons" has been pushed. Something in the words or situation has touched on a very sensitive area of the psyche, which automatically reacts in self-defense. As we come to understand the polar and fluid nature of the psyche, we can remind ourselves that *there is the other side*, and that both we and the other person will probably get to it soon enough.

Hypersensitivity, along with easy and frequent crying, can be part of a grief reaction. Crying at the proverbial drop of a hat, or floods of tears over "nothing," can come out of an inner well of sorrow. The person may be talking reasonably, then suddenly become despondent or begin crying in misery. The fluctuating mood changes are abnormally rapid, and feel different than the normal shifting of feelings in response to life's changes. The emotional condition is *labile*. In the mineral world, "labile" means that a substance readily undergoes chemical, physical or biological breakdown. In the human world, there is the added possibility of emotional breakdown, or of being easily overwhelmed, and feeling weak and teary under stress. This emotional weakness can be the aftermath of grief. Or the lack of emotional resiliency may have its roots in repeated or unresolved hurts, which have undermined the ego-strength.

Filling Old Holes

Unresolved grief leaves an emotional hole, or a sense of deprivation. To transform that feeling, it is first necessary to find out what we really have been deprived of, and then to fill the hole. We may discover that a real emotional deprivation, or an earlier loss or lack of love, *taught us to deprive ourselves*. We may discover an inability to perceive what we need even when it is right in front of us, and an inability to receive, unless we have hit rock bottom. Receiving is not just a passive function. It involves perceiving and then attracting and reaching out for that which we need. Being able to receive is an indication of emotional health and inner vitality. As one client said after work with Lung tonification, "After several tearful releases, for me the major work was on taking and receiving. The crux of it was that I felt I didn't deserve to receive, because I didn't know my own Spirit." Contacting the beauty and wisdom of her inner Self changed that to *knowing* that she deserved to receive, and that she *would* receive what she needed.

Sometimes the old feelings of deprivation come to conscious attention rather dramatically during work with Lung-related tensions. Marjorie, a graduate student in her early twenties, was divorced and had one child. She complained of often feeling vulnerable and subliminally anxious. She tended to be emotionally inhibited. Her chest was somewhat concave and her shoulders a little slumped. During a chest breathing exercise, after work with the neck segment, Marjorie felt "an emotion attacking my heart." As she focused on breathing from the heart center, fully expanding her chest, she felt overwhelmed by sadness. As the ♯30s released, she remembered her mother's death, and felt tears welling up inside. "But the separation from my Mom also left me alone and free to explore my inner being," her adult self said. Suddenly she felt very young. She remembered thinking, "Where's daddy?" As deeper pressure was applied to ♯30 and ♯18, more old sorrow poured out; after that feelings of love were dominant and Marjorie said she felt "very cleansed."

In another session focusing on chest release, work began with the ♯18. Then Marjorie asked for attention to ♯30. What came up was a sense of her father's presence, and then an image of herself as a young girl of about seven. She was dressed in pink, watching her father work in the basement with his "grinding machine." She felt separate from him. She felt herself asking, "Daddy, why aren't you my friend? Why do you make me cry?" Tears welled up, and she felt an overwhelming sorrow in her chest. "Then I saw red, blood red, and felt rage and anger," she said. "A groan began from a really deep place in me and it lasted longer than I thought I had breath for. It was apart from my mind. The groan came again and again as my whole being cleared and felt free! I had the image of my lungs being blue as the sky. As I laughed and squirmed with delight, the red color changed to purple. I felt united with the universe, and particularly with feelings of my father. My heart was full of forgiveness." Afterwards, Marjorie felt refreshed, relaxed and open, clear and revitalized.

What we missed as a child, we missed. We can't go home again, and staying home wouldn't do it either. Nothing can replace the love we missed out on or lost as a child. What can be changed is the *feeling* of deprivation. Marjorie found that remembering the fact of her childhood deprivation led her through hurt and sorrow, into forgiveness and love. She could see her father's love for her more easily now than in her childhood. Then he seemed distant and uncaring, because he didn't know how to show his love, and because a child cannot easily receive invisible love. Marjorie filled some of the old hole by realizing that his love *was* there, in some way, and by visualizing taking that love energy into herself now.

The caring and nourishing parental love that is a normal part of childhood cannot be had later, unless we can learn to receive it from ourselves or from the Mother of the Universe—the Tao. Seeking to fill the old hole by having a mate assume a parent-like role, or by a continued dependence on our parents, is doomed to fail or be emotionally crippling. Only parents have the *responsibility* to love us and care for us, until we are able to care for ourselves. If we did not get or feel their love when we were children, there will be some sorrow about that. As adults, the only way to re-create the helplessness of childhood, and get automatically loved or cared for, is by becoming physically or emotionally ill. Otherwise we must learn to give and receive love as adults, which means with more mutuality than is expected of children. Learning to love as adults is a challenge, because it means learning to lose and find oneself in another.* The opportunity to do so is something we all want. The lack of love is one of the most common causes of deprived feelings.

Feeling Sorry (Sorrow) for Yourself

Denying that we want what we want is not a way out. The feeling of deprivation remains, despite our good conscious intentions to appreciate what we have and to feel grateful for our blessings. When unfulfilled desires are split off from conscious awareness, they tend to take on a life of their own. When they are perpetually ignored and unfulfilled, the sense of deprivation increases and turns into self-pity, dejection and despondency. If we think, or are told, that we *should not* feel sorry for ourselves, this feeling too can be repressed. For example, with deep release of #30 Deborah said that "instantly feelings about being misunderstood and about rejection started to come out like wellsprings." She felt like layer after layer of sorrow was being peeled away, each older than the last. During these rounds of feeling sorry for (and sorrow for) herself, her image was of "being a very wet rag being wrung out over and over

* As pointed out by Erik Erikson, in his description of the stages of psychosocial development.

again." She said, "I feel ashamed and embarrassed to be upset over such mundane things. I've never been beaten or abused, so I have no right to feel neglected and sorry for myself."

I suggested that when she denied her feelings, she denied *herself*. "That was very good timing!" she said later. "It let me begin to trust my own feelings, and trust that I wouldn't get in over my head. Contacting the old sorrows, I was amazed at how quickly even the tiniest and most mundane moment can build up into a large pile of seething hurts and pains, which explode or eat away inside until the body breaks down into disease. I never before had quite understood the relationship between holding in emotion and self-denial, or a self-destructive attitude. It is such a subtle thing, barely noticeable to the conscious mind, and yet so vastly damaging to a growing spirit."

Self-pity is feeling overcome by weakness in relation to difficulties. It is feeling sorry for yourself, or feeling *sorrow* for yourself. I call this the "empty cup syndrome"—the feeling that the world (or another person) is not giving you the support, love or success you need. Its backside is jealousy and envy towards others who seem to have what you think you need. Self-pity can be transformative, if it is allowed to lead you back to the unresolved sorrow or grief from which it may originate. Venting the old grief can lift the onerous feeling of self-pity, and make way for a new openness and receptivity—which frequently attracts new relationships and situations, or makes old ones newly growthful.

Deborah's most dramatic acupressure release involved a rebirthing experience— going back to birth and then consciously accepting the world she was born into. The night before, while trying to go to sleep, she had felt very cold and as though she couldn't catch her breath. She walked around, feeling stabbing pains in her heart center. Memories of being totally alone and helpless flooded her mind, and she was grateful for her roommate's willingness to listen to it all. That night she dreamed: "I was sitting by a river which was flowing swiftly and was extremely muddy. All around me was a beautiful green light, the color of the trees, and as the sun came up, it shone through me as if I were a crystal and reflected rainbows onto the muddy water."

The next day, after she told this dream, what came up was intense sorrow and self-pity over a boyfriend's suicide several years ealier. She remembered "the terror of feeling helpless and of being utterly alone with no comfort or meaning in sight." While the #30s were held, Deborah felt "a kind of horror and pain which made me want to curl up tightly, because of its intensity. I felt every blood vessel pounding in my body and life being forced into me. Living was such a horrifying and terrible thing. Each breath was a struggle. I felt as if there had been a mistake; I wasn't supposed to be struggling this way. In fact, I was an RH factor baby, dying all through the pregnancy and receiving a complete transfusion at birth. I had to undergo a tremendous struggle to survive. I was re-experiencing this struggle." Deborah was moaning and writhing, crying and sobbing. I encouraged her to go through the pain to the other side; I assured her that there was another side to the pain.

"After I had fully experienced the struggle, I relaxed and went to a place where it seemed I had lived before this existence. It was like what Lewis called 'the wood between the worlds.' In this place, the green warmth of the trees lulls and enchants you with its beauty and peace. Eternity could be spent there, lying on the grass,

listening to the trees grow. I experienced myself as one of the trees, with an awesome healing green light all around—like the light I saw in my dream the night before!
As I reached toward the light, I felt that I never wanted to leave that place. Shifting back to reality, I felt that my body was clumsy and awkward, as if I had jumped into the wrong 'puddle.' Meanwhile my hands were feeling numb and not really connected to me, like they were limbs on a tree.

"I was in conflict over which world I wanted. I felt my whole body becoming numb, like I was leaving my body, and then realized that I didn't *want* to leave. I recall asking for help." Deborah was told that the beautiful world of the trees and the healing green light did not have to be separate from her life. Whenever she wanted to, she could go to that place and breathe it into her whole body. "As I did so, I felt my whole body come alive. The numbness left, and I felt encircled by an incredible sensation of warmth and love. I felt as if I had come 'home.' I felt filled, as though I would never again be utterly alone. I still marvel at how much I have opened up since."

Antidotes to Self-Pity and Despondency

To rise from the bog of self-pity may involve dealing with the fear of loss, hurt and deprivation. It may also involve letting go of introjected ideas about what one *should* have, because these tend to enlarge feelings of hurt or deprivation. For example, one "should" be married, have two children and two cars, own a nice home with all the accessories, and have a high-paying job. As long as such messages play on the subliminal stereo system, feelings of deprivation are easy to come by. Their flip side is envy and jealousy.

The alternative is learning to *be naturally*—to live in the way that is natural to oneself, and to let things work naturally. This is "wei-wu-wei." The Taoists suggestion is to shut the door on the opinions of the world so we can find the joy of *what is* and be open to whatever may be unfolding. When the world's opinions or our introjected versions of them are noisy, the following facts may be helpful antidotes to feelings of self-pity and despondency.

Fact 1. The grass is often *not* as green as it looks on the other side.
      Corollary: Happy appearances often hide great difficulties.
Fact 2. The grass is only greener in some spots, or in some ways.
      Corollary: If you could see the whole reality, you probably *wouldn't* rather change places.
Fact 3. There are always people with greater deprivations.
Fact 4. You don't *know* that the introjected messages are right.
Fact 5. You *can* find things to value about who and where you are.
      Corollary: The future *can* be one of increased personal freedom, though the form this takes may not exactly match expectations.

Also, try holding #30 or #36, and ask this simple question: "How am I breathing?" Shallow breathing or suppressing respiration (with the help of chest tension) has the pay-off of reducing acute anxiety or sorrow. The payment is gradual reduction of bodymind energy, until doing and dealing with things becomes difficult, and stress becomes more impactful and more distressing. The "attitude of inhalation," as Reich called it, decreases acute anxiety by reducing metabolic activities, thereby also decreasing available energy and limiting the freedom to act. The anxiety or pain is partly numbed out, but a state of low-grade anxiety replaces it. Anxiety can be a stimulus for suppressing respiration, but it is also an instinctive *response to* obstructions in breathing, because, after all, breathing is a requisite for *being*. The basic desire to *be* wins to the extent that a shallow breathing pattern is established. We breathe a little, have a little energy, and have only a little bit of feeling.

A common reaction to anxiety, if no escape can be found, is to put up the shutters. This is not only a metaphor for closing off the anxiety-producing world, but also it can mean a literal obstruction of inhalation (and so of the intake of new energy). Breathing is difficult, and there may be the feeling that one just can't take in enough air. The result is a low-energy condition, and oppressive feelings or feelings of de-spondency. Despondency is a deep dejection, or state of low spirits, that generally comes from being convinced that further effort is useless—i.e., that there is no escape from distress. Dejection and despondency are extremes of feeling sorry for oneself, because of real or imaginary disappointments and difficulties.

A common cause of despondency is a dysfunctional perception of change; an antidote is learning to *observe* change rather than to put a value judgment on it. Then disappointing or unsettling changes can be stimuli for self-discovery, rather than evidence that effort is useless. Much of the transformation called "growth" has to do with accepting and filling inner "holes," which is a process of turning weaknesses into strengths. With accepting all of the Self, there comes the insight that the cup is already full, or that there is the power to fill it.

Part 4. HYPERACTIVE P'O: stoicism, defensive pride, selfishness, greed, jealousy, envy

The hyperactive feelings of P'o can derive from the same empty cup which causes feelings of deprivation and self-pity to bubble up. Jealousy, envy and greed can be saying that the empty cup needs to be filled. Common to these feelings is the need to feel bigger—by possessing someone totally, by having what others have, or by acquiring more and more. Defensive pride and stoicism are likewise ways to feel bigger or stronger and braver. Why would a person need to feel bigger? Probably because s/he has felt too small, or belittled. Jealousy, envy, and greed can be compensations for feelings of deprivation and self-pity, while stoicism and defensive pride can be attempts to deny any such feelings of weakness.

Holding in or holding on characterizes all of these feelings. There is also a certain compulsiveness about them all. Stoicism and defensive pride are compulsions to "keep face"; greed is the compulsion to accumulate more; envy is the compulsion to have what s/he has; jealousy is the compulsion to keep someone all to oneself. Greed, jealousy and envy may be first felt in the solar plexus center ["C"], which is related to personal power and to the Spleen and Stomach, as well as to the Lung Meridian. Compulsivity is related to I' as well as to P'o and, as discussed in Chapter 10, compulsive behavior helps assuage anxiety. An individual's favorite compulsions often are extremes of actions that would have netted parental approval—for example, a compulsion about cleanliness. Envy and greed can fall into this category, for these compulsions about aquiring things can originate from the need to "make good." Jealousy can be a compulsive attempt to hold onto love—parental love or its replacement. Stoicism and defensive pride can be compulsions to hold things in or back, in order to get approved for being "nice" or strong.

"Oh, I am a prideful man," said Jesse, after release of the ♯30s.* "I think, 'I did that; I let go of that'—it's ego stuff." We were focusing on sedation of the Lung Meridian because of a pulling pain in his right thumb and tight chest muscles, which can be symptoms of hyperactivity of this meridian. As I was first holding ♯36 with ♯30, Jesse said, "That is really painful!" Then he added, "You don't make the pain. It's my own pain." After a deep release of these Lung-related areas and of Large Intestine points in the neck, he said, "I feel like my body has a lot of holes in it now. It's real light, like there's air inside." Then he had the image of a beautiful green meadow and said, "I expect in a very short time that I'm going to be walking on water!" He laughed as I responded that I didn't have that on my agenda. After noticing his "prideful" attitude about the release, Jesse said, "That ain't letting go, I can tell you that!" To let go is to feel the power of the whole Self—which makes defensive pride obsolete. Towards the end of the session, Jesse asked, "Are you going to send me out there again like this?" I asked if he wanted me to help him close down again. "No! I feel like I should have a leather vest or something to put over this openness. But I don't want it closed. I'll take my chances! I want to stop pulling my power."

---

* Jesse is the 45-year-old businessman whom we met in the first part of Chapter 10.

The next week, still bothered by the pulling pain in his thumb and difficulty in breathing, Jesse asked himself, "What am I not letting go of?" What came up were feelings about how he should "help people out" and "save the world." As he focused on breathing through the chest and feeling the relaxation down his arms, I asked Jesse to let his mind be like a blank screen and be open to any images that might come up. He saw himself at about age eleven, being "with the guys." He said that it had something to do with competition, and that "it feels important." Being "one of the guys," and later being "a man," meant not showing weakness. After a while he said, "I've just realized that I've been caught up in a washing machine lately, trying to be brave! It hurts!" Dropping the brave front felt good.

As the chest and diaphragm armoring melted, underneath the brave front Jesse discovered a primitive part of himself that he'd been denying. During release of Spleen and Stomach Meridian tensions in the chest, diaphragm, abdominal and pelvic areas, Jesse began to grunt and snarl, writhing and gnashing his teeth. The good-looking, well-dressed man on the table in front of me began to look like your basic animal! He began jerking and lunging and punching out, his right shoulder lifting off the table in attacking movements. There were no words—only primal sounds. At the next session he said, "I loved last week! One thing I remember is that I felt very strong!"

It was harder for Jesse to accept the very weak part of himself. In another session, I focused on sedation of the Lung Meridian and release of the lower back [holding #16 and Kidney points, including the intercostal points]. "I don't feel fear about what you're doing," said Jesse, "but it feels really uncomfortable." Sarcastically he added, "Poor, poor pitiful me." I asked if he ever let himself feel sorry for himself. "Not if I can help it," he replied. "But I wouldn't even recognize it. Self-pity? *Me*? As soon as I feel that, I snarl. I mean, feeling these sore places, I could go into self-pity. With that, I feel like a piece of damaged meat, having to suffer . . . I don't like that at all. I'd like to just walk gracefully through all the painful stuff. However, as you are pointing out with your finger right now, a person can't always be graceful!" Following his feelings led Jesse back to the foster home where he'd been deposited at age four. "My mother explained the whole situation. Something about being noble and understanding. I bought it. And I learned not to feel sorry for myself. It was important not to, then."

It had been important for Jesse not to get stuck in a place of feeling sorry for himself. Now that was not a danger. He allowed himself to feel sorry, or sorrow, for his child-self, and cried for a while. Then he remembered a friend who'd been "carrying on and on for months and months" because her child had died. "I said, 'Come on, June, stop that shit! How far are you going to carry it?' Probably because it was so important to me to not look at self-pity." At the end of the session, Jesse was feeling a lot more lightness and joy. "It's like somebody had a tree on you for a long time, and then someone lifted the tree up," he said. "It's nice to have the tree gone!"

Letting Go of a Stoical Front

"Stoicism" is more an attitude of emotional indifference than an emotion. This is the opposite of the hypersensitivity described in the preceding part of this chapter.

The impression is of having such a "tough hide" that the world affects us little
—because we feel it little. At an extreme, there is a total lack of sorrow or crying,
regardless of the situation. The attitude is that "nothing bothers me." This "tough"
stance closes down the chest (and the inner Self) as effectively as the opposite "poor
me" or victim stance.

There are societal rewards for not showing feelings, because emotional indifference
can be confused with strength and admired. In fact, society sometimes encourages or
conditions its children into some degree of stoicism. This emotional indifference is
reflected in the expressionless face, or in the constantly smiling mask—which eventually may look a bit grimacing. Even as painful points are pressed, the stoic is
unlikely to utter a sound of protest, or even to change his or her facial expression.
S/he may even take pride in being able to "take it." Therefore, during the first session,
I ask the client to tell me if the pressure is too much, and I define "too much" as
feeling a resistance to my touch, or not being able to "flow with it." The stoical
personality has a lot of trouble saying "too much"—even when directed to do so.
S/he makes little time for relaxing and enjoying, being instead intent on carrying out
work and finishing what s/he starts.

"I have expected too much of myself, and so magnified my imperfections," explained one man, feeling the way his "grim determination" was reflected in his body
tensions. "Even when I am supposedly relaxing, I am punishing myself. When I'm
jogging, I'm not enjoying myself. I'm just moving toward that three-mile goal, even
if I have to punish myself to get there. Otherwise my deficits would be magnified.
When I'm gardening, for another example, I feel driven to get every weed. Maybe it's
okay for my garden to have weeds—literally and figuratively! As long as they're not
choking the plants. And maybe it's both literally and figuratively okay if my kids
don't like my garden!" At the end of this session, with its intensive focus on P'o-
related armoring, George said he felt relaxed—and liked it. "I'm having spontaneous
positive thoughts about myself, and not because of thinking about accomplishments
and congratulating myself on them," he said with wonder.

The stoical attitude is maintained by holding in feelings of hurt or sorrow. This is
accomplished with the help of tension in the chest and abdominal muscles, which in
the chronic case may manifest in intestinal problems like colitis and constipation, or
in chest congestion, coughing or other respiratory problems. George, for example, had
come for acupressure because of bowel problems, hemorrhoids and lower back pain—
all related to the Large Intestine Meridian. (Imbalance in the Lung Meridian was
also reflected in his pulses.) George saw that his physical tensions were protections
against feelings of weakness or hurt. He was motivated to break down his psychic
rigidities, and tolerate ensuing feelings of vulnerability, because he no longer wanted
to tolerate the physical rigidities and related problems. This meant learning to be
aware of, and express, his softer feelings and, similarly, learning to say "too much,"
instead of handling things with grim "determination."

Stoicism is an inability to let down defenses and show weakness or hurt. Because
of this, an accumulation of sorrow may be lurking behind the stoical front. Inability
to grieve or feel sorrow looks like the polar opposite of self-pitying, sorrowful
despondency, but it can be a manifestation of the same central problem: prolonged
sorrow due to incomplete grieving. Grief that has not been worked through can
produce either of these opposite syndromes: a low-energy state of continuous self-

pitying sorrow, or an apparently high-energy absence of tears or complaints. Either form of P'o imbalance is a malfunction in the ability to receive energy and in the ability to eliminate toxic substances, thoughts and feelings.

Ann's symptoms of throat constriction and a chronic dry cough pointed to hyperactivity of P'o. Ann had smoked for many years, but her cough could not be attributed just to that, for she had been afflicted with coughing fits since childhood. Her smoking was a side-effect of a general defense against feeling, which included blocking off any sounds of complaint. During a session focusing on ♯30 and Lung sedation, the therapist questioned Ann about her childhood. Her story was periodically interrupted by coughing fits. As Ann spoke, her throat tightened and closed, making her voice come from her throat with great restriction, so that it sounded like Ann was being choked.

The story that emerged was one of a violent conception and abusive childhood. Ann said that ten years earlier she had learned the truth of her conception—that her mother had been raped and had planned to abort the baby, but at the last minute got up and walked out of the room where the abortion was to be performed. Then the rapist, who was a powerful figure in their social circle, had arranged the marriage of Ann's mother to another man. Ann remembered this man yelling at her when she was a small child, and telling her mother to "make that 'Deigo Kid' shut up." (Ann's biological father was Italian.) The man who was supposed to be her father screaming at her, calling her a "Deigo Kid"—it never felt right, but she couldn't express it. All her life Ann had sensed the lie, but she had no facts to support her intuition. So, she could never ask, "what is the truth?"

During a session after Ann had quit smoking, while pressing deeply into the ♯30s, the therapist asked Ann to make a sound from her belly, doing so herself so that Ann would not be embarrassed by her sound. The sound naturally began to increase in volume. When Ann started to cough, it seemed an indication that she felt she should cut her sound off. She was reminded to keep her throat open and focus the sound low in her abdomen, feeling like she was pulling the sound up from her bowels. After a while, Ann was asked what her sound wanted to say. Her response was, "I want," repeated many times and interrupted by urges to cough. The therapist reminded Ann that it was safe to make her sounds and express her needs. "What is it *you* want, Ann?" she asked.

"I want to live," Ann replied in a stilted voice, like that of a mummy buried in a dark tomb. She was asked to say this over and over, until it sounded natural. "I want to live" was the basic desire of the fetus about to be aborted, and of the unwanted and emotionally deprived child that Ann had been. But now Ann did have her life and had earned it, so what else did she want right now? In a normal tone of voice, Ann said that she wanted respect, love, and sex—but had always felt unable to ask for these things. She cried gently for a while.

Ann's coughing fits could be seen as a censoring device to prevent her from expressing, or even feeling, her desires and wants. When a new thought or desire excited Ann, her self-expression system went into a panic, her throat closed, and the only release was to cough. The *Nei Ching* describes this condition, saying that times of excitement and change create a cough. To cough is to suddenly expel air from the lungs, with an explosive noise. "On the figurative level, the cough is a rejection of something unwanted," says Connelly, "and this capacity to expel something unwanted is associated with Metal" or P'o.[18] Persistent coughing can indicate a need to expel something unwanted, to cough something up or let something out.

Selfishness and Self-Seeking ━━━━━━━━━━━━━━━━━━━━━━━

Greed, or wanting more and more and more, can be a way to maintain defensive pride. Having a lot of things, money or admirers can be a way to demonstrate that "I'm just fine; nothing really bothers me and I don't need anything (or anyone)." Money and acquisitions can be an attempt at filling an inner hole, the existence of which may be denied. Greed is the accumulation of excess, which the Taoists say is the enemy of stillness and simplicity. Yet it is not the accumulation that is the problem, so much as the implied lack of attention to inner holes that cannot be filled by material things. Scrooge is a stereotypic example of the greedy miser. The ghosts of Christmas present, past and future do not just tell Scrooge that his greed is bad. Rather, they show Scrooge that greed cannot get him what he needs. All his money cannot compensate for his underlying lack of love and friendship.

Greed for the things that wo/men want, and devoting oneself to attaining these things, interferes with something else that wo/men want: peace and tranquility. These feelings come from stillness, not from busily rushing around after more and more things, or more and more social acclaim. Trying to find fulfillment in a chase after tangible and intangible possessions is "running blindly into miseries," for it is letting the "ten thousand things" rule. Peace has to do with seeing that things come and go; they exist and then revert back to their origin. Tuning in to this origin of all things, the Tao, yields a real and deep sense of tranquility.

To find this tranquility, Lao Tzu suggests that we "appear in plainness and hold to simplicity; restrain selfishness and curtail desires."[19] A common meaning of *selfishness* is exclusive concern for oneself, or seeking one's own advantage or pleasure without regard for others. Through such hardness and selfishness, the heart grows rigid. Like Scrooge, we become isolated from others, deprived of heartfelt connections and love. Another form of selfishness is *self-seeking*, or seeking the inner Self. The search for this Whole Self can be seen as a kind of *greed for life*—for the feelings and emotions, perceptions and insights, by which to explore and experience the core Self.

Hans Selye points out that accumulating the fruits of our labors seems to be an instinctive drive. Humans tend to collect things—money, buildings, stamps, coins, trophies, cars, records, almost anything. Greed is an inordinate acquisitiveness, or the desire to acquire more than is needed. The desire for acquisitions can instead be directed into collecting intangible things like gratitude, respect, goodwill and all the other forms of love. Such greed is in the service of self-actualization and of personal peace, as Selye explains in his book *Stress Without Distress:*

> "He who follows our doctrine will greedily hoard wealth and strength, not in the form of money or domination of others, but by earning the goodwill, gratitude, respect and love of those who surround him. Then, even if he has neither money nor power to command, he will still become virtually unassailable and safe, for no one would have a personal reason to attack him."[20]

At first reading, this has an omnipotent ring to it. On the last page of this book, Selye endears himself to me by his frank admission that he has not always been perfectly successful in following this philosophy, though the attempt to do so yielded much happiness. Human beings, all of them, have shortcomings. Philosophies are guides for helping to increase the joy of life, not measuring sticks for judging ourselves and others.

> "In closing, let me express the wish that many of you who read these pages will be better at applying my principles than I am, for I should like your success to augment my capital of love, gratitude, and goodwill, which I have so shamelessly admitted wanting to hoard."[21]

Envy and Jealousy: Grievance Collectors

Jealousy and envy are quite human phenomena, but they are perpetually on most lists of unacceptable feelings. Jealousy and envy can make us miserable, but they also have an adaptive purpose—stimulating us to develop our talents and improve our life condition. Jealous or envious rivalry can stimulate self-development, and may have motivated some of mankind's development through the stages of civilization, too, as the movie "Quest for Fire" illustrates. A primitive tribe, which doesn't know how to make fire, is in big trouble when their fire goes out. In quest of fire, a couple of men from this tribe eventually encounter another tribe which has not only learned to kindle fire by friction, but also to make things for increased convenience and pleasure. The feeling that "I want what you have" spurs the first tribe on to acquire new skills and advance their level of civilization.

Envy and jealousy are comparative or competitive feeling states. It is natural to compare ourselves with others, yet comparisons can be self-destructive. Competition can be fun, but when the competition is too serious, it can be dangerous. The Taoists advised avoiding the temptation to vie with others, and suggested looking neither to the right nor to the left, neither at those who are "better" nor at those who are "worse." An inordinate desire for what others have, or for exclusive possession of someone or something, may indicate blindness to natural laws.

> "It is the law of heaven to make fullness empty and to make full what is modest; when the sun is at its zenith, it must, according to the law of heaven, turn toward its setting, and at its nadir it rises toward a new dawn. In obedience to the same law, the moon when it is full begins to wane, and when empty of light it waxes again. This heavenly law works itself out in the fates of men also. It is the law of earth to alter the full and to contribute to the modest. High mountains are worn down by the waters, and the valleys are filled up. It is the law of fate to undermine what is full and to prosper the modest. And men also hate fullness and love the modest."[22]

In its simplest form, *jealousy* is a painful awareness that a rival is receiving more affection or approval then oneself. Insecurity about oneself increases the likelihood that this will feel intolerable, or that one will feel jealous even where there is no real threat to one's position. Jealousy breeds mistrust and apprehension. The result is *suspicious jealousy*—suspecting rivalry and unfaithfulness and fearing the loss of love or of exclusive devotion. In the chronic case, there may develop a distrustful watchfulness or a hostile vigilance; of course, the mistrust and suspicion then give rise to more jealousy.

Anticipatory jealousy likewise illustrates the close relationship between P'o and Chih (the psychic land related to fear and mistrust). Anticipatory jealousy comes from a groundless fear that something is happening, or about to happen, to our relationship with someone whose affection and attention we crave. Investing self-esteem in others sets the stage for wanting their exclusive devotion, and this exaggerated need multiplies the occasions for fearing loss. To help transform anticipatory jealousy, we could interpret it as a warning to appreciate loved ones, and to open up and show love to them. Love cannot be possessed, but only held in an open hand and caressed.

While jealousy has to do with the fear of loss—of approval, relationship or exclusive devotion, *envy* comes from the desire to have more—to have a (more) loving relationship, (more) children, (more) friends or (greater) popularity, or more and better things. "Envy" is defined by Webster as a "painful or resentful awareness of advantage possessed by another and the desire to possess the same advantage." It is somewhat acceptable to admit to envying societally-sanctioned targets of envy, like the upper class or authority figures. To admit to envy of friends is not so common, yet friends often *are* the targets of our envy. If you are feeling deprived on many levels, and a friend tells you how well everything is going with the relationship and the job and the travel plans, envy is quite likely to pop up. Although you may be genuinely happy for your friend, a little child inside says "me, too!"

Envy generally is born of deprivation. It may arise just because things have been hard lately, with not much money for luxuries or even for necessities, and by comparison somebody else seems to "have it all"—or at least to have a very large piece of the pie. Envy may arise just because your relationship or marriage is at a low ebb, or there is not much love in your life, and someone else seems constantly joyful about their love relationship. However, the roots of envy may go much deeper—back to feeling powerless in the face of a true early deficit of things or of love.

Emotional deprivation can be just as devastating as physical deprivation. In either case, though, envy arises not just because of a lack, but because we perceive others as having what we lack. Privation and hardship can bring people closer together, when the lack is a general one. If everyone is poor, nobody is poor. Likewise, in a society where there are no expectations of romantic love, nobody would feel deprived without it. Not only awareness of a lack, but also feelings of injustice and powerlessness are the roots of envy.

When there starts to be the feeling that you don't have what you want or need *because* others have it, a paranoid flavor has been added to the envy. Then not only have you been ripped off or "screwed," while someone else has won, but in so doing they stole the prize from you. This is not a "sick" feeling—or at least, if it is, society is sick. Envy is a societal problem, because our society encourages competition. Envy is a corollary of the attitude that achieving success means grabbing as much as you can, of the limited amount of stuff available, before someone else gets it all.

Today the media assures that we can always hear about people who have more.

The media is also diligent in informing us about the high percentage of marriages or businesses that fail, the high unemployment rate, and other energy-depleting facts. It is easy to know that others have advantages we lack, and to feel powerless in the face of the statistics. Envy can be seen as a modern challenge. The entertainment industry brings that challenge to affairs of the heart, with countless songs, movies and stories of love. By comparison, which is hard to avoid, our own love relationships may seem like mundane affairs. If envy is not transformed back into openness, our relationships in fact and insidiously may start to lose their luster.

Mild, fleeting envious feelings translate into just wanting more for ourselves. In the more extreme case, there is anger about having less, or about others having more. Feelings of envy alternate with self-pity, and are fueled by anger about apparent present and past disparities. One way to deal with the anger is by finding fault with those who have more. Chronic envy can turn us into *fault-finders* and *grievance collectors*.

The *Golden Flower* says that "all sensuous desires and impulses of anger are affects of the anima (P'o)."[23] [Yet acupressure theory correlates anger with Hun, not P'o. An explanation for this seeming conflict is found in the Five Aspects theory, which says that if P'o is imbalanced, it is unable to control Hun, and so anger rises.] P'o gets weakened when the life energies are devoted to the pursuit of unbridled desires. The *Golden Flower* says that the life energies are no longer wasted when there is a liberation from external things. When the desire for external things can be recognized, but not clung to, then P'o can give energy to Hun, and this energy can be used for self-actualization rather than for the angry pursuit of possessions.

During work with the Lung and Large Intestine Meridians, James noticed that his envy of more prosperous peers was shackling his power.* Comparisons were inhibiting his work more than stimulating it. The angry struggle of fighting for his rights was draining his energy and getting in the way of what he really wanted. The envy and jealousy were focused on acquiring recognition and having a better lifestyle, but the basic inner hole had to do with a need for creative self-expression. What James really wanted was the opportunity to manifest and show his talent. As he focused on this, rather than on the subsidiary desires which sometimes masked it, openness and self-assertion began to replace envy and resentment. When feelings of deprivation and envy popped up again, so did the tension in the #30s. James learned to use these Lung points, and the Large Intestine points in the neck area, as barometers to help him notice a defensive closing down before it progressed into defensive pride and envy.

Jealousy, envy and greed can arise to call our attention to some lack in ourselves or in our situation. The true lack must be noticed and dealt with, by setting intentions, making plans and doing things. Otherwise, this lack will continue to generate feelings of deprivation, which will be compensated by feelings of greed, jealousy and envy, laced with anger and resentment. To see the real deficit underlying these feelings is to begin their transformation. This might involve loosening attachments to particular objects, persons, timetables or outcomes, so that there can be an openness and receptivity to the many different ways that voids can be filled.

Jealousy, envy and greed are encouraged by perceiving oneself as separate from

---

* We met James in Chapter 9, Part 3.

other human beings, all of whom are competing for the same limited pot. The opposite, Taoist perception is seeing the self and others as connected and bound together in a common fate. This viewpoint is an antidote to comparisons and competitiveness. Feeling the inter-connectedness of all life is the easiest place from which to accept that voids get filled and excesses emptied. Then openness to life can replace the compulsion to possess and hold onto things and people.

To transform jealousy, envy and greed, the first step is to acknowledge that *you want what you want*. The next step is seeing that you *can* have what you want, in some way and at some time—as long as the desire is in tune with the growth needs of your *whole self*. Transforming feelings of jealousy, envy and greed involves asking, "Why do I want this?" Is it for self-development, or to somehow help wo/mankind? Or is it just to hide some other, more fundamental inner lack by making things *seem* better? When the real inner needs are recognized, the tense knots of P'o-related tensions can relax, as bodymind energy flows more into living, and less into scheming and grasping.

12. The Land of Chih Revisited —Kidney Meridian

Part 1. SYNERGIC STATE OF CHIH: resolution, will(power), trust

The Kidney Meridian is the "strengthening officer." It influences the bones, marrow and brain, and so strengthens the posture. It controls the adaptive or reserve energy, and so gives vigor and stamina to the entire bodymind. Thus the classics say, "When the Kidney energy is strong, the body is in good spirits and intelligence increases." The energic condition of the kidneys affects all life processes from birth onwards. It is important for growth, for the maintenance of vitality, and to prevent premature aging.

The strength and durability of the Kidney energy is important for general vitality and for sexual energy. "Chih" is an apt name for the related aspect of the psyche, because of the similarity to the word for energy: "ch'i." All the meridians transport energy, but the Kidney has the special function of governing the energy reserves which allow adaptation to life's continuous changes. "The Kidneys store essence," say the classics. This essence is the "ching ch'i," or *reserve energy*, which can be released to any organ or part of the body on need, and which influences the amount of available sexual energy. *Resolution* is the psychological edition of this energy, which gives strength to the character and power to the personality, as well as to the body.

A major challenge of life is adapting to change and maintaining homeostasis, or bodymind balance, despite environmental and interpersonal stresses. Stress researcher Hans Selye says that there is an *adaptation energy* which helps us adjust to stressors, and that this energy is somehow different from caloric energy. He says "we have no objective way of measuring adaptability at any given moment; but there appears to be a superficial, readily available, replaceable type, and another more deeply hidden in reserves which can replenish the superficial kind only after some rest or diversion of activity."[1]

The Taoists also talk about two kinds of adaptive energy. The *"ching ch'i,"* or reserve energy, is readily available, for it is produced from the energy we take in by eating and breathing. There is also a deeper *"yuan ch'i"* or primal adaptation energy, which is absorbed before birth. These two kinds of adaptive energy are like two special kinds of fuel—the yuan ch'i is the original fuel for the vital spark of life; the ching ch'i provides the extra bursts of energy for adapting to stressful changes. The Kidneys store the ching ch'i and, through a point called "Life Gate Fire" ["F"], the meridian is in contact with the yuan ch'i [stored in the "hara," internal to "D"]. The classics say that without "Kidney Fire," nothing can grow, because this energy is an important catalyst in the process of energy production. The "fire function" of

Kidney Meridian

Points of the Kidney Meridian

JSD #43—On the sole, find the pain point under the pad of the foot. The point is in a depression between the junction of the second and third metatarsals with the phalanges (toe bones). It is mainly used as a revival point. (Avoid on pregnant women.) ["Bubbling Spring"—K 1]

JSD #10: K—On the inside of the foot, feel for the sensitive spot above the top of the first metatarsal, in a hollow below the navicular bone.
["Blazing Valley"—K 2]

Source point—This point is midway between the tip of the inner anklebone (malleolus) and the "Achilles tendon," where a pulse can be felt.
["Shining Sea"—K 3]

JSD #9—In a depression 1 *chon* directly below the inner anklebone (medial malleolus).
["Illuminated Sea"—K 6]

JSD #39: K—Press down onto the top of the pubic bone, about 1/2 *chon* out from the midline of the abdomen.
["Transverse Bone"—K 11]

JSD #38: K—This point is about 1/2 *chon* directly outside the navel.
["Vitals Associated Point"*—K 16]

---

* *Kidney Associated Point*—see Chapter 8 for explanation of the associated points.

JSD #4: K—This point is inside from JSD #4** and about 2 *chon* out from the midline of the chest, in the third intercostal space. ["Spirit Burial-Ground"—K 24]

JSD #3: K—This point is inside from JSD #3,** in a depression below the bottom of the collarbone (clavicle) and 2 *chon* out from the midline. ["Associated Points Mansion"—K 27]

Examples of Local-Distal Point Combinations

Local point		Distal point
16	+	31, 12,*** 9, 3: K
3: K	+	38: K, 39: K, 9, S.
39: K	+	41, 10: K, S.

S. = Source Point

** See Stomach Meridian, Chapter 6.
*** #31 and #12 help release any of the associated points. (See Bladder Meridian, Chapter 8.)
In the ending neck release, hold #21:B before holding the #22s.

the Kidney Meridian is as important as its "water function"—the regulation of urination.

Selye compares the two kinds of adaptative energy to "two types of sewage-disposal systems," because a side-effect of "the countless chemical processes required for adaptation" is the accumulation of waste products, which can produce exhaustion, diminishing elasticity of the connective tissue, hardening of the blood vessels, hypertension and predisposition to cardiovascular problems like strokes.* Like the Taoists, Selye recommends flowing around unimportant problems, rather than overstressing ourselves and clogging up our systems by using our precious adaptive energies for unimportant things.

According to acupressure theory, when the ching ch'i has been exhausted, the yuan ch'i may be called on for adaptation to stress. That is, when the most readily available, superficial stores of energy have been used up, the deeper reserves must be tapped. Since these deeper reserves aren't easily replenished, it is wise to periodically take account of our existing energy reserves. Forging through difficulties at any cost is not the Taoist definition of resolution, if it means depleting one's vital energy by determined pursuit of egotistical goals. Some Taoists say the amount of yuan ch'i is finite, and its vitality tends to decrease with time. Others say that this precious energy might be revitalized and rejuvenated through "hara breathing," stimulation of Kidney points, visualization and rest. Selye says:

> "Our reserves of adaptation energy could be compared to an inherited fortune from which we can make withdrawals; but there is no proof that we can also make additional deposits. We can squander our adaptability recklessly, 'burning the candle at both ends,' or we can learn to make this valuable resource last long, by using it wisely and sparingly, only for things that are worthwhile and cause least distress."[2]

Sometimes the body has to speak up before we notice that we are frittering our previous energy reserves away on unimportant things. Sometimes it might take pain to get the attention of the psyche, for there are so many things we think we *should* or *must* do. How rapidly many of them lose their importance, when we suddenly are wracked with pain or contorted with tension! Like that summer day some years back, when an intense pain seized my back in the #16 and #17 areas, as I got out of bed. I hadn't "moved wrong" or injured myself. I barely could get into my car; pain was the price of accomplishing that maneuver. X-rays showed slight subluxations, the result of extreme muscular cramping.

The culprit was adrenal depletion, or the exhaustion phase of the stress response. The Kidney Meridian, and so most likely the "ching ch'i," was severely deficient.** For some time, I had known I was under a lot of stress, but I thought I was handling everything just fine. I was greatly surprised by my body's contrary opinion that I had exceeded my available energy reserves in the attempt to adapt, and adapt, and adapt. Since then, the phrase "I'm handling it" has become a red flag to me. It seems that we can get so used to stress that we stop seeing it as stress, and unwittingly deplete

---

* See diagram, "Stages of Reaction to Stress," in Chapter 9, Part 2.

** Hans Selye's theory about the effects of stress, the "General Adaptation Syndrome," was briefly described in Chapter 9, Part 2.

our energy reserves by trying to handle too much, with too little support.

Big stressors are not required for depleting energy reserves; a hectic lifestyle will also do the job. "The more, and the faster, the better"—and the less reserve energy remains. "Hurry up and wait" is a similarly draining attitude. Hurrying uses more energy than calmly flowing along, but even more energy can be wasted by feeling anxious and uptight about waiting, in long lines or traffic jams, while the clock ticks on and deadlines approach.

The forces that mankind has loosed in the world are depleting our energy reserves, as well as those of the planet. Yet a greater culprit behind the general energy leakage may be our attitude towards these forces, for rampant fearfulness burns up the inner reserves. Maybe instead of seething, we can try breathing. We can consciously connect with the center of power from which all movement flows. If we feel apprehensive or weak, we can breathe into the "hara," contacting this energy reservoir and visualizing its replenishment, until we feel more resolute and more able to act when there is the need or opportunity. Hara breathing helps us feel the roots of our energy, and it helps us feel ourselves as part of a larger energic matrix. Similar feelings may come from hiking, riding, climbing, skiing or any activity which requires being physically and psychologically centered and in tune with Nature.

The "hara" is an energy center about two inches below the navel and inside the lower abdomen. To experience the hara is to experience the inner power of the original life center. "For every movement is as though anchored in an immovable centre from which all motion flows and from which it receives its force, direction and measure," Durckheim explains. "The immovable centre lies in Hara."[3] The hara is the body's center of gravity. "Hara breathing" is a way to contact our inner balance-point and feel the power of our adaptive energy. Hara breathing also stimulates the parasympathetic nervous system to relax the body, thus moderating the "fight or flight" response to stressors.

How to Do Hara Breathing

Although this technique can be used to reduce stress under almost any circumstance, it is easiest to practice in a quiet, peaceful place. You can sit on a chair or on the floor, if that is comfortable, or you can lie on your back (bending the knees, if you like, to help relax the lower back). First, breathe naturally and let your shoulders and jaws drop, relaxing your neck and forehead. Then inhale slowly through your nose (counting to five), and gently exhale through your mouth (also counting to five). As you inhale, feel a movement all the way down to your hara. *Allow* your abdomen to expand as your diaphragm moves down in a full breath, then let your abdomen relax as you exhale completely. Breathe continuously, with no pauses between the exhalation and the inhalation.*

* You can also hold the breath for a few seconds *after* the inhalation, to concentrate the energy in the hara, as described in *The Acupressure Way of Health: Jin Shin Do*, Chapter 4. The use of hara breathing as a "channeling" technique is also explained there. Basically, channeling is letting the universal energy flow through you. While giving a Jin Shin Do session, you can visualize absorbing new energy as you inhale into the hara, and then letting that energy flow out your fingers.

Closing your eyes, focus your attention as completely as possible on the hara. If thoughts come, just let them go. Feel the abdomen expanding from the inside out—the skin and muscles expanding as you inhale and relaxing as you exhale. Gradually move your focus into the very center of the lower abdomen.

Really feeling the hara takes some time, so it's helpful to practice hara breathing every day or two, for fifteen minutes or more. You will feel more relaxed, first in the abdomen and lower back. You might feel a warmth inside the hara, and a wonderful deep relaxation in the whole bodymind. You might enter a calm, peaceful, dreamlike state, perhaps with lovely colors to watch inside your mind. After a while, you will feel a renewed vitality. Or you might go to sleep for a little while, if your energy reserves are low. Afterwards, stretch . . . like a cat . . . and get up slowly.

Now might be a good time to try "hara breathing," and perhaps to hold a few Kidney points too. Continue hara breathing for as long as it feels comfortable, or just a little longer (like you would with physical exercise). As hara breathing begins to feel more natural, the general consensus is that the hara energy is strong and powerful. "It's so powerful!" said one man. "I almost don't know if I can sustain the energy . . . it's wonderful!" A woman exclaimed, "It's amazing to feel that I have so much energy! It's like a big reservoir inside me—but I'm only using a little bit of the surface." As her abdomen began to move with her breathing, another woman experienced rhythmic, wave-like body movements which looked orgasmic. At first she was anxious about letting her feelings be so visible. Similarly, she felt anxious about letting go sexually. After a tremendous energetic release, she felt "more than just relief of the low back pain I'd had—a feeling of lightness and freedom." She later reported that doing hara breathing during foreplay and love-making increased her sexual responsiveness.

Balance and strength of the Hara and of the Kidney energy generates power of personality in general, and sexual vitality too. When we feel full of energy, we radiate a vitality that attracts others to us. The classics say the amount of available sexual energy depends on the strength of the ching ch'i, or reserve energy. Hara breathing helps replenish the reserve energy, and holding points of the Kidney Meridian enhances the effect. Hara breathing also helps increase awareness of the pelvic area, and of the external and internal sexual organs, thus enhancing the ability to feel sensual pleasure. Yet hara breathing in itself is a non-sexual, meditative experience which can facilitate deep energic relaxation and awareness of the vital energy.

The Power of the Will

The *Nei Ching* says the Kidneys "are like the officials who do the energetic work, and they excel by their ability and cleverness." Will and resolution are controlled by the Kidney energy.[4] These are feelings which make it possible to do energetic work —to have firmness of resolve and do what is needed. To will something is to have a strong and fixed purpose, and the energy to carry it out. A feeling of resolution awakens an inner power which can be sensed and felt by others, and which is commonly called "willpower." What is this power of will?

The will is "an emergency mechanism under the control of the ego which can on occasion override the emotional response," says Dr. Alexander Lowen. "And in some situations it can be lifesaving." The instinctive impulse upon feeling fear is to escape; will is the force that enables persistence in that escape, or allows other alternatives. "The will, however, does not diminish fear. It enables an individual to stand his ground or advance in the face of his fear . . . When the ego is identified with the body, it will support the body's emotional responses and direct them into effective actions. If a person is afraid, it will function to assure his escape from the danger."[5]

It is often implied that will is the power to conquer our feelings or override our emotional responses. I am instead defining will as a force which enables us to act effectively in regard to a problem that has been highlighted by our emotional responses. The slight difference between these two definitions is important. Will is self-control *in the service of feelings*—particularly feelings of fear. Will begins with *listening to* fear, for fear can arise to inform us about threats and dangers. Will is the determination to act appropriately in regard to situations highlighted by emotional responses like fear.

Self-control begins with self-knowing. What are you thinking, and what are you feeling? If you are feeling afraid, you can estrange yourself from the fear, denying it and carrying on despite it. Or you can do the opposite—which may end up looking the same. You can *allow* the feeling and *follow* it to its source, to discover what events or thoughts stimulated the fear. In life-threatening situations, what is feared is generally obvious. The fear then makes you more alert, and gives you the energy to react to the danger.

In other situations, the source of fearfulness may be less clear. Just listening to fear might modify it, for you might discover that it's coming from an old, negative thought. For instance, fear can come from the threat of rejection, but the present situation may hold no such threat—except insofar as it rings old bells. After paying attention to the fear, you can more easily act resolutely in regard to the real or psychological dangers which the fear has highlighted. This is will. Unlike blind determination, will has its basis in understanding. It is the resolution to survive, go forward and grow. The *I Ching* says:

> ". . . if one is sincere when confronted with difficulties, the heart can penetrate the meaning of the situation. And once we have gained inner mastery of a problem, it will come about naturally that the action we take will succeed. In danger all that counts is really carrying out all that has to be done—thoroughness—and going forward, in order not to perish through tarrying in the danger."[6]

Living without hiding (from oneself or the world) both requires and develops resolution and strength of character. There is danger in the world, and there is danger also from conditioned negative thoughts and habitual defenses. In either case, dealing with fear is learning to appropriately stand one's ground, retreat or advance in the face of that which is feared. This means getting in touch with an inner power which wants to resolve or dissolve difficulties. "Chih" is the aspect of the psyche related to this inner strength, which allows us to move towards being *all* of our changing Selves, in each changing moment.

Strengthening the Kidney Meridian is helpful for any long-term psychotherapeutic process—including the one called "life." However, it can take time to strengthen the Kidney energy, for this means building energy reserves, which depends on well-being

270

in the whole bodymind. The reserve energy of the Kidneys is tapped whenever there is a need for energy in any part of the bodymind. Building reserve energy means learning to take in more energy, and taking care of physical or psychological problems which are draining that energy. Reserve energy (ching ch'i) is the foundation of resolution (Chih).

One of my favorite images of resolution comes from Heather, whom we met while discussing the Gall Bladder, Small Intestine and Spleen Meridians—and tension headaches, allergies, shoulder pain and menstrual problems. Though these symptoms were alleviated, Heather's pulses continued to be generally deficient, and the Kidney particularly so. As she started sharing her problems, the pervasive theme that I heard was fear. Fear of conflict lay behind her continual attempts to "make nice." Fear kept her from living alone and making her own way in the world, though she was frustrated by her dependence on her parents.

One of Heather's dreams was a clear reflection of her lack of self-trust and dependent lifestyle. She was in a big building with all the people in her life. She was about to take the elevator down, but felt afraid of doing so, because it sometimes crashed. Her boyfriend pulled her back just before the doors shut, and then everyone was screaming as the elevator crashed. Fear woke her up. In the dream, her own fear tried to wake her up to danger, but not trusting her own feelings, she depended on her boyfriend to save her.

Heather began to work on becoming self-directed, and she did hara breathing to build up her reserve energy. In one session, as we were focusing on #16 and Kidney-related points, Heather recalled the feeling of plunging into a cold mountain lake, which she had recently done. She said the image of plunging into a cold lake symbolized *resolve*, and made an analogy with other plunges of life—like starting a business or profession, living alone, moving or getting married. "Maybe the anxiety and fear about those plunges makes no more sense than fearing a tidal wave will come from the lake and whomp you," she said "although regarding the lake, it's clearly over when you're out! In life it's not so clear."

In another session focusing on Kidney points, Heather remembered feeling scared of her father when she was little, and hiding in closets. She saw that her continuous attempt to please others was a way of hiding, and that it had seemed easier until now to hide her real self and her desires. "You're told what to feel," she said. "To discover you have your own feelings, that you can feel, is scary." Heather was discovering that she could be the director of her own life. "I used to not trust anyone else to be the director, in my teenage rebellious phase, but I also didn't trust myself, because I was too insecure. So I still depended on others to play the role of the director."

In later sessions, we focused on her very tight abdomen, working with hara breathing and with areas "C," "D" and #38. Heather felt her face relax as her abdomen relaxed. She experimented with making different faces, and found that a perpetual "make nice" smile was an energy blockage. As she let her feelings show, she felt energy moving down out of her shoulders, neck and face. "What a difference, after holding my feelings back out of fear, and knotting up my insides in the process!" After about half an hour of hara breathing, putting her hands over her abdomen, Heather said, "I feel such a power here."

Three weeks later she said, "I've learned that if I'm not being me, *all* of me, then someone else is having the experience! When I'm being constantly fearful and worried, I'm not being all of me. It's not worth it! If I'm being me, people don't take advantage of me so much. I can *feel* the inner strength." Heather's pulses had stabilized and she looked, as well as felt, more resolute. Not long after this, she found a way to be more independent, and terminated therapy due to moving out of the area. "A thousand miles' journey begins from the spot under one's foot," says Lao Tzu. Resolution is the force that allows the journey to continue, towards being one's whole Self, despite fear aroused by unexpected turns along the way or born of fatigue.

Vitality in Health and in Illness

Possible signs of weak Kidney energy include: urinary problems; stiffness or pain in the #16 area; fatigue; deterioration or brittleness of the bones; knee problems; impairment in the thinking processes; general lack of energy and low sexual energy. The Kidney Meridian also influences the sense of hearing. The classics say, "The kidney ch'i penetrates to the ears; if the kidney is harmonious, then the five sounds can be heard." The Kidney energy affects vitality throughout life; all of the above symptoms can be associated with aging. A corollary, according to the Taoist yogis, is that strengthening the adaptive energy related to the Kidneys can slow down aging.

The kidneys indeed do the "energetic work" and are important organs of detoxification. They filter water and waste material from the blood, then selectively reabsorb useful material and most of the water, passing the waste materials and liquids on to the bladder. A principal function is clearing unessential solutes from the blood and conserving those needed by the body. By regulating the excretion of water and solutes, the kidneys help control the volume, composition and pressure of body fluids. Related hormonal mechanisms influence blood pressure, body temperature, and the changing of vitamin D to its biologically active form (which is important for calcium and phosphorus metabolism, thus influencing the bones).* The kidneys also help regulate the electrolyte content of the blood; improper functioning can be a cause of edema.

The kidneys require appropriate fluid intake to perform their functions, and what is appropriate varies with the climate and type of activity. Excess intake of coffee when tired, and alcohol when wired, can weaken the kidneys. So can excessive consumption of salt (which encourages an excess of liquids). As the Zen masters suggested, pay attention to the body—drink when thirsty; sleep when tired; eat (simple foods) when hungry.

Chronic weakness of the kidney energy can correlate with pain or hypersensitivity of the lumbar area or entire spine, deterioration of the bones, weakness of the lower extremities, or blurred vision and dizziness. The *Nei Ching* says the person may be "prone to slip and fall prostrate" and to have breathing difficulties. Often strengthening the Kidney energy will help in such cases, but if the symptoms don't respond easily to acupressure, the need for a thorough medical examination is obvious.

Symptoms need to be noticed and given attention in order to increase bodymind

* Hypertension, or high blood pressure, can also be related to the Liver Meridian, and to the Heart and Pericardium, although if there is chronic excitè all the organs will be affected. Release of neck tension, at #23, #19, #20, #21 and #22, is often helpful.

wellness—that is, for the experience of joyful vitality, not just from fear of disease. Ultimately, to be healed to a new and vital wholeness includes finding a courageous resolution in the face of life or death, since there is no generally applicable magic which can make us exempt from the human condition. Resolution is a force that does not depend on continuous youth, strength, or wellness.

> "This is the way of acupuncture: if man's vitality and energy do not propel his own will his disease cannot be cured."[7]

Speaking of Kidney-related dis-eases, the *Nei Ching* also says, "those who act bravely and courageously will bring (the disease) to an end, while those who are afraid and cowardly (become infected and) fall ill."[7] Illness can be prolonged because of a lack of vitality, resolution and will. On the other hand, sometimes illness just *is*. There is a time to live and a time to die. Some of the most courageous behavior I have witnessed has been in the face of a seemingly senseless selection to the fate of cancer. Need death mean there was no healing? Dr. Albert Kreinheder points out that illness can be a healing on a deeper level than the continuation of bodily form:

> "The symptoms are the crying out of the body telling you it has had enough. The symptoms will tear you apart at the very places where you have held too tightly. . . . The object of healing is not to stay alive. It is to move closer to wholeness. Healing may take place in death; death is the final healing. Whatever comes is ours, and we can handle it.
>
> "When we become ill, it is as if we have been chosen or elected, not to be limited and crippled, but to be healed. The disease always carries its own cure and also the cure for our whole personality. If we take it as our own and stay with this new experience, with the pain and the fear and all the accompanying images, we will be healed to a wholeness far beyond our previous so-called health . . . God does not punish us. He selects us."[8]

A Basic Sense of Trust

A person can be resolute out of an egotistical will to have power over others, or resolution can be empowered by a basic sense of *trust*. Each of us is a child of God, a part of Tao. The more you can trust that this is so, and the more you can trust your core self, then the more resolute you can be about living fully and consciously. The more you can trust the love and integrity of your mate, the more resolute you can feel about reconciling differences and hanging in there through the rough spots. Similarly, the more you can trust that there is a growthful purpose to your life, and that everything can be used for growth, the easier it is to resolutely follow your heart-felt path.

Basic trust can get damaged by introjected negative messages and unresolved emotional trauma. A path back to trust is well-illustrated by some of the insights Louise had while exploring her fear of intimacy. Since a car accident several months earlier, Louise had recurrently suffered from low back pain, in the area above the pelvic bone. She said her neck and shoulders had been feeling really tight during the weekend preceding her first session. The main shoulder tensions were along the Small Intestine

Meridian. I first worked with this area, then with the lower back, using Kidney Meridian points.

Louise said that she was very reserved in relationships, but that earlier in her life, her fear of letting her feelings show had been much more extreme. Others saw Louise as being always nice and calm, but that had ceased feeling like a compliment because she sensed that her constant "niceness" was a general restriction of herself. Through her current relationship, Louise was discovering that she tended to project her "dark side" onto others. She had realized that some of the qualities she sometimes attributed to her boyfriend—like being critical, judgmental or "a bastard"—were qualities of her own that she didn't like. Intellectually she acknowledged her dark side, but she was afraid to really own the part of her that was a "bitch" or a "brat." She was afraid of her anger, because then she felt like a "bitch." She was afraid to express her feelings, because she didn't want to make a fool of herself.

"Why am I so afraid of that?" she asked. She recalled being teased as a child, but not feeling humiliated, and not being self-conscious about calling boys—even if they said "not you again!" "Then right around puberty, something changed," Louise said. "I got real self-conscious, couldn't even say anything around boys, and thought I was really ugly and awkward." Some of that negative self-image was still around, though Louise was in fact quite attractive.

Could there be a relationship between the old negative self-image and fear of the "dark side"? Maybe it's harder to tolerate the "bitch" in yourself, when you're already struggling to overcome an old negative self-image. "That feels right," Louise responded. "It reminds me of how I sometimes react childishly, and even start to whine, if my boyfriend accuses me of being a brat or a bitch. The hurt adolescent Louise takes over again. It's like I already have such a pool of self-criticism that I can't bear for someone else to say something negative." Maybe an angry woman is, in a way, a bitch! "Why deny those parts of myself? They just get more insistent when I do!"

Louise had been a trusting and confident child. Puberty was the onset of a sense of inferiority about her appearance because, by comparison with societal ideals of feminine perfection, Louise thought she came out short. "It was a really terrible time," she said. "I felt miserable. And then my mother died when I was 16. Somehow I felt guilty about that, like I was somehow to blame. She was sick with cancer for about three years before she died, but somehow I always thought she would get well." Though the death might have been anticipated, it was still a shock. "That made it a much more terrible time."

Basic trust is of Self and of Tao, or of God. Trust of others follows from this basic trust; it cannot be attached to expectations about the perfection of their actions or the permanence of their presence in our lives. Trust is in the *essence*. The essence of life is a basic energy or spirit, which is called the Tao in its universal form and the Self in its personal form. Trust must be dynamic, because the Self and the Tao are dynamic. We can only *hope* for something to be static. What we can *trust* is that life will keep bringing changes, and that all of them are somehow part of our unfolding.

It's hard to accept some of the changes, but finding a way to use them for growth builds self-confidence, or trust of Shen. Courage begins with risking, or extending yourself into life, and finding that *you are enough.* You *can* deal with whatever comes

274

your way. You have the courage to *live*. The components of courage are self-confidence, trust and resolution. In other words, courage is the affect of a healthy Shen and a strong Chih.

Louise's pulses indicated a deficiency of Shen as well as Chih (of the Heart, Pericardium and Kidney Meridians). Her chest armoring and shallow breathing suggested some blockage of the heart center. What she was seeking was the courage to feel and live fully, but fear was getting in her way. When we get afraid, we contract—in general, and in particular places. A couple of Louise's particular places were the lower back and the chest.

As she spoke of her mother's death, I held the ♯18s with Pericardium distal points to encourage the release of the feelings that were locked behind her chest armoring. As Louise focused on breathing through the tension, sadness arose along with a desire to close down her feelings out of fear. As she let go to her tears, what came up was wanting her mother, not wanting to experience another loss, and being afraid of an intimacy that could make her vulnerable to feeling such loss again. She felt like her whole body wanted to collapse around the ♯16. Then, as the tension there released, a warmth radiated out from those points, and she felt solid, supported and happy.*

The trust that is developed in early childhood can get impaired by the shock of finding out that it is unrealistic to expect things to always turn out as we wish them to. This amounts to a loss of innocence, and there is a sadness about this loss, for somewhere inside we would like to always live in the light, or in the garden of Eden. Projects of adulthood include finding a balance between the light and the dark, and a trust that embraces both sides of life. I asked Louise if she could feel a basic sense of trust somewhere inside. She said it felt like a small, compressed light inside her chest.

I suggested that her inner Self knew about balanced trust, and that she could let her breathing lead her into contact with that inner Self. "What do you want to know about trust?" I asked Louise. "I guess *how* to trust," she said. I directed her to ask her inner Self about that. "What came up seems easier said than done," she said. "The message I got was to love fearlessly! That seems like step number eight hundred. I was hoping for maybe an easy one, two, three, four!" I suggested she could ask her core Self how to love fearlessly. "Develop a willingness to be hurt" was the message. Was there anything Louise could trust not to hurt her? "Maybe God," she said, "although I really mistrusted God after my mother's death. I had trusted that He wouldn't let anything bad happen."

I asked Louise what she could trust about God, or about life. "Maybe I can trust that everything is for growth," she responded. "Can you trust yourself?" I asked. "It depends on what part of myself," she responded, and then agreed that she could trust her essence. "Maybe your core Self can't really be hurt," I said. "That little light I saw got brighter as you said that," she replied. At the end of the session, Louise said she felt peace with seeing that hurt could be accepted. "I don't need to live with a fear of hurt that causes a fear of intimacy," she said. "There's some sadness with accepting the dark side of myself and of life. But that sadness feels sort of good, because I feel more *alive*."

* This session was described in the first part of Chapter 1.

Part 2. EXTREME EMOTIONS OF CHIH: fear or apprehension

Fear can unleash the energy and resolution needed to resolve difficulties and survive dangers. It can bring the experience of an inner power which is so strong that it enables us to go past our normal physical and psychological limits. Fear generated by the "elements" or forces of nature can also bond people together in the effort to deal with the danger. The experience of overcoming such threats can be revitalizing—which is one reason why people still seek mountains to climb, or take up sports which involve challenging or cooperating with the forces of nature.

With much of our fear, however, the source is not so clear. Many modern fears are characterized by ambiguity, which adds to the stress level—and tips it in the direction of *dis*tress. The result can be a state of low-level fear or anxiety about the future, which amounts to a "fear of fear"—the fear that threatening things will happen that we won't be able to handle.

The emotion of fear can rage from apprehension and agitation to alarm, dread or terror. Sudden fear may be followed by a pounding heart (an effect of adrenal stimulation), and we may break out into a cold sweat. With extreme fear, there may be deep guttural groaning, and there may be a liquid-like sensation down the legs—or even something literally descending (due to urinary incontinence). Fear energizes the organism to flee from the danger; feeling a lot of energy in the legs facilitates this reaction.

Continuous fear, on the other hand, is draining. This constant anticipatory state leads to weakness and exhaustion, for it is like running the bodymind motor too fast and too long. The continual hyperactivity puts pressure on the whole bodymind system, and depletes the adaptive energy. Symptoms can include urogenital problems, blurred vision, high blood pressure, *cardiac arrhythmia*, or an oppressive feeling in the chest, along with a general fearfulness.

Fear releases the reserve energy, or "ching ch'i," to energize the system for necessary emergency reactions. Fear also releases adrenalin, which is like a messenger for liberating the energy reserves and putting the body on "red alert." The functions that the Chinese attributed to the Kidneys (especially "kidney yang") have much to do with the *adrenal glands*, which cover the upper surface of the kidneys and secrete hormones influencing almost all body systems. The *adrenal medulla*, controlled by the sympathetic nervous system, secretes hormones which enable bodily adjustments to emotional states, including two hormones important in fear responses: *adrenaline* and *noradrenaline*.

Anticipatory states, or feelings of apprehension, stimulate the release of noradrenaline (also called *norepinephrine*). This hormone is a vasoconstrictor which elevates the blood pressure and slows the heart. Extreme emotional stress, like that of intense fear, also increases the secretion of adrenaline (or *epinephrine*). This hormone is also a vasoconstrictor and a cardiac stimulant. Adrenaline mobilizes the physiological changes necessary for the "fight or flight" response. These change include stimulation

276

of heart activity and breathing, increased circulation of blood in the muscles, stimulation of the liver to produce more *glucose* (blood sugar) from *glycogen* (starch), and reduction of gastrointestinal activity—because the digestion of food is not essential to dealing with an emergency. The resulting burst of energy enables high-speed responses to danger. This is the adaptive function of fear.

Fear becomes non-adaptive when it is habitual. It becomes destructive when there is no resolution of the fear, and when its energy is not used for constructive action. This might be the case when someone is held captive by tormenting enemies or criminals, or by an abusive family system, from which escape is or seems so dangerous that it is not attempted. Habitual fear can also be the result of our own tormenting thoughts. There is no escape because we believe that our negative, fearful thoughts are the reality. Ellen, for example, was afraid of feeling because she thought that letting herself feel would be letting herself in for a depression, like the one she had experienced ten years earlier. She also had no sexual feelings. Her physical symptoms included *nephritis* (inflammation of the kidneys)* and pain in the left back (both #16 and #17). In the first two sessions, I focused on release of the Gall Bladder Meridian, to relax her very tight neck and shoulders.

In the next session, tears came up during work with the Kidney Meridian, after some release of the neck [#21: LI] and of #18 and #17. Ellen was amazed to notice how she stopped the tears—"like turning off a switch inside."

Before the fourth session, she'd had kidney pain for two days, especially on the left. As I held Kidney points, she gradually began to breathe more fully into the abdomen. After about fifteen minutes of silence, I asked Ellen what she was seeing. "Blackness," she said. What was she feeling? "Fear." After a few minutes, she said the darkness had turned to light. She also said she was afraid of death yet attracted to it. I asked if she'd ever had thoughts of suicide, and Ellen replied that she had during her depression, but not now. "But I haven't felt joy in my life," she said, "except after the last Jin Shin Do session. The smell of the trees was *so* beautiful. I felt joy just looking at them, and at the sky." I asked if she ever went to the country. "No," she replied, "I'm too tired." What would she say if a friend gave her that excuse? Smiling, she answered, "Go to the country."

Ellen had noticed that there was a parallel between controlling her tears and stopping her sexual feelings. "It's like I turn a switch off and stop any feelings of sexual pleasure, too," she said. She had a pervasive fear of losing control, partly because she thought that letting herself feel would open the door to depressive feelings. I explained that depression is more related to non-feeling and non-joy, and asked what precipitated the depression ten years ago. Ellen suddenly looked tormented and said, "I don't deserve to feel pleasure because I killed." What was she seeing? Hesitantly, she told me of a traumatic home abortion twenty years ago. Shortly afterwards, her boyfriend left her and her father died.

There was still some sorrow about these losses, but the main problem was a long-standing belief that she had committed a heinous crime and was wicked. She feared that she had killed a human being, and would be punished for it. How did Ellen *know* that there was a human spirit in the three-month-old fetus? She just felt there was, so I suggested she try to communicate with that spirit now, explaining why she

---

* For which she was under a doctor's care.

couldn't accept a child twenty years ago and saying good-bye. As she did so, her sobs of grief over her loss turned into tears of relief at finally accepting what had happened and letting go of her need to punish herself.

She had overcome a longstanding fear of confronting her feelings about the abortion, and she had discovered that there was joy and strength on the other side of the painful feelings. As she hugged me, I told Ellen that she was a beautiful spirit and deserved joy. If the old chains tried to come back, she could shrug them off. After the session, she felt "very different," and she looked lighter and brighter. Also, her diaphragm had released a lot, though I had only worked directly with the Kidney Meridian and chest release.

The Anatomy of Fear

The Chinese classics say that in fear the energy is drained, or descends to the bowels and lower extremities. That is, the energy descends to the lower chakras (centers of the natural and instinctive life) and to the organs of flight. The sympathetic-adrenal system is charged and mobilized. It's like the psychic antennas go up, too, making for hyper-awareness and hyper-alertness.

Lowen describes fear as "a downward movement along the back [which] results in a pulling in of the tail section and the charging of the legs for flight. In a state of fear one turns tail and runs. If flight is not possible, the excitation is caught in the neck and back, the shoulders are raised, the eyes are wide open, the head is pulled back, and the tail is tucked in."[9] This is the posture of a cornered animal, and it is that of a human being who feels trapped—whether or not the fear is conscious. Tensions which maintain this posture include the lumbar [#16], neck [#21] and intercostal areas.

Fear and anger are related emergency responses, as the phrase "fight or flight" indicates. Fear can give rise to anger. Anger can be a way of releasing the energy stimulated by fear, or of covering up fear. If we can neither flee nor express anger, then both options of the "flight or fight" response are blocked and we are defenseless. Lack of self-trust or the threat of pain from a seemingly superior force can reduce us to this state of helplessness. Fear and anger likewise cannot easily mobilize action if they are responses to persons who seem necessary to our physical or emotional sustenance. Therefore, we may hesitate to express fear and anger to parents when we are children, or to employers or spouses when we are adults. We may try to overcome our feelings of helplessness by attempts at manipulating the environment—like through charm and cleverness, or by teary sulking, sarcasm or subtle put-downs. We can also avoid *feeling* our fear, with the help of abdominal armoring.

When tensions at the Kidney associated points [#16s] release, sometimes underlying fears come up for conscious attention. Staying with the fearful feelings usually leads us to their origin. A renewed feeling of resolution comes from confronting fears which have limited our enjoyment of life. I am reminded of a woman with cancer who suddenly asked "is that fear?" as I was holding #16 with Kidney points. She realized that her fear had been draining her already-depleted energy, and that her fear had a superstitious quality: "It's as though by fearing I can ward off that which I fear, but really the fear gives power to that which I fear." She transformed the fear by finding an inner strength which enabled her to live fully and enjoy the life left to her.

Another woman cried out in fear when the #39: Kidney point and #41 were held. Then, when #13* was held with #16, she felt intense fear "like an electric shock through my body, which jerked my whole being awake." At first she breathed in gasps, as though resisting moving into and through the pain. With any amount of pressure on the points, she whined. A little physical pain seemed to stimulate a lot of emotional pain. Images of her father came up, with the remembered feeling that she was the cause of his unhappiness. Gradually, during work with the Kidney and Lung Meridians, she began to be able to breathe through the pain and confront the old fears.

"Though I had known intellectually that I wasn't responsible for my father, I had never before been able to *know* it deep within the little child part of me," she said. "It was like he was dead inside. I couldn't trust him, and I couldn't tell him that, for fear that I might lose what love I did have from him for whose affection I was starving." She saw that this fear and mistrust had extended into her relationships with men, and into a fear of being emotionally honest.

Just as someone may have a fear of horses after being thrown or kicked by a horse, so someone else may have a fear of intimacy because of a past betrayal, rejection or abandonment, and someone else may have a fear of self-expression because of past humiliations or embarrassments. However, not everyone develops a fear of horses after being thrown, nor a fear of intimacy because of emotional jolts. A person who rides frequently is likely to have fallen or been thrown off a few times. Riding instructors emphasize habits that help prevent this, but also normalize the experience. "Get right back on" is the basic advice after a fall, whether from a horse or a bicycle.

Applied to affairs of the heart, "get right back on" means developing new friendships and renewing old ones, not becoming isolated by pain after a fall from romantic expectations. A therapist may help normalize feelings of hurt and counter feelings of fearfulness, perhaps tracing the fear back to its (childhood) origin. It can be comforting just to be assured that it's not abnormal to have old fears stirred up by new hurts, and that there can be a new resolution of the fear, on a deeper level. Releasing related physical tension [like at #16s] also helps the emotional stress to leave the system more quickly.

Fear and Avoidance Behaviors

How do "neurotic" or debilitating fears develop? Basically, we *don't* get right back on, or go on to new challenges. We develop *avoidance behaviors* which seem to reduce the fear, but which amount to just not confronting it. The fear doesn't get a chance to be extinguished. And so we are not much different from the rats which Miller (in a landmark study in 1948) conditioned to run out of a white room into a black one, to escape electric shocks. At first the rats reacted to the shock with signs of intense fear—agitated running about, squealing, urinating and defecating. Soon they learned

---

* This point helps relax muscular tension, and so is useful in the case of fear of attack. (See Gall Bladder Meridian, Chapter 4.)

to fear the white room and escape into the "safe" black room. They continued to do so, frantically, for hundreds of trials *after the electric shocks had ceased*. By contrast, when rats were conditioned to run down pathways to get food rewards, extinction of this learned response occurred soon after the reward was withheld.

Miller concluded that fear is more than just a response to painful, threatening or alarming stimuli; it is also an acquired drive. Learned fears are at least as powerful in motivating our behavior as are primary instinctual drives like hunger, thirst and sex. Like the rats, though with more sophistication, we tend to continue responses which once seemed to enable us to avoid danger or pain. Like the rats, we may not dare to go back (or on) to discover whether the danger still exists in situations we were conditioned to fear. For human beings, often the learned response is some kind of betrayal of ourselves—a timidity about really *being ourselves*, or a defensive hiding of our feelings (and so ourselves) from others.

Like the rats, we waste a lot of energy in efforts to avoid threats which could be overcome or which are non-existent. Our avoidance behaviors suggest underlying fears—like of rejection, humiliation, shame or embarrassment. There may be reluctance to enter relationships, unless given strong guarantees of uncritical acceptance. There may be a tendency to withdraw from others, even while sorely needing affection. Such avoidance was part of Linda's psychological profile; her pronounced muscular armoring included the ♯16 and ♯18 areas. Avoiding situations which stimulated her fears kept them alive, so that her life was ruled by fear. She was afraid to move into the world except in a limited way. Several times, when an unconscious fear came up during a session, Linda had an almost simultaneous pain or spasm in the ♯16 area.

During one session, what came up was a fear of closed places. [I was working with the Kidney and Large Intestine Meridians.] Linda saw herself as a child, in the bathroom at a gas station. It was dark inside, and she couldn't reach the door knob. Frightened, she was pounding on the door and screaming "Daddy, daddy, daddy!" When he came, he didn't seem concerned about her fear. "I wanted that," she said. "I wanted him to feel sorry for leaving me in there." Instead, his attitude was, "Big girls don't cry." That message reminded Linda of having her forehead stitched, without anesthesia, after a car accident with her father, and having her ears lanced a lot, because of severe earaches. Her association to that was feeling jabbed a lot emotionally.

The next week, there were spasms in the ♯16 area as Linda encountered her fear of being independent. A related fear that her mother would die, if Linda left home, coexisted with guilt about being the cause of her mother's problems. Throughout the session, Linda kept shutting down her breathing; I had to keep reminding her to breathe through the tensions, instead of tightening up more. In another session, while working with abdominal tension [♯16 and ♯38], Linda remembered being forced to ride a roller coaster and go into a "scary house," after which she had nightmares of a woman's face. A couple weeks later, during release of the ♯17 and ♯16 area, Linda began to let go to her anger by pounding the table. That aroused the fear that something would happen to her mother if Linda let herself feel her anger. That seemingly neurotic fear stemmed from a real childhood fear, for Linda's mother had been so sick that she wasn't allowed physical contact with Linda.

A month later, we were focusing on the ♯16 area because Linda had twisted and strained her back. It was like a voice from the past: "It hurts! Oh, don't! Don't go away . . . Don't hit me." The words came out with a throaty and painful sound. After a while, Linda said disgustingly, "I'm a shit! They made me into a nothing." I asked if she was afraid to be something. "It's hard to break the pattern of being miserable, but I want to be well. I don't want to be like this any more."

Her voice was no longer pain-filled as, towards the end of the session, Linda said, "There's nobody out there! Oh, God, I understand. I guess I have to learn to trust myself. The vision that I got was someone holding a trumpet out to me, saying 'play this.' My favorite instrument is the trumpet. I love it. I've always wanted to play it. I said, 'I can't play this. There's no way!' The response was, 'I expect you to play this trumpet. I expect you to, because I want you to play it.' " This was a beautiful symbol for the resolution to triumph over fears and limitations. As Linda began to confront her fear, she discovered that it had helped her avoid pleasure as much as pain. "It's as though I feared that I would like pleasure too much," she said with surprise.*

Kidney points are antidotes to fear, but as Linda's story illustrates, sometimes fear must be traced back to its origin in order to break the pattern of avoidance. We begin to break that pattern just by confronting the old fears that are being mirrored in our current relationships and problems. Often, instead of confronting what we fear, we follow conservative strategies designed just to *minimize* the *maximum* hurt or damage that someone or something can cause us. For example, we may try to minimize hurt feelings or damage to the ego by inhibiting our emotional expression or by avoiding deep emotional involvements. The problem is, such defensive strategies also limit growth.

Human beings tend to quickly learn and long remember stimuli associated with danger. Once, this promoted survival. Today, it often promotes unnecessary or neurotic fears, for we quickly learn and long remember things which are threatening only to the ego. Fears of rejection, humiliation, hurt or embarrassment make us back off from being our whole Selves, in order to protect our precious egos. The ego is basically a limited, though useful, edition of the Self. By discovering that some things we fear are just threats to the ego or self-image, not to the Self, we can re-program ourselves to stop spending so much energy on bolstering the ego. A simple antidote to neurotic fear is knowing and valuing the strong core Self. By experimenting with new ways of responding to fearful situations, we can develop new coping abilities and so a new self-awareness, which gradually decreases our fearfulness.

Fear is essentially a "bodily reaction produced physiologically in response to a situation of danger," says Lowen. "Although neither the secretion nor our bodily reaction to it is subject to conscious control, we are constantly advising our children not to be afraid."[10] Perhaps we could instead teach them, and ourselves, ways to deal with the fear, so that its energy could be used for acting resolutely in the face of dangers and threats. One method of centering the body energy is focusing on the hara. Instead of saying "don't be afraid," we could say, "breathe into your tummy," "find your inner strength," "trust that you'll attract what you need," "trust in God" or "tune into the Tao."

* More of Linda's story is found in Chapter 9, Part 1 and Chapter 13, Part 3.

Life Does Work ————————————————————————

For James, (the artist we met in the land of Shen), chronic Kidney Meridian deficiency
was evidenced by frequent fear, as well as by lower back pain [in the #16 area],
chronic fatigue, and successive sinus, throat and ear infections which he thought were
after-effects of a virus he'd contracted several months earlier. He was afraid that his
body was breaking down. He was afraid of not having enough work, but also of not
being able to handle a lot of work. He was afraid of being trapped in a relationship,
but also of "missing out," so that for a couple years he could neither leave nor
commit to his girlfriend.

James was also afraid of feeling his fear. He said that sometimes the fear was
a stimulus to achievement, but sometimes it was paralyzing. When fear came up, I
asked him to notice accompanying thoughts or images, and breathe into the lower
abdomen. "If I breathe, will it give me more energy, so I won't be so depressed and
anxious?" James asked. "Yes, and if you just let yourself feel and follow the feelings,
they will change," I replied.

At the next session, James said he'd felt fearful during the past week. "But as soon
as I started watching it, the fear seemed to go away. I've been feeling considerably
better since I tuned in on it. I meditated on the fact that I was afraid to get in touch
with it. All it was, was the fear of being broke. And the self-esteem just magically
seemed to come back, for the most part. The scariest thing is that when I feel afraid,
all the other stuff I've accumulated disappears—the feeling good about myself, and
even the memory of it. It was different this time because when the fear came up I
was aware of it, so *it* disappeared instead. And I discovered a new fear! The fact
that I've been feeling good about myself the last couple of months meant that I had
something to lose. Slipping back was twice as painful, because I could lose something of value—my self-esteem." After about fifteen minutes of hara breathing [while
I was holding Kidney points], James tuned in on "a spot of warmth" inside his
lower abdomen. "Is that a chakra?" he asked.

Feeling the hara, the center of adaptive energy, is empowering. Hara breathing is
a tool we can use to help counteract old fears—and sometimes to dig them out at
their roots. One week, while working with the #16 and #15 areas and hara breathing,
James recalled his Mother's fearfulness and anxiety. "There was always the feeling
that people won't produce and things won't work. *The world doesn't work*—that's the
message! It's all very negative." The only safe thing is the conventional, and even
that is questionable. In this psychological legacy, there was no room for a life dream
and the resolution to manifest it.

To pursue his career as an artist, James had to challenge the fearful perspective
that "life doesn't work." "A number of times, I've put a lot of energy into something and gotten nothing back, or ended up having power taken away from me." So
does that mean the world doesn't work? James had the image of his mother putting
out his eyes with two fingers and eating them. This was a dramatic, if disgusting,
symbol of how the introjected negativity distorted James' perceptions, and kept him
from responding spontaneously to life in each changing moment. "It's scary to look
at life fearfully," he concluded.

In another session, James discovered that some of his fear went back to being the
smallest kid in his class in elementary school, and so being afraid of physical con-

frontation. "I've often backed down—not only from fights but just from verbal confrontations too," he said, "and the fear has cost me a lot." After this realization, James decided to confront his fear of confrontation by studying a martial art.

During another session, after a recurrence of low back pain [and while I was holding Kidney and Bladder points], James had the image of a mouse blowing a horn; then an elephant stepped on and crushed the mouse, but the mouse got bigger and strangled the elephant with a pink necktie! "The elephant is fear," he said. "If the mouse doesn't gather his energy and get really determined, the fear will crush him as soon as he starts to blow his own horn." Anger came up with feeling how much fear had crushed him throughout his life. Then came the image of the mouse getting still bigger, and playing his horn until the elephant shrank.

The following week, James said he'd noticed a fear of seeming arrogant. "When my self-esteem starts to increase, I start lowering myself, acting humble, so my self-esteem won't be too out front." Was the bottom line that he didn't trust himself? "Trust myself to *what*?" Just *trust yourself*—your innate energy and spirit, which wants to manifest its potential. After concentrating for some minutes on the hara, James shared this image: "I saw energy rising as something like an electric current, going up from the abdomen into my brain. Then I was riding on a merry-go-round, on a golden horse with a lot of balls flying around, in balance and at the same time out of balance. My horse got very strong and rose above the merry-go-round, and I was looking down on it, controlling where the balls went. I feel very good!"

During sessions focusing on the #16 area and the Kidney Meridian, James had a series of images starring a modern symbol of power: *Superman*! Throughout these sessions, the changing forms of James' Superman illustrated his changing relationship to personal power, and his lower back pain disappeared. At first his Superman was omnipotent and fearlessly combative—like a compensation for James' feelings of inadequacy.

One week James said he had been feeling rich in himself, and was getting in touch with a core inner strength. The "life doesn't work" message was losing its grip. As we focused on deep release of the #16 area, the movie title, "Whose Life is at Anyway?" came into his mind. "We choose life minute by minute," he said. "And we can choose to change how we relate to someone or something at any moment." James was feeling increasingly motivated by "the desire to do something, rather than by the fear of failure," though he still felt compulsive about trying to cover all bases. He had the image of a young Superman parachuting from a plane. A crossbow appeared, and he shot at targets—and hit them all. To confirm that life does work, do we need to hit every target we shoot for?

Six weeks later James complained of fatigue and what amounted to psychic impotency. As we focused on the Kidney Meridian, James saw himself as Mighty Mouse surrounded by a ring of supermen. He had to bore through the ground to get out. "I feel like hurting a lot of people," James said tensely. Was the anger coming from fear? The ground that Mighty Mouse had to bore through reminded me of difficulties we have to go through to carry out our resolutions.

In a later installment of the Super series, Supermouse was flying over the city and turned into Superman, who landed painfully (versus perfectly) on a spire! Then he was inside a building, on a gold merry-go-round. "That's a paradox, because I associate gold with lasting value, and the merry-go-round with the ephemeral nature of life." Superman flew out of the building on a golden horse and plunged into a pool at a party where there were lots of successful people. A black horse emerged from the pool with a black masked rider, who demolished things. In the sky, the horse became golden again, and then turned into a spaceship, which was fighting off little warships!

Abruptly, James turned from this image to his agenda of problems, fears and worries. I pointed out that he seemed anxious and very much up in his head, as I held some Spleen points. "It's as if I need to have something wrong! That's a corollary of the world not working!" Like Superman, we can fly out of our problems, but there are problems even in space. Problems are a fact of life, not a justification for constant apprehension. "That triggered something that went all through me," James said. "Maybe I keep trying to make things wrong. I don't have to do that! When things come up, they're just challenges, to make me grow—not indications that the world doesn't work!"

> "It is only when we have the courage to face things exactly as they are, without any sort of self-deception or illusion, that a light will develop out of events, by which the path to success may be recognized. This recognition must be followed by resolute and persevering action. For only the man who goes to meet his fate resolutely is equipped to deal with it adequately. Then he will be able to cross the great water—that is to say, he will be capable of making the necessary decision and of surmounting the danger."[11]

What is a "superman" anyway? Superman is part of the hero archetype. The Taoists talked about a different kind of hero or super man. The "superior man" did not always confront; in fact, he often followed the path of least resistance and avoided forcing things. The emphasis was on *inner* strength. James' Superman gradually began to feel more like this "superior man," as he began to embrace others instead of aggressively overcoming them. The "macho" Superman was replaced by one who could hold a rag doll and play with a little boy. James concluded that "a Super Man is one who is in full possession and command of his power—who is aware of, and feels free to use, his entire Self."

Rather than avoiding that which is feared, the Super Wo/Man can pay attention to fear before it becomes overwhelming and act resolutely in regard to it. To pay attention to a thing (or a feeling) while it is small is to respect its power. Lao Tzu says:

> "Regard the small as great; regard the few as many.
> Manage the difficult while it is easy;
> Manage the great while they are small.
> All difficult things in the world start from the easy;
> All great things in the world start from the small."[12]

Part 3. HYPOACTIVE CHIH: fearfulness, inadequacy, inferiority, timidity, panic, phobias

The hypoactive feelings of the Chih spectrum are all saying that life feels very powerful in relation to me, and I feel very weak in relation to life. Habitual and unnecessary fear is a giving away of power to that which is "other." Continual apprehension results in excessive adrenal stimulation, producing temporary bursts of energy which ultimately fatigue and exhaust the body. The result is a low energy state of *fearfulness*, in which we feel neither willing nor able to confront and deal with life. Fearfulness is contagious and easily degenerates into panic when a threat does arise. When a crowd is seized by fear the consequences can be downright scary—whether the threat is real or imaginary. At such times, it can be difficult to tune into the real self-felt feelings, and to distinguish between the outer and inner voices, especially if one's general practice has been to avoid rather than to confront fear.

Frequent fear drains the reserve energy or "ching ch'i," and weakens the Kidney Meridian. In this low energy state, one is more vulnerable—more easily triggered by fear-arousing stimuli and more susceptible to fears born of fatigue. Fatigue and chronic fearfulness can allow imaginary fears to proliferate; in turn, imagining threats where none exist is fatiguing. Imaginary fears are the most persistent, for they have no climax in real life, no real resolution. Old "tapes," or introjected negative messages, often are just imaginary fears. "If I let myself be seen, I'll be rejected"; "if I take risks I'm liable to fail"; "if I express myself freely, I'll make a fool of myself"; all because "I can't measure up." We may also have been conditioned to fear certain things which actually pose no real threat, or at least none proportionate to our fear—for example, a certain race, the opposite sex, liberals or conservatives, authority figures, or the free expression of emotions.

Often, fearfulness and anxiety are aroused because the present situation somehow reminds us of unresolved past traumas. For example, Charles, who had felt almost totally unaccepted as a child, was afraid of being visible in social situations.* To him, being noticed was associated with making a mistake and feeling foolish, or being ridiculed and rejected. To avoid doing something wrong and feeling foolish, he avoided all social situations—classes, parties, even movies or concerts.

Old and unconscious fears can be allowed conscious awareness, and we can find a new, healthy resolution of them. As Charles worked through his fears in therapy, he was able to start going to movies, then to classes and parties. As neutral or positive experiences were added to his memory banks, they began to offset the accumulation of old negative ones. Gradually he experienced less fearfulness before and during social situations. Also, coincidentally, his lower back pain went away. Facing that which is feared, and finding it not so powerful as imagined, reduces the fear—and stress—level.

Avoided fears get exaggerated as the imagination works on them. We picture situations as threatening and fearful, and then spend time and energy trying to escape

---

* Some of Charles' sessions are described in Chapters 1 and 2, and in Chapter 9, Part 3.

285

from our imagined fears. Additionally, our cognitive abilities can distort and complicate our fears. Anticipating rejection, for instance, we can experience it *whether or not it really exists*. No matter what others say or do, we can construe their behavior as rejection.

Extinguishing fear responses can be difficult, because fear is such a powerful motivator that we tend not to risk finding out if the danger is real or still exists. Instead, we avoid situations in which the old fears might come up. Avoiding feared situations results in a reduced anxiety level. This is rewarding, so avoidance is continually reinforced. The problem is, avoiding that which we fear does not lessen our fearfulness, but only our *acute* fear.

To transform fearfulness into resolution, it is necessary to face that which is feared. This is the heroic way—the way which enlarges the sense of Self. Overcoming fear can be taken in stages however, as even the heroes of fairy tales met and overcame lesser obstacles on their way to fight dragons or save princesses. *Desensitization* is the psychological name for the repeated presentation of graded fear-producing stimuli, while the person is in a state of relaxation—first the image of that which is feared, and then some representation of it, until the person is ready to confront the feared object or situation itself. Because it induces a deep state of relaxation and the arising of images related to physical tensions, Jin Shin Do can facilitate this kind of "desensitization." When fear or anxiety comes up, it can also be countered with deep breathing, conscious relaxation of muscular tension, and affirmations (positive statements which are antidotes to negative thoughts).

Desensitization, along with insight-oriented psychotherapy, is the treatment of choice for *phobia*—a continuing intense fear of a specific object or situation which does not present an actual threat or danger to the individual, or at least none proportionate to the fear. Psychodynamically, a phobia is a way of controlling fear by displacing it onto a specific object or situation. Dr. Willard Gaylin gives the example of a small child who becomes "terrified of the strength and angers of his parents":

"What in the world is he supposed to do about that? There is no way to conquer *them* . . . Nor can you avoid the source of anxiety, for it resides in the same personna that you cherish and require.

"One of the ways, then, to handle the fear of the parent is to displace it onto a horse, a book, a wolf, the boogeyman, monsters, or what have you. Animal displacements are wonderful. All you need do then to control your anxiety is to make sure to avoid the animal! Displacement not only offers the relief of rationalizing the anxiety—and there is nothing more terrifying than irrational fear—but offers a way of controlling and limiting the fear. How many wolves will a three-year-old encounter in his typical day? The only one he is likely to meet is too preoccupied with Little Red Riding Hood to attend to him."[13]

A phobia may in part be a conditioned fear, as well as a displacement of fear. For example, Joan's fear of snakes seemed to have originated as a displaced fear of her mother, but she also remembered other children tormenting her with garden snakes.* Snakes and wolves are among the animals which have earned man's fear

---

* See Chapter 9, Part 4, "Hyperactive Shen."

over the centuries. Interestingly, many phobias, or persistent irrational fears, are similarly related to things which we seem to be designed to fear. Certain animals, open or closed-in spaces, heights, darkness, foreigners—such common phobias are based on fears which once aided man's survival.

Perhaps we have some inbred tendency to fear things which once were reliable predictors of danger, since phobias to historically neutral stimuli (like hammers or electrical outlets) develop much less readily. Certainly our fears are often disproportionate to actual dangers. The fear of violence is much more widespread than the fear of automobiles, yet three times as many people die in car accidents as by murder. People walk the streets with fear and caution, yet forget to fasten their seat belts or drive in an oblivious trance. A widespread fear of violence from strangers is supported by rising crime statistics, yet as much or more violence takes place in families, because of intense and unresolved frustration.

Panic and Passive Fear

Panic is the degeneration of fear, because of a loss of ego control—or of any control, when one is confronted by a truly overwhelming threat. Panic is the urge to flee blindly. If flight is impossible, the panic may manifest in extreme shaking of the legs. With intense fear, there may also be groaning or hysterical screaming. If both the flight and the sound are blocked, a chronic state of panic can result. The body is tensed as though for flight, locked in the position of inhalation (with an overinflated chest maintained by intercostal tension). The feeling is that of being trapped.

The word "panic" literally means "of Pan." One definition of panic is "sudden overpowering fright . . . often accompanied by mass flight." Another is: "of, relating to, or resembling the mental or emotional state believed induced by the god Pan." Pan was the Greek god of forests, wild animals, fields and pastures.[14] Jungian psychologist Edward Whitmont points out that:

> "Pan and Dionysus, who were demoted to the nether regions of hell by the Medieval church, point to the realm of the orgiastic experience of natural and instinctual life. They represent 'divinities'—namely, autonomous creative drives, independent of man's volition—which are related to the lunar or earthly world of generativeness, joy, lust, sexuality, growth and renewal through life and death cycles of nature, rather than through rationality and mental discipline."[15]

It is interesting that the orgiastic rites associated with Pan involved the dance. Perhaps the freeing movements of Pan's dance were antidotes to bodies tensed as though for flight. Perhaps Pan's dance allowed the release of natural movements that had been blocked by external and internalized prohibitions. The fear of Pan, as exhibited in his demotion to hell, is the fear of the natural instinctive life. Our instinctive drives are *vitalizing forces*. They become destructive when they can find no exit.

The *Nei Ching* says that the mysterious powers of Chih create trembling "in times of excitement and change," and "among the emotions they create fear."[16] Fear and trembling can motivate a person to rise to the occasion and meet the challenge. Trembling can be a release of blocked energy. It can also be the effect of anxiety, and it can degenerate into a bodymind shakiness which makes action almost impossible.

The most yin, or passive, response to fear is fainting. A similarly passive response is a feeling of utter *powerlessness* and debilitating weakness. There is almost no sense of inner strength or energic force. "The force propelling a person toward actually doing something comes from clarity in the Water Element," Diane Connelly explains. "If this clarity is not there, a person can suffer from lack of personal force in life, and get buffetted around by other people's strength and will."[17] The person may seem "wishy-washy" or "weak-kneed," and there may be lower back or knee pain, sexual or urinary problems. As Connelly points out, the Water Element influences all kinds of fluid movement within the bodymind:

> "Brittleness of joints, dryness and thirst, frequency or infrequency of urination, excess or deficiency of perspiration, the lack of flow in thought processes and emotions, feelings and fears of inundation, being overwhelmed by things are just a few of the symptoms the bodymind can throw up to tell us about an imbalance in the Water Element."[17]

Even in a healthy person, periods of low Kidney energy may coincide with feelings of inadequacy, inferiority and timidity, along with fatigue. Fatigue can produce symptoms of dizziness, blurriness, and even fainting. Chronic fatigue can result in a lack of appetite (including sexual appetite) and sleep difficulties—like being too "wired up" to sleep.*

Periods of deficient Kidney energy can also correspond with a tendency to be easily overwhelmed by difficulties, or to be afraid to undertake anything because of consciously or unconsciously fearing that it will fail (or even, sometimes, that it will succeed). When we feel disempowered, old inferiority problems may rear their ugly heads. There may be a lack of astuteness, or of the sensitivity to know what to do in a given situation, along with a physical or psychological clumsiness. Feeling powerless to deal with a situation gives it *more* power, so that we become even weaker in relation to it.

The Transformation of Fearfulness

Fear unleashes a river of emergency energy, but in the process it further depletes the energy reserves. Trying to exert self-control by suppressing the fear is likely to result in *repressing* the fear, or pushing it down to an unconscious level. The healthy resolution of fearfulness is not the *lack* of fear, but rather an *appropriate fear*. The idea is not to extinguish all fear, but to have the fear be appropriate to the relative strength or weakness of oneself vis-à-vis the external threat or danger. Fearfulness of situations or people who pose no real threat is a distorted awareness of relativity, or *inappropriate fear*. Developing a sense of *personal power* allows a less fearful awareness of relativity. Being in touch with our inner power, and the power of the life

---

* Compare with symptoms of depression in Chapter 9, Part 3. Depression usually correlates with deficiency of Shen and Hun, but the disharmony often includes deficiency of Chih (or P'o or I') as well.

energy, allows resolute action in the face of real, or "appropriate," fears. However, fear is a sneaky emotion, often well-protected by rationalizations, or denied and projected onto others. Even when we have largely resolved irrational fears—of rejection or failure, of social situations or snakes or whatever—still they may come up again, in subtle ways.

Beginning to let life flow can bring up the fear of change, and perhaps of newly-conscious feelings. Growth and change bring up the issue of trust—trust of Self, and of Tao or God. As we begin to let ourselves be the Selves which we truly are, old feelings of inferiority may pop up. We may wonder if we really *are* enough, if the inner Self really *is* strong enough to live spontaneously and creatively. This can be a dark time—of feeling like we are in "the valley of the shadow of death." On the horizon, in fact, is death—of a hyperative ego control which would override the Tao if it could. Then comes birth—of an ego more in tune with the inner Self and the Tao. But the ego is afraid to lose control. It chatters away at us, saying "It's risky to let go of control! I've gotten you this far—trust me!" The birth of an expanded Self requires the death of limiting ego-ideals and comforting dogmas based on illusory belief systems. This can be a little scary. Lao Tzu says:

> "Not knowing that one knows is best;
> Thinking that one knows when one does not know is sickness.
> Only when one becomes sick of this sickness can one be free from
>   sickness."[18]

I am reminded of Sarah, a single woman in her late thirties who had received some acupressure prior to our first session. Her pulses were generally weak; the Lung, Heart and Kidney Meridian pulses were especially deficient, while the earth meridians [Stomach and Spleen] were slightly excessive. Asked what she wanted to focus on, Sarah replied "fear, self-doubt and low energy." She said inferiority feelings had been especially bothersome in the past couple of years, since she made a big job change after working for many years with one firm, in the same capacity. "But I have always felt this way, really." Sarah talked of her fearfulness as though it were a mysterious external force which could suddenly overpower her. As I began by holding #21: B and #37, Sarah told me about never really feeling confident about expressing herself, and not trusting that it's really okay to communicate her feelings. "I don't know what I'm feeling," she said, "or else I question it. Am I really feeling that? Is it right to feel that way?"

As Sarah spoke of this long-standing confusion, the pain of not trusting herself was visible in her distressed expression and tears. "It looks to me like you're feeling sad," I observed. She questioned that, and then said, "You're right—I *am* feeling sad!" As she surrendered to the feeling of sadness and let herself cry, the neck points I was holding suddenly became much softer and then completely relaxed. The crying continued while I held the jaw [using #35 as a distal point], and then the #21: LI area [with #3 and Large Intestine distal points]. I asked Sarah if she could remember a time when she hadn't felt fearful—when she had trusted her feelings and her ability to communicate. She recalled a spelling bee when she was about eight. She had to use each word in a sentence of her own. On about the third word, she passed out from fear and anxiety. This phenomenon recurred throughout the rest of her childhood and adolescence. Sarah determined that it would be gone by the time she was twenty. "But obviously the fear behind the fainting isn't gone yet," she said with wry amusement.

The neck segment had by now released enough to move down into Sarah's armored chest. I focused on ♯30 with points for Lung tonification, and then on ♯18 with points for Pericardium and Heart tonification [also holding ♯21 and ♯4]. I asked Sarah what was her earliest memory. "Ballet class at age four," she replied, "and taking the bus alone to go to it." I was astonished that a four-year-old would be allowed to ride a public bus alone. Sarah had recently asked her mother about that memory. Her mother had at first insisted that she was at least seven, but Sarah's memory of their house dated the solo bus rides at the earlier age. "My mother said she didn't know how she let me do it either. Maybe it was because she had trouble finding a baby-sitter for my little baby sister." Her mother had needed Sarah to be very mature, so she had tried to oblige. She remembered being really good with her baby sister—except once when she bit the baby! When her mother came to see about the baby's crying, Sarah denied knowing what had happened. "You really didn't know, on one level," I said. "You knew what you did, but you didn't know why."

Throughout the chest release, Sarah had been crying and sometimes sobbing. With the memory of biting her sister, Sarah seemed to be contacting some internalized anger, so I moved to the ♯17 area and ♯5 [with ♯13 and ♯42 as distal points] to facilitate release of diaphragm tension. After a short silence, Sarah started talking about always feeling inadequate in ballet class, because she couldn't do as well as the others. All of them were at least a year or two older. "Of course you couldn't do as well," I said. "You were too young. Didn't anyone ever tell you that? That you were doing well enough for your age?" More tears came up. After a while I asked, "Are you feeling anything besides hurt?" "A little anger," she replied. Then she growled: "Maybe a lot of anger!" Sarah had quit dance classes within a few years, because of extreme anxiety about performing at a mandatory recital. The dance was gone, but the fearfulness and inferiority feelings which had taken root remained in power for many years.

"You learned failure early," I observed, now holding ♯16 with Kidney points. Sarah cried as she wrestled with the task of coming to a new resolution of the old childhood fears. "You didn't have enough support for your feelings, so you decided the problem was that you were inadequate," I said, "But now you *can* find a new resolution of your fears." I asked if it felt okay to feel weak, like she did right then. She said that it did, and that it felt like the sorrow was "about never really having been a child—free to play and to just *be*." I suggested that she needed to let this sorrow out, and then could start letting her *inner* child out to play. As her chest and abdomen released, Sarah began to feel a warmth inside. "But I still feel cold on the outside," she said. Her armoring and coldness were like a shield. Did she really need that shield now? Was it safe to let herself out now?

After tracing her bewildering fearfulness back to childhood, Sarah began to have a glimpse of alternative feelings like self-trust and resolution. Her fearfulness and inferiority feelings were demystified, because she saw that they were natural results of having felt like a failure. Her inadequate self-image was the result of an outdated self-evaluation, based on failures which no longer even had any importance. Throughout the session, as inferiority feelings came up, I asked Sarah to breathe into the fear, all the way down to the lower abdomen. As she did so, she felt her body relaxing. I suggested that she could increase the fear by giving herself messages like "I can't trust myself," or she could mitigate the fear by countering it with affirmations like "I am adequate." She hesitatingly said, "I'm adequate . . . I'm okay." More confidently, she continued, "I'm adequate . . . I'm intelligent . . . I'm a feeling person . . . I'm sensitive . . . *I'm competent*." She seemed to like the sound of that one, savoring the words as she repeated, "I'm competent."

The joy of feeling began to overcome the fear of feeling. Sarah felt warmth going through her body, then up her spine, as I held a few points of the Central Channel. At the end of the session, Sarah told me how much she appreciated my skill. I replied, "This was a special experience. It happened because you were ready for it. You did it—I just facilitated it. You are a special person—not perfect, but special." She laughed, feeling more joyful, confident and resolute than she had for a long time. However, she also felt tired after this intense hour and a half of inner work. I asked her to rest for a while, and gave her the homework of remembering to *breathe*, and to move her body, by stretching and exercising.

It takes time for the psyche to stabilize around an increased feeling of resolution and self-trust, just as it takes time to build up the reserves of adaptive energy. The release of chest and abdominal armoring allowed Sarah's breathing to be naturally deeper and fuller, so that her bodymind gradually became more energized. In a later session, she wanted to focus on what felt like a "lack of flow" or a "lack of ease in movement from one thing to the next." Where did she feel this? Sarah pointed to the base of her skull [♯22s] and the back of her calves [♯45], and said she felt a band of tension close to the spine. After I held neck and jaw points, she said, "What's coming up is how I disconnect from myself when I start to express myself." How does that feel? Crying, Sarah said, "like what I say is not important." Where does she go then? "To feelings of worthlessness."

I asked, "What if it's *not* important?" She replied, "If it's not important then *I'm not important*." I suggested that maybe the dance of her life is what's important, not the individual performances. I asked her to see how it would feel to say, "I'm important, so what I say is important even if it's not!" It felt pretty good.

Sarah talked about how she had used others to motivate herself or to feel good about herself. Now she wanted not to need others for that, but rather to be able to do it for herself. "The important thing is just being the Self you truly are, because that Self *matters*," I said. "That takes courage!" she replied. I directed Sarah to let her breathing take her down to the core of her energy. She felt a powerful energy inside of "D" and "C." I suggested she could ask her inner Self how to find courage, I held the ♯18s [with Heart distal points], and the ♯16s [with ♯45, the Kidney source point, ♯9 and ♯12]. After a while, I asked Sarah what she was getting. "Humbleness and simplicity!" she said, laughing. "I didn't expect that! Just being myself—that's humble and simple!" I suggested that "being that Self which one truly is, both requires and gives courage." Sarah responded, "I can feel that, and I can feel a lot of tingling in my body, and a flowing sensation through my whole being."

Part 4.   HYPERACTIVE CHIH: mistrust, suspicion, paranoia, superiority, audacity, foolhardiness

Mistrust and fearfulness are two sides of a coin; they are opposite manifestations of fear. In fearfulness, the focus is on one's own weakness and the dominant feeling is of being personally unable to deal with problems. Mistrust projects the fear outward, onto others; the problem is that *they* can't be trusted. When the mistrust is extreme and unrealistic, or unfounded suspicions are rampant, the mood may be described as feeling "paranoid."

Though not the most pleasant feeling, mistrust has its uses in the project of human survival. Blind, naive trust of everyone and everything would not benefit the survival of the species. There *are* dangers in the world which we need to be aware of. Also, experience does not support a trust that others or life will provide exactly what we expect or wish. Although mistrust can have a protective function, chronic mistrust of others tends to boomerang. Often what we get back is *their* mistrust of *us*. In this case, mistrust is not serving a protective function. Instead, it is preventing mutual understanding and the development of realistic trust, and it is inhibiting growthful relationships and a joyful movement through life.

How do we get a basic sense of trust? And how get it back when it has been eroded? Erikson describes the first stage of psychosocial development as "trust versus mistrust." During the first year of life, the main project is developing a sense of *basic trust*, while overcoming a sense of *basic mistrust*, through the mutual experience and regulation of frustration by mother and child. When there is excessive mistrust, then, the most difficult case might be a person who did not develop a basic sense of trust in the first year of life—for example, because of physical or emotional abuse or neglect.

The basic sense of trust can, however, be dented by unresolved trauma at any age. Commonly it is tested in puberty or early adulthood, when many people have a first experience of being rejected, heartbroken or betrayed, or of being disillusioned—finding that someone they idealized is very human, and that society is quite imperfect. A result can be a self-defensive attempt to overcome naivetè, which can also stifle the basic sense of trust.

Where there is mistrust, there also will fear be found; where there is fearfulness, there will also be mistrust. To illustrate the mistrust/fear polarity and its transformation, consider the insights of Rose, an attractive and intelligent woman in her early forties who complained of low back pain [in the ♯16s area]. During her fourth session, I asked Rose about her earliest memory. She remembered her mother telling her what her father had said when she was born: "Now we've got trouble!" She then remembered feeling it wasn't fair that boys could do things that girls could not. She had emerged from childhood with a fair amount of trust, but also some mistrust of her own sex, because of the message that girls were somehow inferior to boys.

When we focused on the painful left lower back with points and hara breathing, an early memory arose of feeling fearless while riding a bike, and then getting her ankle caught in the spokes, which hurt terribly. The injured area was around points of the Kidney Meridian. Rose recalled this same area being injured years later, when a boyfriend threw something at her in anger. She talked about being betrayed by her ex-husband, and feeling rejected as a woman. She was afraid that others—especially men—would be threatened if she were to be all of herself.

"Who can you trust?" she asked. I had her ask herself that question. "You can't trust letting go to others," she declared. I wondered what she might lose if she did that. "Myself," Rose replied. Was this need to preserve her own identity coming from a shakiness of self-trust? Was the mistrust of others aimed at protecting herself? The real protection is paying attention to the inner feelings of the core Self; otherwise, one betrays oneself more completely than anyone else could. "The important thing is to dare to be all of myself, *for myself*," Rose realized. "Maybe sometimes others are picking up on my mistrust and fear, rather than just being threatened by me."

When we feel mistrustful and look around to see what the problem is, usually we look outside of ourselves first. Perhaps that is part of an instinctive defense mechanism—a biological wariness which could protect us from predators or dangerous enemies. But for civilized man, with his conditioned fears and introjected messages of mistrust, the instinctive reaction of looking for external dangers is often not appropriate. Much of the time we are just reading negative meanings into events and words, because of our own inner fearfulness and mistrustfulness.

Thinking that we can't trust someone else may be a cover for not trusting ourselves. To give form to our mistrustful feelings, we may imagine that someone is trying to hurt us or won't "come through" for us—emotionally, economically, physically, intellectually or spiritually. With all these (and more) options, it's not hard to find someone who is somehow threatening us—especially with the help of a little tunnel vision to hide parts of the picture. The problem is, the other person feels sad or mad about not being trusted, and becomes defensive to protect his or her self-image. S/he reacts negatively to our accusatory words, or just because of "picking up on" our suspicious thoughts or mistrustful attitude. These negative reactions in turn seem to justify our mistrust, and so perpetuate the negative cycle.

Self-Trust and Self-Forgiveness

Learning to trust ourselves may involve forgiving ourselves for past mistakes, just as being able to trust others may involve forgiving them for past hurts. In either case, to truly forgive is to accept the fact of being human. Humans make mistakes. Humans misunderstand and hurt each other—sometimes to get revenge, but often just because of ignorance or emotional turmoil. Self-forgiveness involves stopping the belief that past problems or failures *mean* we can't trust ourselves. Self-forgiveness opens the door to self-acceptance and self-trust. When we trust ourselves, we feel less dependent on others to satisfy our needs, so we can perceive others more accurately.

Authority figures are a convenient screen on which to project feelings of mistrust. Experiences beginning with mommie and daddie, and continuing with teachers and bosses, may have demonstrated that authority figures are sometimes unfair, dishonest, manipulative or untrustworthy. If we frequently have problems with various kinds of authorities, it may be because our experiences "taught" us to mistrust authority figures, or to project our mistrust on them.

We can explore these dynamics through some of Sylvia's experiences and insights. In her early thirties, Sylvia had determined to stop drinking and get her life together. Alcoholics Anonymous had been her first step; Jin Shin Do therapy was part of her quest to connect with her core inner strength. She was virtually unaware of an inner turmoil of hurt, resentment and fear. A theme that emerged early in her therapy was conflict with authority. During a session focusing on the Kidney and Bladder Meridians, Sylvia suddenly felt inundated with fear. Its apparent cause was that her love relationship seemed to be ending. She said later, "I then had the revelation that it wasn't the end of my relationship, but merely the end of the relationship as it had been, with the death of my alcoholic self.

"Somehow this moved into a memory of age 17, when I left home to go to college and my mother coerced me into going through Sorority Rush. I purposefully sabotaged being accepted, but felt crushed and humiliated when I wasn't. I relived the memory of a sense of failure, and all the crises I created for myself during that period. Helped by suggestions, I became able to forgive myself, because I saw that I'd done the very best I could. I began to have a vision of my old self dying. I could see her sick and dying, dressed in white, reaching out to me. I told her how much I loved and accepted her, and then forgave her. I could see her beauty and her worth. Then she died and faded away. I cried through all of this, first with rage and anger at my mother, then with love and forgiveness of myself, and finally with grief and pain over the loss and death of my old self.

"A burial was suggested. My vision was of my old self dressed in white on a pyre in a forest grove. I saw myself standing at the foot of the pyre, and felt filled with absolute love and acceptance—as well as grief. Then I saw my father walk into the grove of trees. His presence was very strong. It felt significant that my dead alcoholic father was witnessing the death of my alcoholic self. Afterwards I felt cleansed and purified, but tired and drained. I slept and dreamed that the pyre was burning in a beautiful intense flame. I awoke feeling complete and whole. I thought, so this is the 'satori'—a plateau before descending into the next valley of exploration!" Later, Sylvia said that she still felt awe thinking about this session, but that "the most measurable change came from working through my transference to you as 'Mother,' and learning to see you as just human. This, of course, has expanded my view of my real Mother and of authority in general. She and 'they' have become teachers, friends and peers—not enemies to be subdued."

In her resolution to stop denying and avoiding things out of fear and mistrust, Sylvia was now sometimes audacious about confronting others with her thoughts, feelings and needs. Her audacity was the strength to be different—to trust herself and live creatively, rather than be constricted by limited, outdated opinions of what she "should" be and do. Her trust of self was on a gradual ascent, and she was increasingly respected for her frankness and integrity.

"Audacity" implies directness, boldness and a refusal to be restrained by social conventions. "Foolhardiness," on the other hand, is a rash, extreme audacity that seems to seek or create danger. This recklessness is the opposite of timidity, which is an over-abundance of caution. Foolhardy behavior gives the appearance of fear*less*ness, but may actually be an over-compensation for fear*ful*ness. Foolhardiness is a refusal to listen to fear. As Lowen puts it, the will is being used "to override the fear for ego-gratification."[19]

Foolhardiness may alternate with timidity, just as mistrust may alternate with fearfulness. These polar extremes are just manifestations of the same central problem: lack of resolution and of self-trust. Hara breathing helps increase the reserve energy and resolution that enable adaptation to life's demands. Balance of the Kidney Meridian encourages a sense of inner strength and so of self-trust. Also, the release of fear-related tensions helps decrease resistance to the needs of the Self. To listen to these bodymind needs is to trust the Self.

> "No situation can become favorable until one is able to adapt to it and does not wear himself out with mistaken resistance."[20]

The Urge to Be All of One's Changing Self

Mistrustfulness and fearfulness can be forms of resistance to *being all of one's Self*. During release of the lower back [♯16s] and Kidney Meridian, one client said, "This area has to do with being creative and powerful." Before this, she had been talking about her fear and mistrust of speaking up in groups. While applying pressure to the ♯16s, I asked why the area needed to be tight. "What comes up is trying to protect people by holding myself back. I need to give myself more room to move," Joanne responded. As her back began to release she said, "I'm feeling relief at the thought that I *can* just allow myself to say what I'm thinking or feeling—that maybe I *don't* have to be understood and liked by everyone!" Why is it so important to feel understood? Because of a deep need to feel connected with others? "I have to tolerate the pain of not feeling connected, and not conclude that *it means* I'm not okay."

Joanne began to feel "incredibly expansive . . . just huge!" Then she said it felt like two inner forces were struggling against each other. One was "powerful . . . open . . . creative . . . moving . . . expansive . . . flowing." The opposing force was the fear and mistrust that wanted to limit the expansiveness. "I think I've been afraid that I might abuse power if I took it on—as though there isn't a gentle expansive power, but only being better than some and not as good as others," Joanne said. "What a struggle! The limitations are saying, 'You can't just let go to movement, because you don't know where it's going.' But because of that I'm not going anywhere! I don't want the limitations. I want to trust that this powerful energy and its creative movement are real." After several minutes of hara breathing, Joanne said, "I feel a part of myself crying and reaching back for the part that was crippled—but it doesn't need to be crippled anymore." After this impactful session, Joanne risked speaking up in a group—and found that it wasn't such a risk anymore.

Paranoid Reactions

Overwhelming fear is hard to tolerate, so it is tempting to project the fear onto other persons or forces. Mistrust of these others may be justified by perceiving them as "out to get me." Such mistrustfulness and oversuspiciousness are part of the definition of "paranoid." The underlying dynamics include a lack of trust, and a lot of fear. There may be a general fear of closeness, and more specific fears like of being touched or watched.

"Paranoid" can also refer to a distinctive way of thinking—a *hyperactive mode of cognition*, which Shapiro describes as "an extremely tense and rigid directedness of attention."[21] Nothing out of the ordinary escapes scrutiny. Paranoid perceptivity can be as amazing as what the person *does* with these perceptions—which may amount to mistaking the forest for the trees.

> "Suspicious people are not simply people who are apprehensive and 'imagine things.' They are, in actual fact, extremely keen and often penetrating observors. They not only imagine, but also search. . . . The attention of these people is, furthermore, not only unusually acute and intense, but also unusually active. . . .
>
> "On the one hand, the paranoid person searches intensely for confirmation of his anticipations. On the other hand, those same rigid anticipations of what he will find allow him to feel entitled to discredit and disregard apparent contradiction. Between these two attitudes, he is bound to 'find' what he is looking for. In this process, intellectual capacity, keenness, and acuteness of attention become not guarantees of realistic judgment, but, on the contrary, instruments of bias. This keenness enables suspicious people to make, as they often do, brilliantly perceptive mistakes."[21]

One example of a paranoid thought process is the superstitious linking together of unrelated events. For example, if laughter occurs when one enters a room, the laughter is thought to be related to oneself. If one accidentally cuts one's finger while slicing vegetables, and then sees a neighbor outside, the injury may be perceived as caused by the neighbor's bad energy or hostile intentions. If someone is doing bodywork, and someone who lives nearby gets sick, these events might be linked by superstitiously believing the bodywork released negative energies which in effect zapped the guy who got sick.

Having a paranoid thought is common. Being absolutely convinced that the paranoid thoughts are true, and unwilling to consider other perspectives or to explore one's own feelings, is a problem. This rigid arrogance implies a denial of some basic human impulses. Being unable to accept one's own aggressive impulses, for instance, and instead projecting them onto others, makes for argumentative tendencies. Being unable to accept one's need for affection, and unable to ask for love directly, makes for suspicious jealousy*—and suffering.

There may be some realistic fear behind paranoid thoughts, but a tendency to resist "reality-testing" makes it difficult to get at the underlying fear. It is scary to face a profound inner fear—the fear of death, perhaps, or of life. Likewise, it is scary to acknowledge a hostility that comes from feeling perennially suppressed in life. It feels safer to conceal rage behind a preoccupation with justice or fairness, and to avoid fear by projecting it outward and clinging to delusional thoughts. We all sometimes take this "safe" route, denying any view of reality which includes the painful awareness of fear and aggressive impulses, and then accusing others of these same denied

---

* For more on suspicious jealousy, refer back to Chapter 10, Part 4.

296

feelings. Denial and projection are defenses against fear—defenses which can be taken to bizarre extremes. After a while, the defenses become offensive, for life often manifests that which we fear. Dr. Willard Gaylin explains:

> "We do, then, live in a world partly of our own creation—not just in our imagination. We are capable of actually facilitating that which we dread through defensive maneuvers that are both unnecessary and self-destructive. The suspicious, paranoid person, always expecting to be taken advantage of, always assuming he is, whether he is or not, eventually invites exploitation. He asks for it—and we are inclined to oblige. Because we have the power to create the world that we will be forced to live in, our anticipation can be a dangerous instrument."[22]

For another example, the suspicious, paranoid person, always fearing that s/he is being watched, invites others to watch him or her. After some reality-testing, she might realize that "sometimes people are looking at me because *I'm* watching *them* to see if they're watching me!" Underlying the paranoid tendencies there may be a feeling of inferiority, perhaps stemming from early experiences of shame and humiliation, or from introjected messages like "you're incompetent" or "you're disgusting." Paranoia can be a strange sort of compensation for inadequacy feelings, wherein you become important by having other people always watching you or "out to get you." Perhaps an antidote is accepting the ways you're important—and the ways you're not.

The "Superiority Complex"

An exaggerated sense of superiority is "false pride," just as an exaggerated sense of inferiority is "false reserve." We tend to mistrust people who are always demonstrating their low opinion of themselves, but we also tend to feel suspicious of people who are always bragging about their accomplishments or their fabulous connections and famous friends. The need to feel superior suggests a large, and perhaps largely unconscious, inferiority complex. This is such common knowledge that Webster defines a "superiority complex" as a feeling of exaggerated self-importance, or an excessive striving for or pretense of superiority, *which compensates for feelings of inferiority*.[14]

Since arrogance or superiority feelings defend against inferiority feelings, they take us another step away from the central problem of trusting Self and Tao—which is the problem of willing to be *all* of one's changing Self, in this changing world. To resolve this problem, the Taoists recommend humbleness, which is somewhere in between humility and arrogance. "Be humble and you will remain entire," says Lao Tzu.[23]

Chuang Tzu tells a story about how the Lord of the Yellow River overcomes a superiority complex.[24] During the time of the autumn floods, when a hundred streams pour into it, the Lord of the Yellow River thinks that he is really swell, and that all the beauty in the world belongs to him. Then he comes to the North Sea. There he sighs and says to Jo, the god of the North Sea:

> "The common saying has it, 'He has heard the Way a mere hundred times

but he thinks he's better than anyone else.' It applies to me. . . . Now, however, I have seen your unfathomable vastness. If I hadn't come to your gate, I should have been in danger. I should forever have been laughed at by the masters of the Great Method!"

Jo replies, "You can't discuss the ocean with a well frog—he's limited by the space he lives in. [Similarly] you can't discuss the Way with a scholar—he's shackled by his doctrines." The river lord had felt superior when he was the biggest fish in a small pond. "Now you have come out beyond your banks and borders and have seen the great sea—so you realize your own pettiness. From now on it will be possible to talk to you about the Great Principle." Jo continues:

> "Of all the waters of the world, none is as great as the sea. Ten thousand streams flow into it—I have never heard of a time when they stopped—and yet it is never full. The water leaks away at Wei-lu—I have never heard of a time when they stopped—and yet the sea is never empty. Spring or autumn, it never changes. Flood or drought, it takes no notice. It is so much greater than the streams of the Yangtze or the Yellow River that it is impossible to measure the difference. But I have never for this reason prided myself on it. I take my place with heaven and earth and receive breath from the yin and yang. I sit here between heaven and earth as a little stone or a little tree sits on a huge mountain. Since I can see my own smallness, what reason would I have to pride myself?"

If I can see my own smallness, then I don't need to feel superior. If I can also see my own power, then I don't need to feel inferior, either. The general idea is to develop an unconditional acceptance of oneself and others, rather than needing to make one thing (or oneself) better or more "right" than others. Everything has its bigness and its smallness, its usefulness and its uselessness, its right and its wrong. Therefore, why should we see one thing (or person) as better or worse than another? Jo exclaims:

> "Now do you say that you are going to make Right your master and do away with Wrong, or make Order your master and do away with Disorder? If you do, then you have not understood the principle of heaven and earth or the nature of the ten thousand things. This is like saying that you are going to make Heaven your master and do away with Earth, or make Yin your master and do away with Yang. Obviously it is impossible. If men persist in talking this way without stop, they must be either fools or deceivers!"

To justify the rightness (or righteousness) of our words and actions is to say that we are superior. To maintain the illusion of orderly rightness, we must project all wrongness onto others, which is tantamount to seeing them as inferior. The Great Wo/Man, by contrast, knows that all of us are *all* things. Instead of seeing things as Right or Wrong, s/he sees just different—and changing—natures, with differing preferences of behavior. Jo explains:

> "There is no end to the weighing of things, no stop to time, no constancy to the division of lots, no fixed rule to beginning and end. Therefore great wisdom observes both far and near, and for that reason recognizes small

298

without considering it paltry, recognizes large without considering it unwieldy, for it knows that there is no end to the weighing of things. It has a clear understanding of past and present, and for that reason it spends a long time without finding it tedious, a short time without fretting at its shortness, for it knows that time has no stop. It perceives the nature of fullness and emptiness, and for that reason it does not delight if it acquires something nor worry if it loses it, for it knows that there is no constancy to the division of lots."

"Well then, what should I do and what should I not do?" asks the Lord of the River. "How am I to know in the end what to accept and what to reject, what to abide by and what to discard?" Jo says from the viewpoint of the Way (or Tao), nothing is noble and nothing is mean. "Do not hobble your will" by trying to pick out what you *should* be "or you will be departing from the Way!" Don't be hedged in by limitations. "Be broad and expansive. . . . Embrace the ten thousand things universally. . . . This is called being without bent."

Jo has complete trust that everything changes, by itself and without the need for interference. You can trust nothing, for nothing stays the same. Yet you can trust everything; by accepting and being in tune with the changes of life and self, you can respond appropriately to changing situations.

"He who understands the Way is certain to have command of basic principles. He who has command of basic principles is certain to know how to deal with circumstances. And he who knows how to deal with circumstances will not allow things to do him harm . . . he distinguishes between safety and danger, contents himself with fortune or misfortune, and is cautious in his comings and goings. Therefore nothing can harm him."[24]

Even if the body is harmed, or the feelings are hurt, difficulties need not harm the inner self. The Great Wo/Man is the Natural Wo/Man, who avoids unnecessary strain by letting both Self and others *be*. S/he tries to stay in touch with the *essence* of self, others, and life. Guarding that essence is the ultimate focus of caution. The feeling is one of basic *respect*—for oneself, others, and the wholeness of Life.

13. *The Land of Hun Revisited —Liver Meridian*

Part 1. SYNERGIC STATE OF HUN: self-assertion, motivation, response-ability

According to Webster, "liverish" means "displaying a sour disposition; peevish; cross." Bile is the bitter, sour fluid secreted by the liver and stored in the gall bladder; "bile" also means bitterness of spirit or anger, while "bilious" means bad-tempered or cross. These definitions point out the long-standing popular association of the liver with the temperament, and with temper.

In the Chinese tradition, too, anger is the emotion associated with the liver. Acupressure theory says that anger stimulates the liver, and that symptoms of Liver Meridian imbalance include irritability or easy arousal to anger. The *Nei Ching* says that excessive or chronic anger is injurious to Yin in general, and to the liver in particular. The liver "brings forth animal desires and vigor," yet at the same time "the liver has the functions of a military leader who excels in his strategic planning." The related aspect of the psyche, called Hun, "grants the capacity for control" during "times of excitement and change." Hun "controls the soul, or spiritual faculties."[1] It is the active, yang part of the psyche, which directs the conscious and unconscious thinking activities, as Wilhelm points out in *The Secret of the Golden Flower*, where he translates "Hun" as "the animus" or intellect—the yang, masculine, assertive aspect of the psyche.

Acupuncture theorist Felix Mann says, "A general sense of well-being and energy is more often dependent on the liver than any other organ in the body—at least in my experience." He speculates, "Perhaps this is because the liver is the centre of metabolism, which is after all the most important aspect of life."[2] *Metabolism* is the process by which assimilated foods are converted into components of the body or used for fuel, and broken down into simpler substances that can be eliminated. In this way, energy is released for all vital life processes. Metabolism is like an instinctive biophysical planning and controlling process, directed by the organismic intention to *live*.

The liver has much to do with fulfilling this intention. The bile that it secretes is necessary for the digestion of fats and fat-soluble vitamins (A, D, E and K). The liver neutralizes various poisons (including drugs and alcohol), synthesizes several kinds of proteins, and helps regulate the blood sugar level. The Chinese classics say the liver stores blood; in fact, all blood from the stomach, spleen and intestines goes to the liver, which serves as a detoxification center. The liver also stores glycogen (starch), changes it into glucose (sugar), and then releases it when the bodymind needs energy. Since the brain does not store any glucose, the liver's steady supply is crucial to mental activities. Thus, there is a physiological basis for the traditional view that the liver is vital to conscious and unconscious thinking processes, and for classical

Liver Meridian

Points of the Liver Meridian

JSD #42 (Source point)—Trace up from between the first and second toes, to a sensitive spot a little below the junction of the first and second metatarsal bones.
["Supreme Rushing"—Lv 3]

JSD #7: Lv—This point is about 2 *chon* higher than and about 1 *chon* inside of JSD #7,* between the muscles (vastus medialis and sartorius).
["Yin Wrapping—Lv 9]

JSD #6: Lv—This point is inside and below JSD #6, in the flexure of the groin (inguinal groove), and about 1 *chon* below the upper border of the pubic bone.
["Quick Pulse"—Lv 12]

JSD #5—Feel for a little hollow at the bottom of the rib cage, just inside from the nipple line (at the junction of the ninth rib cartilage to the eighth rib). Press up into the rib cage.
["Gate of Hope"—Lv 14]

HUN

self-blame guilt | irritability resentment

Self-Assertion Motivation Will to Become Response-Ability

lack of motivation boredom impotency depression

Frustration, Anger

hostility bitterness vengefulness

---

* See Spleen-Pancreas Meridian, Chapter 10.

Examples of Local-Distal Point Combinations

Local point		Distal point
5	+	"D" area, 41, 42
6 or 6: Lv	+	7: Lv, 41, 42
17	+	13,** 42, 5, 21***

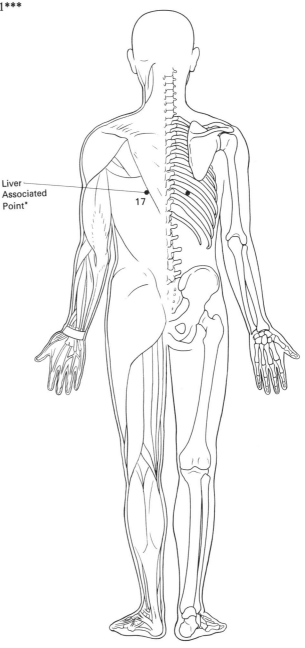

Liver Associated Point*

17

** See Gall Bladder Meridian, Chapter 4; #13 helps relax muscular tension.
*** *Be sure to do an ending neck release.* (See the last part of Chapter 1, "The Whole Session.")
— 1986 by Iona Marssa Teeguarden
† *Liver Associated Point*—see Chapter 8 for explanation of the associated points.

associations of the liver with the "soul"—the actuating force, or the part which moves the organism into action.

To the Chinese, the "Liver" refers not just to the organ, but to a set of energically-related functions, all of which have something to do with planning and control. For example, the body parts related to the Liver are the tendons and ligaments, which hold us together physically and control physical movement. *Tendons* connect muscles to bones, and *ligaments* bind the ends of bones together. These fibrous connective tissues allow us to mobilize the body or limit body motion.

A branch of the Liver Meridian goes to the eyes, so the sense related to the Liver is sight, and the related body fluid is tears. Diane Connelly explains the relationship of the eyes with planning: "The *eyes* are considered to be vessels of vision integrating the outside and the inside of a human being. When we *see* we take into ourselves information which we use as a guide for what we do, and how we think." Migraine headaches, which are accompanied by disordered vision, can indicate "a sort of frustration within the system because plans were not laid out or being followed."[3] This sort of frustration can bring us to tears—and sometimes the tears can help relieve the frustration.

The *Golden Flower* poetically explains the connection between consciousness, the eyes and the liver: "The animus [Hun] lives in the daytime in the eyes; at night it houses in the liver. When living in the eyes, it sees; when housed in the liver, it dreams." Hun "is of the nature of light" and "loves life." Hun is the will to return to the Creative, or the Light of Consciousness.[4] This inner light is experientially correlated with the "third eye"—the energy center associated with *Yuan Shen* or spiritual consciousness, and related to the pineal body and Pituitary gland (the master gland of the body, attached to the base of the brain behind the eyes).* The Liver Meridian is said to particularly influence the pineal body. At any rate, Hun is related to spiritual consciousness, as well as to gut impulses like anger. Perhaps these are not mutually exclusive. Perhaps they are two sides of the human coin.

The liver itself is the largest organ in the body. It is located beneath the diaphragm, mainly on the right side but also extending into the left. A density of tension in Liver-related points #5 and #17 can correlate with Liver disharmony and with tension in the diaphragm—the muscular partition between the chest and abdomen. Both Liver Meridian imbalance and diaphragm armoring can reflect anger problems, or excessive restraint of assertive and expressive impulses. Free movement of the diaphragm allows the lungs to expand downward with inhalation, causing a slight expansion of the abdomen. Diaphragm tension limits the free movement of the lungs and inhibits full respiration. Functionally, it divides the body in half, cutting off awareness of the lower parts of the body, and segregating the "lower" gut impulses from the "higher" impulses of the heart. Integrating these opposing internal forces is a prerequisite for expressing one's Whole Self.

---

* Also see the discussion of Yuan Shen, the "primal spirit," and Shih Shen, the "earthly spirit," in Part 2 of Chapter 9—"Modern Stress Theory and the Extreme Emotions of Shen."

"Will to Become"

Hun is the motivation to become that Self which one truly is, and to express that Self appropriately. The symbol for Hun is wood, or the tree—an archetypal image for the process of psychological growth or self-actualization. Jung compares the powerful innate urge for psychic growth or "individuation" to the force which causes a seed to grow into a pine tree. Just as the "seed of a mountain pine contains the whole future tree in latent form," so the Self is like an "inborn germ of wholeness." Wo/Man differs from the pine tree, however, in possessing an ego. To manifest the whole inner Self, first the ego must *notice* this "inborn but hidden totality of the psyche" which "brings about a constant extension and maturing of the personality." To develop into this whole Self, "our attitude needs to be like that of the pine tree."

> "It does not get annoyed when its growth is obstructed by a stone, nor does it make plans about how to overcome the obstacles. It merely tries to feel whether it should grow more toward the left or the right, toward the slope or away from it. Like the tree, we should give in to this almost imperceptible, yet powerfully dominating impulse—an impulse that comes from the urge toward unique, creative self-realization."[5]

To grow around obstacles, the mountain pine tree bends a little one way, then another. If it were not well-rooted, these imbalances might topple it over, or it might be blown down by a storm. To grow at all, the mountain pine has to be able to create roots. Similarly, to grow and be strong we need to be able to create roots for ourselves. For human beings, roots are close ties not only with the earth, but also with other people. To be "well-rooted" is to have established close connections with people and places which nourish us.

In the body, the legs are like roots which extend downward from the "hara" center in the lower abdomen. Free movement of the diaphragm allows us to be in touch with the "hara," the embodiment of the primordial life force. To be in touch with the hara is to be rooted in Nature, or connected with the primal unity of Life. The Japanese say that the man in touch with hara is the man with "center," who is not easily thrown off balance.[6]

Jung says that in cultures "more securely rooted than our own," people have less trouble giving up the "attitude of conscious planning in order to make way for the inner growth of the personality." It is as though our culture has tried to sink roots into egotistical accomplishments. There is not a lot of cultural validation for the arduous work of *becoming your Self*, although this is the most important thing one can do. Jung recalls an elderly lady who complained that she had not "done" anything with her life, though she had "made a good marriage with a difficult husband, and had somehow developed into a mature personality." In reply, he told her this story from Chuang Tzu:

"A wandering carpenter, called Stone, saw on his travels a gigantic old oak tree standing in a field near an earth-altar. The carpenter said to his apprentice, who was admiring the oak: This is a useless tree. If you wanted to make a ship, it would soon rot; if you wanted to make tools, they would break. You can't do anything useful with this tree, and that's why it has become so old.

"But in an inn, that same evening, when the carpenter went to sleep, the old oak tree appeared to him in his dream and said: 'Why do you compare me to your cultivated trees. Even before they can ripen their fruit, people attack and violate them. Their own gifts bring harm to them, and they cannot live out their natural span. That is what happens everywhere, and that is why I have long since tried to become completely useless. You poor mortal! Imagine if I had been useful in any way, would I have reached this size? Furthermore, you and I are both creatures, and how can one creature set himself so high as to judge another creature? You useless mortal man, what do you know about useless trees?'

"The carpenter woke up and meditated upon his dream, and later, when his apprentice asked him why just this one tree served to protect the earth-altar, he answered, 'Keep your mouth shut! . . . The tree grew here on purpose because anywhere else people would have ill-treated it. . . .' "

From his dream, the carpenter saw that the tree had fulfilled its destiny, though it appeared useless in worldly terms. Jung says the tree gives "a lesson to our short-sighted ego." The tree symbolizes the process of psychological growth or individua-tion. The earth-altar symbolizes the need to "surrender consciously to the power of the unconscious, instead of thinking in terms of what one should do, or of what is generally thought right, or of what usually happens. One must simply listen, in order to learn what the inner totality—the Self—wants to do here and now in a particular situation." Chuang Tzu's tree berated the carpenter for thinking it should be like other trees. Similarly, says Jung, it is "futile to cast furtive glances at the way some-one else is developing, because each of us has a unique task of self-realization." In his opinion, the elderly lady had "done" something with her life. Realizing oneself is no small accomplishment.⁵

Feelings of frustration, and eventually an inner rage, may be the penalty for not growing into one's Whole Self. The powerful inner urge for self-actualization does not just die when it is blocked off; rather, it seethes inside. To become one's whole Self, it is necessary to assert and express that Self. Not doing so builds up an inner frustration and anger. Doing so also nets some frustration and anger, however, for like the pine tree one is bound to encounter obstacles to growth. Learning to deal with anger and frustration is part of learning to assert and express oneself.

To have an "anger problem" is to feel anxiety about the presence of anger—one's own anger or someone else's—or to have difficulty communicating angry feelings. Often, assertion is confused with aggression, so that it is hard not only to express anger, but also to be self-expressive in general. The main alternatives are being non-expressive or explosive. It takes time and work to learn assertiveness skills, and to overcome the anxiety that arises with letting more of oneself show. Gradually, through the commitment to *being and expressing oneself*, awareness and self-esteem increase, and so does the ability to express anger and other feelings appropriately, as they come up—rather than days or months later.

Individuation is realizing who we really are. It is coming to know our Whole Self. It is integrating the opposite aspects of the personality: the masculine and feminine, the adult and the child, the "good" and the "bad," the "higher" and the "lower," and all our seemingly opposite thoughts, feelings and emotions.

According to Jung, a double tree symbolizes "the individuation process in which the inner opposites unite." The circle symbolizes "the all-important center of the psyche," or unification of the Whole Self.⁷

Letting Feelings Be

The main prerequisite for expressing feelings is *feeling* them. In a session focusing on release of anger-related tensions [the diaphragm, the Liver Meridian and the jaw], one client said the #17s felt like "a garbage can that was stretchable but tight, with all the unacceptable stuff held down." Jill had expected that therapy would teach her how to just make undesirable feelings go away. "I never suspected that it wasn't a matter of 'dealing with' or 'handling' emotions, but feeling them! Powerful emotions—but only in my head! I used to pride myself on being *so* understanding. I figured if I tried to understand someone, s/he would try to understand me. Meanwhile I was *so* angry that I wasn't getting enough for me!"

"The Angel" was Jill's nickname for the perpetually understanding part of herself. As the diaphragm armoring began to release, she said it felt like the Angel was struggling with the "Beast of Rage." It looked like the Beast wanted to growl, but felt inhibited. I probed, saying, "People don't want you to be uncivilized." Growling and hissing, she replied, "Well, I fucking well *am*!" The hissing sounded like a serpent. Jill's associations to a snake were "respect" and "hate." She said, "You don't pet a snake unless you've worked at getting to know her, or you're likely to get bit! I think I've always been a 'secret snake'—afraid that self-assertion would call up the same kind of hatred toward me as the snake's dangerous independence calls up in many people. The snake is my powerful, formidable self which can handle the threatening outside stuff."

After feeling this powerful, assertive self for a while, Jill said, "Snakes usually don't attack if you don't threaten them. I need to *know* that feelings, in themselves—like the snakes—are not dangerous. I have to deal with and handle my actions, but my emotions are just there, so I might as well let them *be*! I've cut off my power along with my emotions."

Letting our feelings *be* implies letting them be expressed spontaneously—through sounds, gestures, actions or words—and letting them be transformed naturally. To do this, we must know that to communicate feelings, including anger, is to care about and respect ourselves and others. A nice result is feeling like we've "cleared the air." What gets in the way of this is repressing the anger because of seeing it as "bad," or holding onto the anger because of seeing ourselves as "right" and someone else as "wrong." What needs to happen is accepting the polarities in ourselves and in our relationships, so we can see the whole picture. Trying to eliminate half of a polarity doesn't work. What works, according to Chuang Tzu, is abandoning the struggle between right and wrong, and instead seeking the "true light"—the light of inner awareness.

> "What use is this struggle to set up 'No' against 'Yes,' and 'Yes' against 'No'? Better to abandon this hopeless effort. . . .
>
> "The wise man therefore, instead of trying to prove this or that point by logical disputation, sees all things in the light of direct intuition. He is not imprisoned by the limitations of the 'I,' for the viewpoint of direct intuition is that of both 'I' and 'Not-I.' Hence he sees that on both sides of every argument there is both right and wrong.
>
> ". . . Hence he sees the limitless possibilities of both 'Yes' and 'No.' Abandoning all thought of imposing a limit or taking sides, he rests in direct intuition. Therefore I said, 'Better to abandon disputation and seek the true light!' "[8]

Expressing ourselves doesn't need to mean arguing, and arguing doesn't need to mean that someone wins and someone loses. When we find ourselves arguing, sometimes in the next moment we can see something that is funny about the argument, or realize that it's not so serious. When we can see that there is right *and* wrong both on our side *and* on the other guy's side, we can let go of our angry feelings and "abandon disputation."

Anger that *won't* go away, even after it's been expressed, may be a clue to some underlying conflict. When upset feelings are persistent, acupressure therapy can help uncover the real source of the distress, thus clearing away the cobwebs so that we can "see the light." The release of withheld feelings often has the therapeutic effect of reducing bodymind tension, so that we react less intensely to irritating stimuli. To stay relaxed and avoid accumulating new bodymind tensions, we need to learn how to express our feelings in ways that let ourselves and others *be.* Western psychology provides a wealth of information on effective communication and assertiveness techniques. Some of the basics are summarized in the following section.

A Miscellaneous Collection of Self-Expression and Self-Assertion Guidelines

• *Safety valves:*   How do you release pent-up emotional tension? Your repertoire of safety valves might include walking, running, exercising, playing sports, shadow boxing, punching a pillow or hitting it with a tennis racket, chopping wood, gardening, writing, drawing, and playing or listening to music. There is also great release value in humor. (After all, whatever the problem, it's usually not the end of the world.) A simple and ancient release for strong feelings is the poison-pen approach; it's especially effective if you then crumple the letter and vigorously throw it in a wastebasket. Even simpler is this Eastern-type release: the "Bah!" exercise. This safety valve requires no props, and takes little time, but you need to be alone or with an acceptant companion. (Under duress, you can excuse yourself to go to the bathroom.) Inhale deeply and, as you exhale, forcefully shout (or if need be whisper) "BAH!" Repeat. And repeat again. It's a simple way to let off the steam of accumulated frustrations and irritations—and maybe even find a smile.

Self-expressive communication is a safety valve, too, because it allows letting feelings out simply and clearly, before they build up more steam. How well you can communicate your feelings depends on the intimacy of the relationship. Hopefully, you can be relatively free and spontaneous with your mate, family, and friends, whereas it might be foolhardy to express feelings with intensity to your boss. (Emotional ventilation is probably not part of your job description.)

• *The bugaboo of blaming:*   A "bugaboo" is something that causes needless or excessive anxiety, and blaming certainly does that. It also gets in the way of understanding, and so of communicating. How can we instead just let each other have our feelings, and maybe help each other to let them flow (or go)? A big first step is to stop judging feelings, and accept the frustrations that are part of the natural tension of opposites. It helps to remember that your feelings are just that: *your* feelings. Even if your frustration or anger (or whatever) was stimulated or intensified by what others said or did, it's *not* their fault that you feel as you do. (It's not your "fault" either; feelings are not failings.) You are participating in the conflict, in some way, so it might be a good idea to reflect on how you are making or allowing the problem.

• *The luxury of labeling:* Labeling is a tempting way to let anger out: the target of your anger is suddenly "an asshole," "a bitch," "a bastard," "a jerk," "a bum," "a bad apple" or a stupid fool. *Nobody* is all bad, or stupid in every way. Even severely retarded persons have something to teach us—like appreciation of the simple things of life. Everyone has an asshole, and everyone is sometimes a jerk or a bum, a "bitch" or a "bastard." A couple of problems with labels are that they are insulting, and that they can be self-fulfilling prophecies. Repeatedly call someone a lazy bum, and s/he might just get lazier; call someone crazy, and s/he might act crazier. If s/he's going to be hung for it anyway, s/he might as well *be* it.

Labeling puts someone else in the negative side of a polarity, so that you get to stay in the positive side. Labeling is a way of polarizing conflicts. Two people stand on either side of an imaginary dividing line, with each taking one side of a polarity, and waiting for the other to agree that it's the *right* side. What needs to happen is joining hands and making a circle. One way to do that is to examine the labels, asking "What's so bad about that?" For example, "You are a useless lazy bum!" What is the underlying upset? Is it that the laziness leaves things undone? Or is it that you hate your own lazy streak, which is minimized when someone else becomes the embodiment of laziness? Or is it that you would really like to be lazier yourself, but circumstances (or yourself) won't let you be?

Laziness, like most things, has its rewards. Uselessness can be useful. Someone once tried to insult Chuang Tzu by saying his teachings were as useless as a gnarled, distorted, crooked tree that no carpenter would even look at. "No one will try to cut that tree down," was his response. "Nothing will harm it since it has no use. You can just rest in its shade. Useless? Then why be anxious about it?"

• *The vice of violence:* Have you ever hit or thrown something at someone, or felt such rage that you suddenly knew you were *capable* of physical violence? Having violent and aggressive impulses, or having sometime acted them out, does not mean you are "bad." Feeling an impulse to strike out or hit back just proves that you are a human being—with animalistic impulses as well as spiritual consciousness. Denying aggressive feelings and instead projecting them onto others can also be an act of violence; it can be liking striking others with a violent gust of self-righteousness. True non-violence requires owning and being current with feelings—that is, somehow expressing them before an inner rage builds up.

• *The role of forgiveness:* Apologizing can help heal emotional wounds, and forgiveness can help the scars be less noticeable. Apologizing can be saying "I'm sorry," or it can take the form of a loving touch, a considerate question, a positive statement. Without such antidotes, hurtful words or actions are like poisons; the longer they are allowed to act on the bodymind system, the more toxic are their effects. "Will you forgive me?" A powerful question, and perhaps an anxiety-producing one. To "forgive" means literally to "give away." "I forgive you" means "I give up anger against you, and I give up any claim to a right to punish you." To forgive is to accept what has happened, and so be able to use it as a stepping stone to something else.

• *You shouldn't say "should" and "shouldn't":* "You shouldn't do this" means about the same thing as "you are *wrong* to do this." "You should do this" is the equivalent of "You would be *right* to do this." Why? "Because this would be fair, and that would be unfair." According to whom? According to which rules? What seems unfair according to my set of rules may seem quite fair according to yours. There are no universal rules except those of Nature, and one of Nature's rules is that everything changes. Nature doesn't have "right" and "wrong," "fair" and "unfair," "should" and "shouldn't." There is yin and there is yang; there is one thing and there is its opposite. Neither side of a coin is right or wrong; both sides just *are*.

> "When we look at things in the light of Tao,
> Nothing is best, nothing is worst.
> Each thing, seen in its own light,
> Stands out in its own way . . .
> All things have varying capacities."[9]

It makes no more sense to say "you should be reasonable" or "you shouldn't be angry" than to say "it should be bright and sunny today" or "there shouldn't be a thunderstorm now." Perhaps you would *like* it to be sunny, and you would *like* the other person to be "reasonable" (as you define it, of course). The storm may inconvenience or threaten you, but it would be silly to say that Nature *shouldn't* be creating thunder and lightning around you. Likewise, you may not like the fact that someone is angry at you, but thinking "this shouldn't be happening" is not likely to stop the psychic storm. Being told that you "shouldn't" be angry might cause you to "make nice," if your self-esteem is weak or you are susceptible to guilt-tripping. But most likely the inner tempest will go on, hidden by a cloak of niceness.

What if you program yourself not to label someone when you get upset, but then *s/he* labels *you*? At a peak of anger, s/he yells, "You're just a pain in the ass, you creepy asshole!" You reply, "You shouldn't call me names. You should express your anger better." Oops. The "shoulds" and "shouldn'ts" just got you. Maybe the other guy has a different rule book. Maybe nasty names are unacceptable *to you*, and you need to make that clear. Maybe you can remember that, being human, you may sometimes *act like* a "creep" or an "asshole"—but that's hardly what you *are*. Neither are you just an angel, so there's no reason why you *should* always respond perfectly. Verbal attacks can push old buttons. When old tapes start playing, the inner light may temporarily go dim, or blink out.

• *Exaggeration and escalation:* "Speak the truth and do not exaggerate; then you will not be harmed," says Chuang Tzu.[10] Anger and distressed feelings tend to escalate when we exaggerate the importance of an upsetting incident, or attach exaggerated negative meanings to it. For example, my son tells me he doesn't have homework; then, when it pops out of his pocket, he says he just forgot. This makes me angry, but the anger can be easily intensified with thoughts like, "He *never* does what I tell him," or "he *always* tries to get out of doing his work" or "this *means* he'll *never* learn to be responsible." Behind such exaggerated thoughts lies fear—often obsolete old fear. The words "never" and "always" are clues to exaggerations. Nobody "always" does anything—at all times and without exception. Likewise, we cannot know that we would *never* do something—in no way, to no degree, under no circumstance.

• *Assertion and acceptance:* Functional communication means striking a balance between assertiveness and receptiveness, and between concern for yourself and concern for others. Assertiveness means clearly expressing your own thoughts and feelings. Receptiveness means listening to the other person, without interrupting, and trying to accept their thoughts and feelings. "But how can I accept something I don't agree with? How can I not interrupt when what s/he's saying isn't true?" It may not be easy, but acceptance does *not* mean agreement. Listening and being receptive rather demonstrates simply the *willingness to tolerate* a different point of view.

• *"I-Messages" vs. "You-Messages":* One of the simplest and most clear ways to initiate and respond to communication is to begin with "I": "I feel," "I think," "I hear," "I see," "I believe," "I value." An "I-Message" is a direct statement of thoughts and feelings, likes and dislikes, desires and needs. An "I-Message" reflects your awareness of your inner reality, whereas a "You-Message" often conveys a value judgment or negative interpretation of another's words and behavior. Begin a statement with "I" and you are more likely to own part of the problem; begin with "you" and blaming the other person follows more easily. For example, consider these possible responses when your husband or wife (or mother or father) asks or tells you to do something:

> "You act like I'm your slave!"
> "You're always so bossy!"
> "You never consider *my* feelings. You don't really love me."
> "You should be more considerate of my needs."
> "You shouldn't always try to make me do things your way."

Notice how easily "you" is followed by always/never, should/shouldn't or labeling? In these statements, the tone is accusatory. Between the lines we read, "It's your fault!" "I-Messages," on the other hand, are attempts to describe your inner reality. Because you are saying what you really feel, your verbal and non-verbal messages tend to be *congruent*—that is, your words and body language are in harmony. This avoids confusion, conveys confidence and inspires respect. For example:

> "I feel annoyed by that demand."
> "I really don't want to do that right now."
> "I would enjoy doing something else."
> "I love you, and I feel upset when it seems like you're ordering me around."
> "I need to take care of some other things today."

Sometimes your "I-Messages" will inspire not only respect, but also resistance and defensiveness. The other person may disagree reasonably or sarcastically. S/he may pout or get angry, look shocked or hurt, leave or hang up. S/he may blame or label you, and say you are wrong or unfair. It is easy to go on the defensive, or to attack back. A happier solution is to just stand on your feelings. For example, "I'm sorry it upsets you, but I really feel I need to do some other things today." By re-asserting your need or feeling, you are in effect saying, "It is important that *I* get heard and *my* needs get met." However, what the other person might hear is, "I don't care how it affects you!" In that case, you might want to say some good stuff, like that you *do* care. Or, it might be time to just be receptive.

• *Questions vs. assumptions:* Ask questions to clarify the other person's message. Find out exactly what s/he wants or means, rather than reacting to what you think s/he thinks. Ask questions before making ultimatums. It is amazing how often we jump to hurtful conclusions, hearing something as proof of our fears or confirmation of our hopes. "But I just assumed s/he meant. . . ." It has been pointed out that "assume" means to make an "ass" out of "u" and "me." Assumptions are the doorway to confusion and misunderstanding. Asking questions gives the other person a chance to vent feelings, and can prevent escalation of the conflict. For example:

> "Why do you want me to do that?"
> "What are you feeling?"
> "What is upsetting you?"
> "Why does that bother you?"
> *"What do you mean by that?"*

• *Listening is a skill:* "Active listening" means trying to get a sense of what someone is feeling or experiencing, and then checking back in with them, for example by saying, "It sounds like you're feeling. . . ." Active listening says, literally or in effect, "Here's my understanding of what you're saying. Have I understood you or not?" After listening and trying to empathize with the other person, you give feedback so that misunderstandings can be corrected before they get exaggerated. Basically, you are re-stating what you heard: "Are you saying that you think. . . ." or "Do you mean. . . ?" The idea is to try to avoid judging, criticizing or defending, and instead to verbalize your understanding of the other person's message—its *content* or the actual words, and its *context* or the accompanying feelings and behavior.

• *Saying No:* A discussion of assertiveness would hardly be complete without considering the automatic yes and the fearful no. Perhaps you have been asked to contribute work for a charitable cause, loan money to a friend, or baby-sit for your sister's kids. How often do you reluctantly say "yes," and then find yourself muttering and fuming about the extra work or strain? Why the automatic yes? Reasons might include: not wanting to seem selfish, not wanting to hurt others, needing to be liked, or feeling obligated. Duty and reciprocity can be positive forces, but they can push you into a non-assertive position. The element of surprise can also cause an automatic yes response. An alternative might be: "I need to think about that."

If you do need to say "no," saying instead "I'm too busy" or "I can't" may just postpone the problem. Part of self-assertion is being able to sometimes say, "I don't want to" or "I have decided not to," without defending or explaining yourself. It is not a sin to be selfish. However, you may want to give a reason, in effect telling the other person, "I am saying 'no' so that I can meet some legitimate needs of my own, not because I don't care about your needs." (There is no guarantee that the other person will *like* this, especially if you have always said yes before.) When you decide to say yes, you might also want to give a reason, in order to communicate that you really want to and aren't just giving in.

The opposite problem is the automatic no. Determined not to be taken advantage of or "used," you may have learned to just say "no" to most requests, especially when they feel like demands. Meanwhile, in your own way, you may be doing things that, to you, demonstrate that you care. To the other person, however, your automatic no may demonstrate the opposite, and so may be pushing people away from you as effectively as insults or sarcasm. The automatic no is reminiscent of an adolescent's rebelliousness. The rebellion may be important, but it is equally important to know what you are rebelling against—which may not be the targeted person.

Saying both "yes" and "no" consciously, together with active listening and questioning, will often dissolve problems by helping to clarify ambiguous situations. Ambiguity is at the root of many misunderstandings and conflicts. When a situation is left vague and undefined, people more easily project their old conflicts into the situation and attribute negative thoughts and feelings to each other. The present conflict escalates as each person reacts to what s/he *thinks* the other person thinks or feels. These opinions often derive from myths about what *should* be happening.

• *Exploring dysfunctional myths:* One such myth is: if you really love someone, you should just *know* what s/he feels and needs. Not so. Love confers neither psychic powers nor continual bliss. Paradoxically, happiness depends on challenging the myth that your relationship should make you happy by satisfying all your needs, and conflict resolution depends on challenging the myth that all conflict could be avoided, if you did everything right.

Conflicts are evidence of unmet needs or unresolved feelings; they need not be power struggles in which one person comes out feeling like the loser. Before investing your energy in working through a conflict, you might want to evaluate its importance. Is this something you could just drop, or will it upset you until it's resolved? And is the present conflict exaggerated because of unresolved past conflicts? In an intimate relationship, you might talk about these psychic dynamics. For example: "I suspect it's not entirely what you're doing, but partly my fear of being used." Your boss, on the other hand, may not appreciate being taken on a journey through your psychic depths.

• *Agreeing to disagree:* What if you have communicated as clearly as possible, but the conflict has not been resolved? What if you feel you must say no, and the other person says that's not acceptable? Besides blowing up or pouting, about all that you can do is to further define the nature of the problem. "It seems our problem is that I feel I need . . . while you feel you need. . . ." When the problem is crystal clear to everyone involved, you may want to consider possible solutions, and agree to try one of them. Or you may want to just acknowledge the impasse, and agree to disagree! Abandoning the attempt to fix things, or to change each other, can sometimes break an argumentative cycle as effectively as finding points of agreement. Sometimes, when we get out of the way, things fix themselves. In short, just about any interruption of a dysfunctional communication pattern is an improvement. Often the negative interactional *pattern* is more the problem than the specific *content* of the disagreement.

• *Placating, Computing and Leveling:*   Since the other person is not likely to be totally wrong, finding something to agree about does not mean being dishonest. Being really honest usually means acknowledging at least two sides of a coin: both positive and negative feelings. Often, we ignore one or the other. At an extreme, ignoring the seemingly negative feelings, and just agreeing about everything, can amount to *placating:* pretending to agree with others so they won't get mad. Placating can be a lethal game in which "everyone agrees with everyone else, at the expense of his own needs and satisfactions," says Virginia Satir. "This is a common interactional pattern in families which develop a high incidence of psychosomatic illness." An alternative is "growth vitality games," in which "each person includes self and others in inter-action by expressing himself and also permitting others to express themselves." "Growth games" involve learning to tolerate disagreement and to level with each other.[11]

A couple basic ways of expressing feelings are *showing* them or *explaining* them. Always suppressing emotional words and gestures, and patiently explaining your feelings, is what Satir calls "computing"—using ulta-reasonable words that discount your feelings. Computing is a defense against the anxiety of being more openly as-sertive and communicative. But it is not a very effective way of getting understood. How can the other person empathize with your *feelings* when all s/he is getting is words?

To always follow any guidelines, including the ones described above, would be "computing." Guidelines can be helpful, but the goal is spontaneity. The Taoists emphasized being responsive to the needs of the moment—being receptive or asser-tively standing your ground as the situation requires, instead of trying to figure out in advance what will work. Chuang Tzu says that "struggling or giving way . . .may be at one time noble and at another time mean. It is impossible to establish any any constant rule."[12]

> "Don't listen with your ears, listen with your mind. No, don't listen with your mind, but listen with your spirit. Listening stops with the ears, the mind stops with recognition, but spirit is empty and waits on all things. The Way gathers in emptiness alone. . . . Let your ears and eyes communi-cate with what is inside, and put mind and knowledge on the outside. Then even gods and spirits will come to dwell, not to speak of men!"[12]

Part 2.   EXTREME EMOTIONS OF HUN: frustration or anger

Often people will more readily admit to feeling frustrated, irritated or annoyed than to feeling angry. It is as though the word "anger" were a red flag, which might activate a mad bull, or as though *getting* mad were equal to *going* mad. The message is that the ideal or good person doesn't get angry. Is this true? Was Jesus being less than his ideal Self when he angrily pushed over the tables of the money-changers at the temple? Or was he just acting angry to make a point? I doubt it. Pretense and masterhood don't seem to go together. Perhaps the point is that while much of life needs to be peacefully accepted, anger can be an appropriate reaction to that which seems unacceptable.

People don't like anger, so they'll like you better if you don't express any. Is this true? If expressing anger equals acting out, it may be, but releasing anger need not mean being obnoxious or aggressive. "But I had a bad temper," or someone else did, "and it scared me, so I learned to control my anger." Great, but have you also learned how to express it? There is a fine line between controlling anger and containing it. Resentment, guilt and depression are clues that what seemed like great self-control was actually just suppression. Like the guy who was being sarcastic and snapping at everything I said one morning. "You seem angry," I said. "No, I'm not angry," he replied. "Since I took the ABC Training, I don't get angry any more." Not until he slugged his girlfriend during an argument a couple months later, that is.

Trying to overcome a "bad temper" by never getting angry again rarely works. Anger is a normal human experience, not evidence of a demonically destructive force. Anger generates energy, which almost begs for some kind of action. The opposite of a "bad temper" is not the absence of all anger, but rather the ability to let anger out appropriately, and to channel its energy constructively. This is part of self-actualization, as Maslow points out:

> "My opinion is that the weight of the evidence so far indicates that indiscriminately *destructive* hostility is reactive, because uncovering therapy reduces it, and changes its quality in 'healthy' self-affirmation, forcefulness, selective hostility, self-defense, righteous indignation, etc. In any case, the *ability* to be aggressive and angry is found in all self-actualizing people, who are able to let it flow forth freely when the external situation 'calls' for it . . . Presumably, then, a child should learn not only how to control his anger, but also how and when to express it."[13]

Mandy's story (continued from part two of Chapter 11) illustrates the process of transforming anger by learning to release it appropriately. Mandy came for therapy largely because of her "crazy-acting temper tantrums." She also felt constantly guilty and frequently depressed. Her "uncontrollable anger" was usually directed at her husband—through yelling, screaming and throwing objects around. She was afraid her husband would leave her if she couldn't do something about her explosions—and she wanted desperately to have her I.U.D. out and become pregnant. "When I calm down," she said. "I can't imagine myself doing and saying the things that I have. My temper gets worse when I drink liquor—then I go into rages and crying fits." Alcohol directly affects the liver; it also lifts inhibitions so that internalized angers can spew forth. After her angry explosions, Mandy felt guilty and alternated between feeling sorry for herself and obsessing on house-cleaning.

Mandy's idea of a cure was to never get angry. However, she'd already tried that and it hadn't worked too well. I suggested that she could instead learn to express the anger more appropriately, by finding some outlet for it—like physical exercise. She also could be aware of when an angry explosion was coming up, by paying more attention to her body feelings. She could then excuse herself, go into another room, and let the anger out safely—like by hitting pillows or yelling and crying. The next week Mandy reported that her husband liked this approach, but doubted she could learn to control her feelings "because they are so strong." Yet, when she felt herself getting angry at a party that week, she *had* gone into another room to vent her feelings. Was she going to let her husband's statement sabotage her attempts? She decided to give herself permission to be angry—in a different way.

Mandy tended to alternate between the extremes of acting nice and then exploding. She couldn't think of any in-between behavior. I suggested that the middle way might be learning to express and assert her feelings as they came up. She agreed that might be better than staying mad all night and then exploding a day or two later. She worked on learning to express what she was feeling by making "I statements"—like "I feel angry when you . . ." or sometimes even "I feel angry about . . . although I think it might be silly!"

In the third session, I began using acupressure along with psychotherapeutic techniques.* After some neck and chest release, while we were focusing on the diaphragm area, what came up was Mandy's anger at her mother for not allowing her to go to her father's funeral when she was twelve. Then, for the first time, she got in touch with her anger at her father for abandoning her by dying. This old but very real anger was a source of her "uncontrollable temper" and "constant guilt." Not being in touch with it, she had directed all the anger at her mother, whom she had seen as the "cause of my problems," and she had displaced anger onto her husband. Determined not to be weak, Mandy had also displaced feelings of hurt or sadness into anger. The images which arose during the diaphragm release allowed her to work through some of the old anger, and to move into the process of finally grieving her father's death.

For some time before this, Mandy had not been on speaking terms with her mother. Part of her anger at her mother was for not understanding her father; since Mandy strongly identified with her father, downing him felt like downing her too. As she accepted her mother's limitations and began communicating with her, Mandy learned a confusing "fifteen-year secret"—that it was her *father* who had not wanted her to go to his funeral. Remembering her father's spiritual beliefs, like reincarnation, Mandy saw that he might have wanted her to communicate with his spirit, not mourn his dead body. At the end of this session, Mandy said she felt more in touch with her father's personality than she had for a long time. "It's like finding a missing part of myself!"

---

* This session was more fully described in Chapter 11, where the relationship between unresolved grief and depression was explored. Although sometimes useful with depressive symptoms, such an early focus on diaphragm and anger release is not generally recommended.

In her first sessions, a constant theme was that Mandy saw herself as all bad, and her husband as all good. Her former abuse of drugs, along with the temper tantrums, had helped her to paint that picture. She idealized her husband, giving him power by making him all right. But that led to frustration and anger, followed by guilt. Besides being the effect of unresolved old anger, her tantrums could be seen as an attempt to gain power. But then she got labeled as "bad" or "sick" by both herself and her husband.

Feeling that dysfunctional communication patterns might be stimulating some of Mandy's anger, I asked her to bring her husband for a joint session. He refused. When Mandy wanted to bring a tape he had once made of a tantrum, so that I could hear how bad she was, her husband said, "I want to listen to it first. Maybe I said something that made you mad!" He'd never before admitted that he might have a role in the tantrums. This new feedback was a turning point, because Mandy's anger became a shared problem. Her husband was *not* all good, and she was *not* all bad.

For many years after her father's death, Mandy had used drugs to provide her with all kinds of mood changes. Since the liver is a detoxification center, it is affected by drug or alcohol abuse. According to acupressure theory, Liver imbalance makes for easy arousal to anger. Fortunately, the liver has great powers of recovery, if demands on it are kept to a minimum. At first it was hard for Mandy to stay off drugs, because they made life more exciting by enhancing her sensory awareness. She found that acupressure could similarly awaken her senses, and the accompanying endorphin release provided her with some of the "high" feelings she had missed. She also learned simple relaxation exercises and started exercising at a health spa. In a follow-up conversation about six months after termination of therapy, Mandy said, "I've been working like a dog and am feeling really good about myself—finally!" Her marriage had become stable, and she was pregnant.

Noticing images and thoughts that accompany our angry feelings, sometimes we discover that our anger is not so much caused by the present situation, as by an unresolved past conflict that it has triggered. Mandy, for instance, often got furious when her husband criticized her, because she feared this meant that he would abandon her. For another example, Shirley got so angry that she terminated therapy after I had to end a session while she was still in a very emotional place. Wanting to support her, I had already kept my next client waiting for half an hour. But because Shirley was not in touch with her deep feelings of rejection, from being an unwanted and abused child, she projected her mother's cruelty onto me. A year later, when she resumed therapy, she said, "I had to discover that you were not *causing* the feelings, but they were *mine*."

Bodymind Dynamics of Anger and Frustration

"When animals face death, they do not care what noises they make. They growl fiercely and snarl, and then they attack. In the same way, if a man is pushed too far, he turns and strikes without knowing why."[14]

Awareness of the dynamics behind anger moderates the impulse to act it out through physical or verbal hostility. Anger can be a response to a real or imagined threat. It can also be a response to frustration—that feeling of irritable uptightness (and literal tightness in the shoulders, neck and back) which arises when we feel hindered or pressured. Frustration can come from feeling thwarted, being excessively limited, or being pushed too far. Therefore, basic Taoist advise is: "Don't force things." Human beings have limited frustration tolerances. Forced beyond those, they will become angry. Continued frustration turns into an anger that wants to overcome obstacles. Frustration is not likely to be eliminated from our lives, nor is anger likely to be excised from our personalities. (My cat agrees, meowing vigorously to be let outside again. Whichever side of the door she is on, it is the wrong one.)

Frustration is woven into the very fabric of life, because life is a tension of opposites. An apparent conflict between opposites is part of the relative world—the world of activity and passivity, light and shadow. Frustration results from and calls our attention to conflict. Frustration has an adaptive purpose, for this seething sense of unrest demands that we change our situation or ourselves, instead of just putting up with what feels intolerable. Frustration can be temporarily diminished by winning an argument, but the victory is an empty one, and the frustration a recurrent phenomenon, until the underlying conflict is resolved. And then there will be another conflict with the outside world, or we will become aware of another internal conflict.

We could avoid the frustration of conflict and opposition if we could accept all of life's polarities. Growth is gradually seeing the ways that all things are right *and* wrong, good *and* bad—or neither. It is integrating the polar aspects of oneself so that there is less inner conflict. But the aim is not a static balance, with the absolute absence of conflict and the perfection of complete integration. How can a limited being integrate every aspect of Self and Universe? Yet we want, even crave, wholeness and harmony. The urge to wholeness, together with the seeming conflict of opposite forces, is the formula for growth, as well as for a kind of existential frustration. Without conflict, we would not exercise our Selves; without the compensating urge to wholeness, we would be torn apart by the conflict of opposites.

Integrating the opposing feelings and forces of life presumes accepting them. "Just let it all be!" I can hear the Taoists saying. Otherwise, we are distressed by an unnecessary frustration *about the existence of conflict and frustration.* This reminds me of a family therapy case where the presenting problem was the oldest son. The mother complained that he was always causing upsets with the younger children. The boy maintained that he sometimes, but not always, was at fault. As they compared their memories of quarrels, the mother saw that she was often frustrated just by the existence of conflict. She thought that family members *should* always be nice to each other. Since it didn't feel "nice" to express frustration or show anger, she ended up placating. When she stopped being upset about the existence of conflict, she started being able to channel her frustration into assertiveness, and was able to more effectively set limits for her children.

An archetypal example of the tension of opposites is the polarity of the masculine and the feminine. We encounter this basic polarity within relationships and social interactions, and in our own psyches. Part of maturity is accepting the differentness of the opposite sex, and accepting the "masculine" (active, assertive, analytical) and "feminine" (passive, receptive, intuitive) aspects of ourselves. In Jungian terms, growth or "individuation" requires this integration of the "animus," or more masculine aspect of the self, with the "anima," or more feminine self. We need *both* the partners within every polarity for wholeness.

Growth also involves accepting the "shadow"—the parts of ourselves which feel dark and which we don't like. Part of the shadow is our animalistic self. No matter how sophisticated or spiritually developed we become, we remain also animals, with primitive instincts and primal emotional responses. Anger is a non-angelic, but natural, response to threatening situations. Anger and fear are the primary emergency emotions. Both stimulate the adrenal glands and the sympathetic nerves to provide the extra energy needed to fight for survival or flee for our lives. With anger and fear, the muscular system is charged and mobilized for action—though in different ways, since different muscles are required for fighting against or fleeing from danger.

Acupressure theory says that in anger the energy rushes upwards and becomes strong in the head and shoulders. Lowen also describes anger as an upward movement of energy. When we get very angry, we become not unlike a dog seized by the impulse for confrontation: the fur along the neck and back is raised, the shoulders are lowered, and the head moves forward.

> "In the feeling of anger, the excitation charges the muscular system along the back of the body, mobilizing the powerful movements of attack. The main organs of assault are located in the upper and front end of the body, because this end is directly connected with the search for and seizure of food. Anger is experienced, therefore, as a surge of feeling upward along the back of the body and into the head and arms. This surge of feeling is associated with a strong flow of blood to these parts, which accounts for the fact that some people literally see red when they become intensely angry."[15]

Nature has arranged things so that this emergency emotion gives us the energy to confront or stand up to threats. The secretion of noradrenaline raises the blood pressure and helps prepare us for aggressive action. When the emotional reaction is more intense, the secretion of adrenaline mobilizes the changes needed for fight or flight, which include increased heart activity and breathing, and an increase of the blood sugar level resulting from the liver's production of glucose (sugar) from glycogen (starch).

Fear and Anger: Intertwined Emotions

Fear and anger are alternative emotional responses; the one can change into the other. Anger can be a way of covering up anxiety-producing feelings like fear and vulnerability, or the expression of anger can be blocked by fear. Fear can give rise to anger, but the hyperactivity of chronic anger drains the reserve energy and so gives rise to easier or more frequent fear, which in turn can breed more anger. [In Five Elements terms, Chih breeds Hun, and Hun in turn influences Chih.] The anger in turn produces a feeling of excitement; the longer it brews, the more excitable or anxious we become. [Hun breeds Shen.]

Fear and anger are potent defensive drives. Theodore Lidz says that these emotions are "crucial forces in human motivation," and that they are modifiable, or can be controlled and channeled.

"These built-in automatic defenses against danger, which arose early in the evolutionary process to implement the capacity to fight enemies, flee danger, and mobilize resources in emergencies, are only slightly less important to the preservation of the animal than the drives arising from tissues needs. As soon as danger is sensed the bodily processes alter almost instantaneously to prepare for fight or flight without the intervention of conscious decision. Such defenses are crucial to survival in a world filled with enemies and in-animate hazards. . . . The human being is heir to these physiological re-sponses, even though they may impede as often as they help in dealing with dangers in civilized society."[16]

In most modern situations, neither physical violence nor running away is in the interests of conflict resolution. Since attacking is not societally acceptable (except in war or to control criminal activities), people usually don't release the excitation of anger with primitive actions like striking, biting or hitting. However, alarming statistics of child and spouse abuse might indicate that we aren't as civilized as we like to think. An old-fashioned pillow fight, anyone? If the energetic charge of anger is not somehow released, tension accumulates in the muscles that have been mobil-ized for action: in the shoulders, arms, neck, and jaw. The head may begin to feel like a pressure cooker, and tension headaches may develop. Frustration and anger may also "talk" to us through mid-back pain or abdominal discomfort, especially around points #17 and #5. The diaphragm contracts in response to anger, and its armoring then functions to hold down assertive and expressive emotions.

As an example of the tension that can accumulate with residual anger, I am reminded of a middle-aged man who had made an appointment because of his chronic mid-back pain. From my office window, I could see him quarreling with his wife before they came in. In checking the primary reflex points, I noticed that not only was his back tense in the diaphragm [#17] area, but also he had a lot of tension along the trapezius in the shoulders and neck, in the upper arms, and in the jaw. Points of the Liver and Gall Bladder Meridians were hyper-tense or hyper-sensitive.

As the session progressed, David began to talk about a very stressful period in his life, when he had been betrayed by business associates and publicly humiliated. "That would make almost anyone angry!" I observed. Starting over can be a frustrating business. But David's distress had been intensified because, not seeing a way to release and resolve his anger, he had turned it against himself. He was plagued with guilt at the stress he had inadvertently put his family through. Midway through the session, he said, "I don't know why I'm telling you all of this!" Since we had been releasing tension at points that often record unresolved anger, it was not so mysteri-ous that he was baring his angry psyche to me.

Just feeling that I understood and accepted his feelings was enough to let David see that they were okay. He listened to what his body was saying, and realized that his body tensions had been a response to his anger and guilt. He explored the fear that he had unwittingly hurt his family through his involvement with associates who turned out to be unethical. What had changed because of the crisis? Were the results all bad? A loss of wealth and social status had made David retreat into a very simple lifestyle. He felt a deep appreciation for his family's love and for the beautiful rustic place in which they lived. He saw that his anger was obsolete, for he no longer even wanted the things that he had once been so angry about losing, and so afraid of never having again. He felt good about how he was raising his children. The trade-off had been a growthful one; there was nothing to feel guilty about. After this session, both David's wife and my secretary were amazed at his changed appearance, saying he looked ten years younger.

Letting go of anger-related tensions often requires more than just self-awareness and verbal expression. Bodywork is very helpful for getting the release started, but some kind of energetic activity is also an important part of anger therapy. The primitive, animalistic part of ourselves isn't satisfied with words; it needs to *act*. Without a physical outlet, the energy tends to stay bound in the related musculature. It's not hard to find a constructive use for this energy: you can exercise or go jogging, walk or hike, wash dishes or clean house, pull weeds or mow the lawn, wash the car or dog or horse—or help me clean the corral!

The mutual aerobics of love-making is another outlet, but using sex just to relieve pressure distorts its psychological and biological purposes: connecting and procreating. Compulsive sexuality can be a way of avoiding the anger component of frustrating situations. Acupressure theory says that "excessive sex" is energy-draining; sex involves a lot of emotional energy, and can drain the reserve energy stored in the Kidneys. On the other hand, repression of the sexual instincts can produce inner stress and frustration. [Imbalance in Chih breeds imbalance in Hun.] And if it's a choice, making love *does* sound more attractive than making war.

Considering the Source

"It's not worth it to get mad," says common opinion; "just consider the source." Not bad advice, except that it often implies contempt for the person who has "caused" the anger, and so considering that it's not worthwhile to resolve the contention. "What do you expect from him (or her)?" The anger may not even be all related to the other person; some of it may be a cover-up for anxiety-arousing feelings like vulnerability, hurt and fear. When psychotherapists advise considering the source of the anger, they mean looking at how the present situation is stimulating unresolved conflicts, triggering old fears and igniting repressed angers—or looking for interactional or communication patterns which are causing escalation of the anger.

Sometimes the source of the anger may be just that two people have different ways of perceiving things. Three main modes of perception are the auditory, visual and kinesthetic; each of us perceives in all these ways, but often one mode will be dominant and another less developed. For instance, person A might be an auditory type; being more sensitive to sound, s/he might really tune into the *sound* of person B's voice. Person B might remember the content of the conversation, while person A remembers its tone. For another example, person A might be a visual type, while person B is more kinesthetic. In a relationship, person A might be reacting more to how things *look*, while person B is more sensitive to how they *feel*. When unrecognized, these differences can be sources of anger or frustration.

When the Taoists suggested considering the source, they were referring to *the* Source—the Tao. Taoist texts make few direct references to anger, but there is much talk about resolving conflicts—between right and wrong, yes and no, good and bad.

The Taoists say judgments of right and wrong make for faster and feebler arguments; endless distinctions lead to chaos and confusion. Avoiding judgments reduces conflict, because as long as there is a right and a wrong, people will take sides. As soon as I take one side and you another, we are in conflict. To stand in the center between right and wrong is to see how these (and all) opposites converge. It is to rest in the Source.

> "Suppose you and I argue. If you win and I lose, are you indeed right and I wrong? And if I win and you lose, am I right and you wrong? Are we both partly right and partly wrong? Are we both all right or both all wrong?
>
> ". . . Waiting for changing opinions is like waiting for nothing. Seeing everything in relation to the heavenly cosmos and leaving the different viewpoints as they are, we may be able to live out our years. . . . Forget time; forget distinctions. Enjoy the infinite; rest in it."[17]

One of the best ways to increase anger is to deny it or be dishonest about it. Take the example of a woman who is afraid to express anger to her husband. Instead she feels like a victim or martyr, or complains about being misused and misunderstood. The anger and frustration, having no direct outlet, begin to ooze out in "passive aggressive" behavior. She "forgets" to pick up what her husband needed from the store or to give him a message, ruins his favorite shirt in the wash, has a "headache" when it's time to go to bed, or goes into the ultimately passive routine of silence. Her husband, and everyone else, can *feel* her anger, whether she owns to it or not. Disguising anger with sweet or clever talk just tends to confuse others and make them more frustrated and angry. They *feel* that something is wrong, but can't do much about it when the internally angry person is busy denying it.

> "What was simple in the beginning becomes grotesque in the end. Words are like the wind and the waves; action involves the risk of gain or loss. The wind and the waves are easily set in motion; risk easily turns into real danger. Hence, anger comes from nothing more than clever words and half-truths."[17]

Why disguise the anger with clever words and half-truths, which just end up stimulating more anger until it all becomes grotesque? Why not simply say "I feel angry?" The person who is afraid to make waves by admitting to anger might reply, "But I don't know if my anger is right; I don't know if it's justified." In the beginning, the feeling is quite simple. Trying to figure out whether the anger is right or wrong generally complicates things. The unexpressed anger grows while it is being analyzed, justified, explained, rationalized or defended against.

Anger just *is* when it is. It is neither right nor wrong. It doesn't need to be justified. The attempt to justify anger is one of the easiest ways to pervert it into a foul state of resentment, for the quickest way to justify anger is to blame others for it. The longer we sit on anger, the more energy gets invested in the feeling, and the more desire there is to justify it by finding things that are wrong. Disliking anger can waste as much energy as liking anger would. Disliking and avoiding anger, rather than processing it, is like burying a bomb. Disallowing any expression of anger is like shortening the fuse. Avoiding small blow-ups can produce big ones—which might start over a little thing, so that later we can't even remember what the fight was about. The dam broke, that's all. We were emotionally too full, so we belched.

Felt anger is finite. Anger which is accepted is self-limiting. Anger which is suppressed is self-generating. Heather, for example, thought she had a "bad temper" because she so often felt angry. While she tried to be understanding and placate others, her anger seethed inside her very tense abdomen, and turned her shoulders into rocks. "I just try not to get mad, because I don't like to get mad. I try to be reasonable and agreeable, but then after a while I lose it and get mad. When I get mad, I don't really say anything. It's not a good kind of mad. I don't express myself well. So when I get really upset, I just leave." The problem wasn't so much a bad temper, as that the anger Heather was afraid to express built up inside, and sometimes broke out.

Getting in touch with internalized anger can be an intense experience. "As I let go to the anger," while breathing through the diaphragm, "it felt like a huge dark cloud coming out of me. The energy was tremendous. Then I had the image of a sun breaking through dark clouds, as my whole body relaxed. I felt like I had somehow gotten down to feeling the core of myself." The universal law is to live from that core. "I've been side-stepping that law by being afraid to assert myself, and I'm the loser for it." A big discovery is: "Facing the dark side doesn't mean less of the light side, but more intensely feeling the light side too! This flower looks *so* beautiful to me right now. It reminds me of how deeply I felt things like that when I was a child."

Letting go to the energy of anger can bring an exhilarating sense of power and joy. A therapeutic situation is a safe place to vent anger. It may feel more dangerous to express anger in a relationship, perhaps because of a fear that expressing anger will end a relationship. In *The Angry Book*, Dr. Theodore Rubin speaks to this concern:

> "This seems obvious, but it isn't to many people: anger doesn't kill relationships, and it certainly does not kill people. . . . Anger of course does make waves and kills the neurotic kind of 'love' that depends on a show of 100 percent complete harmony. But this isn't love at all; it is neurotic dependency and only confused with love. Feeling anger and exchanging angry feelings strengthen true love and are actually life-affirming. . . . It isn't anger that kills; people kill—people who are often completely divorced from all their feelings, especially warm human ones that would give them the wherewithal to empathize with their fellows."[18]

A relationship is at least as likely to blow up, or wither on the vine, if anger is *not* expressed and the emotional air is not cleared. To put it bluntly, as Rubin does: "If a relationship is destroyed by a show of anger, then there's an excellent chance that it was a sick, destructive affair and that all parties are better off for its termination."[18] It would probably have died anyway, from toxic deceptions and emotional poisoning. It might already have been dead, as far as a real intimate, feeling connection—which is a lot of what we mean by "love." Sharing feelings demonstrates confidence in the strength and importance of the relationship. Deep down, most people are relieved by a sharing of real, honest feelings. What people generally *don't* appreciate is an eruption of repressed old feelings, especially when they spew forth under the guise of sarcasm, blaming, put-downs or insults.

Feel it and accept it without judgments, and the anger might just change by itself. Often it changes to amusement, laughter and joy. [Hun breeds Shen.] Vent your anger, like by kicking some stones around or yelling nonsensical curses, and you might find yourself chuckling—if only at your own actions. After a fight with your mate, you might find a smile teasing the corners of your mouth, and feel a desire to be hugged building up. Maybe anger is not so terrible, if its expression can so easily be followed by laughter and mirth.

Part 3. HYPOACTIVE HUN: self-blame, guilt, lack of motivation, boredom, impotency, depression

Excessive guilt feelings can be highly distressing. "Pop psychologies" sometimes imply that guilt is an unnecessary feeling, which should be chucked if we want to get on with growing. Buying this, we could feel guilty about feeling guilty. Is guilt a useless feeling? In Old English, the word *gylt* meant "a sin or offense." Leaving the question of sin aside, guilt is a painful feeling of self-blame, stemming from the belief that we have done something wrong. It can be a signal that we *have* offended somebody, according to our own standards or those we have been trained to uphold. Guilt is *not* just a useless, neurotic feeling. The ability to have ethical standards, and reproach oneself for violating them, is a quality which distinguishes the normal person from the "sociopathic" or antisocial personality—who has little conscience and can't consistently care about others.

However, "guilt-tripping" heads the list of distressing psychological states. Not only do we reproach ourselves for perceived offenses, but we also sit in trial on ourselves and condemn ourselves to be punished—by the self-torture of guilt, if nothing else. The guilt is often way out of proportion to the offense, which may even be nonexistent. For instance, a client tells me that a masseur tried to stimulate her sexually. She is angry. Then her diaphragm and abdomen tense up as she starts blaming herself: "I should have checked to see if he was licensed. I should have scheduled an appointment earlier in the day. I should have known." Why? That we may learn something from a difficult experience doesn't mean that we *should* have known it already. We are all guilty of being human. Human beings don't know everything.

They don't even remember everything, and besides that they make mistakes. Like the time I was relaxing in the desert sun and suddenly remembered I hadn't given a key to a colleague scheduled to teach at my center the night before. As I pictured him and the students standing outside a locked door, sudden guilt constricted my shoulders and sent a nauseating feeling through my upper abdomen. I called to apologize, and as he said I was forgiven, I asked, "Aren't you angry?" He replied, "Well, I was at first, but then I thought, 'Are you allowed to make a mistake, Iona?'" I still feel a welling up of teariness remembering that simple but impactful question. Although I insisted *other* people not put me on a pedestal, I still expected perfection of myself. In my own book of rules, there was the entry, "Thou shalt not make dumb mistakes." Guilt was a penalty I imposed on myself for breaking that rule.

Lowen says, "The original feeling of guilt arises from the sense of being unloved. The only explanation a child can formulate for this state of affairs is that he is not deserving of love."[19] Feeling disapproved and unloved, the child concludes that s/he does not deserve love because s/he is "bad." Or, at least, s/he is "good" only insofar as s/he follows the rules, one of which is not to get angry at the rule-makers. Punishment or shame is the consequence of breaking the rules, which often seem to be stacked against seeking pleasure. So the unconscious equation becomes: pleasure=

sin=guilt. A decreased capacity for pleasure and a compensating over-emphasis on productivity are characteristic of unconscious guilt, as Lowen points out.

> "Any feeling or emotion can become a source of guilt feelings if a negative moral judgment is attached to it. Generally, however, it is our pleasure feelings, sexual or erotic desires and hostility that are colored by such judgments, which stem directly from parental attitudes and ultimately from social mores. A child is made to feel guilty about his pleasure strivings in order to make him into a productive worker, he is made to feel guilty about sexuality to subdue his animal nature, and he is made to feel guilty about hostility to render him obedient and submissive. In the course of such training his creative potential is destroyed."[19]

If we are made to feel guilty about "wasting time," then gradually guilt may make it impossible to fully enjoy relaxing. The spaces between activity are fruitful, not barren wastelands. The time we take for rest and relaxation is time *spent* on nurturing ourselves, not time *wasted*. The times of "doing nothing" are often the times of sudden insights, creative ideas and "just" pleasurable feelings. When unconscious guilt is telling us we *should* instead get something done, we can't really unwind, and so don't feel ready to get busy again. Guilt might make us get going, but resentment builds up, whether or not we are conscious of it.

What happens if guilt becomes attached to pleasurable or erotic feelings? Guilt about eating turns having a delicious dessert into an act fraught with anxiety, rather than a simple pleasure. Because food is not really enjoyed, there may develop an inordinate desire for more, as in binge eating, or an anorexic inability to nurture oneself with food. Similarly, guilt about sex prevents full surrender to the pleasure of making love. Because love-making is not wholly satisfying, there may develop strong cravings for new sexual partners and experiences, or various sexual dysfunctions may arise. Lowen explains how a lack of sexual satisfaction can result from and then intensify guilty inhibitions.

> "When emotion is fully expressed and the excitation of the emotion released, one feels good. . . . However, when an emotion is not fully expressed, the residual undischarged excitation leaves one feeling dissatisfied, unfulfilled, and bad. This bad feeling can be interpreted as guilt, sin, or wickedness, depending on the moral judgment. . . .
>
> "Guilt creates a vicious circle. If a person feels guilty about his sexual desires, he will be unable to give in fully to these desires . . . The unconscious holding back enforced by the guilt, introduces a painful element into the experience, and one comes out of it with the feeling that it was somehow 'wrong.' "[19]

Meanwhile, anger simmers in the depths of the psyche. Anger results as naturally from the frustration of pleasure-seeking, which is the betrayal of the body, as it would from betrayal by a lover. The "sexual revolution" has helped dispel some of the old guilt, by countering the message that sexuality is bad or shameful, but sometimes the emphasis on sexual responsiveness has generated new guilt—about episodes of frigidity or impotency, not orgasming easily, or not being able to "give" an orgasm to one's partner. New sexual diseases have also restimulated guilt about sexuality

326

(along with renewed interest in sexual fidelity). Under this guilt, there is anger—at oneself or a sexual partner, at social mores, or at the disease itself. Similarly, under guilt about sexual performance, there is anger and anxiety about being judged according to that performance—which hardly helps it.

Guilt can also be a way of keeping aggressive feelings down, or the result of suppressing anger for so long that the anger gets turned against oneself. Evidence of this is the fact that after people really get in touch with and release their anger, often their guilt miraculously diminishes. After the hostility has been vented, in its place comes new acceptance and affection. Guilt is using the energy of anger to beat up on oneself, instead of beating up on the other guy or assertively standing up for oneself.

Guilt can be physically as well as emotionally distressing. Vicki, for example, was suffering from nausea and dizziness, and headaches that were getting worse and worse. She felt guilty about her lack of sexual desire, and resentful of her husband for calling her frigid. "Every time I think about making love, I get a headache." A psychologist diagnosed the problem as depression, and told her to express her anger rather than playing into the guilt.

"I decided to write, to see if any anger was really in me. What a revelation! I felt like I'd been used as an emotional punching bag. I wasn't frigid, but angry about being lied to. I knew I had to get the pent-up anger out, because the headaches were debilitating. There was so much pain that I had to lie prone—feeling powerless and stuck. Finally I started doing Pal Dan Gum, and when I did the angry punching I would yell, if nobody was around. Afterwards I felt great. I even stopped a headache that way. And I stopped blaming myself and feeling guilty all the time. I realized I can't allow anybody to run my life! No way am I going to be a bird in a glass cage with a headache!"

Guilt and Resentment: A Polarity

Guilt is anger directed against oneself; resentment is anger deflected outward. "Whenever you feel guilty, find out what you resent, and the guilt will vanish and you will try to make the other person feel guilty," Perls says cryptically. [20] For instance, you might feel guilty because you're not living up to someone's expectations, but underneath you might resent the unrealistic or burdensome expectations. Trying to make the other person take the blame might help you climb out of the quicksand of guilt, but it's not a permanent solution. It merely shifts the polarization of blame.

Guilt is blaming yourself; resentment is blaming others. Guilt is feeling that you owe something to someone; resentment is feeling they owe you something. An antidote to both feelings is to stop putting shoulds and shouldn'ts on life, and start accepting *what is*—for example, paying attention to and honoring your own needs and abilities. Fritz Perls points out that the turning point is to move from guilt into responsibility and acceptance.

> "Responsibility means simply to be willing to say 'I am I' and 'I am what I am—I'm Popeye, the sailor man.' It's not easy to let go of the fantasy or concept of being a child in need, the child that wants to be loved, the child that is afraid to be rejected, but all those events are those for which we are not taking responsibility.

"But there's always the question of accepting or not accepting, and accepting is not just tolerating. Accepting is getting a present, a gift. The balance is always greatfulness for what *is*. If it's too little, you feel resentful; if it's too much, you feel guilty. But if you get the balance, you grow in gratefulness. If you make a sacrifice, you feel resentful; if you give a present, you give something surplus and you feel fine."[21]

If I am the person who feels unloved and unaccepted, then I am not just the child who was made to feel unacceptable. I am also the adult who doesn't love and accept myself. If I am the person who frequently feels guilty, then I am also the person who condemns myself. Adults don't have to buy someone's set of shoulds and shouldn'ts, and condemn themselves accordingly. "Since the feeling of guilt is a form of self-condemnation, it can be overcome by self-acceptance," says Lowen. "Subjectively, one is what one feels. To deny a feeling or emotion is to reject a part of the self. And when a person rejects himself, he is left with a feeling of guilt."[19]

This brings us to "existential guilt," or feeling bad because we are not being "that self which we truly are." We each have a wide range of physical, mental, emotional and spiritual potentialities. Confronting the need to fulfill these potentialities can make us anxious. To escape the anxiety, we may retreat from the responsibility of being our whole Selves, but guilt is a consequence of denying our potentialities. Since we all somehow and sometimes fail to fulfill our potentialities, or take our time about doing so, this kind of guilt is basic to human existence—that is, it is "existential." Existential psychologists say it arises because we *forget* to be our whole selves; we lock up our potentialities by conforming, instead of being authentic. "If you lock up potentialities, you are guilty against (or *indebted to*, as the German word may be translated) what is given you in your origin, in your 'core.' "[22]

"Neurotic guilt" can result from unconfronted existential guilt. One way to make peace with guilt is to take it seriously, by looking for ways we are forfeiting some of our potential—by not being our whole selves or not understanding our fellow man. For example, feeling guilty about your body might be a nudge towards getting into a better relationship with your body, and exercising it. Feeling guilty about your children might be a nudge towards getting into a better relationship with them, or towards giving your own inner child more time to play. Rollo May says existential guilt is a potent source of "a sound humility and an unsentimental attitude of forgiveness toward one's fellow men," as well as "sharpened sensitivity in relationships" and "increased creativity in the use of one's own potentialities."[22]

Psychic Impotency

Just as guilt or shame about sex can lead to suppression of sexual desire and sexual impotency or frigidity, so guilt about ourselves can lead to general emotional suppression and psychic impotency—until we can neither feel nor do much of anything. This is the ultimate in self-deprecation, and the beginning of depression. To bolster self-esteem, we might substitute illusion for reality—the grand illusion being that happiness will follow from external recognition, acceptance and approval. The fall of this illusion can be the onset of depression. The reality is that we must accept and approve *ourselves*.

328

Psychodynamic theory says that depression, like guilt, can actually be anger or aggression turned inward. It is normal for a child to have ambivalent feelings of love and anger towards the parents. If expressing the anger is forbidden, s/he may learn to turn it inward. From another viewpoint, hostility turned inward is secondary to the experience of losing a "love object" (i.e., person). Resolving the loss involves working through grief, which in turn means confronting anger about being abandoned.*

Lack of motivation and frequent feelings of boredom and fatigue can be precursors of depression. We cannot be bored if we take responsibility for being our whole selves, relating to others with authenticity, and connecting with Nature. There is always more of oneself to discover and more of life to explore. Not being able to find anything interesting is like being emotionally dead; it is majoring in self-torture. Perls speaks to this condition:

> "Instead of saying, 'I'm bored,' and finding out what you're actually interested in, you suffer and stay with what is boring to you. You torture yourself with staying there, and at the same time, whenever you torture yourself you torture your environment. You become a gloom-caster. If you *enjoy* the gloom-casting, if you *accept* it, that's fine, because then the whole thing becomes a postive experience. Then you take responsibility for what you're doing. If you enjoy self-torture, fine."[21]

If you don't enjoy boredom or psychic impotency, you need to take responsibility for getting in touch with self, body and environment. Linda, for instance, complained that she wasn't doing the things she really wanted to do, and that her parents were always putting her down and saying she was the cause of their unhappiness.** Yet when she thought about leaving, she felt guilty—either about abandoning her grandfather, whom she took care of, or because her mother would ask her to stay. Her dependency was tied to an inability to express anger or assert herself, yet she felt guilty about feeling anger. Fearing her parents' wrath, as a young child Linda had learned to suppress her anger by turning it against a safer target—herself. Because of the guilt, she remained a depressed and internally angry thirty-year-old little girl.

At the beginning of one session, Linda complained of a pain in her diaphragm area. As I held #17 with Liver distal points, she complained of being angry "at how the world is" and always feeling rejected. "I wanted to get away," she said, "But I couldn't get mad. I couldn't do anything!" She hit her head, then said, "Ow! That wasn't too smart! I already had a headache; I didn't have to give myself more pain!" Similarly, she was beating up on herself by believing her parents' negative messages. "My mother always tells me she risked her life for me. She had pneumonia when I was born, and wasn't allowed to touch me for weeks. Then she thought the hospital had given her the wrong baby, and she actually tried to exchange me! She tells the story like it's real funny. All I've wanted all these years is 'I love you.' "

As the #17 area began to release, Linda had the image of a baby calf. "They're trying to catch it and brand it," she said. "It's running away. It doesn't want to be

---

* An example is Mandy's story, in the previous section. Depression was also discussed in Chapter 9, Part 3.

** More of Linda's story is found in Chapter 9, Part 1 and Chapter 12, Part 2.

caught." Moaning and grimacing, she said, "They're holding the feet down and branding it. Ohhh! It *hurts*!" What else was she feeling? "Anger at being held down." What did she want to do? "I want to kill them because I can't get away," she said, pounding the table. Who branded her? "Everyone. Everyone's laughing at me, calling me a big creep. They don't pick me for games and they won't let me play. My brother has a club—he's president and I'm the slave! I have to do what he wants, and then *I have to take the blame if anything goes wrong.* I want to run away, but I'm afraid. I'm just a little kid. I can't ask for anything . . . I couldn't ask for *any-thing*!"

The next week, Linda still felt the pain in the diaphragm area, but more "on the inside." I asked her to breathe into the pain and tell me what it felt like. "It's burning hot," she said. "It's like a flame that wants to come out. Oh, I want it to come out!" She talked about a recent round of insults from her parents. When she started to sound angry, she swallowed and stopped the feeling. "That's what I've always done—swallow it down. Where does it go when I swallow it? I wish I had a magic wand to make the problems go away." Craving her parents' approval kept her enslaved, and kept a lid on her anger. Letting go of her need for that approval could be like waving a magic wand.

For the next several weeks, her back was better but Linda had occasional headaches. The Gall Bladder pulse was excessive and the Liver deficient, a pattern consistent with her guilty attempt to control and suppress anger. Acknowledging the anger could give her the energy to live her own life. "I want to be the way *I* want to be!" she finally shouted. "I don't want to be what *people* want me to be. Everybody wants me to be something—especially my parents. But no matter what I do, they're *still* not happy! It's never good enough! That's what makes me mad. Who I am, that's who I am. Sometimes I have to change, to like myself, but people have to like me for me." After crying for a while, she said, "I didn't even know that was there! I felt like I was being squashed under someone's thumb. It's not fair!" Indeed, life often isn't fair. "But the guilt hurts worse than the squashing. Not to feel guilty, to just think of being happy—that would be amazing!"

Linda's role was that of scapegoat. The original "scapegoat" served only on the Day of Atonement, when the Jewish high priests confessed the sins of the people over its head, then allowed it to escape. Human scapegoats, on the other hand, may get pressed into service daily. By focusing on Linda as the dysfunctional cog in the family system, and finding ways that she wasn't good enough, her parents could avoid looking at their own problems.

When she began talking with her mother about her real feelings, Linda finally got to hear her say "I love you." Her father, however, still intimidated her. After a towel-wringing catharsis of anger, I asked what her father had taken from her. "My self-esteem." How? "Through fear and guilt." While we worked with the Gall Bladder and Stomach Meridians, she had the image of ugly, rough, repulsive hands tearing her apart inside. One was named "Fear" and the other "Guilt." But there was another image too. A lovely lady in white appeared, surrounded in light. She said, "Now you must love yourself. It's hard and it takes time, but I'll teach you." Loving yourself and cherishing the beauty inside yourself is something you will never regret. If you *can* change things but *choose* not to, a nagging feeling of guilt may try to wake you up to yourself and to life, so that you don't postpone being and loving your whole Self.

Part 4.   HYPERACTIVE HUN: irritability, resentment, hostility, bitterness

Unexpressed anger or accumulated frustration builds up pressure. Without an escape valve, the mounting irritability and resentment can turn into a pervasive hostility or cold bitterness. These are not innate feelings; our intrinsic core emotions are simpler ones, like love, fear and anger. Vengeful desires come from old anger that was thwarted, by circumstances or by our own internal restraints. When the anger can't break through obstacles, it may seek outlet through hostile behavior, as Maslow explains:

> "Destructiveness, sadism, cruelty, malice, etc. seem so far to be not intrinsic but rather they seem to be violent reactions *against* frustration of our intrinsic needs, emotions and capacities. Anger is not *in itself* evil, nor is fear, laziness, or even ignorance. Of course, these can and do lead to evil behavior, but they needn't."[23]

If we have difficulty directing anger towards its source, we tend to internalize it. Malicious behavior may amount to displacing the anger onto people to whom it does not belong, because they are *safer* targets or just *available* ones. The backside of a venomous spewing-forth is guilt, unless one has a sociopathic personality or has an "explosive disorder" (being unable to resist performing a harmful, destructive act, and then feeling pleasure or relief of tension). Another perversion of anger is passive-aggressiveness; though more subtle, it can be as destructive as overt aggression.

Feeling anxious and guilty about the presence of anger can lead to avoiding its expression until it becomes putrid and resentment accrues. If a feeling *needs* to be expressed, energy builds up behind that need and intensifies it, until the thought of expressing it makes us more and more uncomfortable. Resentment is one of the most common unexpressed experiences, says Perls:

> "This is the unfinished situation *par excellence*. If you are resentful, you're stuck; you neither can move forward and have it out, express your anger, change the world so that you'll get satisfaction, nor can you let go and forget whatever disturbs you. Resentment is the psychological equivalent of the hanging-on bite—the tight jaw. The hanging-on bite can neither let go, nor bite through and chew up—whichever is required. In resentment you can neither let go and forget, and let this incident or person recede in the background, nor can you actively tackle it."[24]

Resentment can speak through chronic jaw and neck tension, as well as through diaphragm armoring. Clenching and tensing the jaw helps hold back the expression of anger through biting or biting words. "Compressing the lips and setting the jaw are the way one can clamp down to shut off any sound from breaking through to the outside," says Lowen. "Setting the jaw, regardless of its position, is equivalent to saying, 'Thou shalt not pass.'"[25]*

Excessive self-control can be related to "TMJ" (*tempo-mandibular joint syndrome*), with symptoms of jaw pain and nocturnal teeth-grinding. "TMJ" and tension in the diaphragm area were Sheryl's presenting problems. When I asked what was going on in her life, she said her marriage was stuck in a boring routine and her husband seemed chronically depressed. She felt resentful of the limitations that had been imposed on her—first by her parents and then by her husband and three children. What were the jaw and neck [#21: LI] tensions saying? "I want my own life, but I hold myself back." Then, over and over, she said passionately, "I want freedom, life, feeling!" Her hands began to feel numb. What did they want to do? She began to make reaching movements, her breathing became faster, then her body began to move convulsively. To assist her release of rage, I held the #17s with Liver distal points.

The physical catharsis gained momentum and Sheryl's neck rose off the table with the convulsive body movements. Her throat tensed up and her head kept thrusting forward until she was red in the face. She was making choked little noises, so I encouraged her to let the sound come from deeper inside, until it was coming from the diaphragm. Her hands were still numb. What did they want? Sheryl covered her chest with her hands, like she was protecting herself. As she held this posture, she began to feel tension in the jaws and deltoid muscles. "Don't go up in your head; *feel* it," I directed. She made an angry face and struck out timidly with her hands. "How do you feel about not living and not feeling?" I probed. She punched vigorously for some time, then relaxed. Suddenly her diaphragm and jaw were much looser!

This release brought up some early childhood stuff, like being told not to tell her mother after a neighbor told her about sex, then frequently having nausea, and needing her mother to rub her back so she could sleep. "I shouldn't have had so much trouble with whatever my neighbor told me, as a child of this age," Sheryl said self-critically. Who says so? "As a child, I was very full of life," she said, remembering screaming and singing outside but later feeling bad when she figured out that her parents disapproved. Obediently, she learned to hold herself back, but subliminal resentment was the aftermath of frustrating her innate desire for free expression.

Demands and Appreciations

Perls suggests a threefold exercise for letting go of resentments, and so letting ourselves grow. 1) Evoke the person you resent by saying his or her name, then say "I resent" whatever, out loud, as though you were really trying to get the person to hear you. This is likely to make you realize "that you don't dare, really, to express your anger, nor would you be generous enough to let go, to be forgiving." If you dared express your anger or could really forgive, you wouldn't be tortured by resentment. 2) "Behind every resentment there are demands," so the next step is to express those demands out loud, imagining that you are openly telling the other person about them. 3) Now remember what you resented, and repeat those things—substituting the words "I appreciate" for the words "I resent." "Appreciate what you resented be-

---

* Tensions in the jaw and along the sternocleidomastoid muscle can reflect blockage of the Stomach and Large Intestine Meridians, which can correlate with anxiety about expressing "negative" feelings.

fore," says Perls. "Then go on to tell this person what else you appreciate in them," because "if there were no appreciations, you wouldn't be stuck with this person and you could just forget him. There is always the other side."[24]

Anger which has solidified into resentment blocks off appreciation. Since resentment is an "unfinished gestalt," it keeps gnawing at us. Somehow we can't quite get to an assertive attitude and deal directly with the problem, nor can we get to a receptive attitude and forgive it. "Resentment is an emotion of central importance," says Perls. "The resentment is the most important expression of an impasse—of being stuck. If you feel resentment, be able to express your resentment. A resentment unexpressed often is experienced as, or changes into, feelings of guilt."[24] In effect, resentment is being addicted to anger, unable to either let it go or let it fly. The gears are stuck, so the emotional kaleidoscope can't revolve naturally from anger through assertiveness on to amusement or appreciation. Instead, we go back and forth between the equally distressing states of resentment and guilt.

The word "resentment" derives from the Old French *resentir*, meaning "to feel or perceive again." Unresolved anger is felt again and again, until we feel bitter indignation and a sense of having been injured. Resentment goes beyond a simple displeasure at an offense, and can lead to smoldering ill will or eventual embitterment. Keeping the fires of anger burning uses up a great deal of energy, so eventually fatigue might prevent us from carrying out resolutions, even if we *feel* motivated to bring problems to some kind of completion. The fires of rage deplete the energy reserves until there's not enough energy to feed the fires of integrity. [Hyperactive Hun drains Chih.]

Demands underlie resentment. They might be blatant and presumptive: "The world owes me love and a living. If you don't give me what I want, as much as I want, when and how I want it, then I have a right to resent you." Or they might be more reasonable: "If you would just be more cooperative (understanding, fair, communicative, ambitious, responsive, etc.), then I wouldn't always be getting angry at you." The resentment would vanish if we could just get our demands met, but no matter how clearly or cleverly we present our demands, the other person is not always going to comply immediately. S/he is not always going to comply at all (darn it). To give up our resentment, we may have to give up some cherished demands, but just the process of acknowledging and expressing the demands can lead us back to appreciation.

Whose Fault Is It Anyway?

"All that stuff about communication and growth is hard work," a friend responds. "I have always found it easier to blame one person." Surprised, I reply, "Yes, it *is* easier to just blame someone else. Who do you blame, then?" "Murphy! Some day I'm going to catch up with that son-of-a-gun! Boy, he'll be in trouble then! That guy is responsible for so much hassle in this world!" Have you met Murphy? He's the guy that made up "Murphy's Law": If anything can go wrong, it will—at the worst possible moment!

Another perspective is that everything is the fault, or credit, of the Tao. Chuang Tzu tells the story of how Masters Ssu, Yu, Li and Lai reacted to events which ordinary men might have resented. Master Yu suddenly got a bizarre disease, and Master Ssu went to see him. Yu said:

> "Amazing! The Creator is making me all crookedy like this! My back sticks up like a hunchback and my vital organs are on top of me. My chin is hidden in my navel, my shoulders are up above my head, and my pigtail points at the sky. It must be some dislocation of the yin and yang!" Yet Master Yu seemed calm and not really concerned. Ssu asked, "Do you resent it?"
>
> "Why no, what would I resent? If the process continues, perhaps in time he'll transform my left arm into a rooster. In that case, I'll keep watch on the night. Or perhaps in time he'll transform my right arm into a crossbow pellet and I'll shoot down an owl for roasting. Or perhaps in time he'll transform my buttocks into cartwheels. Then, with my spirit for a horse, I'll climb up and go for a ride. What need will I ever have for a carriage again?
>
> "I received life because the time had come; I will lose it because the order of things passes on. Be content with this time and dwell in this order and then neither sorrow nor joy can touch you. In ancient times this was called the 'freeing of the bound.' There are those who cannot free themselves, because they are bound by things. But nothing can ever win against Heaven —that's the way it's always been. What would I have to resent?"

Suddenly Master Lai grew ill unto death. His family gathered around him and began to cry. "Shoo! Get back! Don't disturb the process of change!" said Li, who had come to visit. Lai responded that having had "the audacity to take on human form once" did not give him the right to demand of the Creator, "I don't want to be anything but a man! Nothing but a man!" That would be as ridiculous as a piece of metal saying to a skilled smith, "I insist upon being made into a Mo-yeh!" (Mo-yeh: a famous sword, like a Chinese Excalibur.) Master Lai concluded:

> "So now I think of heaven and earth as a great furnace, and the Creator as a skilled smith. Where could he send me that would not be all right? I will go off to sleep peacefully, and then with a start I will wake up."[26]

With no resentments mucking up the psychic works, Masters Ssu, Yu, Li and Lai had no vengeful fantasies interrupting their calm acceptance of fate. Ordinary wo/men, not yet having received badges of sagehood, do sometimes have angry fantasies. One of my favorites was imagining dumping a truckload of manure on someone's doorstep. (Somebody actually did that. I think maybe it was on the steps of some city department of health and sanitation.)

Just allowing ourselves to complete vengeful fantasies in our imagination, and being assured they're not terrible, can be a relief. Expressing "dark" feelings— through images, sounds and body movements—can be deeply releasing. Often people will stop this process to assure me (or themselves) that they're not all bad. The basic premise is that you're *not* bad. You have a 'dark' side and a 'light' side, and some conflicts between the two. When you just let go to the 'bad' feelings, and let them release in some appropriate way, they'll change. More joyful and harmonious feelings will come up naturally.

Vengeful images are especially common during release of armoring in the diaphragm [♯17/5] area. James, for example, saw himself "dropping rocks on people." He said, "I'm getting the feeling that I want to knock some people's heads off!" After some diaphragmatic breathing, he said, "I was knocking people's heads off, and then I saw Superman becoming huge, monstrous, towering over the landscape and just kicking people aside with his feet." Feeling the powerful energy of the suppressed anger, he said, "I wish I could let it out in the appropriate places! There are so many places where I can't. When I resent things that happen or don't happen to me professionally, I can't just let the shit hit the fan! The politics are very sensitive—all that damn ego stuff! But if I don't get it out somehow, I go back and forth between being angry at *them* and then blaming or putting down on myself."

When circumstances or lack of assertiveness makes us hesitate to express resentment, it may intensify as we go back over the situation, adding editorial comments like: "It's not fair! I've been had!" We may embroider the memory by inventing responses that might have "shown him (or her) a thing or two!" We may imagine ways to "get even," inventing scenes in which we embarrass or hurt our tormentor(s). Shocking! Doesn't fit the nice person image at all. We may begin to feel guilty. "Maybe there's something wrong with me. Maybe a bad person like me deserves to be punished. Maybe feeling angry just proves that I'm warped." So guilt pushes the anger down.

Guilt and resentment are a well-known psychic polarity, and a vicious emotional cycle. Resentment puts the blame on someone else, to avoid having it assigned to us. "The irony is that even when there is no fault at all, we defensively assume 'someone' must be to blame," says Gaylin. "Because of the fear that somehow we may have had some responsibility . . . we defensively fix responsibilities somewhere other than ourselves even where no responsibility is involved."[27] Resentment says: "If s/he hadn't. . . ." Guilt replies: "But I shouldn't have. . . ." If someone must be to blame, and the other guy won't take the rap, the anger is liable to spiral right back in on ourselves. Guilt can be a way of punishing ourselves, and as such can even bring a sense of relief.

Resentment is frozen anger. Like love, but in a different way, anger is a warm feeling. Anger and love are closely connected, for we can get the most angry at the people we love, including ourselves. Anger wants to break down old forms so that we can grow. Hostility and hate are anger and love grown cold. This withdrawal of feeling not only punishes the other person (assuming s/he cares), but also circumvents joy, as Lowen explains:

> "The blood leaves the skin and the surface of the body, producing a sensation of coldness. All hostile feelings are cold. The hostile person withdraws his affection and turns cold toward another individual. He loses any erotic desire he may have had and is repelled by any idea of physical contact. All hostile feelings represent, therefore, the withdrawal of feeling."[28]

When you feel resentment, try asking yourself what you're angry about and whether you've expressed it. Did you know you felt angry? Did it feel unsafe or wrong? Did you feel anxious or guilty? Did you fear retaliation or rejection? Did the anger get stuck inside you? What would happen if you let it out?

In therapy, people often get in touch with some hostility towards their parents, stemming from abuse, rejection, criticism or negative judgmental attitudes. While love fades in the absence of pleasure, it is betrayal which changes love to hostility. When the betrayal can be forgiven, the hostility melts and genuine affection returns. The sense of betrayal can be ancient: "I didn't ask to be born, and I *sure* didn't ask to be born to *them!*" How do you *know* you didn't ask to be born, and to them? In any event, discharging old emotional tensions can open up new vistas which include respect for the struggles of preceding generations, and awareness of how their behavior was also conditioned by their upbringing. Emotional honesty can bring a sense of forgiveness, reconciliation and acceptance, plus an increased love in the balance.

Whether directed at mother or father or both, a resentment that goes back to childhood may be quite unconscious. Sylvia, for example, said she had been depressed and "virtually unaware of an internal turmoil of rage and resentment." During work with the Liver Meridian, she felt irritable and hostile towards the therapist who seemed, like a parent, to have the power to disapprove. "I connected with my rage as I realized that my mother continuously disapproved of me, verbally and nonverbally, as a child and as an adult," Sylvia said. "At first, the pressure at the points below my ribcage [♯5s] felt like a branding iron being pressed into my diaphragm. I got the picture of myself with angry eyes exuding hostility and resentment, in a manipulative and carefully guarded manner. All those years of frustration without resolution!" She realized that poisoning herself with alcohol and drugs had been a way of stifling her anger towards her mother in particular and authority in general. "My rebellion was a way to anesthetize myself against the disapproval—and to avoid my own rage and resentment."*

Feeling Is Healing

"This is my experience, as I recall it," another client said, some time after a particularly dramatic but largely non-verbal session. "It started when you pressed points on my jaw. It was very painful there, and that pain was all I felt at first. As I got into that pain, I became aware also of sorrow. There was so much sorrow in that pain. These feelings started to grow within me and I began to cry, and then the tears transformed into screams or cries from deep down in my belly."

The focus was now on the ♯17s and Liver Meridian; periodically, I returned to the neck and jaw points. "There was the feeling of having wild animals roaring at the greatest frustration," she said. "I had the impression that these sounds were there since ages ago. I began to remember resentful feelings I did not or dared not express, but the reasons for their suppression were too far away to recall. It's okay to feel it! How healing! I cried some more, and felt so very sad, because I felt so lonely, almost deserted. In my mind I went back to my early childhood. 'Why, Mother, did you not hold me tight and hug and touch me? What was wrong with me? Why didn't you love me?' Suddenly it was clear how I had been so afraid of not being liked or being rejected, and how this translated to always doubting myself in relation to others.

---

* Working through her conflict with authority involved confronting her fear and mistrust. (See Chapter 8 and Chapter 12, Part 4.)

"All these ideas went through my mind as I started to sense great bursts of warmth running through my body. Especially around my ankles and wrists, the energy or heat was just spurting out. My whole body was trembling, and I sensed tremendous heat waves running from my feet towards my head. Feelings of joy and love overwhelmed me. There was a knowingness that I had always been loved by such an infinite love, as we all are. At that moment I cried of joy, and felt so much love, forgiveness and compassion for every being. That was what happened inside me. I remember all of it very clearly. I felt so alive! And so very grateful to be living."

14. Acu-Exercise

In 1975 and 1976, I learned various "internal" and "external" Taoist yogic exercises from Sung Jin Park, who had studied under the guidance of a Taoist master in Korea. "*Hara* breathing" (described in part 1 of chapter 12) was the core of the "internal" or meditative techniques. "*Pal Dan Gum*"—the set of exercises shown in this chapter—was the primary part of the "external," physically strengthening, techniques. It was obvious to me that these "Eight Silken Movements" were a nice way to stretch the body and improve the posture, but it was years before I realized just how powerful they are.

Master Park said that the Eight Silken Movements have been used for thousands of years in China and Korea, for promoting radiant health and aiding spiritual development. "But, most importantly, they can be practiced by anyone willing to take ten minutes a day for the development of improved health and increased awareness. If performed once or twice a day, the Pal Dan Gum exercises will recharge the inner organs and will purify all the psychic channels and organ meridians. They will promote improved blood circulation to all parts of the body. The muscles and joints will become more flexible and resilient. The posture will improve and many of the common everyday ailments that plague most people will gradually disappear. This is the secret art of Chinese and Korean sages."

Strong claims! Although I found that my body was in better alignment from doing these exercises, I did not practice them daily after Master Park returned to Korea. Still, I found that even irregular practice was helpful. One day, I reviewed my notes on what organ meridians are benefited by these eight movements. While doing Pal Dan Gum, I could feel stretching and stimulating effects along other meridians as well. Compiling this information, I was surprised to notice how strongly these eight movements affect all twelve organ meridians. They facilitate the release of blockages throughout the entire meridian system. They are truly "acu-exercises"—exercises which help open and balance the acupressure meridians. And they are easy to learn.

Morning is a wonderful time to do these acu-exercises, so as to get your energy flowing in preparation for the day's activities. After doing them, you will feel refreshed, relaxed and energized. The exercises are more beneficial if you concentrate completely on your motions, posture and breathing. After you have learned the movements, flow smoothly from one exercise to the next, doing them slowly and as accurately as possible. Breathe in through the nose and out through the mouth, as directed below. It will take about ten to fifteen minutes to complete the entire series. If you like, you may do more repetitions of exercises you feel a need for, and you may add other stretching movements.

As you do each movement, focus your attention on the parts of your body that are being stretched. STRETCH, DON'T STRAIN! If you push yourself too hard, you may reach a point where an exercise may become painful. In that case, release the tension so that you still feel a stretch, but it feels pleasurable. In general, stretch just *a little* past the point of comfort. Gradually, you will find that the limits of what is comfortable are stretching.

If you have an injury or a chronic problem in some area, do the exercises which affect that area gently; in severe case, skip them while the area is healing. When you feel tension or soreness, pause for a moment and *breathe through the tension*. The breath is the key to release and relaxation.

When some part of you is tense and blocked, it may be difficult to breathe fully. Suppressing the breath is a primary defense mechanism, but shallow breathing just helps maintain the muscular blockages and armoring. The blockages may be due to a physical injury or disability, or a long-term lack of stretching. The blockages may stem from anxiety or other distressed feelings, and they may be related to defensive attitudes. They may also have arisen from the repression of emotions like grief, anger, fear and excitement. Whatever the cause, breathing into the blocked areas will help you let go of the tension. As you breathe through the tension, you might ask "what is this about?" Just *be open* to any answer that might come up from your inner Self.

The breath is a powerful tool for reducing physical and emotional stress, and for increasing physical and emotional well-being. Deep breathing improves the energy level by increasing the amount of oxygen in the system and the release of carbon dioxide from the system. If not eliminated through the respiratory process, carbon dioxide changes into carbonic acid, which must then be filtered by the kidneys. This taxes the organs which, according to the Taoists, are the storehouses of reserve energy ("*ching chi*"). By breathing deeply, all the way down into the lower abdomen or "*hara,*" you can increase your reserve energy. In the process, you will probably become aware of areas which resist moving freely with your breath. The parts that are hard to breathe into may be sites of chronic tension.

To release tension and reduce stress, the first step is to really *contact* yourself, and *feel* which parts of your body are tense or blocked. As you tune into these parts while doing the following exercises, you may be able to discover the messages behind your physical tensions. Really feeling the body can be a way to explore the psyche. The more aware you become of yourself—*all* aspects of your Self—the more awake and alive you will feel. Just by concentrating your attention on the blocked places and sending your breath into them, you will find yourself gradually moving away from the *fear of feeling*, and towards the *joy of feeling*.

Acu-Exercises—"The Eight Silken Movements" ───────────────────────

I. "Upholding Heaven with the Two Hands"

This exercise helps relieve fatigue. It strengthens the Triple Warmer Meridian, and so improves circulation and helps the organism to absorb and transform the vital energy.

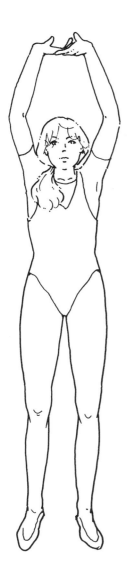
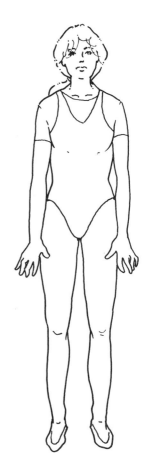

1. Stand erect with your feet shoulders' width apart, toes pointing forward, and arms at your sides.
2. Turn your hands so that the palms are up, and breathe in while you slowly raise your hands above your head. As your hands meet above your head, interlock your fingers. Your palms will now be facing downward.
3. Keeping your fingers interlocked, turn your hands so that the palms are facing upward, and push upward with your hands. At the same time, stretch upward on your toes, so that your heels raise slightly off the ground. Look upward.
4. Maintain this upstretched position for a few seconds, then breathe out as you come back down on your heels and let your arms come back down to the sides.
5. Repeat two more times.

II. "Opening the Bow"

This exercise strengthens the muscles of the chest, shoulders and arms. It expands the chest, increasing lung capacity, and it stimulates the entire route of the Lung Meridian.

1. Stand erect, then take one big step to the left. Bend your knees to assume "horse-riding position." (The more you bend your knees, the more strenuous this position will feel.) Be sure that you are not leaning forward or backward, and that your pelvis is not tipped forward.
2. Cross your arms in front of your chest at the wrists, left arm in front of the right. Clench your fists, then extend the index finger of the left hand.
3. As though holding a bow in your left hand and the bow string in your right, push out the left arm until it is straight. At the same time, pull the right hand out to the side, as though you were pulling a bow string. Inhale deeply during this movement. Concentrate your attention on the tip of the left index finger, following its movement with your eyes.
4. Exhale while you relax the arms, crossing them in front of your chest again —this time with the right arm in front of the left and the right index finger extended.
5. Open the bow again, this time to the right side.
6. Repeat two more times.

III. "Raising the Hands Separately"

This exercise stimulates the Large and Small Intestine Meridians, which flow along the sides of the outer arms. It also helps to harmonize the energies of the Stomach and Spleen Meridians.

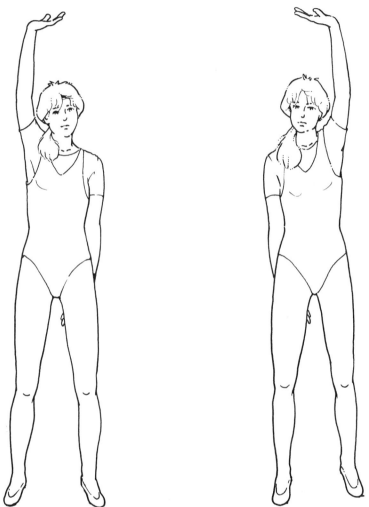

1. Stand erect, as in exercise I. Raise your hands to the solar plexus, with your palms up and your elbows straight to your sides. The fingertips will touch slightly.
2. Raise your left hand above your head, rotating the arm so that the palm faces upward, fingers pointing inward. At the same time, lower your right hand, with the palm facing downward and the fingers pointing inward. Inhale as you push up with your left hand and down with your right hand. You may let your eyes follow the palm which is pointing upward.
3. Exhale as you return to the starting position.
4. Do the same movement on the other side, pushing upwards with your right hand and downwards with your left hand.
5. Repeat two more times.

IV. "Looking Backwards"

This exercise strengthens and tones the muscles of the chest and upper back, while stretching the muscles in the sides of the neck. It was traditionally said to relieve fatigue in the yin organs—the Heart, Pericardium, Lungs, Spleen-Pancreas, Liver and Kidneys.

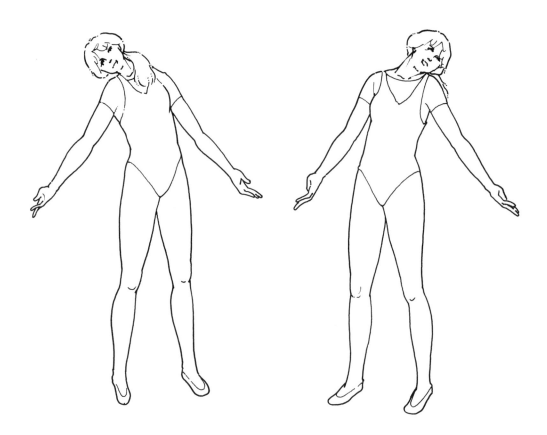

1. Stand erect, as in exercise I. Cross your hands in front of your face, with your left hand in front of your right hand.
2. Inhale while pulling your hands to the sides and back, with your arms straight and your palms forward. Turn your head to the left as far as it will go without rotating the waist. The left shoulder will dip slightly. Feel the stretch in the muscles over the right chest.
3. Exhale while you return to the starting position, but this time with your right hand in front of your left hand.
4. Do the same movement on the other side.
5. Repeat two more times.

V. "Swinging the Trunk and Head"

This exercise helps to loosen the lower back, stimulates digestion and circulation, and benefits the nervous system. It especially stretches the Gall Bladder, Bladder and Stomach Meridians.

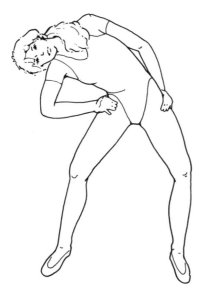 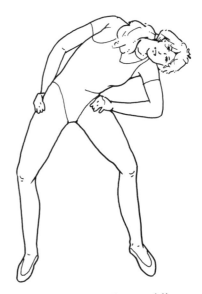

1. Stand erect, then take one big step to the left, assuming a "horse-riding position," as described in exercise II. Place your hands on your thighs.
2. Exhale while you bend your body to the left side, allowing your shoulders and head to tilt to the left so that you feel a stretch all the way down the right side of your body.
3. Inhale while you return to starting position.
4. Exhale while you bend body and head to the right side.
5. Inhale while you return to starting position.

6. Exhale while you bend your torso and head forward.
7. Inhale while you return to starting position.
8. Place your hands behind your back, with your thumbs below the buttocks to support yourself. Exhale while you stretch backwards. (If you have a back problem, skip this movement or do it gently.)
9. Inhale while you return to starting position.
10. Repeat one more time.
11. To relax the shoulders, slowly rotate them, making several circular motions forwards, and then backwards. (You may straighten your legs while doing this, if you like.)
12. To relax the neck, bend your head towards your left shoulder, breathing through the tension in the trapezius muscle; then bend your head to the right shoulder. Put your hands behind your head and slowly pull your head forward, feeling a stretch in the back of the neck. Slowly straighten your neck. Then move your head slowly in half-circles from side to side, breathing through the tight spots. You may also, very slowly, rotate the head several times, counterclockwise and then clockwise; if you have neck problems, skip this.

VI. "Standing on the Toes"

This is a great centering exercise. When you feel more centered, you are more able to withstand disharmonious conditions and unsettling influences. This simple exercise particularly strengthens the Stomach and Kidney Meridians.

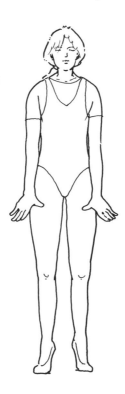

1. Stand erect, with your hands at your sides and your feet slightly apart.
2. Inhale deeply as you raise your heels up slowly, until you are standing on your toes. Hold this extended position for a few seconds.
3. Exhale as you slowly return the heels to the ground.
4. To make this exercise more challenging, you can close your eyes while you do it. You may be surprised at how much more difficult this is! To keep your balance, it will be helpful to inhale into the "*hara*"—the energy inside the lower abdomen (about two and a half inches below the navel). Feel your body rising from this center, and be sure that neither your head nor your pelvis are tipped forward.
5. Repeat this movement ten times.

VII. *"Punching with Angry Eyes"*

This acu-exercise helps relieve frustration and pent-up anger, so you might want to do it several times during days when internal or external conditions are making you feel "uptight" and irritable. This invigorating exercise helps to strengthen metabolism and increase body vitality. It particularly helps relieve blockages of the Liver and Gall Bladder Meridians. The movements need to be very firm, not yielding.

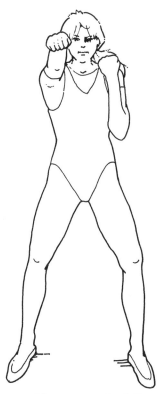

1. Stand erect, then take one big step to the left, assuming a "horse-riding position," as described in exercise II. Place your clenched fists at your waist, palms up.
2. Open your eyes very wide, as though you were angry, directing energy out from your eyes. Bare your teeth, in a growling expression.

3. With utmost firmness, punch forward with the left fist, turning the fist over so that it is facing downward when fully extended. While you are punching, it may be more releasing to make a noise (like "huh!" or "ha!") as you exhale. Return the fist to the left side.
4. Punch forward with the right fist, then return to the right side.
5. Punch to the left side with your left fist, then return.
6. Punch to the left side with your right fist, then return.
7. Punch to the right side with your left fist, then return.
8. Punch to the right side with your right fist, then return.
9. Repeat each movement once more, if you like.

VIII. "Holding the Toes and Stretching Back"

This acu-exercise stretches the spine and increases the flexibility of the back, waist and legs. It helps give the body fresh energy, and increases circulation to the brain. It particularly stimulates the Kidneys, and so enhances the body's ability to expel toxic accumulations. It also stretches the Bladder, Gall Bladder, Stomach and Spleen Meridians.

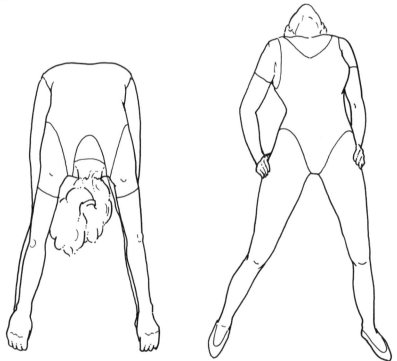

1. Stand erect with your feet shoulders' width apart and your hands at your sides.
2. Exhale as you bend your body forward, keeping the knees straight. Touch or hold your toes with your fingertips, or come as close to them as possible.
3. Inhale as you slowly straighten back up, and place your hands on your back hips to support yourself.
4. Exhale as you arch your head and back backwards. (If you have a back problem, skip this movement or do it gently.)

5. Inhale as you return to the starting position.
6. Repeat two more times.
7. Exhale as you bend your body forward once more, this time having the knees slightly bent and just letting your torso hang down. Let your back relax and let your head droop, arms dangling. Inhale deeply, all the way down into the pelvis. As you slowly exhale, visualize all the tension running out of your back and arms. Inhale and exhale a few more times, relaxing your jaw, and letting your head become heavy.
8. When you are ready to, slowly roll up, keeping your knees slightly bent. First roll the pelvis up and back, then slowly straighten the back, putting your attention into each vertebra from the lower back up to the shoulders. Roll your shoulders back, then slowly raise the neck, vertebra by vertebra. Finally, feel your head resting, balanced, on top of your spine.*

Relaxing After Exercising

After completing these eight acu-exercises, you may want to shake out your arms and legs, and make a few circular movements with your wrists and ankles, to loosen them. Then it is useful to take a couple of minutes to just relax. A simple way to do that is to sit in a squatting position, covering your ears with the palms of your hands and just letting your body relax, while breathing slowly and deeply into the lower abdomen. The squatting position is similar to that of the fetus in the womb. It is a way to let yourself feel small, and let go of your adult attitudes. The squatting position also helps straighten the spinal cord and strengthen the leg muscles. Even a minute or two of peaceful relaxation will increase physical and emotional well-being.

A short walk is a simple way to continue your moving meditation, if you have the time. Walking aids the free circulation of blood and energy, and increases the intake of oxygen (particularly if you can walk in the country, where the air is fresh and the sights of nature are refreshing). While walking, breathe into the *"hara"* center in the lower abdomen, and feel your body moving from this center. Let your whole body be relaxed, arms hanging down and moving freely.

After exercising, it may be very enjoyable to lie down for a few minutes, arms by your sides, closing your eyes, letting your whole body relax completely. Wiggle your toes and rotate your ankles to relax your feet. Gently shake your legs, letting go of the tension in your calves and thighs. Tighten your buttocks muscles for a moment, then move your pelvis from side to side, letting it relax. Take several deep breaths into your lower abdomen; as you exhale, let your belly relax and let your back sink down. Feel the tight muscles expanding as you inhale, and relaxing as you exhale. Let go of any disturbing thoughts that may come up, by keeping your focus on your breathing and on your body.

Breathe deeply, through your chest and down into your tummy, letting your chest and abdomen relax. Wiggle your fingers and gently shake your arms to relax them. Let your head roll loosely from side to side. Breathe into your shoulders and neck,

* Tapes of the acu-exercises in this chapter are available from the Jin Shin Do Foundation for Bodymind Acupressure, P.O. Box 1800, Idyllwild, California 92349.

visualizing the tension melting. As you exhale, visualize the released energy flowing down your arms and warming your hands. Tell your throat and cheeks to relax. Move your jaw up and down, and from side to side, then let it hang loosely, with your lips slightly parted. Let go of the tension around your ears, nose, eyes, and temples. Wiggle your forehead, and let go of the tension there. Enjoy the feeling of relaxation throughout your whole body.

If you want to really treat yourself to some self-nurturing, you can stay in this relaxed position and hold acu-points for the blocked areas which you have discovered. Or you can do "*hara* breathing meditation" (as described in Part 1 of Chapter 12) for ten minutes or so. Keep your attention focused at the point between your eyes and behind them (the "third eye" energy center), or on the "*hara*" center inside the lower abdomen.

Before getting up, stretch your arms above your head and point your toes, feeling a stretch in your whole body. Gently stretch any parts of your body which feel like they want to be stretched. Get up slowly.

Taking a little time each day to relax is being good to yourself. Deep relaxation is a surrender to your Self. In a state of deep energetic relaxation, you may feel like you are floating into some very comfortable and enjoyable mental place, yet are simultaneously fully aware of your body. As you let go of physical, mental and emotional resistance, you can become aware of your oneness with Nature or the Tao—the whole of life. This experience of oneness can help you to *find your joy*. It can help give you the resolution needed for living fully and joyfully.

Reference Notes

Chapter 1
1 Thomas Merton, *The Way of Chuang Tzu*, 1965, New Directions, N.Y., pp. 104, 113.
2 Gia-Fu Feng & Jane English, *Chuang Tsu: Inner Chapters*, 1974, Vintage, N.Y., pg. 26.
3 C.G., Jung, *Modern Man in Search of a Soul;* 1933, Harcourt, Brace and World, Inc., N.Y.
4 Information on skin temperature and electrical resistance is based on reports by Katsusuke Serizawa, M.D. and colleagues at the University of Tokyo School of Medicine: "Studies on Clinical Scientific Approach in Acupuncture and Moxibustion Treatment," 1966; "Individual Pattern Changes in the Distribution of Skin Temperature and Electric Resistance," 1964; "The Distribution of Skin Temperature and Point-Meridian Phenomena," 1976.
5 Merton, Ibid., pp. 129–133.
6 Burton Watson, *Chuang Tzu: Basic Writings*, 1964, Columbia University Press, N.Y., pp. 42, 103.
7 Merton, Ibid., pg. 80.
8 Kok Yuen Leung, *Chinese Medical Philosophy and Principles of Diagnosis*, The North American College of Acupuncture, 1971, "The Cause of Disease," pp. 9–10.
9 Feng & English, Ibid., pg. 89.
10 Rollo May, *Man's Search for Himself*, New American Library, N.Y., 1953, pp. 91–93.
11 Dunbar, *Psychosomatic Diagnosis*, 1943, pg. 657.
12 Carl Rogers, *On Becoming a Person*, 1961, Houghton Mifflin Co., Boston, pg. 147.
13 May, Ibid., pp. 94–96.
14 Iona Marsaa Teeguarden, *The Acupressure Way of Health: Jin Shin Do*, 1978, Japan Publications, distributed by Harper & Row, Scranton, Pa.
15 "Experimental Study on the Main Meridian Line," by Rokuro Fujita, M.A., The Japan Society for Oriental Medicine, 1964; and "Study on Meridians, Second Report," 1952.

Chapter 2
1 *Tao Teh Ching*, translation by Ch'u Ta-Kao, 1970, George Allen & Unwin, Ltd., London, pg. 13.
2 Fritz Perls, *Gestalt Therapy Verbatim*, 1969, Real People Press, N.Y., pg. 18.
3 Burton Watson, *Chuang Tzu: Basic Writings*, 1964, Columbia University Press, N.Y., pp. 35–36.
4 Philip Slater, *The Pursuit of Loneliness—American Culture at the Breaking Point*, 1976, Beacon Press, Boston, pg. 8.
5 *The I Ching or Book of Changes*, Richard Wilhelm translation, 1950, Bollingen Series XIX, Princeton University Press, pg. 201, Hexagram 52—"Keeping Still, Mountain."
6 Carl G. Jung, *Memories, Dreams, Reflections*, 1965, Vintage, N.Y., pp. 349–350.
7 Ibid. pp. 196–197, 207–208.
8 *The Secret of the Golden Flower*, Richard Wilhelm translation, 1931, 1962; Harcourt, Brace & World, Inc., N.Y., pg. 136.
9 Watson, Ibid. pp. 32–33.
10 Carl Rogers, *On Becoming a Person*, Houghton Mifflin Co., Sentry Ed., 1961, pp. 163–164.
11 Abraham H. Maslow, *Toward a Psychology of Being*, 1968, D. Van Nostrand Co., N.Y., pp. 40–41.
12 Watson, Ibid., pp. 34–45.
13 Perls, Ibid., pg. 53.

350

14 Maslow, Ibid., pp. 91–92, pg. 136.

15 Watson, Ibid., pp. 46–47.

16 John Blofeld, *The Secret and the Sublime—Taoist Mysteries and Magic*, 1973, E.P. Dutton, N.Y., pg. 155.

17 Benjamin Hoff, Ibid., pg. 68.

18 John Blofeld, *TAOISM, the Road to Immortality*, 1978, Shambhala pg. 10.

19 Benjamin Hoff, Ibid., pg. 6.

20 Maslow, Ibid., pg. 55.

21 *Tao Teh Ching*, pg. 20.

22 Story by John Smolowe, M.D., in *Holistic Medicine—Harmony of Body Mind Spirit*, 1982, Reston Publishing Co., Reston, Virginia, pg. 199.

23 *Nei Ching*, (Yellow Emperor's Classic of Internal Medicine), Ilza Veith translation, 1970, University of California Press, Berkeley and Los Angeles, Cal., pp. 118–120, 189, 195, 200.

24 *Nei Ching*, pg. 181.

25 According to the current psychiatric diagnostic manual, the DSM III, in the category of "Psychological Factors Affecting Physical Condition."

26 Gia-Fu Feng and Jane English, *Chuang Tzu: Inner Chapters*, 1974, Vintage, N.Y., pg. 117.

27 Ibid., pg. 22.

28 Thomas Merton, *The Way of Chuang Tzu*, 1965, New Directions, N.Y., pp. 42–43.

Chapter 3

1 Gia-Fu Feng & Jane English, *Chuang Tzu: Inner Chapters;* 1974, Vintage, N.Y., pg. 30.

2 Thanks to family therapist Virginia Satir for her definition of maturity.

3 Thomas Merton, *The Way of Chuang Tzu*, 1965, New Directions, N.Y., pp. 136–137.

4 John Blofeld: *Taoism, the Road to Immortality*, 1978, Shambhala, Boulder, Colorado, pp. 11–12.

5 *I Ching*, Richard Wilhelm translation, 1950, Princeton University Press, pp. 102–103, Hexagram 25, "Innocence (The Unexpected)."

6 *Tao Teh Ching*, Ch'u Ta-Kao translation, 1970, Allen & Unwin, London, pg. 93, Chapter 78.

7 *Nei Ching*, Ilza Veith translation, pp. 189, 222.

8 *Tao Teh Chung*, Ibid., pg. 79, chapter 44.

9 *The Secret of the Golden Flower*, Richard Wilhelm translation, pp. 26–28, 51.

10 Carl Rogers, *On Becoming a Person*, 1961, Houghton Mifflin Co., Boston, pp. 170–175.

Chapter 4

1 Alexander Lowen, M.D., *Bioenergetics*, 1975, Penguin Books, N. Y., pg. 114.

2 Wilhelm translation, *The Secret of the Golden Flower*, 1931, 1962; Harcourt, Brace & World, Inc., N.Y., pp. 25, 38.

3 K. Durckheim, *Hara: the Vital Centre of Man*, 1962, Allen & Unwin, London, pg. 19.

4 Most of these traditional names are from *The Treatment of Disease by Acupuncture*, by Felix Mann, William Heinemann Medical Books Ltd., 1975, London.

5 *Nei Ching*, Ilza Veith translation, pg. 133.

Chapter 5

1 *Nei Ching* (The Yellow Emperor's Classic of Internal Medicine), Ilza Veith translation, 1970, University of California Press, Berkeley and L.A., pg. 133.

2 Denis and Joyce Lawson-Wood,; *The Five Elements of Acupuncture and Chinese Massage*, Health Science Press, England, 1965, and *Acupuncture Vitality*, 1959, Health Science Press, Rustington, Sussex, England.

3 *The Secret of the Golden Flower*, Richard Wilhelm translation, 1931, 1962, Harcourt, Brace & World, Inc., N.Y., pg. 38.

4 Ibid., pg. 98.

5 Karlfried Durckheim, *Hara—the Vital Centre of Man*, 1962, Allen & Unwin, London, pp. 17–18.

6 *Nei Ching*, Ibid., pg. 165.

Chapter 6

[1] *Nei Ching*, Ilza Veith translation, pg. 133.

[2] See *The Acupressure Way of Health: Jin Shin Do*, by Iona Marsaa Teeguarden, Japan Publications, 1978, pp. 61–62, 118–119.

[3] Felix Mann, *Meridians of Acupuncture*, 1964, William Heinemann Medical Books Ltd., London, pg. 43.

Chapter 7

[1] *Nei Ching*, Ilza Veith translation, pg. 133.

[2] *Tao Teh Ching*, Lao Tzu, Ch'u Ta-Kao translation, pg. 72.

Chapter 9

[1] The anonymous "Desiderata," found in Old Saint Paul's Church in Baltimore, dates from 1692.

[2] Alexander Lowen, *Bioenergetics*, 1975, Penguin Books, pg. 33.

[3] *Tao Teh Ching*, Ch'u Ta-Kao translation, 1970, Allen & Unwin, pg. 47, chapter 33.

[4] Denis & Joyce Lawson-Wood, *The Five Elements of Acupuncture and Chinese Massage*, 1965, Health Science Press; Rustington, Sussex, England; pg. 89.

[5] Rollo May, *Man's Search for Himself*, 1953; Signet, New American Library, N.Y., pg. 84.

[6] Hans Selye, *Stress Without Distress*, pp. 18, 108.

[7] *Nei Ching*, Ilza Veith translation, pg. 133.

[8] Kok Yuen Leung, *Chinese Medical Philosophy and Principles of Diagnosis*, The North American College of Acupuncture, 1971, "The Cause of Disease," pp. 9–11.

[9] Hans Selye, M.D., *Stress Without Distress*, 1974, New American Library (Signet), N.Y., pp. 15–26.

[10] *Nei Ching* or "The Yellow Emperor's Classic of Internal Medicine," Ilza Veith translation, 1970, University of California Press, Berkeley, L.A., pg. 139.

[11] Selye: Ibid. pp. 77–78.

[12] Ibid., pg. 54.

[13] Jean-Paul Sartre, *The Emotions: Outline of a Theory*, 1948, Philosophical Library, N.Y., pp. 68–70.

[14] Alexander Lowen, M.D., *Pleasure: A Creative Approach to Life*, 1970, Penguin Books, N.Y., pp. 174–175.

[15] *Nei Ching*, pg. 119.

[16] Lowen, *Pleasure*, pp. 78–79.

[17] Soren Kierkegaard, *The Sickness Unto Death*, Alfred Knopf, 1976 as quoted in *Feelings: Our Vital Signs*, by Willard Gaylin, M.D., 1979, Harper & Row, N.Y., pg. 106.

[18] Paul Zweig, *Three Journeys*, pp. 149–150, as quoted in *The Culture of Narcissism*, by Christopher Lasch, 1979, W.W. Norton & Co., Inc., N.Y., Warner Books edition, pg. 60.

[19] Rollo May, *Man's Search for Himself*, 1953, W.W. Norton & Co., Inc., N.Y.; Signet edition, pp. 22–23.

[20] Lowen, *Pleasure*, pp. 25–26.

[21] *I Ching*, Richard Wilhelm translation, 1950, Princeton University Press, pp. 181–182, Hexagram 47, "Oppression (Exhaustion)."

[22] Alexander Lowen, M.D., *Depression and the Body*, 1972, Penguin Books, N.Y., pg. 28.

[23] *Nei Ching*, pg. 117.

[24] Dianne Connelly, Ph.D., *Traditional Acupuncture: The Law of the Five Elements*, 1979, Centre for Traditional Acupuncture, Inc., The American City Building, Columbia, Maryland 21044, pg. 52.

[25] Fritz Perls, M.D., *Gestalt Therapy Verbatim*, 1971, Bantam Books, pg. 52; 1969, Real People Press, P.O. Box F, Moab, Utah 84532.

[26] Ibid., pp. 32–33.

[27] Ibid., pg. 3.

[28] Lowen, *Pleasure*, pp. 76–77.

[29] Gaylin, *Feelings*, pg. 27.

[30] Perls, *Gestalt Therapy Verbatim*, pp. 50–51.

[31] David Shapiro, *Neurotic Styles*, 1965, Basic Books, Inc., N.Y., pg. 131.

[32] Ibid., pp. 115–119.

Chapter 10

[1] Thomas Merton, *The Way of Chuang Tzu*, 1965, New Directions, N.Y., pp. 123–124.

[2] From Merton pp. 52–53, 110–111 and Watson, *Chuang Tzu: Basic Writings*, 1964, Columbia University Press, N.Y., pp. 126–127.

[3] *Tao Teh Ching*, translation by Ch'u Ta-Kao, 1970, George Allen & Unwin, Ltd., London, XX, pg. 32 and XXV, pg. 37.

[4] Fritjof Capra, *The Tao of Physics*, Bantam Books edition, 1975, Shambhala Publications, Inc., P.O. Box 271, Boulder, Colorado 80302, pp. 69, 129.

[5] Ibid., pp. 196–197.

[6] Merton, *The Way of Chuang Tzu*, pp. 38–39.

[7] *Nei Ching*, pg. 148.

[8] Dianne Connelly, *Traditional Acupuncture: The Law of the Five Elements*, 1979, The Centre for Traditional Acupuncture, Inc., The American City Building, Columbia, Maryland 21044, pp. 65–66.

[9] Watson, *Chuang Tzu: Basic Writings*, pp. 121–122.

[10] *Nei Ching*, pg. 133.

[11] *Nei Ching*, pp. 119–120, 189.

[12] Kok Yuen Leung, *Chinese Medical Philosophy and Principles of Diagnosis*, The North American College of Acupuncture, 1971, "The Cause of Disease," pp. 10–13.

[13] *Nei Ching*, pg. 181.

[14] *The Secret of the Golden Flower*, Richard Wilhelm translation, 1931, Harcourt, Brace & World, Inc., (A Helen & Kurt Wolff Book), pp. 35–36.

[15] Erich Fromm, *The Sane Society*, 1955, Holt, Rinehart and Winston, N.Y., pg. 120.

[16] Dianne Connelly, *Traditional Acupuncture: the Law of the Five Elements*, pg. 72.

[17] Burton Watson, *Chung Tzu: Basic Writings*, 1964, Columbia U. Press, N.Y., pg. 111.

[18] Dianne Connelly, *Traditional Acupuncture: the Law of the Five Elements*, pg. 66.

[19] Erich Fromm, *The Sane Society*, pp. 196–204.

[20] Rudolph Ballentine, M.D., *Diet & Nutrition: a Holistic Approach*, 1978, Himalayan International Institute, Honesdale, Pennsylvania, pp. 485–491.

Chapter 11

[1] *Tao Teh Ching*, Ch'u Ta-Kao translation, 1970, George Allen & Unwin, Ltd., London, Chpt. XLIV, pg. 59.

[2] Ibid., Chpt. XXII, pg. 34.

[3] Evan Morgan, *TAO the Great Luminant—Essays from Huai Nan Tzu*, 1974, Ch'eng Wen Publishing Company, Taipei, pp. 21–22.

[4] *The Secret of the Golden Flower*, Richard Wilhelm translation, 1931, Harcourt, Brace & World, Inc., (A Helen & Kurt Wolff Book), N.Y., pg. 26.

[5] *Huang Ti Nei Ching Su Wen—Yellow Emperor's Classic of Internal Medicine*, Ilza Veith translation, 1949, University of California Press, Berkeley, L.A., 1970, pg. 189.

[6] *Golden Flower*, pp. 41, 45.

[7] Ibid., pp. 16–17.

[8] *Nei Ching*, Ilza Veith translation, pg. 120, 133.

[9] *I Ching*, Richard Wilhelm translation, Hexagram #61: "Inner Truth," pg. 238.

[10] Merton, *The Way of Chuang Tzu*, pg. 86.

[11] *I Ching*, Hexagram #62, "Preponderance of the small," pg. 241.

[12] Gia-Fu Feng & Jane English, *Chuang Tzu: Inner Chapters*, pg. 93.

[13] Ibid., pg. 128.

[14] Another version is found in Watson, *Chuang Tzu: Basic Writings*, pg. 113.

[15] Rollo May, "Contributions of Existential Psychotherapy" in *Existence*, edited by Rollo May, Ernest Angel & Henri Ellenberger, 1958, Touchstone Book, Simon & Schuster, N.Y., pg. 52.

[16] As Erich Fromm pointed out in his book by this name.

17 David Viscott, M.D., *The Language of Feelings*, 1976, Pocket Books, Simon & Schuster, N.Y., pp. 78–79.

18 Dianne Connelly, *Traditional Acupuncture: the Law of the Five Elements*, pg. 88.

19 *Tao Teh Ching*, Ch'u Ta-Kao translation, Chpt. XIX, pg. 31.

20 Hans Selye, *Stress without Distress*, pg. 6.

21 Ibid., pg. 144.

22 *I Ching*, Richard Wilhelm translation, Hexagram #15, "Modesty," pp. 63–64.

23 *The Secret of the Golden Flower*, Richard Wilhelm translation, pp. 15, 28.

Chapter 12

1 Hans Selye, *Stress Without Distress*, 1974, Signet (New American Library); J.B. Lippincott Co., 521 5th. Ave., N.Y., pg. 94.

2 Ibid., pg. 28.

3 Karlfried Durckheim, *HARA: The Vital Centre of Man*, 1962, George Allen & Unwin Ltd., London, pg. 26.

4 *Nei Ching*, Ilza Veith translation, pp. 133, 189.

5 Alexander Lowen, M.D., *Pleasure: A Creative Approach to Life*, 1970, Penguin Books, N.Y., pg. 183.

6 *I Ching*, Richard Wilhelm translation, Hexagram #29: "The Abysmal (Water)," pg. 115.

7 *Nei Ching*, Ilza Veith translation, pp. 152, 195.

8 Dr. Albert Kreinheder, in *Holistic Medicine*, ed. Tracy Delimon and John Smolowe, M.D., 1982, Reston Publishing Co., Reston, Va., pp. 218–219.

9 Alexander Lowen, M.D., *Pleasure: A Creative Approach to Life*, pg. 181.

10 Lowen, *Pleasure*, pg. 167.

11 *I Ching*, Richard Wilhelm translation, Hexagram #5: "Waiting (Nourishment)," pg. 25.

12 *Tao Teh Ching*, Ch'u Ta-Kao translation, Chpt. LXIII, pg. 78.

13 Willard Gaylin, M.D., *Feelings: Our Vital Signs*, pp. 36–37.

14 According to Webster's Seventh New Collegiate Dictionary and Webster's New World Dictionary, 1982, Simon & Schuster, N.Y.

15 Edward C. Whitmont, *The Symbolic Quest*, 1969, C.G. Jung Foundation, Princeton University Press, Princeton, New Jersey, pg. 44.

16 *Nei Ching*, Ilza Veith translation, pg. 120.

17 Dianne Connelly, *Traditional Acupuncture: the Law of the Five Elements*, pp. 97, 106.

18 *Tao Teh Ching*, Ch'u Ta-Kao translation, Chpt. LXXI, pg. 86.

19 Alexander Lowen, M.D., *Pleasure: A Creative Approach to Life*, pg. 183.

20 *I Ching*, Ilza Veith translation, Hexagram #17, "Following," pg. 72.

21 David Shapiro, *Neurotic Styles*, 1965, Basic Books, N.Y., pp. 58 and 60.

22 Willard Gaylin, *Feelings: Our Vital Signs*, 1979, Harper & Row, N.Y., pg. 26.

23 *Tao Teh Ching*, Ch'u Ta-Kao translation, Chpt. LXXXI, pg. 96.

24 *Chuang Tzu Basic Writings*, Burton Watson translation, 1964, Columbia University Press pp. 96–104.

Chapter 13

1 *Huang Ti Nei Ching Su Wen* (The Yellow Emperor's Classic of Internal Medicine), Ilza Veith translation, 1970, University of California Press, Berkeley and Los Angeles, Cal., pp. 117–118, 133, 139, 189.

2 Felix Mann, *The Meridians of Acupuncture*, 1971, William Heinemann Medical Books Ltd., London, pg. 106.

3 Dianne Connelly, *Traditional Acupuncture: The Law of the Five Elements*, 1979, The Centre for Traditional Acupuncture, Inc., Columbia, Maryland, pp. 28–31.

4 *The Secret of the Golden Flower* (A Chinese Book of Life), Richard Wilhelm translation, 1931, 1962, Harcourt, Brace & World, Inc., New York, pp. 26–28.

5 Carl G. Jung, *Man and His Symbols*, 1964, Doubleday & Co., Inc., Garden City, N.Y., pp. 161–164.

354

[6] Karlfried Durckheim, *HARA, The Vital Centre of Man*, 1962, George Allen & Unwin Ltd., London, pp. 18, 49.

[7] Jung, *Man and His Symbols*, pp. 187, 165.

[8] Thomas Merton, *The Way of Chuang Tzu*, 1965, New Directions, N.Y., pp. 42–43.

[9] Ibid., pg. 87–88.

[10] Gia Fu-Feng and Jane English, *Chuang Tsu: Inner Chapters*, 1974, Vintage, N.Y., pp. 73–74.

[11] Virginia Satir, *Conjoint Family Therapy*, 1967, Science and Behavior Books, Inc., Palo Alto, California, pg. 186.

[12] *Chuang Tzu Basic Writings*, Burton Watson translation, 1964, Columbia University Press, pp. 101, 54–55.

[13] Abraham H. Maslow, *Towards a Psychology of Being*, 1968, D. Van Nostrand Co., N.Y., pg. 195.

[14] Gia Fu-Feng and Jane English, *Chuang Tzu: Inner Chapters*, 1974, Vintage, N.Y., pg. 74.

[15] Alexander Lowen, M.D., *Pleasure—A Creative Approach to Life*, 1970, Penguin Books, N.Y., pp. 180–181.

[16] Theodore Lidz, *The Person: His and Her Development Throughout the Life Cycle*, 1968, 1976, pg. 30.

[17] Gia Fu-Feng, Ibid., pp. 46, 74.

[18] Theodore Isaac Rubin, M.D., *The Angry Book*, 1969, Collier Books, Macmillan Publishing Co., Inc., N.Y., pp. 169–171.

[19] Alexander Lowen, M.D., *Pleasure*, pp. 189–192, 199.

[20] Perls, *Gestalt Therapy Verbatim*, 1969, Bantam Books, N.Y., pg. 51.

[21] Ibid., pp. 70, 75–76.

[22] Rollo May, "Contributions of Existential Psychotherapy" (including quote from Medard Boss), in *Existence*, edited by Rollo May, Ernest Angel and Henri Ellenberger; 1958, Touchstone Book, Simon & Schuster, N.Y., pp. 53–55.

[23] Abraham Maslow, *Towards a Psychology of Being*, pp. 3–4.

[24] Fritz Perls, *Gestalt Therapy Verbatim*, pp. 51–52.

[25] Alexander Lowen, *Bioenergetics*, pp. 275, 277.

[26] *Chuang Tzu: Basic Writings*, Burton Watson translation, 1964, Columbia University Press, N.Y. and London, pp. 80–82.

[27] Willard Gaylin, *Feelings: Our Vital Signs*, 1979, Harper & Row, N.Y., pp. 53–54.

[28] Alexander Lowen, *Pleasure*, pp. 175–179.

Bibliography

Academy of Traditional Chinese Medicine, *An Outline of Chinese Acupuncture*, 1975, Foreign Languages Press, Peking.

Elsworth Baker, M.D., *Man in the Trap*, 1967, MacMillan Pub. Co., Inc., N.Y.

Rudolph Ballentine, M.D., *Diet & Nutrition: a Holistic Approach*, 1978, Himalayan International Institute of Yoga Science and Philosophy, Honesdale, Pennsylvania.

Herbert Benson, M.D., with Miriam Klipper, *The Relaxation Response*, 1976, Avon Books, N.Y.

John Blofeld, *Beyond the Gods: Buddhist and Taoist Mysticism*, 1974, E.P. Dutton, N.Y.

John Blofeld, *The Secret and the Sublime—Taoist Mysteries and Magic*, 1973, E.P. Dutton, N.Y.

John Blofeld, *TAOISM, the Road to Immortality*, 1978, Shambhala Publications, Inc., 1123 Spruce St., Boulder, Colorado 80302

Jean Shinoda Bolen, M.D., *The Tao of Psychology: Synchronicity and the Self*, 1979, Harper & Row, N.Y.

Fritjof Capra, *The Tao of Physics*, Bantam Books edition, 1975, published by arrangement with Shambhala Publications, Inc., P.O. Box 271, Boulder, Colorado 80302.

Dianne Connelly, Ph.D., *Traditional Acupuncture: The Law of the Five Elements*, 1979, Centre for Traditional Acupuncture, Inc., The American City Building, Columbia, Maryland 21044.

Tracy Delimon and John Smolowe, M.D., editors (including chapter by Dr. Albert Kreinheder), *Holistic Medicine—Harmony of Body Mind Spirit*, 1982, Reston Publishing Co.; Reston, Va.

DSM-III (Diagnostic and Statistical Manual of Mental Disorders, Third Edition), 1980, American Psychiatric Association, Washington, D.C.

K. Durckheim, *Hara: the Vital Centre of Man*, 1962, George Allen & Unwin, Ltd., London.

Ken Dychtwald, *Bodymind*, 1977, Pantheon Books, N.Y.

Gia-Fu Feng & Jane English, *Chuang Tsu: Inner Chapters*, 1974, Vintage Books, A Division of Random House, N.Y.

Marliyn Ferguson, *The Aquarian Conspiracy: Personal and Social Transformation in the 1980s*, 1980, J.P. Tarcher, Inc., L.A.

Erich Fromm, *The Sane Society*, 1955, Holt, Rinehart and Winston, N.Y.

Rokuro Fujita, M.A., "Experimental Study on the Main Meridian Line," The Japan Society for Oriental Medicine, 1964; and "Study on Meridians, Second Report," 1952.

Willard Gaylin, M.D., *Feelings: Our Vital Signs*, 1979, Harper & Row, Publishers, Inc., 10 East 53rd. St., New York, N.Y., 10022

Lionel Giles, *Taoist Teachings (Translated from the Book of Lieh-Tzu*, 1912, 1959, John Murray, 50 Albemarle St., London.

James Hillman, *EMOTION: A Comprehensive Phenomenology of Theories and Their Meaning for Therapy*, 1964, Northwestern University Press, Evanston, Il.

Benjamin Hoff, *The Tao of Pooh*, 1982, Penguin Books, Ltd., 40 W. 23rd. St., NY, NY 10010.

Carl G. Jung, *Memories, Dreams, Reflections*, 1965, Vintage Books, a division of Random House, N.Y.

Carl G. Jung, *Man and His Symbols*, 1964, Doubleday & Co., Inc., Garden City, N.Y. (First printed in Yugoslavia by Mladinska Knjiga Ljubljana)

Carl G. Jung, *Modern Man in Search of a Soul*, 1933, A Harvest Bk., Harcourt, Brace & World, Inc., N.Y.

Carl G. Jung, "Psychological Commentary on Kundalini Yoga," Lectures One, Two, Three and Four, 1932, SPRING: An Annual of Archetypal Psychology and Jungian Thought, 1976, Spring Publications, 28 E. 39th. St., N.Y. 10016.

Ted J. Kaptchuk, *The Web that has no Weaver: Understanding Chinese Medicine*, 1983, Congdon & Weed, N.Y.

Christopher Lasch, *The Culture of Narcissism*, 1979, W.W. Norton & Co., Inc., N.Y., Warner Books edition.

Denis & Joyce Lawson-Wood, *Acupuncture Vitality*, 1960, Health Science Press, Rustington, Sussex, England.

Denis & Joyce Lawson-Wood, *The Five Elements of Acupuncture and Chinese Massage*, 1965, Health Science Press; Rustington, Sussex, England.

Johng Kyu Lee, M.D., *Acupuncture*, 1974, Kai Chuk Sa Publishing Co., Korea.

Kok Yuen Leung, *Chinese Medical Philosophy and Principles of Diagnosis*, The North American College of Acupuncture, 1971, "The Cause of Disease."

Theodore Lidz, *The Person: His and Her Development Throughout the Life Cycle*, 1968, 1976, Basic Books, Inc., N.Y.

Alexander Lowen, M.D., *Bioenergetics*, 1975, Penguin Books Ltd., 625 Madison Ave., N.Y., N.Y. 10022

Alexander Lowen, M.D., *Depression and the Body*, 1972, Penguin Books, 625 Madison Ave. N.Y., N.Y. 10022

Alexander Lowen, M.D., *Pleasure: A Creative Approach to Life*, 1970, Penguin Books, N.Y.

Felix Mann, *Acupuncture: The Ancient Chinese Art of Healing and How it Works Scientifically*, 1973, Vintage Books, Random House, N.Y.

Felix Mann, *Meridians of Acupuncture*, 1964, William Heinemann Medical Books Ltd., London.

Felix Mann, *The Treatment of Disease by Acupuncture*, 1974, William Heinemann Medical Books, Ltd., London.

Abraham H. Maslow, *Toward a Psychology of Being*, 1968, D. Van Nostrand Co., 135 W. 50th. St., N.Y., N.Y. 10020

Kiiko Matsumoto and Stephen Birch, *Five Elements and Ten Stems*, Paradigm Publications, P.O. Box 539, Higganum, CT 06441.

Rollo May, "Contributions of Existential Psychotherapy" in *Existence*, ed. Rollo May, Ernest Angel & Henri Ellenberger, 1958, Touchstone Book, Simon & Schuster, N.Y.

Rollo May, *Man's Search for Himself*, 1953, A Signet Book from New American Library, 1301 Ave. of the Americas, N.Y., 10019, published by arrangement with W.W. Norton & Co., Inc., 55 Fifth Ave., N.Y., 10003.

Thomas Merton, *The Way of Chuang Tzu*, 1965, New Directions, N.Y., 333 Sixth Ave., N.Y. 10014.

Evan Morgan, *TAO the Great Luminant—Essays from Huai Nan Tzu*, 1974, Ch'eng Wen Publishing Company, Taipei.

Fritz Perls, *Gestalt Therapy Verbatim*, 1971, Bantam, N.Y. Copyright 1969 Real People Press, P.O. Box F, Moab, Utah 84532.

Wilhelm Reich, *Character Analysis*, 1945, Touchstone Book, Simon and Schuster, N.Y.

Wilhelm Reich, *The Function of the Orgasm*, 1942, 1973, A Quokka Book, Pocket Books, Simon and Schuster, N.Y.

Martin Reymert, ed., *Feelings and Emotions: the Mooseheart Symposium in cooperation with the University of Chicago*, 1950, McGraw-Hill Book Co., Inc., N.Y.

Carl Rogers, *On Becoming a Person*, 1961, Houghton Mifflin Co., Boston.

Theodore Isaac Rubin, M.D., *The Angry Book*, 1969, Collier Books, Macmillan Publishing Co., Inc., N.Y.

Sartre, Jean-Paul, *The Emotions: Outline of a Theory*, 1948, Philosophical Library, N.Y.

Virginia Satir, *Conjoint Family Therapy*, 1967, Science and Behavior Books, Inc., Palo Alto, California.

Maggie Scarf, *Body, Mind, Behavior*, 1976, Laurel Ed., Dell Pub. Co., N.Y.

Hans Selye, *Stress Without Distress*, 1974, A Signet Book from New American Library, published by arrangement with J. B. Lippincott Company, 521 Fifth Ave., N.Y., N.Y.

Katsusuke Serizawa, M.D. and colleagues at the University of Tokyo School of Medicine: "Studies on Clinical Scientific Approach in Acupuncture and Moxibustion Treatment," 1966; "Individual Pattern Changes in the Distribution of Skin Temperature and Electric Resistance," 1964; "The Distribution of Skin Temperature and Point-Meridian Phenomena," 1976.

David Shapiro, *Neurotic Styles*, 1965, Basic Books, Inc., N.Y.

Philip Slater, *The Pursuit of Loneliness—American Culture at the Breaking Point*, 1976, Beacon Press, Boston.

Ch'u Ta-Kao, translator, *Tao Teh Ching*, 1970, George Allen & Unwin, Ltd., London.

Iona Marsaa Teeguarden, *The Acupressure Way of Health: Jin Shin Do*, 1978, Japan Publications, Inc., Japan, N.Y.; distributed by Harper and Row, Scranton, PA 18512.

Raymond Van Over, *Taoist Tales*, 1973, Mentor Book, New American Library, N.Y.

Ilza Veith, translator, *Huang Ti Nei Ching Su Wen*, (The Yellow Emperor's Classic of Internal Medicine), 1970, University of California Press, Berkeley and L.A.

David Viscott, M.D., *The Language of Feelings*, 1976, Pocket Books, a Simon & Schuster division of Gulf & Western Corporation, 1230 Avenue of the Americas, N.Y., N.Y. 10020

Burton Watson, *Chuang Tzu: Basic Writings*, 1964, Columbia University Press, N.Y.

Edward C. Whitmont, *The Symbolic Quest*, 1969, C.G. Jung Foundation, Princeton University Press, Princeton, New Jersey.

Richard Wilhelm translation, *The Secret of the Golden Flower* (A Chinese Book of Life), 1931, 1962, Harcourt, Brace & World, Inc., New York.

Richard Wilhelm, translator, *The I Ching or Book of Changes*, 1950, Bollingen Series XIX, Princeton University Press.

Henry Woollerton and Colleen J. McLean, *Acupuncture Energy in Health and Disease*, 1979, Thorsons Publishers Ltd., Wellingborough, G.B.

Appendix of Terms

In this book, the Wade/Giles transliterations are used. The following table gives the corresponding terms in the Pinyin transliteration.

Wade/Giles transliteration:	*Pinyin transliteration:*
Ch'i	Qi
Ching Ch'i	Jing Qi
Yuan Ch'i	Yuan Qi
Tao	Dao
Tah Teh Ching	Dao De Jing

Index

50, 69, 199, 219, 296, 303,
313, 332
chyme, 115
circulation, 82, 97, 152, 158,
169, 172, 337, 338, 343, 346
Circulation-Sex Meridian,
101, 158
cold, 97, 161, 214, 232, 247
colitis, 127, 255
collective inconscious, 196
colon, 127, 232
communication, 49, 158, 189,
307, 316, 320
compassion, 57, 93, 102, 152,
336
completion, 58, 68, 223, 253
computing, 313
concentration, 200, 213
concern, 55, 56, 119, 121, 202
conditioning, 30, 31
conflict, 47, 56, 80, 118, 158,
188, 270, 312, 317
Confucianists, 19
confusion, 65, 127
Connelly, Dianne, 183, 199,
287
conscious, 44, 92, 232
consideration, 57, 67, 68, 200
constipation, 106, 127, 135,
232, 255
contemplation, 200, 206
contentment, 147
control, 69, 81, 89, 90, 92,
134, 144, 171, 276, 302
control issues, 85
core, 17, 20, 22, 23, 27, 48,
49, 80, 152, 206, 322
core Self, 61, 83
core spirit, 65
core tendencies, 75
coughing, 255
courage, 33, 159, 273, 290
creativity, 51, 74, 75, 179,
187, 235, 302
crying, 81, 110, 155, 156, 238
cycles, 20, 43, 166, 206
cystitis, 140

death, 272
decision-making, 90, 92
decisions, 73
defense,80, 125, 155, 188,
206, 209, 211, 233, 242, 247,
296, 319
defense energy, 247
defense mechanism, 44, 131,
233, 241, 338

defensive attitudes, 83, 92,
106, 131
defensive pride, 46, 57, 131,
132, 134, 253,
deficiency needs, 50
deflation, 182
dejection, 249, 252
demands, 331
denial, 44, 45, 60, 63, 131,
241, 243, 296
dependent, 159, 184
depression, 23, 28, 29, 44, 46,
57, 66, 74, 97, 101, 122,
127, 169, 172, 175, 178,
182, 243, 287, 314, 326,
327
deprivation, 57, 59, 184, 248,
251, 253, 259
desensitization, 285
desires, 68, 69, 232, 235, 260
despair, 57, 65, 174, 182
despondency, 57, 249, 252
diaphragm, 31, 81, 83, 85, 86,
89, 109, 120, 158, 185, 212,
243, 302, 315, 319, 322,
328, 330, 334,
diarrhea, 106, 127
diet, 22, 122, 140, 223
difficulty giving and receiving,
57
digestion, 67, 115, 127, 208,
343
digestive problems, 55, 83, 97,
106, 122, 203
discharge, 68, 70, 76, 81, 235
discouragement, 57, 173
dis-ease, 33, 66, 167, 231
disease, 30, 35, 272
distal points, 40, 41, 83–85
distress, 120
dizziness, 188, 245, 271, 287,
326
Do, 20
doubt, 173
dramatics, 189
dreams, 180
Dychtwald, Ken, 22

ear infections, 281
ears, 56, 70, 103, 115
earth, 58, 67, 198
eating disorders, 121, 325
edema, 271
ego, 20, 22, 52, 103, 131, 242,
253, 269, 288, 303
elation, 57, 182
elimination, 55, 68, 83, 127,

131, 231
emergency, 165, 276, 277, 318
emotional spectra, 56
emotions, 20, 21, 27, 30, 31, 33,
54, 55, 59, 63, 155, 157, 318
emotions, dominant, 162
emotions, evil, 162
emotions, extreme, 28, 56, 58–
60, 64, 68, 70, 72, 75, 162
emotions, negative, 53, 63, 65,
155, 230
emotions, synergic, 28, 30, 56,
59, 60, 75
empathy, 56, 57, 60, 162, 191,
194, 197, 204, 206
emptiness, 19, 31, 57, 65, 163,
174, 183
empty cup syndrome, 250, 253
endorphins, 23
energic tendency,64, 67, 68,
70, 72
energy, 8, 20, 23, 24, 27, 34,
36, 47, 55, 69, 71, 82, 83,
97, 100, 108, 110, 124, 162,
165, 186, 194, 200, 219, 221,
232, 241
energy, reserve, 71
energy centers, 82, 101, 115,
157, 205
enlightenment, 54, 231
enthusiasm, 190
envy, 57, 59, 69, 236, 250,
253, 258
epinephrine, 275
euphoria, 183
excitement, 55, 56, 64, 66, 162,
163, 169, 186, 318
exercise, 22, 205, 235, 337
exhaustion, 97, 164, 165, 266,
275
expectations, 65, 131, 134,
169, 178, 186, 326
explosive, 330
expression, 31, 80, 82, 243,
320
extreme emotion, 56, 58, 64,
67, 68, 70, 72
extremities, 81
eyes, 56, 72, 80, 85, 115,174,
241, 302

face, 232
failure, 239, 288, 289
fainting, 287
fascial adhensions, 32
fatigue, 32, 35, 81, 100, 197,
166, 202, 208, 232, 271, 281,

361

itching, 220

jaw, 80, 85, 100, 103, 131, 134, 212, 233, 234, 288, 319, 330, 331, 335
jealousy, 57, 59, 250, 253, 258, 295
Jin Shin Do, 15, 17, 19, 21, 27, 35, 36, 37, 54, 83, 160, 206
joy, 19, 20, 31, 41, 49, 53, 56, 57, 60, 64, 65, 70, 140, 151, 160–163, 166, 169, 186, 323, 336, 348
joy of feeling, 160, 161, 338
Jung, Carl, 16, 22, 47, 196, 303, 304

ki, 36
Kidney Meridian, 55, 82, 83, 111, 133, 135, 142, 165, 168, 199, 221, 232, 344
kidneys, 56, 58, 70, 71, 271, 338, 343, 346
Kierkegaard, Soren, 54, 189
Klaus, Marshall, 67
Kok Yuen Leung, 30, 204
ku chi, 115
Kundalini, 184

lack of concentration, 57
Lao Tzu, 25, 44, 50, 73, 147, 197, 227, 257, 271, 283, 288
large intestine, 56, 68, 232
Large Intestine Meridian, 83, 119, 142, 234, 236, 331, 341
laryngitis, 243
laughter, 155, 157, 183, 323
Lawson-Wood, 151
left brain, 60
legs, 82, 85, 95, 108, 118, 133, 346
lethargy, 118
letting come and letting go, 57
letting go, 56, 68, 230, 253
ligaments, 56, 72, 302
listening, 311
liver, 56, 58, 72, 106, 222, 276, 299, 302, 316, 342
Liver Meridian, 55, 82, 83, 85, 91, 271, 299, 345
local points, 40, 41, 83, 84
logic, 45, 155
longings, 70
love, 17, 80, 93, 132, 134, 151, 154, 158, 160, 161, 169, 180, 191, 196, 201,

239, 249, 257, 259, 322, 334, 336
Lowen, Alexander, 22, 80, 147, 288, 368, 318, 325, 327
Lung Meridian, 55, 82, 83, 133, 202, 339
lungs, 56, 58, 68, 231, 342

magic, 161, 163
mandala, 54,77
mania, 119
manipulation, 85
marrow, 56, 70, 263
martyr, 214, 321
Maslow, Abraham, 16, 50, 53, 314, 324, 330
maturity, 58, 67, 68
May, Rollo, 31, 32, 35, 151, 175, 245, 327
meditation, 27, 100, 206, 217, 233, 235, 268, 347
memory, 200, 213
menstrual difficulties, 199, 218
menstruation, 59, 203, 209
mental fatigue, 57
meridians, 16, 23, 36, 55, 59, 80, 82, 84, 337
metabolism, 299
metal, 58, 69
Miller, 278
mistrust, 57, 59, 71, 258, 291, 294
moderation, 70
morphic resonance, 196
motivation, 73, 238, 303
mouth, 56, 67, 115, 131
mucus, 56, 68
muscles, 32–34, 56, 67, 77, 107, 109, 141, 200, 337

Nature, 20, 26, 30, 48, 53, 58, 65, 72, 74, 197
nausea, 326
neck, 24, 80, 82, 85, 89, 103, 108, 118, 131, 134, 142, 155, 157, 180, 187, 220, 224, 288, 319, 330, 335, 342
neck release, 41, 95, 100, 144
neediness, 124
negative attitudes, 130
negativity, 281
Nei Ching, 16, 72, 75, 91, 160, 166, 172, 183, 198, 200, 203, 268, 271, 272, 286, 299
nephritis, 276
nervousness, 165, 220

nervous system, 233, 267
non-attachment, 54, 57, 69
noradrenaline, 275, 318, 275
nose, 56, 68, 115
nourishment, 67, 68, 115, 118, 122, 133, 200, 219
numbness, 32, 145, 209, 211, 251, 331

obesity, 59
obligation, 85
obsession, 57, 127, 223
obsessiveness, 57
obstinacy, 223
ocular segment, 80, 101
old shit, 127, 130, 132
oneness, 49, 67, 68, 191, 196
openness, 56, 57, 60, 68, 76, 162, 170, 231, 236, 250, 261
opposites, 44, 47, 48, 50, 61, 195, 305, 317
oppression, 57, 69, 232
optimism, 170
organ, 63
organ meridians, 97
orgone energy, 36
over-concern, 56, 57, 67, 68, 162, 202
over-joy, 56, 162, 169
over-sympathy, 57, 202
over-thinking, 57, 67, 216

pain, 19, 23, 34, 43, 54, 59, 66, 133, 141, 154, 158, 170, 173, 185, 188, 211
Pal Dan Gum, 337
Pan, 286
pancreas 58, 68, 106, 115, 199, 222
panic, 57, 284, 286
paranoia, 57, 259, 291, 294, 295
partner yang organ, 56, 64, 67, 68, 70, 72
passions, 33, 64, 70, 86, 163, 166
passive-aggressiveness, 46, 242, 321, 330
peace, 49, 70, 108, 155, 257
pectoral muscles, 77
pelvis, 81, 83, 85, 97, 118, 133, 135, 137, 157, 212, 218, 268
perception, 320
pericardium, 58, 64, 158, 342
Pericardium Meridian, 55, 56, 83, 92, 100 160, 271
Perls, Fritz, 44, 50, 186, 326, 328